Learning, Teaching and Researching on the Internet:

A Practical Guide for Social Scientists

S. D. Stein

Faculty of Economics and Social Sciences
University of the West of England

 **LONGMAN**

Pearson Education Limited
Edinburgh Gate
Harlow
Essex CM20 2JE
England

and Associated Companies throughout the world

Published in the United States of America
by Addison Wesley Longman Inc., New York

Visit Addison Wesley Longman on the World Wide Web at:
http://www.awl-he.com

The programs in this book have been included for their instructional value. They have
been tested with care but are not guaranteed for any particular purpose. Their publisher
does not offer any warranties or representations nor does it accept any liabilities with
respect to the programs.

Many of the designations used by manufacturers and sellers to distinguish their products
are claimed as trademarks. Addison Wesley Longman Limited has made every attempt to
supply trademark information about manufacturers and their products mentioned in this
book. A list of trademark designations and their owners appears on xiv.

First published 1999
Second impression 1999

ISBN 0 582 31935 8

British Library Cataloguing in Publication Data
A catalogue record for this book is available from the British Library

Library of Congress Cataloging-in-Publication Data
Stein, S. D. (Stuart D.)
    Learning, teaching, and researching on the Internet: a practical
    guide for social scientists/S.D. Stein.
      p. cm.
    Includes bibliographical references and index.
    ISBN 0-582-31935-8
    1. Social sciences--Computer network resources. 2. Internet
(Computer network) I. Title.
H61.95.S73   1998
025.06'3--dc21
                                       98-8739
                                        CIP

Set in 10/12pt Times
Typeset by 42
Produced by Pearson Education Asia (Pte) Ltd.,
Printed in Singapore (KKP)

Contents

Preface   xi

PART I   Internet preliminaries   I

Chapter 1   **A very brief introduction to the Internet   3**

            1.1   Local Area Networks   3
            1.2   Wide Area Networks and the Internet   6
            1.3   The World Wide Web   8

Chapter 2   **Web browsers   11**

            2.1   Introduction   11
            2.2   The browser interface   13
            2.3   The toolbar   14
            2.4   Downloading files   15
            2.5   Backtracking   17
            2.6   Manipulating accessed documents   19
            2.7   Frames   21
            2.8   Bookmarks   22
            2.9   Working the Net with the browser   26
            2.10   Offline browsers   30

Chapter 3   **Internet addresses   31**

Chapter 4   **Referencing Internet materials   37**

            4.1   Introduction   37
            4.2   Underlying principles   39
            4.3   Electronic mail   43
            4.4   FTP (File Transfer Protocol)   43
            4.5   Gopher sites   44

v

4.6	Mailing list messages	44
4.7	Synchronous/asynchronous communications	45
4.8	Telnet	46
4.9	Newsgroups	46
4.10	World Wide Web resources	47
4.11	Conclusion	49
	Bibliography (Web sites)	49

PART II   **Searching the Internet**   **51**

Chapter 5   **Subject directories**   **55**

5.1	Introduction	55
5.2	Major subject directories	57
5.3	Conclusion	63

Chapter 6   **Search engines and searches**   **65**

6.1	Introduction	65
6.2	Basic search query principles	67
6.3	Some search engine sites	70

Chapter 7   **Searches: basic**   **71**

7.1	Introduction	71
7.2	Basic searches	72
7.3	Refining simple searches	77
7.4	Some summary remarks	79

Chapter 8   **Searches: advanced**   **83**

8.1	Introduction	83
8.2	Boolean operators	84
8.3	Parentheses	86
8.4	Ranking of queries	87
8.5	Sundry matters	88
8.6	Other search engines	88
8.7	Addendum	89

PART III   **Exchanging views on the Internet**   **91**

Chapter 9   **Locating mailing lists**   **93**

Chapter 10   **Mailing list commands and exchanges**   **103**

10.1   Introduction   103
10.2   Subscribing and unsubscribing to lists   104
10.3   List information   105
10.4   Regulating mail inflow   106
10.5   Contributing to mailing lists   109
10.6   Other mail management/services commands   112

Chapter 11   **Mailing list archives**   **113**

11.1   Introduction: mailing list archives as a
resource   113
11.2   Mailing list archive database commands   115
11.3   Summary and conclusion   124

Chapter 12   **Reading the news: newsgroups**   **127**

12.1   Introduction   127
12.2   Newsgroups and Usenet   128
12.3   Configuring the newsreader settings   130
12.4   Netscape newsreader interface   132
12.5   Accessing discussion groups   133
12.6   Reading the news   134
12.7   Posting messages   135
12.8   Newsgroup archives   136
12.9   Graphics and software programs   141
12.10   Commercial newsreaders   142

PART IV   **Social Science subject resources**   **143**

Chapter 13   **General reference resources**   **147**

13.1   General reference desks   147
13.2   Biographical resources   149
13.3   Encyclopedias   153
13.4   Country and geographic resources   153
13.5   Language resources: dictionaries, thesauri, etc.   155
13.6   Articles and printed books   156
13.7   Miscellaneous   157

Chapter 14   **Electronic texts and reviews**   **159**

Chapter 15   **Data archives**   **165**

Chapter 16   **Statistical resources**   **177**

Chapter 17   **Social Science funding**   **185**

Chapter 18   **Current news online**   **189**

        18.1   Introduction   189
        18.2   General electronic newspaper resources   190
        18.3   Newspapers and agencies   193
        18.4   Television and radio news   197

Chapter 19   **History resources**   **201**

        19.1   General history   201
        19.2   Ancient history   206
        19.3   Medieval history   208
        19.4   Eighteenth century history   209
        19.5   American history   209
        19.6   Twentieth century history   212

Chapter 20   **Human rights resources**   **217**

        20.1   Introduction   217
        20.2   Treaties, declarations and other instruments   218
        20.3   General resource sites   218
        20.4   Human rights in particular countries   219
        20.5   The United Nations and human rights   222

Chapter 21   **Philosophy, sociology and psychology**   **225**

        21.1   Introduction   225
        21.2   General resource sites   226
        21.3   Journals   230
        21.4   Mailing lists   234
        21.5   Miscellaneous   234
        21.6   Subject areas   235
        21.7   Texts, bibliographies and thinkers   238

Chapter 22	**Political Science and government resources**	**243**
	22.1 Introduction	243
	22.2 General resource sites	244
	22.3 Country politics (non-UK)	249
	22.4 Country politics (UK)	252
	22.5 Elections	255
	22.6 Subject areas	256
	22.7 Texts	257

Chapter 23	**European Union resources**	**259**
	23.1 Institutions	259
	23.2 Policies	263
	23.3 Publications and documents	263
	23.4 Other European Union resources	266

Chapter 24	**Resources for economists**	267
	24.1 Mailing lists and newsgroups	267
	24.2 Current economic news	268
	24.3 Journals and working papers	271
	24.4 Guides and lists	273
	24.5 Multiple topic sites	274
	24.6 Specialized topic sites	277
	24.7 Miscellaneous	282

PART V	**Closure**	**283**

Chapter 25	**Ancillary computing skills**	**285**
	25.1 Introduction	285
	25.2 Using the mouse	287
	25.3 Program Manager (Windows 3.X)	288
	25.4 File Manager	290
	25.5 The clipboard, copying and pasting	294
	25.6 A note on saving files	295

Chapter 26	**Additional techniques, applications and resources**	**297**
	26.1 Configuring Netscape	297
	26.2 Locating, downloading and installing software	305
	26.3 Bookmark applications	309
	26.4 Keeping abreast of additions to Web resources	310

Glossary 313

Bibliography 327

Index 329

Preface

This book is aimed at students and academic staff whose recourse to Internet-based resources is likely to be essentially pragmatic. The questions that they are likely to be interested in include the following:

- 'What resources are available?'
- 'How can I find them most efficiently?'
- 'What type of Internet forums exist?'
- 'What do those participating in these forums do?'
- 'How do I locate potentially useful forums, mailing lists and newsgroups, for instance, that deal with subjects relevant to me?'
- 'How do I manage participation in these forums, such as subscribing, unsubscribing, retaining anonymity, searching archives of past exchanges, etc.?'
- 'Should I have mailing list messages sent individually or in a weekly or daily digest?'
- 'Which are the primary Web sites dealing with my subject specializations?'
- 'How do I reference Internet materials?'
- 'How do I keep up with new additions to Web resources?'
- 'Should I use a subject directory, Yahoo or SOSIG, for instance, or a search engine to locate a specific document?'
- 'What search syntax should I employ in order not to have to sift through thousands of records?'
- 'How do I efficiently bookmark Web sites?'
- 'How can I track down a resource that I found earlier but which cannot be accessed from the same Web address subsequently?'

These are some of the questions that are addressed in this book. It is not aimed, therefore, at students or staff who wish to become experts on all matters associated with the Internet and its varied forums, although it does provide a useful foundation for those who would wish to do so. Throughout I have assumed that most students and academic staff who will want to explore the uses of the Internet will wish to do so in order to accomplish more efficiently their primary interests in teaching, learning and researching. It is entirely feasible to track down subject-specific materials located on computers linked to the Internet, to manage participation on mailing lists, to learn how to reference resources accessed over the Internet, and to keep abreast of new developments, without having to become an Internet expert. Moreover, it is not necessary to have had any prior experience of using information technologies.

My own experiences in integrating the use of Internet resources and electronic platforms in modular delivery have convinced me that they can be deployed to improve the teaching, learning and research experiences of both students and academic staff. The courses that I teach on the Holocaust and Comparative Genocide at the Universities of the West of England and Bristol rely extensively on students and lecturers using materials accessible over the Internet, as well as a conferencing system. Another module that I have taught is Human Rights and their Violation in the Twentieth Century. On this course the majority of the materials used by students are accessed from Internet sources.

Some of these resources are not available in our library. Some are not available in any library as there is no printed version of the original material. In other cases they are available in a more useful format from Internet sources, or can be accessed more easily. Frequently, commentary, reports and hard copies of legislation take months if not years to find their way into the library, if at all. By the time some of them have cleared through ordering, purchasing, cataloguing and labelling there are often topics of more immediate interest to pursue. Internet forums also provide valuable opportunities for exchanging views and collaborating with students, researchers and teachers with similar interests at other locations. They also provide ample scope for locating informants and information that can be used in the context of social scientific research.

The first part of the book provides a basic overview of the infrastructure of the Internet and its relation to other networks, explores the use of Web browsers, and includes chapters on Internet addresses and the referencing of Internet resources. Many students and staff will already be familiar with the use of Web browsers and Internet addresses, the latter in the sense that they regularly type them into the location boxes, or select hyperlinks. In my experience many of those using browsers and other Internet applications use them less efficiently than they could, to their detriment in terms of time lost and the failure to track down resources being sought. Only a relatively small number of users appreciate that the Internet address of a resource is a potentially valuable piece of information for tracking it down if it can no longer be accessed at its previous location. Few students or academic staff are conversant with the conventions for referencing Internet resources, something which probably prevents many from using them in the context of teaching and research.

Part II focuses on the development of search skills. After a review of some of the more important subject directories and their uses, I explore briefly the workings of search engines and then concentrate on the development of basic and advanced searching techniques using them. There are now hundreds of different types of search engines available. Typing in a word and returning a list of records that meet the query syntax is not difficult. What does require some experience and knowledge is the technique of filtering out unwanted records. The volume of information accessible over the Internet in conjunction with the way in which search engines parse files can result in hundreds of thousands of hits, that is documents that match the search syntax. No one has the time or the mental energy to sift through all of this chaff. If you construct your query carefully you should be able in many instances to ensure that the information that you require is included in the first 30 or 40 records returned. If not, as I argue later, you should construct a different query. With experience and some experimentation you should narrow this down to the first 10. Experts can narrow it down to three. Anyone who works their way through these chapters can become quite expert. The savings in time will be considerable.

Part III explores Internet communication forums, namely mailing lists and newsgroups. Many commentators, students and academic staff still tend to think of the Internet primarily as a large, somewhat inchoate database of information. There are, however, also many electronic forums, and more are appearing all the time, that facilitate exchanges and clarification of view, communicative interactions relating to unfolding events, pressure group advocacy, and collaborative research and teaching endeavours. Mailing lists and newsgroups are also valuable sources of information on many issues, as well as useful research sampling frames in some instances.

Part IV, which is the largest section, provides annotated guides to social scientific resources under 12 separate headings. These do not exhaust those available across the Internet. Nor do the categories that I have included. I have, however, been scouring the Internet for some years now and many of the sites that I have annotated are, to my mind, among the most useful that are currently available. I would have liked to include separate chapters on sociology, psychology and women's resources, among others. However, the current Web offerings in many subject categories do little justice to these fields of enquiry and I have sought not to waste the time of readers for little return. Some others have been left out because they did not fit easily under any of the headings included.

Under each of the subject headings that I have employed I could have added many more resources. My objective has not been to provide an exhaustive listing of resources – something, moreover, which is not attainable. The reason why the major Internet tool today includes the word *Web* is because nearly every resource on the Web is linked to every other, however circuitous the route. What I have sought to do is to identify the major cluster nodes. From these the reader should be able to fan out and locate other individual resources or nodes. More significantly, if I have been successful in earlier parts the reader will be able to track down resources under any category. My attention has been primarily directed at mapping the underlying grammar of the Internet.

Part V closes the book from opposite ends of the information technology skills continuum. One chapter deals with some introductory Windows skills whilst the other explores more advanced topics, including browser configuration, how to locate and install software, and how to keep abreast of that which it is virtually impossible to keep abreast of, the Internet. The Glossary provides definitions/explanations of all the major terms used in the book.

After all the toil the first pleasure is that of being able to thank those who have helped the enterprise along, and it gives me great pleasure to be able to do so. I cannot claim to be what is now referred to as an 'early adopter'. The growth of the Internet during the seventies and eighties did not impinge upon me at all. In the late eighties and early nineties I was preoccupied with matters relating to Eastern Europe. Consequently, I had a lot of catching up to do. I would never have accomplished this without the patience of many of those working in the Information Technology Services department at the University of the West of England. They endured incessant telephone enquiries which no doubt distracted them from more important things, but which they tolerated with much forbearance. Others spent time assisting me in configuring the many PCs and applications that I ran through over the years. My profound thanks and gratitude, therefore, to Andy Mason, Mike Herrin, Peter Whyton, Paul Richards, June Coffey, Neil Marshall, Julie Hudson, John Saville and Martin Ubank. In my own faculty I owe much to John Hatt, who encouraged me in my quest to develop IT skills and facilitated their deployment in teaching and research, as well as providing assistance in obtaining the necessary hardware and software resources. I am grateful for his friendship. Professor Peter Glasner, himself not an early adopter, invariably senses the way things are flowing. He provided encouragement and authorized the allocation of resources necessary to integrate the use of electronic platforms in teaching. My thanks also to Elaine Scurr, our Social Science librarian, who assisted in the speedy acquisition of many volumes, proving that the era of hardcopy materials is not yet at an end. I am also very pleased to acknowledge the assistance of Chris Harrison, Publishing Director, first at Longman, then at Addison Wesley Longman, who at the other end of our email connection piloted this work through from idea to publishing.

Notation

In the text all URLs, Internet addresses, are enclosed in angle brackets, <*http://www.demon.net*>, for instance. The angle brackets should, of course, be omitted when typing the URL in the browser location/address box.

Trademark notice

The following designations are trademarks or registered trademarks of the organizations whose names follow in brackets: Adobe Acrobat, Adobe Exchange (Adobe Systems Inc.); Alta Vista (Digital Equipment Corporation); AMD (Advanced Micro Devices Inc.); Archie (Bunyip Information Services); Cyrix (Cyrix Corporation); Excite (Excite Inc.); Explorer (Texas Instruments Inc.); IBM PC, OS/2 (International Business Machines Corporation); Excel, Infoseek (a service mark of Infoseek Corporation); MS-DOS, Internet Crossroads, Internet Explorer, Internet Lexicon, Microsoft, Microsoft Excel, Microsoft Frontpage, Microsoft Peer (Microsoft Corporation); Java (Sun Microsystems Inc.); Logos (Logos Corporation); Lycos (Lycos Inc.); Macintosh, Macintosh System/ Finder (Apple Computer Inc.); Mosaic (University of Illinois); Pentium, Pentium Pro (Intel Corporation); Postscript (Adobe Systems Inc.); Reveal (ICL); UNIX (licensed through X/Open Company Ltd.); WordPerfect (WordPerfect Corporation, registered within the USA); Yahoo (Yahoo ! Inc.)

PART I

Internet preliminaries

Chapter 1   A very brief introduction to the Internet   3
Chapter 2   Web browsers   11
Chapter 3   Internet addresses   31
Chapter 4   Referencing Internet materials   37

CHAPTER 1

A very brief introduction to the Internet

1.1   Local Area Networks   3
1.2   Wide Area Networks and the Internet   6
1.3   The World Wide Web   8

Most people who drive a car, use the telephone or watch television manage to do so despite the fact that they understand little about the workings of a car engine, digital exchanges or television transmission. It is equally feasible to locate and download information from Internet sources without comprehending its structure or how data is carried over it. This chapter offers a brief overview for those who are interested in understanding the way in which the Internet is structured and how information is transmitted over it. Those readers who have neither the time nor the inclination to delve below the bonnet can quite easily skip this chapter without impacting on their ability to locate, download, and manipulate information accessible over the Internet. Some of the terms explained here crop up in other chapters. The Glossary provides brief definitions of them and the Index makes reference to the pages where more detailed information is available.

1.1   Local Area Networks

The Internet is not one network, but a network of networks. It constitutes a network by virtue of the fact that a large number of separate networks can be linked to each other and data can be exchanged between computers attached to them. The communication and exchange of data between machines attached to the separate networks can take place because the computers on them employ identical software and each network is attached to devices that route data between them. The software comprises a collection of protocols called the *TCP/IP Protocol Suite*. A protocol is essentially an agreed standard that is implemented in software programs so that the connecting computers can exchange data with each other, order it, and check that the data dispatched corresponds with the data received. An electronic mail message, for example, is sent from one computer to another, sometimes through holding computers en route. All the computers in the chain must include software that manipulates and orders the data identically so that the recipient can read the message in a format and order that corresponds to the data that was transmitted by the sender. The same applies to software applications that are moved over the Internet, to newsgroup messages and to Web documents. This is achieved through agreed protocols.

Before looking at the way in which data is exchanged between different networks it is necessary to explore briefly the operation of those smaller networks that link up jointly to form the Internet. The smallest form of self-contained network is referred to as a LAN, an acronym for Local Area Network. The network illustrated in Figure 1.1 represents some of the components on a LAN that you are likely to encounter in a small enterprise. This network comprises the workstations of employees, the network infrastructure between them, which is likely to be some form of cabling, a common server on which various programs and files are stored which can be accessed from the workstations, two printers and a modem.

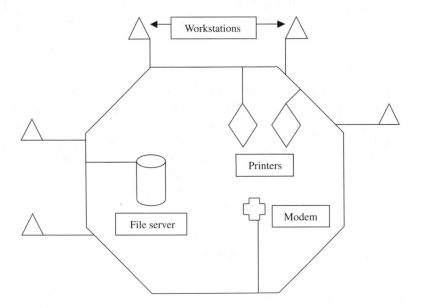

Figure 1.1 *Local Area Network.*

In a large organization the computer network might consist of a number of inter-connected LANs. So, for example, a sizeable university might have separate LANs for each of its major faculties and servicing departments. Communication devices link LANs. One such device is a *bridge*, whose function it is to copy data from one LAN to another. Another device that effects a similar outcome is a *router*. This is illustrated in Figure 1.2.

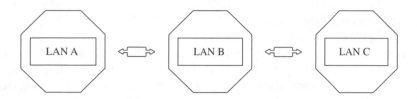

Figure 1.2 *LAN interconnectivity.*

In order for the separate components of a LAN to work seamlessly together exchanging data, it is necessary that all the devices attached to the network can communicate with each other. This is achieved through the use of network operating software. This 'controls the data traffic flow in the network, converts transmission and reception speeds, translates different data codes produced by different computers, detects and corrects errors, forms data messages and performs user access functions. In its simplest terms the network software may be seen to behave like a form of operating system which makes resources dispersed across the network appear to be local to each user's workstation.' (Anderson, 1996, Foundations of Computer Technology p. 327). In other words, the network operating software ensures that the data that is being exchanged across the network arrives at the appropriate destination in the format that it is supposed to be in, that all of the data is transmitted and that it is in exactly the same order as it was before being sent. Network operating software also allows those connected to the LAN to share and exchange data files, to access common programs and peripherals such as printers, CD-ROM drives and modems, and to receive and send electronic mail.

The network infrastructure (cabling, microwave, radio signals), hardware (work-stations, printers, modems, file servers) and software applications (word processors, spreadsheets, databases, etc.) are all means to an end, the production and distribution of information by and between those connected to the network. A key factor, therefore, is the means by which information is moved over a network. Data can be transmitted over Local Area Networks through a number of different mechanisms, namely through circuit switching, message switching and packet switching. Here I will be concerned only with the latter, as packet switching is the means by which information is also moved over the Internet.

With packet switching the data that is to be transmitted from one part of a network to another, say the contents of a word-processed file, a Web page or a spreadsheet, is divided up into small packets of data. The packet includes some of the data that is to be transmitted and header information. The header information consists of control and address codes that specify where the packet is to be delivered and provide for the control of errors, for instance loss of data in the course of transmission from one part of the network to another. If the file is being sent over a network on which there are a number of file servers the header specifies to which one the packets of data are to be sent. A schematic representation is illustrated by Figure 1.3.

CHECK BITS	DATA BITS	CONTROL BITS

Figure 1.3 *Packet file components.*

As on a typical medium-sized to large LAN a significant volume of data will be regularly transmitted across its segments, it is necessary to ensure that all users can uninterruptedly access and transmit data. To avoid the creation of bottlenecks arising from the transmission of large bodies of data, most network operating software implements a sharing arrangement. This is achieved by limiting the volume of data that can be transmitted in each packet and ensuring that, when data is being transmitted from a number of sources on the network simultaneously, the data packets from one source alternate with those transmitted from others. In other words, a turn-taking procedure is implemented. This arrangement is known as *packet switching*, and a network that implements it is referred to as a packet switching network. The Internet is a packet switching network.

To summarize, a Local Area Network links together workstations and peripherals (file servers, printers, modems, etc.) for the purpose of accessing and transmitting data. Some form of cabling links the component parts. Network operating software monitors and controls the transmission of data across the network. Most LANs are packet switching networks. The data in a packet switching network is moved across the network in packets. These packets include portions of the data to be transmitted as well as control and addressing codes that ensure that the packet arrives at the correct destination, that the data is free from errors and that it is in same format and order as intended by the sender. Finally, LANs can be connected to each other.

1.2 Wide Area Networks and the Internet

From the above description of the workings of a LAN it might appear that creating a worldwide network is relatively simple. As LANs can be linked to each other, why not link all the LANs that exist in separate organizations to create a large network across which information can be transmitted and accessed? There are a number of reasons why this cannot be done. First, there are constraints on the size of a Local Area Network in terms of its cabling length. That is one of the reasons why a large organization is likely to have a number of LANs that are linked through communication devices as described earlier. The physical limitations on a LAN vary with the LAN technology that is used. However, 500 metres or less is not atypical. This, of course, militates against connecting LANs that are separated by distances greater than this. There are other reasons why an organization might set up a number of LANs irrespective of whether cabling constraints are operative, including the need to implement different levels of security on them and the use of alternative LAN technologies to meet the different requirements of component parts of the organization. There are a large number of different LAN technologies that meet different specifications regarding performance and scalability. They also vary in terms of cost.

A network that links LANs over large distances is referred to as a Wide Area Network or WAN. For two or more Local Area Networks to constitute a WAN they require a dedicated medium (cabling, satellite, microwave or radio transmission) across which the data is transferred. They also need a special dedicated computer-modem arrangement at each end that connects to a computer on their respective LANs, as illustrated in Figure 1.4.

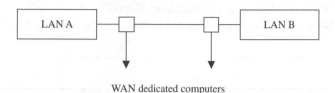

WAN dedicated computers

Figure 1.4   *Wide Area Network connectivity.*

Although it is possible to link LANs to each other within an organization and LANs that are dispersed over large distances by means of WAN technologies, this is still a long way from creating a large network that can link hundreds of thousands of LANs and WANs so that data can be transmitted seamlessly between them. The reason why this cannot be done is that the different WAN technologies, like many LAN technologies, are incompatible in the sense that you cannot just cable them together and transmit data between them without having some other components in place that enable this to happen.

Two essential components that need to be in place are *routers*, which are computers that direct data being sent over networks linked by some form of infrastructure to a specified computer, and software that allows computers sending and receiving commands and data to communicate with each other. During the 1960s and 1970s the necessary software, referred to as the *TCP/IP Protocol Suite*, was developed in the United States. TCP is an acronym for *Transmission Control Protocol* and IP stands for *Internet Protocol*. The suite consists of more than just these two protocols, it being a bundle of many programs that interact with each other. The Internet evolved as rapidly as it did because this protocol suite was made freely available so that the developers of all operating systems (see the Glossary) could incorporate it. The result is that all computers, regardless of type (IBM PC, Macintosh, mainframe and minicomputer), or the software operating systems that they are using (UNIX, Windows, LINUX, etc.) can exchange data if they are linked through some infrastructure medium.

The Internet, therefore, is not a real network in the sense of a LAN or a WAN linking different parts of an organization. Local and Wide Area Networks are owned by some entity which manages them in the sense of deciding on their infrastructure, how many workstations are connected to them, their rate of expansion, the mode and speed of connectivity to other networks and so forth. The Internet is a network of networks, hence inter-net. It is a means of linking networks together so that those connected to one network can exchange data with those on others.

To summarize, the Internet links computers to each other, both those of individuals not connected to a network and those connected to smaller Local Area Networks, through the technologies of Wide Area Networks and a commonly employed suite of protocols.

The efficiency of the Internet is dependent on the rate at which the data can be transmitted. Both in the United States and in other continents and regions high bandwidth infrastructures, that is infrastructures that can transmit large volumes of data per unit of time, have been set up to connect major population centres, or institutional sectors, based on Wide Area Network technologies. In the United Kingdom academic institutions are linked through a Wide Area Network called JANET (Joint Academic Network) or Super-JANET. European countries are linked through EBONE. The highest level network in a country or region, that with the highest carrying capacity, is referred to as the *backbone network*. EBONE stands for European Backbone Network.

The way in which this all ties together is illustrated in Figure 1.5.

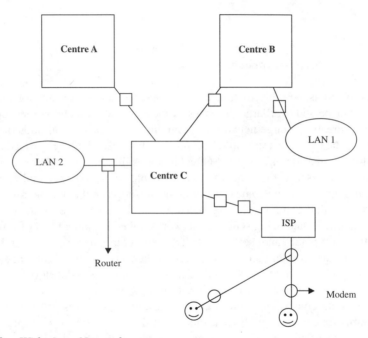

Figure 1.5 *Wide Area Network setup.*

The centres A, B and C represent part of the backbone which is linked through routers to LANs. Internet Service or Access Providers link individuals through modems to the Wide Area Network/Backbone. Of course, the figure is a very schematic representation of a very complex network involving advanced hardware, networking and software technologies. In principle, however, it represents the way in which data can be transmitted around the globe between millions of individual users, whether connecting through a service provider or a network.

1.3   The World Wide Web

Most users connecting to the Internet are interested in doing one or more of the following: (1) accessing files that are of interest, (2) making data that they think may interest or influence others accessible to them, and (3) communicating with other users. All of these things are accomplished by using various software applications that are frequently referred to as Internet tools or services. The Internet applications that are most widely used at present are electronic mail, FTP, newsreaders and World Wide Web browsers.

The operation of all of them is based on the relationship between two complementary software applications. Their complementary operation is referred to as distributed client–server computing. One component, the *client*, issues commands. The other, the *server*, executes them if appropriate. Let me illustrate with reference to the File Transfer Protocol (FTP) client and server. A large proportion of all software that is distributed over the Internet is downloaded from computers through a software application called an FTP server. This program, among other things, will display the names of files accessible from the server and download them if it is given the appropriate commands. The commands are issued by the complementary software component, the FTP client. The server and the files that are downloaded from it may be on a remote computer at the other side of the world, or in the next room. The client software will be on the hard disk of the user's PC or on a file server on the network the user is connected to. Figure 1.6 illustrates the relationship.

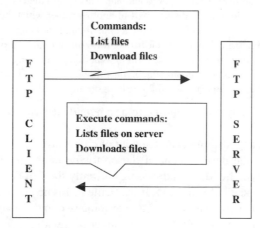

Figure 1.6   *Client–server computing.*

Similarly, Web pages are downloaded to the computers of those requesting them in response to the issuing of a command in a client application called a browser. This is transmitted to a Web server that responds by downloading the relevant file if appropriate. Computers that hold files that are manipulated through a software application that constitutes the server side of client–server distributed computing are referred to as servers. Thus, it is common to refer to Web servers, file servers and FTP servers.

When a command is issued through a client application to a server requesting, for instance, the downloading of a file, the data packets that are sent include in the header information the address of the computer that it is being sent to, as well as that of the computer that it is being sent from, so that the computer that receives the command can send back the requested file. Every computer linked to the Internet has its own unique address, referred to as its IP (Internet Protocol) address. Files sent over the Internet are split up into data packets. These data packets do not all take the same route through the network.

In addition, most Internet services, ftp, gopher, electronic mail, and the World Wide Web do not maintain an open connection with the servers they are issuing requests to. Thus, if you request that a file be downloaded from a server in Australia, the command may arrive there in a number of data packets that have taken different routes over linked networks. It is then processed by the server which responds by dispatching a large number of packets that travel along different network pathways until they are processed and ordered by the computer that sent the original command. At no time is there an open connection between the computer that sent the command and the computer responding to it.

The rapid growth in the popularity of the Internet since 1989 is due largely to the development of the World Wide Web and graphical browsers. The World Wide Web was developed in 1989 by Tim Berners-Lee at CERN, the European Laboratory for Particle Physics, situated in Geneva. Berners-Lee was interested in facilitating the exchange of documents between scientists engaged on collaborative research. Although it was by then already possible to transmit files by way of ftp servers, Berners-Lee went further, suggesting

> 'that you could actually link the text in the files themselves. In other words, there could be cross-references from one research paper to another. This would mean that while reading one research paper, you could quickly display part of another paper which held directly relevant text or diagrams. Documentation of a scientific and mathematical nature would thus be represented as a "web" of information held in electronic form on computers around the world. This Tim thought could be done by using some form of hypertext, some way of linking documents together by using buttons on the screen which you simply click on to jump from one paper to another.' (Raggett *et al.*, 1996, Electronic Publishing on the World Wide Web pp. 3–4).

The World Wide Web is therefore referred to as a hypertext-based distributed information system.

Although this application generated a lot of enthusiasm and interest, it did not take off significantly until the development of the prototype of the modern Web browser in 1993. This was produced by Marc Andreessen, currently the CEO of Netscape Communications Corporation, Inc., and Eric Bina. It was called Mosaic and was in widespread use until being supplanted in popularity by Netscape some two to three years later. Although it was revolutionary and a very efficient tool, in comparison with the functionality of today's browsers it was rather primitive.

The initial version of the protocol that underpins the Web, called *Hypertext Transport Protocol* (HTTP), was also rather basic, as was the markup language in which Web documents were written. All have been substantially developed since the beginning of the decade. Today's leading Web browsers incorporate newsreading and electronic mail applications and can access a variety of Internet services, including ftp and newsgroup servers. Whereas previously it was necessary to employ a number of different clients (e.g. ftp, electronic mail) to access files stored on different types of Internet-accessible servers this is no longer necessary. You can now send electronic mail, read newsgroup messages, download files from ftp servers, download and read files from gopher servers, download and read html documents, and view video clips and documents in many different formats through the use of Web browsers. In the following chapters I explain how to exploit some of their important features.

CHAPTER 2

Web browsers

2.1	Introduction	11
2.2	The browser interface	13
2.3	The toolbar	14
2.4	Downloading files	15
2.5	Backtracking	17
2.6	Manipulating accessed documents	19
2.7	Frames	21
2.8	Bookmarks	22
2.9	Working the Net with the browser	26
2.10	Offline browsers	30

2.1   Introduction

Graphical Web browsers are client-side software applications that have been developed for the purpose of accessing files on the World Wide Web. By client-side is meant that through them the user sends instructions to a Web or other server requesting that particular files be downloaded on their computer. Browsers now also act as message centres. With many browsers you can read and send electronic mail, and read and post discussion group messages. Often they are referred to simply as Web browsers, or just browsers. They are graphical inasmuch as the interface includes various buttons, images, scroll bars and pop-up menus that are largely manipulated with the aid of a mouse.

Although there are a number of different Web browsers available, two of these dominate the market. Netscape, developed by Netscape Communications Corporation, was an early market leader whose browser was probably the one most widely used between mid-1994 and early 1997. Since the release of Windows 95, Microsoft's Internet Explorer has made very substantial inroads on Netscape's market position. Although both companies currently claim that their browser is the one most widely used worldwide, it is extremely difficult to be certain what the current position is. A significant number of users employ both.

Despite the fluidity of the current browser market, in discussing their features and uses I will illustrate the use of a browser principally, but not solely, by reference to Netscape Navigator 3.01/Gold. My justifications for this are threefold. The majority of institutions of higher education in the UK use one or other version of Netscape. In the summer of 1997 I carried out a survey of approximately 33% of universities in the UK. I asked their system administrators what browsers were used by staff and students, and what plans they had for changing to Microsoft's Internet Explorer if they were using one or other version of Netscape. The overwhelming majority of those interviewed stated that they were currently using Netscape. There were no immediate plans for change.

Secondly, Netscape and Internet Explorer are remarkably similar in what they do, and how the user implements particular features. The terms employed for the same features may not be identical (bookmarks/favorites), the interfaces look slightly different, but not radically so, and some functions (sending electronic mail) may be more complicated to perform with one or other browser, or version thereof. Such differences are largely inconsequential. The manner in which essential features are carried out, those that you will be performing most of the time, is virtually identical. Moreover, the logic of software development and marketing is such that what is characteristic of Internet Explorer today is adopted with minor changes and improvements by its competitor three months down the road.

Finally, browsers, along with all other software applications (word processors, graphics packages, databases, spreadsheets, etc.) are upgraded with new features frequently. Few students or members of academic staff are likely to have the time to spend reading new manuals and help files, both of which increase in size dramatically with each upgrade. The only way to benefit from the constant upgrading without diverting too much time to the development of peripheral skills is to build on knowledge of generic interfaces and common functions. Whichever word processor you are using it is likely that its Edit menu will have selections for copying, cutting, pasting and finding, and that the File menu will enable the opening, saving and printing of documents. Similarly, browser interfaces and functions are sufficiently alike to enable users who employ one brand to master similar features in others relatively effortlessly. I am assuming, therefore, that if you happen to be using Internet Explorer you will be able to follow the ensuing discussion without undue difficulty.

I do not cover all features of the Netscape browser. To do so would necessitate writing the equivalent of another book. There are many books already that focus exclusively on documenting the varied features and uses of one or other version of the browsers developed by Netscape and Microsoft. In my experience many students and academic staff have neither the time nor the desire to plough through extensive treatises on particular browsers. These are regularly supplanted by upgraded versions and the earlier treatises are replaced with lengthier ones, usually before the user has had time to master the contents of the earlier manual.

In this chapter I focus on most of the main features of browsers that are used for accessing files stored on Internet-linked servers as efficiently as possible. I am assuming that most readers want to access files rather than become experts in either the manipulation of a particular browser or all facets of the Internet.

2.2   The browser interface

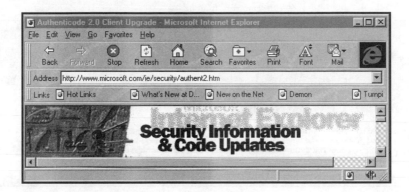

Figure 2.1   *Internet Explorer interface.*

The similarities between the interfaces of Internet Explorer, Figure 2.1, and Netscape, Figure 2.2, are apparent. The top part includes buttons (e.g. *Back*, *Stop*, *Print*), menus (e.g. *File*, *Edit*, *View*) and a text box in which the address of the file you want to download is inserted, designated by *Address* in Figure 2.1 and *Go to* in Figure 2.2. To the right and bottom of the interface, where you can see left/right and up/down arrows in Figure 2.1, are the scroll bars. Figure 2.2 only displays those for scrolling the document up and down because the document loaded in it fits into the window. The area in the middle of the interface is the document loading window in which is displayed the file that you have accessed.

Interpretative key for Netscape interface

Drop-down menus – Offer choice of browser actions/configurations.
Buttons – Replicate some of the action choices on drop-down menus.
Navigation bar – Address of document currently loaded or to be requested.
Stop button – Halts online activity of the browser.
Directory buttons – A selection of online resources compiled by Netscape, Inc.
Exit – Select to exit browser in Windows 95/NT; top left for Windows 3.X.
Netscape icon – When animated signifies document is loading, site sought, or connection being established. If you double click on it, Netscape's home page will load. Internet Explorer has its own icon in an identical position.
Status bar – Indicates state of downloading. Also, when mouse cursor is placed over hyperlink, the URL, or address, is displayed in it.
Progress bar – Graphical indicator of status of downloading.
Document window – Files loaded in this space.
Security key – Displays the security status of site that has been accessed. A site with maximum security displays an unbroken key.
Scroll bars – Used to move documents in the display window up, down or across.

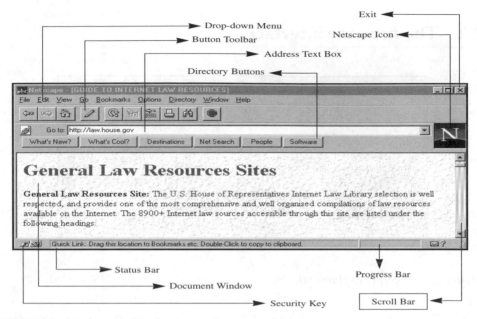

Figure 2.2   *Netscape Navigator interface.*

2.3   The toolbar

The toolbar is illustrated in Figure 2.3.

Figure 2.3   *Netscape toolbar.*

The *Back* and *Forward* buttons are used for opening (displaying) in the document window files that have already been viewed during the current session. By the current session is meant the interval between launching and shutting down the browser. Once the browser has been closed down, the session has ended. You cannot reload every document that you have viewed in the current session by using a back or forward button, only those with the same lineage, as explained below.

The *Home* button reloads the page that is loaded in the document window when you first launch the browser, which is referred to as the home page. You can alter which page this is in the *Options* menu, as described in Chapter 26, Section 26.1.

The *Edit* feature loads the Netscape Navigator Gold editor application. This provides some basic editing capabilities so that users can write their own Web pages, or edit others that they have downloaded. This feature is not available with earlier versions of Netscape, and its use will not be covered in this volume.

The *Images* button toggles between images being downloaded, and image downloading being turned off. This is best activated from the *Options* menu by toggling the

Auto Load Images feature. Graphic images frequently take up a lot of data volume. The speed with which a page downloads is a function of its size. If it includes large graphics files it will take much longer to download than a file that consists primarily of text. If the network is very slow, and if the graphics are not essential to understanding the content, turning the graphics downloading off is worth considering. On such a page you will see the outline position where the graphics would have been displayed had you not turned their loading off. If you want to see a particular graphic, place the cursor over it, click with the right mouse button, and select *View image*. The image will now be downloaded to its allocated position in the file.

The *Open* button replicates the location box. The *Print* button is used for printing the file in the document window. The *Find* button replicates this option on the Edit menu. It is useful for locating information on a lengthy document without having to scroll through it. The *Stop* button is coloured red when the document is downloading. To interrupt downloading, click on the button.

Beneath the *Go to* box there are a number of Directory buttons. These point to Web pages authored by Netscape Communications Corporation that link to various Internet resources. The *Net Search* and *People* pages are of some limited use for tracking down resources and persons accessible over the Internet.

The *Help* menu provides guidance on the use of various Netscape Navigator features. This is not, however, a help file that is bundled with Netscape in versions of the browser earlier than Netscape Communicator 4.0. When you choose this option the browser will try to access help files stored on Netscape's servers. Thus, you need an open connection to the Internet to access these files.

The Netscape and Internet Explorer icons in the top right-hand corner of the interface are hyperlinked to Netscape's and Microsoft's home pages respectively. You may find these links useful for locating additional information on features of the browser, how to configure various options or for obtaining recently released upgrades or information thereon.

2.4   Downloading files

From an address

The primary use of a Web browser is to download files from remote servers, that is, from servers linked to the Internet. To do this you need to know the precise address of the file, its URL. URL is an acronym for Uniform Resource Locator. Internet addresses are discussed in greater detail in the next chapter. The URL is inserted in the address text box of the browser, Figure 2.2. To do this you need first to delete the address that is already showing in the box. Insert the cursor at the end of the address already displayed in the box and use the backspace facility to delete it. Usually, when you click anywhere in the box with the cursor the existing address will be highlighted. If you press the delete key once it is, it will be removed.

Next you need to insert the URL of the file that you want to download. Web addresses take the form

<http://www.microsoft.com>

the http:// being the protocol scheme used for transmitting the file. As Web browsers were developed for downloading pages accessed with the http protocol, this is the default protocol. Consequently, you do not need to insert it in the address with most later versions of browsers. Thus, to access the home page of the United Nations you only need insert

<www.un.org>

without the http:// prefix. For many organizations you do not even need to insert this abbreviated URL. If you just type **un** for the United Nations main page, or **netscape** or **microsoft**, the browser will access the main pages of these organizations.

Having inserted an address you then need to hit the Enter/Return key to activate the browser. When you do so, the browser sends a command to the remote server instructing it to send the file referenced in the address box back to your PC. You can usually follow the sequence of events that takes place after you hit the Return key in the status bar, at the bottom left of the interface. The stages generally are:

● connect/contacting <site address>

● waiting for reply…

● 7% of 3K … 97% of 25K (at 560 bytes/sec)

● document done.

The figures denote the rate of download relative to the size of the data being downloaded. As a file is downloaded in a series of packets of data, you frequently will see a large number of these figures rapidly flashing across the status bar.

During the downloading process the browser icon in the top right-hand corner of the interface is animated and the mouse cursor changes from an arrow to an hourglass if situated in the document window. You can stop the downloading process at any time by selecting the *Stop* button on the button bar.

Summary: Downloading a file from an address

1. Load browser.
2. Place cursor over the address box and click with left mouse button.
3. Delete existing address by pressing delete button, or selecting *delete* on right mouse button, or using the backspace.
4. Type in the address (URL). If you are accessing a Web address, one preceded by http://, you do not usually need to type in http:// The browser assumes that you will most frequently be typing Web addresses and these are always preceded by http://
5. Hit the Enter key.
6. Browser will now attempt to access the site and download the file.

Example: If the address is *http://www.slaughterhouse.com* you only need to type *www.slaughterhouse.com*

From a hyperlink

Most Internet users locate resources (download files) by selecting the hyperlinks embedded in files they have downloaded. Hyperlinks are embedded addresses. They point either to another file on some server, or to a different position in the same document. When you select them by clicking on them with a mouse the browser is activated and requests that the file specified in the address be downloaded from the server on which it is stored, or that the document scroll up or down to the position indicated.

Hyperlinks are most frequently highlighted in blue if you have not selected them previously. Once you select a link, and the document begins to download, it ordinarily changes colour for a period of time specified in your browser configuration settings, as explained later. This feature is designed to assist users in recalling whether they have downloaded a particular file within the time frame specified. You should be aware that not every Web page author abides by these conventions and that hyperlinks on some pages may be in other colours, and may not change colour after you have accessed the files that they point to. Graphics (icons, buttons and images) can also be hyperlinked. When you select them another file is downloaded, or the document scrolls. Graphics do not change colour once selected, although the colour around the border of the icon may change.

From a bookmark

If you locate a file that you think you may want to access again, you can *bookmark* it, the procedures for which will be detailed below. When you bookmark a file, it places the address of the site in a file named <bookmark.htm>. By default this file is stored in the Netscape directory. You can open your list of bookmarks by selecting the *Bookmarks* menu or button, or either, depending on the version of the Netscape browser that you are using. In Internet Explorer the term used is *Hot Favorites*, for which there is either a menu or a button, or both in more recent versions. To access a bookmarked file you select its address from the bookmarks or hot favorites list with the mouse cursor.

2.5   Backtracking

Typically, Web pages provide links to other files, some of which are on the same server while others are on other servers linked to the Internet. If you move forward along a particular hyperlink trajectory, say P–F–K–R in Figure 2.4, and you subsequently want to access page L, which is referenced from page P, you will need to get back to P to select it.

There are a number of ways of doing this. If you have not moved many pages beyond the opening one of the series, you can select the *Back* button repeatedly until you get back to P, then select L. Quicker still with Netscape, click the right mouse button in the document window and select *Back*. If you have gone back and want to go forward again, select the *Forward* button on the button bar, or select *Forward* on the right mouse button.

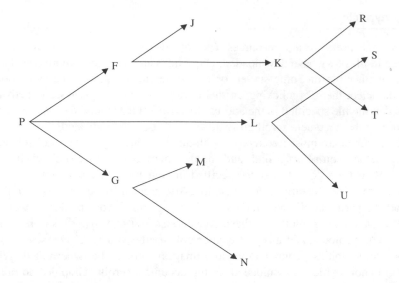

Figure 2.4　*Hyperlink pathways.*

To quickly upload again a file that you have already seen during a session, you need to use the *Session history* option. This keeps a record of all the sites that you have visited during the session, a session being the interval between opening and exiting the browser. In both Netscape and Internet Explorer, click on the ▼ button to the right of the address text box.

Address	http://www.un.org/Overview/rights.html	▼
	http://www.tufts.edu/departments/fletcher/multi/humanR ▲	
	http://164.11.32.97/~paul_dowdall/address.htm	
	http://164.11.32.97/~paul_dowdall	
	http://www.io.org/amnesty/ailib/aipub/index.html	
	http://www.umn.edu/humanrts/ins/inservie.htm	
	http://lcweb2.loc.gov/frd/cs/cshome.html	
	http://www.intac.com/PubService/human_rights/	

Figure 2.5　*Session History drop-down box.*

Select the file that you want from the list, as in Figure 2.5. Note that this just lists sites, not files within a site. So, for example, if you have accessed the United Nations home page and then downloaded the UN News file, only the former will be listed in the pull-down section of the location box.

Both Netscape and Internet Explorer compile history files that list addresses of documents accessed over more than one session. The extent and time period covered depends on the way in which this feature of the browser's functions has been configured. You access it in Internet Explorer by choosing the Open History Folder on the Go menu. If you are using Netscape you will find a list of the most recently visited sites tagged onto the bottom of the Go menu. If you have visited many sites, the Go menu will not list all of them. Instead, open the Window menu and select History. If you are working in a computer lab it is likely that the history file will be overwritten each time the operating system (e.g. Windows) is shut down. If you are reviewing many files in a particular session, consider bookmarking those that you think you might want to look at again. Bookmarking a file takes less than five seconds. At the end of the session you can easily delete the bookmarked files if you do not think that you will need them again.

2.6   Manipulating accessed documents

Having accessed a file that appears to be useful, your choice is between printing it, reading it online or saving it whole or in part for subsequent use, or some combination of these. If you possess an offline browser, an inexpensive application that I highly recommend purchasing, discussed on p. 30, you can open files that you accessed during a session after you have gone offline. This is convenient, often saves time and is cheaper than either accessing them again or reading them online if you have to pay connect charges.

Copying

Copying is relatively straightforward. Block (select) the data that you are interested in, select the Edit menu, and copy it to the clipboard (see p. 294) by selecting *Copy* from the Edit menu or by holding down the Ctrl key and pressing the C key. Now switch to the open application you want to copy the text to and paste it in by selecting *Paste* from the Edit menu, or holding down the Ctrl key and pressing the V key.

Printing

Before you can print a document the browser must have stopped loading. A partially loaded document can also be printed. The *Print* command is on the File menu. There is also a *Print* button. Choose the appropriate printer from the list by selecting the ▼ button. In Netscape you can also select which pages of the document you want to print. To do so you need to select *Print Preview* from the File menu. Graphics and tables will print satisfactorily on most printers. The procedures are similar for Internet Explorer, versions to 3.01, with the exception that there is no print preview facility. You cannot, therefore, readily determine the page numbers to print if you want to print only a portion of the document, portions of the first and last pages excepted.

Adjustments to page margins may be made in the Page Setup window, which is accessed from the File menu. Ensure also that the boxes under Header and Footer are all checked, as illustrated in Figure 2.6. This ensures that on each of the printed pages the title of the document, its location or URL, the date it was printed and its page number will be included. The first three of these are important for referencing purposes, as indicated in Chapter 4. It is very easy to lose track of where you located documents and it may be impossible to locate them again. Even if you can, this will take up unnecessary time. It is worth noting that the page numbering cannot be used for referencing purposes as individual users may have different margins, page sizes and fonts configured.

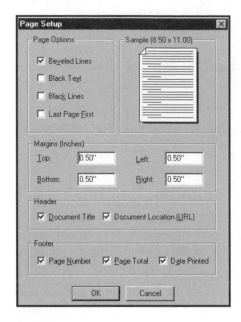

Figure 2.6 *Page Setup dialog box.*

The procedures for Internet Explorer are similar with the exception that the header and footer variables are set, not with check boxes, but by typing in codes that are detailed in the help facility.

Saving documents

It is unwise to assume that files that you manage to locate at one point in time will be accessible later. Even if they are still available somewhere on the Internet, you may have to spend scarce time locating them. Disk space is relatively cheap and getting cheaper by the week. Deleting files does not take long if they have been ordered systematically. If you locate interesting materials that you believe you may want to consult subsequently it is probably worth saving them to disk.

Documents are saved from the File menu by using the *Save As…* option. This opens a window like that illustrated in Figure 2.7. First choose the drive and folder (G) that you want to save the file to. On PCs the drive letter for floppy disks is usually A. If you are saving to hard disk, usually C, you may want to create a special directory for html files. Next choose the file format (F) that you want the document saved in. There are two choices, html and text, the default being html. HTML is an acronym for *Hypertext Markup Language* and is the coding used for authoring Web pages. When a file is saved in html format you can open it in your browser. You can then print it, as well as save it again as a text file. You should, therefore, save it as a text file only if you are certain that you will not want to open it in or print it from the browser. Saving a file in html allows you much greater flexibility than saving it as a text document.

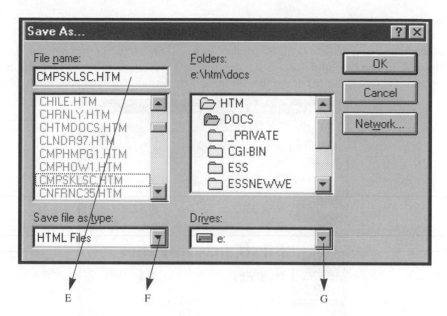

Figure 2.7   *Save As dialog box.*

When you save the file in text format all the html codes are stripped out. Also, a text file contains only minimal formatting. If the original file included html formatting commands for bold, italics, print sizes, headers, etc., these will not be visible in the text document. In addition, information that appeared in forms or tables will not be arranged as systematically as in the original. Frequently these will be very difficult to interpret in a text file.

When you save an html file it is only the text content that is saved. If the document includes graphics (buttons, images, lines and icons), these will not be saved, regardless of whether the file is saved in html or text format. Graphics need to be saved separately. To save a graphic place the cursor over it and click the right mouse button. On the menu select *Save Image As...* This will open up the *Save As...* window (Figure 2.7). The subscript to the file name will usually be *.gif*, sometimes *.jpg*, both of which are graphic file formats. If you are saving a graphic because you want it to be loaded into a browser along with the text of a file that you have saved, you should save it to the same directory as the one that you saved the html file to. Unless you do so you will need to rewrite sections of the html coding in the master document. You should be aware, however, that you might need to alter the coding even if you save it to the same directory.

Having determined the directory to which you want to save the file, and the file format, you need to decide on the file name, E in Figure 2.7. The default name, the one that will appear in the File Name box, is the one that the original author will have given to it. You may want to change this to something that will make it easier for you to recognize its contents.

2.7   Frames

A relatively recent addition to Web page design has been the introduction of frames. These divide the browser document window and interface into a number of sub-areas, in each of which a separate document is loaded. Invariably one of these is an index to the component documents of the presentation, as is the left-hand frame in Figure 2.8. If you select any of the headings listed there, a document linked to it will be loaded in the frame on the right. This modification to html formatting was initially greeted with some enthusiasm as it increased the rather limited design possibilities then available to Web page compilers.

Figure 2.8   *Frames displayed in Internet Explorer.*

2.8   Bookmarks

One of the most difficult aspects of working the Net is keeping track of those sites and files that you find useful. The bookmark feature allows you to keep a permanent record of the sites that you consider important, to organize them into categories and to include additional information relating to the file bookmarked. Having bookmarked a site, to download it subsequently you only need to select its title from your list of bookmarks. Competent management of bookmarks will enable you to easily locate links to information and resources that you consider are important to your own study, teaching and research interests. It is worth remembering that within a decade many users of the Internet may have bookmark files running to thousands of items.

In the discussion below I distinguish between those users who have access to the same computer all the time, and those who are likely to work on different computers each session. The latter will need to save their bookmark file to floppy disk at the end of each session and load it into the correct directory when they start a new one, as detailed below. Even those readers who have their own computer may need (when changing computers or jobs) to save their bookmark file to disk. A bookmark file contains useful information that may have taken considerable time to accumulate. It should be treated like any other important file and backed up on either another network drive or at least two portable disks.

Adding a bookmark

Bookmarking a file is relatively simple. Once you have accessed a file (site) that you consider it is likely that you will want to access again in the future you have two options.

The easier, and quicker, with both Internet Explorer and Netscape, is to place the cursor anywhere over the document window and click the right mouse button. From the options on the menu select *Add Bookmark...* in Netscape, or *Add To Favorites...* in Internet Explorer. Alternatively, select the Bookmarks menu in Netscape or the Go Favorites in Internet Explorer and then choose the *Add* option.

Particulars relating to the file will be saved to the bookmark file in Netscape or to the favorites file in Internet Explorer. These include the title of the page and its URL. The first few addresses that you have bookmarked on your list can be accessed from the Bookmarks/Favorites menu. When you select either of these the addresses bookmarked will be listed, as in Figure 2.9 (Netscape) or 2.10 (Internet Explorer).

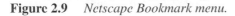
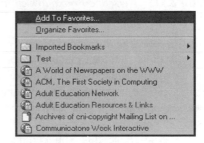

Figure 2.9   *Netscape Bookmark menu.*

Figure 2.10   *Internet Explorer Favorites menu.*

To download a file on the list, move the cursor over it and release the mouse button. When the list gets too long, you access the remainder by selecting the *Go to Bookmarks/ Organize Favorites* option on the menu. This opens a window in which your bookmarks are listed in alphabetical order of bookmarks, or of folders if you have created these, as illustrated in Figure 2.10.

Organizing bookmarks

It does not usually take long to accumulate a lengthy list of bookmarks. The problem then becomes one of organizing them so that you can locate them easily. One of the easiest ways of doing so is to arrange them by subject. To do so you need to select the *Go to Bookmarks/Organize Favorites* options, Figure 2.9/2.10. The discussion below focuses on the organization of bookmarks in Netscape. The procedures are quite similar for Internet Explorer, but you may need to refer to its help file for detailed guidance.

Folders

Figure 2.11 is a graphic of one of my Netscape bookmark files displayed in the Bookmarks Interface. It includes two types of objects: folders, e.g. History, which are holding units for groups of bookmarks arranged by subject, and individual bookmarks, e.g. Teaching and Learning on the Net. You can, of course, classify folders on any basis that you think appropriate.

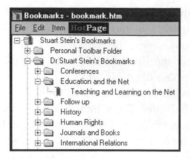

Figure 2.11   *Netscape Bookmark editing interface.*

To create a folder, place the cursor anywhere below the root folder where you want
to create one and either select the Index menu and then choose *Insert Folder...* or click on
the right mouse button and do the same. In the *Name:* text box of the dialog menu that
appears, type the name you want to give to the folder. If you want to give it a description,
do so in the box provided.

Having done this you can move bookmarks into appropriate folders. This is
accomplished by first placing the cursor over the bookmark that you want to move into a
particular folder. Depress the left mouse button and then move the cursor (drag it) until it
is over the folder you want to drop the bookmark into. When the pointer of the cursor is
over the folder you are selecting, releasing the mouse button drops the bookmark into it.
Double click the folder, if it is not open, to see whether the bookmark dropped into the
right folder, or click on the + sign to the left of the folder icon, expanding its contents. You
may need to play around for five minutes getting the hang of this. Once you get the feel for
it you should find the procedure very simple. By using the same procedure described
above you can also create folders within folders. So, for instance, in the History folder in
Figure 2.11 I might want to create folders relating to historical periods (subdivided by
country and era), bibliographies and so forth.

Folders can be copied or cut by clicking on them, then selecting these options from
the Edit menu or by choosing these options from the pop-up menu on the right mouse
button. The latter is quicker. If you think it is necessary you can insert a separator between
a folder and the one above or beneath it by highlighting it and selecting *Insert Separator*
from the right mouse button or the Item menu. I have never found much use for this
feature as it merely results in having to scroll down a lengthier file.

Bookmark properties

Locating a particular bookmark, or a folder that contains a specific category of bookmark,
can be made easier by adding details to the folder and bookmark properties descriptions,
as illustrated in Figure 2.12. This dialog box is accessed from the *Item* menu on the Bookmarks interface, or the pop-up menu on the right mouse button. Highlight a folder or
bookmark, select the *Properties* option from the *Index* button, or the menu on the right
mouse button, and fill in the details.

Figure 2.12   *Bookmark Properties dialog box.*

After you have added the bookmark, select *Edit Bookmarks* from the Bookmarks menu. Locate and select the bookmark by right clicking on it. From the pop-up menu select *Bookmark Properties*. Complete the details in the Description box, Figure 2.12. You can also use this opportunity to provide an alternative name for the file. The default name is frequently insufficiently detailed to serve as a pointer to the contents of the file. Sometimes it is just the URL.

You can use the procedures outlined above to add a bookmark without accessing the file it points to. Having opened the Bookmarks interface, right click anywhere and select *Insert Bookmark* from the pop-up menu, or make this selection from the *Item* menu. This opens the *Bookmark Properties* dialog box, Figure 2.12. Complete the details and select OK.

Bookmarks may be moved between folders by drag and drop, as described earlier. You can also delete, copy and change their properties. At times you will want to have a bookmark for the same file in more than one folder. Select the bookmark, copy to the clipboard and then select the folder you want it placed in and paste it in. On other occasions you may want to change the URL of a file because its address had changed.

Saving the bookmark file

Regardless of whether you work permanently on the same PC or not, it is advisable to periodically save your bookmark file to some drive other than the one that the browser saves it to by default. This is usually the hard disk of the PC that you are working on. By default Netscape saves the bookmark file, named bookmark.htm, to the Netscape directory. If you work mostly in a computer laboratory you will need to save your bookmark file to a floppy disk after each session during which you have added more. Next time you may be using a different PC. Other users may have added, deleted or rearranged bookmarks, or the configuration of the browser may have been set up so that each time the operating system is closed down the bookmark file is overwritten. Although it may not occur very often, hard disks do crash and need to be replaced. If this happens and data becomes corrupted it is extremely costly and difficult to retrieve it. In my experience it is rarely worth the effort of trying.

If you have accumulated bookmarks over a considerable period of time it is folly not to make arrangements to back them up adequately. 'If things can go wrong they will go wrong' may be a cliché, but it is also an everyday reality in matters relating to information technology. If you doubt this, ring up your help desk for confirmation.

If you are working in a lab, at the end of a session locate the bookmark file on your hard drive and save it to floppy disk. You can do this by using the *Search* facility in File Manager (see p. 293) or Explorer with the query <bookmark.htm>. At the beginning of the next session overwrite the existing bookmark file by replacing it with the bookmark.htm file that is on your floppy disk. You can do this using drag and drop in File Manager/Explorer. At the end of the session repeat the saving to floppy disk procedure. If you work all the time on the same PC, save the bookmark file periodically to a floppy disk or a file server, overwriting the old one periodically with a more up-to-date version.

In Internet Explorer your Hot Favorites are located in a folder called Favorite. To locate it use the *Find* facility in File Manager or Explorer. Move it between the hard disk and floppy disks by drag and drop in exactly the same way as you would a file.

2.9   Working the Net with the browser

The ease with which you will be able to connect to a site and download documents will depend very much on the timing of your sessions and the bandwidth of your connections to the Internet. Many of the resources mentioned in Part IV of this book are found on servers in North America. After 11:30 a.m. the links across the Atlantic and the US backbone network become congested. This is also the time of day when the UK network is under maximum load. Between 11:30 and 19:00 the process of downloading documents is likely to be more time consuming than at other times.

If your browser is configured properly, discussed on pages 297–305, accessing and manipulating files should be relatively straightforward. If you type the address in the location box and hit the Enter key, or select a bookmark or a hypertext link, the browser will attempt to access the file requested. If you have typed in the URL make sure that you have done so accurately. Mistyping is probably the most frequent cause of error messages. It is easily done as the font is small and dots do not show up all that clearly, particularly when inadvertently you have typed two of them.

Increasing Net searching productivity

Large files will obviously take longer to download than smaller ones, whatever the state of network connectivity. When it is poor, even relatively small files may take some time to download. You can improve your session output by adopting a number of strategies.

- *Turn the images off by deselecting Auto Load Images on the Options menu.*   Graphics take up an inordinate amount of file space compared to text. By instructing the browser not to load images your documents will load much faster. If you find that you need to see most of the graphics, turn images on and reload the document. Remember that if you have turned *Auto Load Images* off, you can view particular images in the document that was downloaded by right clicking on its position and selecting *Load This Image* from the pop-up menu.

- *Open more than one browser window.*   If you select the *New Web Browser* from the File menu, another browser interface window will open. Whilst a file is loading in one browser window you can be reading a different one in another. The number of windows that you can have open simultaneously is a function of the memory specification of your PC and its configuration. It is, however, very difficult to manipulate effectively more than three windows at a time. Also, there is degradation in speed associated with many windows being open simultaneously. If you are working on a network with many users and everyone opens two or more browser windows the degradation will become noticeable.

- *Stop and reload.*   If a document that is relatively small in size is taking a long time to download, stop the process and then use the *Reload* button.

- *Stop and refresh.*   As an alternative to reloading you should in some circumstances try refreshing the document. The difference between reloading and refreshing is that the former operation causes the browser to download the file again, whereas the latter procedure downloads the file contents that are already in your PC's memory. Sometimes the file has been downloaded to the computer but for some reason it has not been transferred to the browser document window. If you select the *Stop* button and/or the *Refresh* option from the View menu, the contents of the file in memory should be displayed in the browser document window. Try selecting *Stop* first, and then *Refresh*.

- *Access a file with identical content from another site.*   Many files with the same content are deposited on more than one server. Some can be found at tens of sites. Of course you have to make an assessment as to whether this is likely with respect to the file that you want to access. In many cases this is quite easy. So, for instance, if you cannot get through to The Marx/Engels Archive to access a file of a Critique of the Gotha Program, stop the download procedure, access Alta Vista and type in the query <Critique +Gotha +Program*>, see Chapter 7. The records returned will list alternative locations. Doing this should take less than a minute.

  You should commit the address of Alta Vista (www.altavista.digital.com) or HotBot (www.hotbot.com) to memory. In the latest versions of the Netscape and Microsoft browsers, URLs that you have accessed before are held in a file on disk. When you type in part of the URL, say www.al…, the rest will automatically be filled in.

- *View documents offline.*   Frequently you will access a Web page with links to many documents that you will want to have a look at. Some of these will be on the same server, others elsewhere across the Internet. To view all these documents you would need to use the *Back* button frequently to get back to your starting point to access those other documents that you are interested in looking at.

A solution for this is to copy the URL of the source, or starting point page, to the clipboard. When you want to return to the source page, instead of using the *Back* button paste its URL into the location box and hit Enter. As the file is already in memory, it will load much faster than it did on the first occasion. Now you can select the next link that you are interested in, and as many links as you want further along this chain. Repeat this procedure until you have exhausted all the pages that you want to view from this source page. You can now also disconnect from the Internet if you do not have an open connection through a network. If you use the *Back* button now you will be able to view all the pages that you have downloaded sequentially.

- *Save the file directly to disk rather than downloading it first.* Frequently you will know in advance that a file that is linked to from a page that you have downloaded is one that you will want to save. One way of doing this has been described earlier. Click on the hyperlink, wait until it is loaded in the document window and save it. A quicker way is to save it directly without downloading it. There are two ways that you can do this. The first is to click on the hyperlink with the right mouse button and choose *Save Link As…* which will open the *Save As…* window. Select drive, directory, file format and file name as described earlier. The second method is to hold down the Shift key and click on the hyperlink with the left mouse button. This opens the *Save As…* window. Both methods work with Netscape, but only the first with Internet Explorer.

Malfunctions

If you attempt to access a server or download a file, and the message illustrated in Figure 2.13 appears, there are a number of possible explanations.

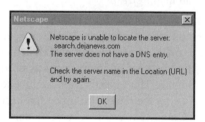

Figure 2.13   *Error message.*

1.   You have typed in the address incorrectly. Check the address. If it is not an address with which you are familiar, quickly type in one that you are familiar with that you have not accessed recently. If you still get the same message, assume first that there is something wrong with either your network or your browser configuration. Check the configuration options, as discussed on pages 303–4.

2.   If you are working in a laboratory look around and see if anyone else is using a browser. If they are accessing files successfully it is likely that there is something wrong with the configuration of the PC that you are using, the configuration of the browser, or both (unlikely). Either check the browser settings and reconfigure if

necessary, move to another PC, or contact your system administrator or help desk. If you are connecting through an Internet access provider, check that you are still connected or use the Finger application to check the status of access to the Internet.

I recommend having access to more than one brand of Web browser on the same PC. This allows comparisons as far as speed and ease of use are concerned and provides a check on where the fault is most likely to be located. If you fire up the other browser and do not have a problem accessing the same server with it, it is most likely that something has gone awry with the configuration of the browser you first used.

3. The message in Figure 2.13 sometimes appears when the server you are trying to connect to is out of operation. Servers are frequently taken offline, usually only for short periods of time so that hardware or software can be added, changed or upgraded. Sometimes you will receive a similar message with the suggestion that you try again later.

If you type in an address such as

<http://www.gemini.org/a/home/index.html>

and receive the message

File Not Found

The requested URL <http://www.gemini.org/a/home/index.html> was not found on this server

this indicates that the file has been either moved or deleted. In other words, the server address is active and correctly typed, but the file is not available in the specified directory <a/home/index.html>.

Web managers are forever setting up new servers and moving home pages, between either servers or directories on them. The best thing to do when you encounter this type of problem is to work yourself back from the end of the address. In other words, in this example, use the blocking facility to lop off index.html, and then try again. If you have no luck with this, go further back along the URL pathway. On any of these files, if they exist, you may be able to locate a link to the file you are after. It is least likely that the main entry point to the presentation, the root file, will have moved, in the example <www.gemini.org>. If you see no link there you may find an email address of the author of that file. Send the author a request for information on its location. Alternatively, if you are looking for a file with known content, try and track it down through the use of a search engine.

Occasionally you may type in an address, or select a link, see indications that something is happening, the hourglass will be visible in the document window and nothing in fact occurs. The system is said to be frozen/hanging/crashed. If you are working in a Windows environment you will sometimes receive the message *General Protection Fault*. In these circumstances usually the only way forward is backwards. You will have to go out of Netscape and fire it up again. In Windows 3.X this frequently necessitates rebooting the system. If you are using the Windows 95 or NT operating system you can shut down the browser by selecting simultaneously the Alt, Ctrl and Del keys. This will bring up a menu from which you should select the *Task Manager…* and then highlight the browser application. Select *End Task*. This brings up another menu from which you may be required to select *End Task* if this does not occur automatically. The browser should shut down. You can then restart it and try again.

2.10 Offline browsers

As noted earlier, by using an offline browser you can substantially reduce the time you spend online. Even if you do not incur connectivity charges, you can increase your productivity if you download files during those times of the day when the bandwidth logjam is not so acute. Generally, offline browsers are easy to install and use and most are relatively inexpensive. For further information try the software download sites reference on page 306. However, I would recommend either MSICE (Miscrosoft Internet Explorer Cache Explorer) or NSCE (Netscape Cache Explorer) from MWSOFT at <http://www.mwso.com/>. The cost, July 1998, is only $20. Either one will import the cache of the other browser.

CHAPTER 3

Internet addresses

The movement of files across the Internet requires three functioning components:

1. Host computers on which are stored files that are available for downloading by anyone who wants to access them.

2. Users who have access to hardware and software that enable them to access these servers.

3. The network infrastructure that connects 1 and 2, over which instructions between PCs and servers are transmitted.

The browser and server are the constituent components of what is referred to as a client–server application. With the aid of the browser, which is the client, a user issues a command to another computer on which there is a software application that services the request. The software that receives and services the request is the server side of the client–server application. The command is transmitted through the network infrastructure. The server processes that command and sends back the file requested. Estimates of the number of publicly accessible Internet-linked servers are necessarily somewhat speculative. The figure now, however, is well over 750,000.

How, then, does a user go about locating a particular server, or specific files stored on it? Files on Web servers are arranged in the same manner that they are on a hard or floppy disk, in directories or subdirectories. Every computer linked to the Internet has a unique address, its IP (Internet Protocol) address. Every file accessible over the Internet also has a unique address. This address, known as its URL, an acronym for Uniform Resource Locator, identifies the computer (server) on which it is located and the directory in which it is stored. If you want to download a specific document, for instance the Maastricht Treaty, you need to identify a computer that it is stored on, and then the directory on that computer in which it is located. The URL of the document will identify both. A file with specific content may have a large number of associated URLs as it may be stored on a large number of servers.

In the normal course of events you will probably not give much attention to URLs. You may locate the URLs of files through using a subject directory or search engine, or you may obtain the address from an email message, a book or magazine, by word of mouth, or in a newspaper or television advertisement. It is entirely feasible to access documents by keying in URLs in the location boxes of browsers, or by selecting links on downloaded documents, without having to have any understanding of what their different components refer to. On the other hand, acquiring some understanding of these matters takes only about 15 minutes and is likely to make navigating the Internet much easier and more efficient in a number of ways.

- From URLs you will be able to infer what type of Internet server the file is stored on, or the protocol used to access the resource. The URL will indicate whether the file is stored on a Web, gopher or ftp server, or whether the resource you are attempting to access requires remote login through Telnet. This information will provide some indication of the type of file stored there, as well as how recent the information included on it is likely to be. There are still quite a few gopher servers around, but many of the files stored on them were uploaded years ago. Similarly, although there are a large number of graphic, text and video files stored on ftp servers, they are most frequently accessed for software applications that are stored on them, rather than for text files.

- From a URL you can invariably determine the nature of the organization on whose server the document is loaded. You can, for instance, frequently establish from the address whether it is a military, commercial, educational, international, governmental or other (residual) organization, or a network (e.g. an Internet Service or Access Provider). If you have located a list of potentially relevant files through the use of a search engine and have thousands to choose from, knowing the type of organization that has uploaded the document may assist you in deciding which of these to access. You may, for instance, require statistical information relating to labour markets. Files that include information on this subject that have been provided by governmental organizations, or educational establishments, may be more relevant to your needs than those contributed on a mailing list or newsgroup, or by an NGO.

- From the URL it is frequently possible to ascertain the identity of the organization that has made a particular file available. This can assist you in establishing its relevance and usefulness. You may, for instance, be interested in downloading documents relating to world population growth. From the address you will be able to determine whether documents returned for a particular search string have been made available on servers managed by the United Nations, the World Bank, particular universities, NGOs, or commercial organizations. Although the organization making the document available is not always the originator, you can at least exercise the option of only downloading files that are on the servers of a particular type of organization, or a named one.

- Frequently you will attempt to access documents and receive a message that indicates that the document is not available, or that the server does not exist. You can use the address to work out a strategy for attempting to establish whether the document is in fact no longer available or whether it has just been moved and where it has been relocated.

- One of the reasons why you may receive such a message is that the URL has been entered incorrectly in the document in which it is embedded. Web page compilers do make typing errors and some are not as familiar with the correct construction of a hyperlink as perhaps they should be. To be in a position to establish whether the URL is correctly entered, you need to have some idea of what a correctly constructed URL should look like. For instance, the URL

<http://lyre.mit.edu/~deering/dwhpmc//vsu/dwhpmc.htm>

has two forward slashes before vsu. This is undoubtedly a typing error. If you select such a link you will receive an error message. If you simply delete the second forward slash before vsu, you should be able to access the file. Such knowledge, of course, is not a remedy in instances when the format is correct but the content is not. If the file name should have been dwhpmf.htm rather than dwhpmc.htm, removing the forward slash error will not enable the browser to locate the file.

Below are three examples of Internet addresses. I have refrained from using the adjective 'typical'. Each Internet address is unique, so 'typicality' in the present context is meaningless. However, these addresses are well within the range of those that you are likely to encounter.

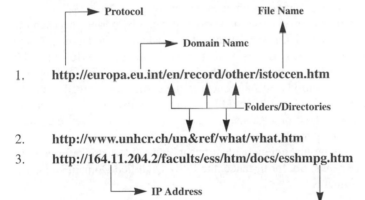

The first component of the URL is the protocol. This is separated from the rest by ./ / This is the only place in a URL in which you should have more than one forward slash. In all the addresses above, the protocol is http (Hypertext Transfer Protocol), which signifies that the resource being accessed is a file on a Web server; in other words, it is a Web page. As you can access files on gopher and ftp servers through the Web (i.e., by means of the hypertext transfer protocol), the protocol at the beginning of the address could also have been gopher:// or ftp:// The Internet Protocol Suite also supports Telnet, so you could also encounter a URL of the form

<telnet://164.11.32.95>

If you selected such a link a separate window should open allowing you to remotely login to another computer. The protocol, therefore, indicates the type of software server that is being accessed. Generally, but not always, ftp files accessed via the Web tend to be software applications and image files. Gopher servers are increasingly being phased out and replaced by Web servers. Files stored on them tend to be of older vintage.

The component of addresses 1 and 2 that immediately follows the protocol, europa.eu.int and www.unhcr.ch, is referred to as the domain name. It is an alphanumeric system that pinpoints networks, organizations and individual computer systems. Generally, the domain name is read from right to left. It consists of blocks of characters separated by periods. The top-level domain, which corresponds to a major branch of the Internet, is at the extreme right of this component. The fields to the left of it are subdomains, those of the organization, the computer, and directories on it.

Taking www.unhcr.ch, the domain name of address 2 above, this breaks down into three parts. Moving from right to left, *ch* signifies the country, which is Confederatio Helvetica (Switzerland), *unhcr* signifies the organization, the United Nations High Commission for Refugees, and *www* is the name of its Web server. If it had two or three Web servers, as many large organizations do, the others might be addressed as *wwwa* and *wwwb*. In address 1 above, europa.eu.int, the *int* signifies an international organization, the *eu* the name of the organization, the European Union, and *europa* is the name of one of its Web servers. The domain name www.bristol.ac.uk signifies that the address is based in the UK, that it is an academic institution (*ac*), that it is the University of Bristol (*bristol*) and that the Web server is *www*. Domain names are not case sensitive.

In address 3, unlike the other two, four numbers separated by periods succeed the protocol. This is the IP address, which is the numerical equivalent of the Domain Name System. IP stands for Internet Protocol. In this particular case, the numbers 164.11.204.2 resolve into www.uwe.ac.uk, which is the URL of the University of the West of England. The Domain Name System was introduced subsequent to the earlier widespread use of IP addresses because it was recognized that it would be easier for most users to remember blocks of characters signifying type of organization, country, name of server, etc., than strings of numbers separated by periods.

The address of a computer that uniquely identifies it on the Internet is referred to as its *Fully Qualified Domain Name*. So, for instance, the Fully Qualified Domain Name for the server at 10 Downing Street is

<www.number.10.gov.uk>

Every Fully Qualified Domain Name (such as <www.unhcr.ch>) has an IP or similar resource record that locates it. When you place a URL in the address box of the browser in the format of a Fully Qualified Domain Name and then hit the Enter key the browser connects first to a Domain Name Server. The Domain Name Server is a software application that sits on a computer and resolves Fully Qualified Domain Names so that the appropriate servers can be located. Only after the IP address has been resolved does the browser attempt to connect to the host computer on which the requested file is stored.

If you now examine address 2,

<http://www.unhcr.ch/un&ref/what/what.htm>

you should be able to draw some useful inferences. This URL indicates that the file is a Web document, the organization is UNHCR, the file is located in a directory probably abbreviated from United Nations and Refugees (*un&ref*), in a subdirectory called *what*. The document most probably describes some of the activities of the UNHCR. It is also a reasonable inference that the subdirectory named *what* may include other files that offer explanations relating to the activities of the UNHCR. It should be possible to access these by deleting *what.htm* from the URL, leaving

<http://www.unhcr.ch/un&ref/what/>

and attempting to download this Web page by hitting the Enter key. This will probably index various documents included in that subdirectory. When you attempt to locate files with the assistance of search engines, you will frequently retrieve from the database pointers to hundreds of documents. Scrutinizing the URL is one way of sorting out those that you consider might be worth consulting.

Web hyperlinks may point to a file on the same server, to a file on a different server, to a different position in the same file, or to a particular position in another file, rather than to the top of that file, which is the default position. A link to a different position in the same file, or to a particular position in another file, can be recognized by the # at the end of the URL succeeded by some alphanumeric characters that identify the precise position that is linked to. So, for instance, the URL

<http://www.demon.net/netiquette/flames.htm#origins>

points to a file named *flames.htm* on the Demon server, in a directory named *netiquette*, and to a position in it that has been named *origins*. Many Web files include numerous errors relating to internal links within them, the most frequent manifestation being that when you select one you find yourself at the top of the page rather than at the position where the Web page compiler intended you to move to. Use the *Back* button to get back to where you were and then either scroll down, or use the *Find* facility to locate the appropriate position.

Top-level domains are arranged in two groups: types of organizations and countries. The designations below are for top-level domains in the United States. Where those of the UK differ, this is noted. The primary organizational domains are:

- com = commercial organizations (e.g. www.microsoft.com). In the UK, commercial organizations are also designated by co (e.g. www.demon.co.uk).

- edu = educational establishments (e.g. www.cmu.edu). In the UK educational establishments are designated by ac (e.g. www.ic.ac.uk). Frequently, working out the name of the organization is not difficult; the two examples above refer to Carnegie Mellon in the United States, and Imperial College in the UK.

- int = international organizations. There is an overlap between this category and the one immediately below. The Web server address of the United Nations, for instance, is www.un.org

- org = organizations not included in the other categories, such as NGOs and research organizations (e.g. aclu.org, the American Civil Liberties Union. Note that this organization's Web server address consists of only two blocks of characters separated by a period).

- gov = governmental institutions and organizations (e.g. www.senate.gov, the home page of the US Senate's Web presentation, or www.number.10.gov.uk).

- net = networks and organizations in charge of networks that are constituent parts of the Internet (e.g. www.cybercom.net or www.demon.net).

Geographically-based Internet domains, using a standard developed by the International Organization for Standardization, are country oriented. Each country is designated by two characters (e.g. jp = Japan, il = Israel, ch = Switzerland).

Files are always being moved on and between servers linked to the Internet. It is virtually impossible to ensure that all the links that are embedded in a particular file (document) are live, in the sense that if you select the link you will be able to download the document to which it points. If files are moved to another directory or server, the new address may be downloaded when you attempt to access a file with the original URL. Alternatively, you may be automatically redirected to the new URL, immediately or after a short time lag. Unfortunately, those moving and deleting files do not always leave pointers to their current location. In these circumstances the previous URL may in many instances assist you in trying to track its current location. If you move back along the URL, from right to left, deleting in blocks between forward slashes (/***/), you may find clues useful.

Thus, to take one of my earlier examples, if you attempt to locate the file at

<http://www.unhcr.ch/un&ref/what/what.htm>

and you receive an error message that suggests the file is no longer available, remove *what.htm* and hit Enter. If this does not work, remove *what* and then, if necessary, also *un&ref*. Somewhere along the line back you may find pointers to the location of the file that you are endeavouring to locate. At the very least you may be able to find an email address of a Webmaster/author, to whom you can direct questions concerning the whereabouts of the file you are seeking. Of course, this does not always work. Moreover, at times it may be quicker to conduct another search via a search engine.

Because files are regularly being moved between servers and directories on them, or are being updated, it is worth bookmarking them (see Section 2.8) and, using the facilities available in Netscape, associating significant details relating to the file with the bookmark. These should include, minimally, the title of the file and the name of the author if available. Academic authors frequently move between institutions and move their Web presentations as well. Knowing the name of the author is one of the easiest ways of tracking down the file with a search engine.

Many URLs end with a forward slash, as in <http://www.demon.net/>. Note that it is not necessary to include the last forward slash. Including it, however, may reduce the download time marginally.

CHAPTER 4

Referencing Internet materials

4.1	Introduction	37
4.2	Underlying principles	39
4.3	Electronic mail	43
4.4	FTP (File Transfer Protocol)	43
4.5	Gopher sites	44
4.6	Mailing list messages	44
4.7	Synchronous/asynchronous communications	45
4.8	Telnet	46
4.9	Newsgroups	46
4.10	World Wide Web resources	47
4.11	Conclusion	49

4.1   Introduction

Collectively, files stored on Internet-linked servers comprise the largest database of publicly available data in digital format. The range and volume of this data is considerable and is extensively augmented daily. Most Internet users now have access to a range of materials that it is unlikely that they could obtain with such immediacy from any other source. It includes electronic versions of some primary and secondary materials for most Social Science disciplines, refereed electronic journals, current news reports, statistical data, maps, organizational agendas, and much more. There are tens of thousands of articles and books available for downloading. An increasing volume of information and reports produced by governments, international agencies, courts, political parties, pressure groups, social movements and other organizational entities are available in electronic format. While it may take months, or even years, for printed versions of these documents to be made available in libraries, many are available for downloading from Internet servers immediately they are released. Hardly any library could afford the costs of purchase or storage of printed versions of the wide range of materials currently available in electronic format without cost.

It is clear, therefore, that in the future Internet-accessible files will be used increasingly as source material in Social Science research and in the communications of those practising it, in exactly the same way as printed resources are currently relied upon. The balance between resource availability in digital and printed formats is likely to tip increasingly in favour of the former for a variety of reasons, two of the most important being ease of access and cost. Accordingly, there is probably no need to convince either Social Science staff or students of the need for some form of standardized referencing of these resources.

There are certain characteristics associated with the way in which digital materials stored on Internet-accessible servers are typically manipulated that have implications as far as referencing them is concerned. Once a book, thesis, journal article, news clip or similar is published in hardcopy, their contents are regarded as permanent. Invariably it is possible to locate an original and examine it in detail. Anyone with access to such resources can, at the very least, state with reasonable confidence that the author made a specific statement at a particular place in the manuscript or document. Those printed sources most widely consulted are available in thousands of copies, each of which is assumed to be an exact replica of all others. There may be disagreements over the meaning attributed to specific content, but ordinarily there is no reason to question the fact that it was so written. If changes are made in subsequent editions it is not especially complicated to note the differences.

Digital files accessible over the Internet diverge in important respects from this model. Invariably the original version, if it can be traced at all, is not in the user's possession in the same sense that a book, thesis, article or even photocopy of the same may have been. It is most probably a file on a hard disk on the author's PC, on a network file server, or on a floppy disk, if the 'original' exists at all. The originator may have been responsible for uploading the file on some server, or may have authorized this through an intermediary who usually would not read or scrutinize its content. This applies not only to those instances in which individuals are the creators of the contents of files, but also to those when they merely act as intermediaries by scanning the materials into digital format and arranging for them to be uploaded on servers.

There is nothing to prevent those who scan in documents, upload files, or manage Web servers from moving, altering or deleting files. Security on the Internet is currently a major issue in connection with electronic commerce, but it has implications for non-commercial transactions and issues as well. If some computer users can hack into files on servers whose owners take extensive precautions to ensure that they are secure, much less of a problem is posed to them by the overwhelming majority of Internet hosts where issues of security are not considered to be particularly important.

Anyone who uses the Internet over an extended period of time discovers that documents that were at some point in the past known to be located in a particular directory on a server with a specific URL can no longer be downloaded. There may be various reasons for this. Web presentations are regularly being reorganized and files moved or deleted. Files can just as easily be altered as they can be eliminated or moved. Frequent modification of electronic documents is considered to be a *sine qua non* of a competent and well-managed Web presentation. The cost of modification in comparison with printed documents is negligible. This allows Web authors to add further information, update relevant sections and incorporate new links to resources that have become available subsequent to an earlier modification. Very few Web authors keep older versions of documents on a server along with modified ones. Frequently there is no information detailing when modifications were made, or these are overwritten by subsequent modifications.

For all these reasons, then, references to electronic files do not carry the same implications concerning permanency and accuracy ordinarily associated with printed or handwritten documents. When authors make a point, or authenticate a statement by reference to printed materials, they are suggesting that the reader can confirm the correctness of their interpretation by examining this same source. When someone makes a reference to an electronic text it is far from certain that the reader can confirm this reference as the document may have been permanently withdrawn, moved or modified. In all such cases it would not be possible to authenticate elements of a copy of the document from the original source. The suggestion, made by some commentators, that students, for instance, should submit printouts of the original with their essays, dissertations, theses, etc., is not practical in terms of costs or the time of academic staff. Moreover, for reasons just outlined, frequently there will be no means of verifying that the printout is an exact copy of the file it purports to point to. Any document that is downloaded can be altered prior to printing it out.

4.2   Underlying principles

Internet-accessible resources are located on servers that are accessed via a number of different protocols – http (Web pages), gopher (various files on gopher servers), ftp (various files on ftp servers), nntp (newsgroup communications). Many files that have identical content have different URLs because they have been placed on numerous Internet hosts. Also, digital files do not have the same degree of permanency that hardcopy materials ordinarily do. Accurate and comprehensive referencing of digital resources on Internet servers is, therefore, probably more important than it is with respect to printed materials. Of course, both should be accurate. However, inaccuracies that occasionally arise in connection with the referencing of printed materials frequently do not prevent the identification of the source material. If the addresses of files on Internet hosts are not referenced properly it may be impossible to trace them, or to pinpoint which edition/modification they represent.

Unfortunately there is at present no agreed standard for referencing Internet resources. In the present context it is probably pointless to delve in detail into the merits of the alternative styles of referencing Internet resources that have been advanced. The recommendations I advocate below build on some of the suggestions made by authors of the documents referenced at the end of this chapter.

My approach is essentially pragmatic. Given a lack of consensus on this matter, the main underlying principles of importance to be adopted as far as referencing is concerned should be:

●   To provide as much information as is necessary for another user to access the same resource.

●   To provide information enabling the user to contact the originator, if appropriate.

●   To follow, as far as possible, the order of referencing that is commonly followed in hardcopy academic referencing (i.e., originator, title, date, etc.).

These are relatively easy principles to formulate, but their implementation is some-what more difficult given the variety of Internet resources that are available and the variable rights of access that users have to them. I adopt the following conventions, some of which are attributable to the authors mentioned in the bibliography at the end of this chapter.

1.   Electronic addresses should be enclosed in angle brackets. One of the difficulties associated with referencing Internet materials is that of distinguishing between the address of a file and the command sequence to access it. For instance, any file that can be downloaded through ftp (file transfer protocol) will necessarily be located in a specific directory. The sequence of directories that you need to move through in the directory structure to get to it is the command sequence you need to use, not the address. Harnack and Kleppinger recommend placing an address in angle brackets and signifying a command sequence by emboldening the protocol (e.g. gopher, ftp), following this by a white space and then the pathway necessary to access the resource. So, in fact, the two would look very similar to each other. The first example below is that of the address of an ftp (file transfer protocol) resource, and the second is the command sequence, which follows their recommendation.

<ftp://sunsite.doc.ic.ac.uk/packages/netscape/pub/navigator/2.02/windows/N16202.exe>

ftp sunsite.doc.ic.ac.uk/packages/netscape/pub/navigator/2.02/windows/N16202.exe

The differences between the two pathways in the above examples are that when an address is stipulated it is placed between angle brackets. When it is a command sequence the protocol, **ftp** in the example, is emboldened and has white space following it, and it is not succeeded by a colon and two forward slashes.

Because there is so little typographical difference between the two formats, I recommend placing both, command sequences and addresses, in angle brackets. If the protocol is succeeded by a colon and two forward slashes (ftp://, or http://, or gopher://, or telnet://) you know that you can copy this to the address box of a graphical browser in order to access it. If a white space and then the equivalent of the rest of an address follow the protocol, this indicates a command sequence. If you place that in the location box of your browser and endeavour to access the file, an error message will be returned. It is, therefore, very important to note that the command sequence cannot simply be changed into an address and entered into the location box in Netscape or some other graphical browser.

Let me illustrate with an example. The document "IHR: A Layman's Guide to the Institute of Historical Review" is located on an ftp server. To access it with a graphical browser the following address should be inserted in the location box:

<gopher://ftp.std.com:70/ORO-18491-/obi/book/Holocaust/IHR>

If, on the other hand, you were to access this document directly from the ftp server, the command sequence would be as follows:

< ftp ftp.std.com/obi/Holocaust/IHR>

As you can see, the two are very different from each other. If you were to enter the above command sequence as an address in a graphical browser, by transforming it into <ftp://ftp.std.com/obi/Holocaust/IHR>, when you try to access it you will receive an error message.

Unlike the referencing of hardcopy materials, the title of the immediate document is always placed in double inverted commas, regardless of whether it is an article or a book. In the case of electronic mail messages, or postings to Usenet newsgroups, the subject matter of the message, i.e. that which appears in the subject line, is placed in double inverted commas.

2. If the title of a larger work to which the document is linked in some way is referred to, it is italicized.

3. Most of the normal punctuation that is found in hardcopy referencing is dispensed with. There are two reasons for this. First, punctuation is included in electronic addresses (e.g. full stops and question marks). Ending an address with a full stop, for instance, would simply add a component to it that did not exist in the original.

<http://www.microsoft.com>

is an electronic address. To render it as

http://www.microsoft.com.

so as to separate it from the next part of the reference, would render it inaccurate. In other words, if you inserted such an address in the location box and hit Enter an error message would be returned.

4. Page numbers are not, as a rule, included in electronic documents. Greenhill and Fletcher suggest that the page numbers included in a printout could be used to pinpoint the position that an author wishes to draw attention to. This, however, is not very practical as the page numbering will vary according to the word-processing/html printout selections chosen by users. It is also unnecessary. All browsers and word processors include a *Find* feature, usually on the Edit menu. If you include a quotation from the document, or keywords, placed in brackets after the address, readers can use this facility to locate the place of reference much more rapidly that they could by printing out the document and finding the correct page, for example (keywords: Cacioppo and Perry, 1969). Accordingly, if the document is a lengthy one and you wish to draw the attention of the reader to a specific passage, include a sufficiently unique keyword, or string of words, so that someone else accessing the document can easily identify it. Of course, if this is done

endlessly in a short communication it could become somewhat tedious to both author and reader.

5.   It is very important to be precise about the addresses, names of originators, titles or subjects and dates. All of these can be employed by readers to access documents referred to. In addresses, a slash, stop, or white space out of place will make it difficult, if not impossible, for the reader to access the document referred to.

6.   If the reference is to a software package, it is helpful if you indicate how large it is as this may influence the reader in deciding whether to access the resource using a particular protocol or at a particular time, for instance (5.7Mb, 654K). The same applies to lengthy documents, e.g. I Kant, "Critique of Pure Reason" (2.7Mb).

7.   As the referencing of electronic resources is of recent origin and there is no consensus on the appropriateness of a particular style of referencing, the author should provide some indication as to what the component parts of a reference signify. Many readers will probably not be particularly familiar with a whole range of matters relating to the Internet. Some of the proposals that have recently been advanced fail to recognize the difficulties many will face in interpreting what the component parts stand for. Let me illustrate the importance of this by reference to an example from Harnack and Kleppinger. They rightly point out that with respect to Internet resources, for some of the reasons I have given earlier, it is necessary to include the date at which a resource was accessed as well as the date at which the resource was composed or last modified. They suggest including the latter at the end of the reference and the former after the title/subject. Although this is eminently sensible, at this stage most readers encountering the reference in Figure 4.1 are likely to encounter some difficulty in trying to understand what the various components signify. Accordingly, you should indicate somewhere, such as in an introductory note to the bibliography, what the various component parts of your electronic references signify.

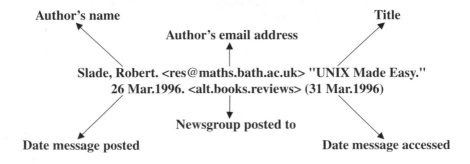

Figure 4.1   *General referencing components.*

Below I provide model examples for the referencing of different types of Internet resource.

4.3   Electronic mail

The components that should be included are originator's name (it could be an individual, company, government organization, etc.), originator's electronic address (in angle brackets), the subject of the posting (i.e. that which appears in the Subject line), and the date the message was posted. All of these components should be listed exactly as they appeared in the message header (Figure 4.2).

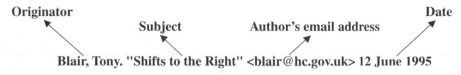

Figure 4.2   *Electronic mail.*

4.4   FTP (File Transfer Protocol)

It is possible to download files from ftp servers with a Web browser. That is, you can use a graphical browser such as Netscape or Internet Explorer to do so. However, it is much more common to download files directly using an ftp client. As ftp files can be downloaded in these two ways, this means that the reference can include either an address or a command sequence. This was discussed at greater length above (see pp. 40–1).

The components that should be included when referencing an ftp URL include the originator's name (if known or applicable), the resource name (it could be the title of a document, or the product or file name of a software package – e.g. Netscape Navigator Gold 3.0 Beta), the date the resource was uploaded on the server or modified, the date when accessed, and the resource size if the file is a software package. The latter gives the reader some indication of how long it will take to download the file. If the resource is a text file which is sizeable this should be indicated if possible. Frequently Web authors indicate the size of files next to the hyperlink used to download them, although not often enough. This is illustrated in Figure 4.3.

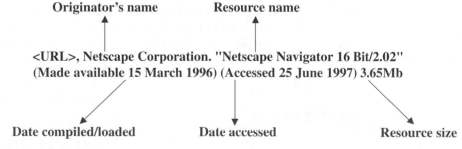

Figure 4.3   *File size.*

The components that should be included in an ftp command sequence are the protocol, followed by the command sequence (i.e., the pathway through the ftp directory structure) and the date the resource was accessed/downloaded. This is illustrated in Figure 4.4.

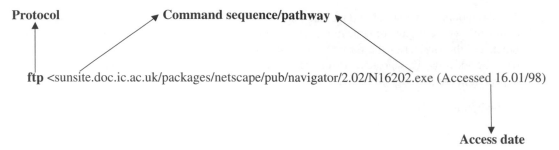

Figure 4.4   *ftp command sequence or pathway.*

4.5   Gopher sites

The information required is identical to that mentioned above in connection with ftp resources, as illustrated in Figure 4.5.

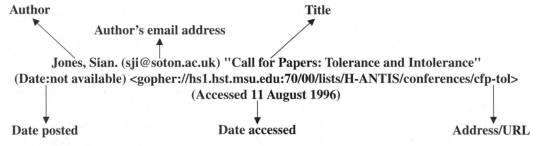

Figure 4.5   *Gopher address.*

I have included the electronic address of the originator after the name, in addition to the address of the resource. Whether this is necessary in particular instances is a matter of judgement. The general principle should be to provide essential information to allow another user to access the material, from either the site, or the author, or the person who placed it on the server.

4.6   Mailing list messages

The referencing of postings made to mailing lists poses somewhat different problems from those discussed in connection with ftp, electronic mail, and gopher resources. First, the address of the originator, and the address where the message can be accessed from, if it can at all, are different. Second, mailing list messages are organized by subject. The same subject can give rise to many messages, and on the same day it is possible that there will be a number of postings from the same individual on the same subject. There is no way of giving a reference to one of a number sent on the same day, by the same author, on the same subject, unless you also enter the time that the message entered the database so that this can be used to access the message. Accessing mailing list messages requires intermediate level skills and can be time consuming for those not familiar with the techniques involved (discussed in Chapter 11). In addition, you invariably have to subscribe to a list before you can access their archives.

In addition to the information components employed in the model examples included above, in referencing mailing list messages you also need to include the administrative address of the mailing list as well as the name of the list. The administrative address is necessary in order to retrieve a copy of the message from the archives. Although some authorities recommend inclusion of the list address (that is, the address to send messages to so that subscribers can view them), I do not think that this is necessary as there is no use to which that can be put in relation to accessing the message. The referencing of mailing list messages is illustrated in Figure 4.6.

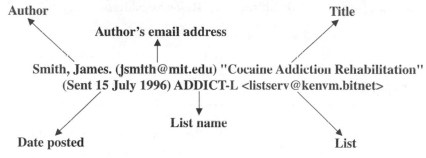

Figure 4.6   *Mailing lists.*

I have not included the date the message was accessed, as recommended by Harnack and Kleppinger, among others. In my view this is not particularly important in this context as archived messages are, as far as we know, not subject to modification. Moreover, the date of access can be different from the date of dispatch for reasons that are entirely irrelevant as far as the objectives of referencing are concerned. Many messages remain unopened on file servers for lengthy periods of time due to the absence or lack of interest of their addressees, neither of which circumstance is relevant to resource citation.

4.7   Synchronous/asynchronous communications

Examples of synchronous electronic communications are some of the exchanges that occur in conferencing systems, or in such Internet-based forums as Internet Relay Chat, MUDs and MOOs (see Glossary). The latest versions of both Netscape's and Microsoft's browsers include conferencing facility applications. Although the current output of Internet-based synchronous exchanges may not be particularly rich in immediate information useful to most social scientists, this situation is bound to change before long. Both synchronous and asynchronous communications are likely to be used extensively for exchanges between experts in various subject areas as text-based and video conferencing systems become more widely available and used.

The information that should be included, if possible, are the name of the individual whose comments are being referenced, the electronic address of the author, the subject of the exchanges, the type of resource on which the exchanges occurred, the electronic address of the resource if it exists and is known, and the date the exchanges took place. This is illustrated in Figure 4.7.

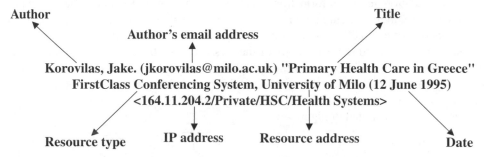

Figure 4.7   *Synchronous communication resources.*

4.8   Telnet

The information that needs to be provided for this resource is similar to that mentioned earlier in connection with ftp and gopher references, for example:

> Washington University Libraries. "comp.infosystems.www.users" (Modified 20 March 1995) telnet <library.wustl.edu 8/3/2/5> (Accessed 11 August 1996)

The address here indicates that you first telnet to: library.wustl.edu and then choose in sequence menu options 8/3/2 and 5, which brings you to "comp.infosystems.www.users".

4.9   Newsgroups

The model for referencing newsgroup communications parallels that provided earlier for mailing lists and should apply equally well to other discussion groups, including those on Local Area Networks. Of course, as far as the latter are concerned, you will need to give some indication of where the resource is located, despite the fact that the communications may not be publicly accessible. The information that should be provided includes the name or alias of the author of the communication, the author's electronic address, the subject of the communication, the date of the communication and the name of the news-group. There is no real need to provide the date of access as once posted the author cannot alter the message. More important than the date of access can be the time of the posting of the article. This is relevant when the author sends a number of postings on the same date, under the same subject heading to the same newsgroups. Newsgroup articles are threaded, which means that all responses to a particular message are part of the same thread. If an author makes more than one of these in a day, then there will be more than one article with the same author name, date and title. They may, however, be differentiated by having a number on the subject line indicating its place in the sequence of messages. The only way of distinguishing between them effectively is by including the time of the posting as well as the date: (13 July 1996 GMT 15:35:25). This is illustrated in Figure 4.8.

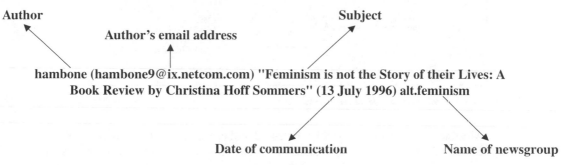

Figure 4.8   *Newsgroups.*

4.10   World Wide Web resources

Web pages are written in Hypertext Markup Language (HTML). Figure 4.9 is part of an html document, as it would appear in the Netscape Communicator browser.

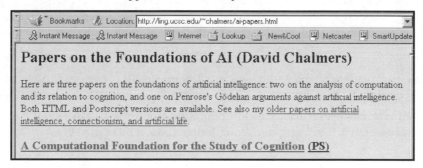

Figure 4.9   *Web page as displayed in browser.*

Figure 4.10 is a part of the html source document illustrated in Figure 4.9. This can be accessed by selecting *View Source* on the browser Edit menu.

The characters and text enclosed in angle brackets are tags. They indicate to the browser how the text that appears after the angle brackets, or between sets of angle brackets, should be formatted. So, for instance, <H2> indicates that the text following should be a header, size 2, and </H2> that this feature should be turned off.

One of the first problems encountered in connection with the referencing of html documents relates to the title. In html the inclusion of a title is a minimal requirement for a document to be readable by a browser. However, by title is meant everything that is enclosed between the <TITLE> and </TITLE> brackets, which appear towards the top of the document, as in Figure 4.10. The document in the browser has the same title in this case but need not do so.

```
Source of: http://ling.ucsc.edu/~chalmers/ai-papers.html - Netscape        _ □ ×

<!DOCTYPE HTML PUBLIC "-//W3C//DTD HTML 3.2//EN">
<HTML>
<HEAD>
    <TITLE>Papers on the Foundations of AI (David Chalmers)</TITLE>
    <META NAME="GENERATOR" CONTENT="Mozilla/3.0Gold (X11; U; SunOS 4.1.4 sun4
</HEAD>
<BODY TEXT="#000000" BGCOLOR="#FFDEAB" LINK="#0000EE" VLINK="#551A8B" ALINK=

<H2>Papers on the Foundations of AI (David Chalmers)</H2>
```

Figure 4.10 *Web page so484urce code.*

Most academics would probably contend that the document title is more important than the html <TITLE>...</TITLE> title, as the former relates to the substance of the document, whereas the latter is merely an html reference point. Generally speaking this is a reasonable position to take. However, what appears between the <TITLE>...</TITLE> tags is what counts as the title of the document as far as search engines are concerned. Land recommends that 'Should the title given in the header elements vary substantially from that in the <TITLE> element, it may be listed also, following the <TITLE> part, and separated by a semicolon'. Land, therefore, gives greater emphasis to the <TITLE> element than to the header element. While recognizing the merit of his argument that there is a problem here, I think that at present it is impractical to expect most academics to follow this line. I suspect that many would not know where to locate the <TITLE>...</TITLE> in the source file if their browser only displays it in part because the length exceeds the display default. In the example illustrated in Figure 4.11, I include the document title rather than the html title.

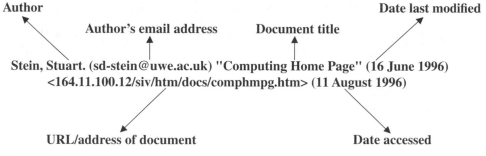

Author   **Date last modified**

      Author's email address   **Document title**

Stein, Stuart. (sd-stein@uwe.ac.uk) "Computing Home Page" (16 June 1996)
        <164.11.100.12/siv/htm/docs/comphmpg.htm> (11 August 1996)

      URL/address of document   **Date accessed**

Figure 4.11 *WWW pages.*

There is another general point made by Land that merits consideration. Some files that can be accessed over the Internet can only be viewed or heard online if users have the necessary software applications (viewers for postscript or .pdf files, for instance) and the appropriate hardware (sound cards for audio files, for instance) and they have configured their browsers appropriately. A very significant number of text files available over the Internet are written in formats that require special viewers in order to read them. Many users may not be aware that a particular file requires special hardware or software, and if they did, they may be inclined not to attempt to download it. Land suggests that when reference is made to such files, the reader should be informed that they are audio, video, graphic or text files that require special hardware or software. He suggests that this be indicated in brackets after the title, as follows:

Oasis: "Cast No Shadow"
<http://www.sony.dreammedia.com/Epic/Clips/AIFF_WAV/Oasis/CastNoSh.wav>
(Audio file, .wav format) (Accessed: 11 August 1996)

4.11   Conclusion

Although the examples given above take into account the most important Internet resources and platforms, they by no means exhaust them. There are various commercial databases, reference materials (the *Encyclopaedia Britannica*, for instance), and numerous electronic journals and magazines which, although accessible over the Internet, can only be downloaded by subscribers. Without subscribing to these databases it is not possible to access the documents that may be referred to by some users. These databases have their own directory systems that may require variations from the recommendations made above. In the future there are likely to emerge other electronic platforms that will require different formats of referencing from those considered above.

Bibliography (Web sites)

Greenhill A, Fletcher G. "A Proposal for Referencing Internet Resources." (Last modified 01 February 1996) <http://www.gu.edu.au/gwis/hub/hub.acadref.html> (Accessed 18 August 1996)

Harnack A, Kleppinger G. "Beyond the MLA Handbook: Documenting Electronic Sources on the Internet." (Last modified 11 June 1996) <http://falcon.edu.edu/honors/beyond-mla/> (Accessed 18 August 1996)

Land T. "Web Extension to American Psychological Association Style (WEAPAS): Proposed Standard for Referencing Online Documents in Scientific Publications." (Last modified 31 May 1996) <http://www.nyu.edu/pages/psychology/WEAPAS/> (Accessed 18 August 1996)

PART II

Searching the Internet

Chapter 5   **Subject directories**   55

Chapter 6   **Search engines and searches**   65

Chapter 7   **Searches: basic**   71

Chapter 8   **Searches: advanced**   83

Those who have not had extensive opportunities to explore the variety of resources accessible over the Internet are inclined to view it principally as a vast repository of information. There are millions of data files that can be readily accessed: text, graphic, moving image, binary and audio. Billions of data packets move across the network every day. The extraordinary rate of growth in the number of files that can be accessed has been facilitated by the rapidly falling costs of data storage and management. This, and the decline in the costs of digitizing printed materials and the perceived marketing benefits of an Internet presence, for both individuals and organizations, have all contributed to the exponential growth in the volume and range of publicly accessible materials that are stored on Internet servers.

No one is in a position to quantify the overall volume of data, or the data in particular categories stored on Internet-accessible servers. Every second of the day files are being uploaded, deleted, moved or altered. Millions of other files are sent in the form of messages to newsgroups and mailing lists. Nearly all of this material is stored for lengthy periods of time on servers and can be downloaded, just as can articles in electronic journals or magazines, parliamentary statutory orders, financial, economic and other statistical series, reports, legislation, books, software packages and many other categories of data in digital format. Currently there are hundreds of millions of files stored on Internet-accessible servers. Alta Vista, one of the larger databases of Internet files, processes 33 million. DejaNews, an archive database of messages sent to newsgroups, stores 1 Gb of new data a day and this excludes quantification of the graphic images which are regularly posted on some newsgroups.

While many of those commentating on the Internet point to its data warehousing features, many others draw attention to the communicative relationships which it has fostered and facilitates. From the point of view of the pragmatic social scientist, the two are not mutually exclusive. On the one hand there are plenty of files out there that can be traced, downloaded and utilized. On the other, there are millions of Internet users whose knowledge can be tapped, with whom views can be exchanged, who can proffer assistance on where to locate on the network required information, and with whom it is possible to set up joint teaching, learning and research projects. On one plane the Internet may be regarded as a large database, much like a library, although its content is radically different. On the other, it is an interactive knowledge and information community, infinitely more intricate, multidimensional and vibrant than any that has existed hitherto.

It is extremely unlikely that you will be able to think of many subjects for which it would be impossible to locate some file that includes information relating to them. Of course, not all information is necessarily usable or useful. Even if we impose the latter restrictions, the requirements of most users will currently be catered for to some degree. The important thing to remember in this context is that what is available currently is but a pointer to the volume and range of materials that are likely to be increasingly accessible over the next five to ten years. In a few years' time the numbers of files currently measured in hundreds of millions will be reckoned in billions.

Having a large volume of material to choose from that extends to virtually every conceivable subject, topic and issue, is all very well. The problem, and it is a serious one, is how to track down and access efficiently that which is of immediate interest to you. Over the past 500 years, during which the printed text has been the primary vehicle for the dissemination and storage of information, libraries have been the warehouses of knowledge. Librarians developed sophisticated classification systems for different categories of text or near-text (microfiche). The classification system had a physical counterpart. Journals, newspapers, reference materials, discipline and subdiscipline, topic and subtopic, all had their assigned portions of physical space. If you were studying politics, economics, history, sociology or law, you went to designated rooms and shelves where information relating to these specialisms was housed. Once there you could browse the available materials, peruse indexes and tables of contents and, sometimes with a bit of guidance from the librarian, invariably locate information pertinent to your task at hand. A similar arrangement of materials obtained in archives of historical documents. Although I may have exaggerated the extent of the orderliness of the arrangement of printed (written) information, it is currently very systematically arranged in comparison with Internet resources.

On the Internet you can find many files in digital format that have printed counterparts in libraries, archives, bookshops and private collections. There are numerous others which have no counterpart in print, just as there are many printed resources that have no digital equivalent. Unlike a library, the Internet has no organization to speak of, no systematic arrangement of materials, no central cataloguing system and no agreed standards for the classification of resources. If you are seeking a report of the World Bank on irrigation projects in Malaysia, or of a rapporteur to the UN Human Rights Commission on human rights in East Timor, or a copy of the Hungarian constitution, or anything else, there is no central catalogue to consult and no librarians.

Locating information in digital format stored on Internet resources is, therefore, considerably more problematic than finding printed materials in a traditional library. For a start, you cannot be certain that what you are seeking is available at all. More frustrating still, even if you spend hours being unsuccessful in a particular quest, you can only be sure that you have been unable to track it down, not that it is unavailable. Although this may apply to printed materials as well, the scale of the problem is vastly different.

Despite these handicaps, those using the Internet have various means available to them that if used effectively will assist in the rapid, efficient and economic location of required information. I emphasize here rapid, efficient and economic because it is possible, although not certain, that a user who has unlimited time and is not constrained by economic considerations will triumph eventually in locating specific information. Most of us, however, have limited time available, and many are constrained by the costs of online time. If the same information can be located in a library more rapidly, the incentive to download files from remote servers is removed.

There are four major tools available to assist in the tracking of information, though only two are at present sufficiently effective to merit attention.

- **Subject directories** (Chapter 5).   These are compilations of links to resources classified by discipline, subdiscipline, topic and subtopic. Some are basically lists of hyperlink titles, whereas others are annotated. Essentially, they are an attempt to transfer to the Internet the classification and physical arrangement model of the print-based library. Subject directories are very useful for obtaining an overview of the resources available in particular discipline areas.

- **Search engines** (Chapter 6).   These are the front-ends of massive databases. Users can key in search strings which when submitted return hyperlinks to records that include matching content. There are thousands of such search engines available, ranging from those that cover files lodged at a particular site, to those that regularly process tens of millions of files distributed on servers dispersed across the world. Some search engines target specific types of resource, such as electronic mail addresses or newsgroup messages, whereas others process files covering a variety of types of resource. Search engines are a highly efficient means of tapping the wealth of resources already stored on Internet-linked servers.

- **Push technology software applications**.   These are relatively recent additions to the range of Internet information tools. They are designed less for when users want to locate a specific file/document (say a report of a government agency, NGO, software application, graphic, etc.) than for the regular updating of particular types of resource or information. Instead of the user keying in periodically particular search strings in some search engine, or revisiting a particular site, the user specifies documents to be updated, news items to be downloaded and sites to be searched for specified content. The user can also schedule the intervals, time of day, quantity and type of information to be downloaded (text/graphics) and similar. While these applications are likely to be of increasing importance in the future, at present they are still very much under development.

- **Intelligent search agents**.   These are software applications that can work either in the background while the user is doing something else on the PC, as long as the PC has an open connection to the Internet, or over a period of time specified by the user. In the latter case, which is still in the realm of *under construction*, the intelligent agent will roam the Internet and deposit pointers to information as specified in the queries entered by the user on some remote server. Later the user can collect the list of links found that meet the query formulated for the agent to implement. In all instances the user keys in a search string and the software processes the instructions so that the Internet is trawled to locate files that match the query or queries submitted. Usually the user has the option of having the complete files downloaded or just their titles and URLs. In the latter case, the user can scroll down the list and select those to be retrieved immediately or later.

Chapter 5 describes the organization and uses of the major subject directories and Chapter 6 describes the way that search engines operate. Chapters 7 and 8 outline how to formulate effective search queries.

CHAPTER 5

Subject directories

5.1 Introduction   55
5.2 Major subject directories   57
5.3 Conclusion   63

5.1 Introduction

A subject directory is a catalogue of Internet resources spanning a range of subjects arranged by topic. During the first few years of the Web, when search engines, robots and wanderers were things of the future, subject directories were an essential guide to Internet resources. Although today experienced Internet users will invariably use a search engine in preference, subject directories are still a very useful resource for obtaining an overview of what is available in particular subject areas.

Figure 5.1 displays the (December 1997) home page of Yahoo, which is currently the largest and most frequently accessed subject directory. Yahoo arranges links to Internet resources in 14 subject-based hierarchies. If you select any of the categories shown (e.g. Education, Science), the file that is downloaded will include links to subcategories, which, in turn, include links to further subdivisions lower down the subject tree. Figure 5.2 displays the main subdivisions that need to be traversed (early December 1997) to locate the UK Labour Party home page from the main subject heading Government.

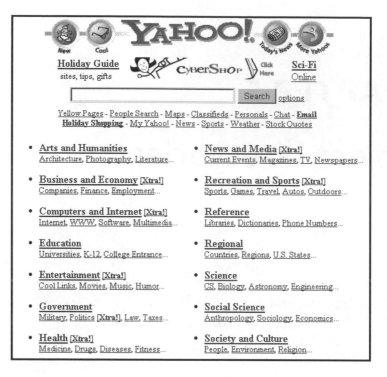

Figure 5.1 *Yahoo interface.*

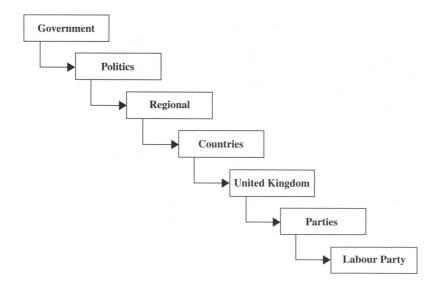

Figure 5.2 *Yahoo subject directory tree.*

5.2 Major subject directories

Yahoo

<http://www.yahoo.com>

The most comprehensive and frequently accessed subject directory is Yahoo. As noted already, each of the 14 main subject areas is further divided and subdivided. As you move down the subject tree hierarchy the volume of subdivisions, or, at the penultimate level, volume of files, is indicated by numbers in brackets. The subdivisions subsumed under Social Science (6 December 1997) are reproduced in Figure 5.3.

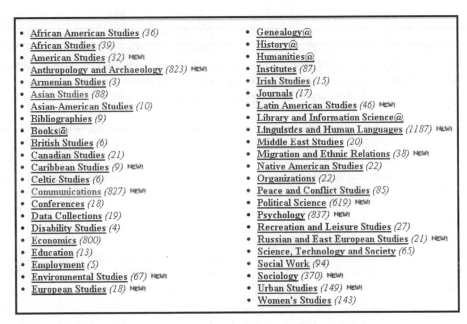

Figure 5.3   *Yahoo Social Science subject listing.*

The figures that appear in brackets designate the number of entries that appear under each subcategory. The entries under some headings are extensive. There are 1187 for the subcategory Linguistics and Human Languages, whereas there are only three under Armenian Studies and 32 under American Studies. The figures are arrived at from a totalling of the number of subcategories and files subsumed. The four entries referred to in Figure 5.3 under Disability Studies are all for files (documents). Under the Economics heading, on the other hand, most of the entries at the next level are to the subdivisions displayed in Figure 5.4.

These subdivisions, in turn, may refer either to other subdivisions or to files. You can move through a large number of subdivisions before you arrive at the level where you are able to identify whether the information you are endeavouring to locate is available.

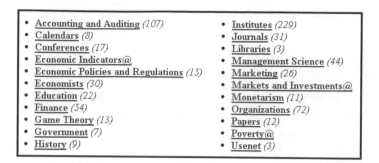

* Accounting and Auditing *(107)*
* Calendars *(8)*
* Conferences *(17)*
* Economic Indicators@
* Economic Policies and Regulations *(15)*
* Economists *(30)*
* Education *(22)*
* Finance *(54)*
* Game Theory *(13)*
* Government *(7)*
* History *(9)*
* Institutes *(229)*
* Journals *(31)*
* Libraries *(3)*
* Management Science *(44)*
* Marketing *(26)*
* Markets and Investments@
* Monetarism *(11)*
* Organizations *(72)*
* Papers *(12)*
* Poverty@
* Usenet *(3)*

Figure 5.4   *Economics subject subdivisions.*

Where the @ character appears this indicates that the subject is included under some other general subject/category heading. In the above list, for example, History is a subcategory of Humanities, which, in turn, is subsumed under the general subject heading of Art. Accordingly, if you are attempting to locate information that you consider belongs under a heading for which there are surprisingly few or no entries, you should investigate whether the subject is subsumed under one of the other main headings or their subdivisions.

On many of the Yahoo pages there appears the entry Indice. This is located above the sections for subdivisions and files, usually superseded by a number in brackets. This is a link to a document that includes hyperlinks to other listings on the Web dealing with a particular subject. Using the above illustrations, selecting Social Science (Figure 5.1) and then Economics (Figure 5.3) provides links to 800 references, one of which is the Indices page. This file includes links to 29 compilations of economics resources prepared by other organizations or individuals. Each of these compilations lists numerous Internet resources touching on economics subjects.

Yahoo includes links to numerous resources that are likely to be of interest to social scientists. Although, as I noted earlier, subject directories are very useful for providing a feel for what is available on the Internet in particular subject areas, locating a specific resource by traversing the many routes to the same destination available through their subject tree hierarchies can be time consuming and frustrating. This is as true of Yahoo as of other subject directories. You may spend considerable time finding out that what you are looking for is not easily tracked down. It may very well be there, but under which heading is not always clear, particularly as the cross-referencing is not always adequate.

If you are looking for a particular document or information relating to a specific topic, you can use the Yahoo search engine as an alternative to moving down the subject tree hierarchy. The search engine interface illustrated in Figure 5.5 appears on every page.

Figure 5.5   *General search engine dialog box.*

To locate a resource (e.g. Magna Carta/Versailles Treaty) type a word or phrase into the text box and select the *Search* button. You can focus the search by selecting

Options, to the right of the *Search* button. This will bring up the search engine dialog
boxes featured in Figure 5.6.

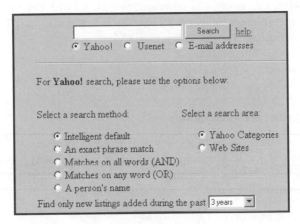

Figure 5.6   *Search engine options dialog box.*

For detailed guidance on the search syntax that can be employed with this search
engine, select *help* to the right of the *Search* button. Also, consult Chapter 6 on search
engines.

- If you are searching for a phrase, include it in double quotes: "historical materialism".

- If you want to ensure that a word is included in the documents that are returned,
  place a + before it. If you want to ensure that a word is excluded, place a − before
  it: dialectical + philosophy | Marx − Groucho.

- t: restricts the search words in the query to the title of the document. For instance,
  if you are searching for the electronic text of Plato's *The Republic*, you could try
  the search query t: Republic. Although not an infallible rule, it is likely that the title
  of the document that is included in the first page of the electronic text will include
  the word Republic. In this context, title refers to the html title of the document.
  Invariably, this is the same as the title of the document (see pp. 47–8).

- u: restricts the search to the URL. This is particularly useful for tracking down
  companies or organizations as their name frequently appears in the URL, for
  instance u: microsoft | u: UN | u: WHO.

- Use wildcards to return documents with variable endings for the letters entered:
  crim* for crime(s) | criminal(s) | criminality | criminalization | criminalisation |
  criminogenic.

- You can use compound search queries if you employ the query variables in the correct order, which is + − t: u: "" * For example, to track down information relating
  to the ruling of the Supreme Court of the United States on the Communications
  Decency Act (CDA), I used the following search query:

    +CDA t:decency u:eff.org "Supreme Court" (December 7, 1997)

I assumed that a good place to search would be the Web site of the Electronic Frontier Foundation (EFF) which monitors issues relating to freedom of information, and which had conducted a vigorous campaign against the CDA. The records returned when this query was submitted included an EFF page with the title EFF "Censorship – Internet Censorship Legislation & Regulation (CDA, etc.)" Archive at the top of the list.

Galaxy

<http://galaxy.einet.net/galaxy.html>

One of the pioneer subject directories that still features prominently in many Internet resource guides is Galaxy. It is organized on similar principles to Yahoo, being divided into a number of main categories, which, in turn, are subdivided and then subdivided further into lower-order directories. The main categories are:

- Business and Commerce
- Humanities Reference
- Engineering and Technology
- Law

- Science
- Medicine
- Social Science
- Government

Its coverage of Web space, in terms of both breadth and depth, is somewhat disappointing. Some important subcategories are missing. For instance, under Law there is no entry for International Law. The Sociology subcategory of Social Science does not include any subdivisions. Instead there is a long list of links, mainly to Departments of Sociology at various universities. The scope of coverage of some other topics, history and human rights, for instance, is not reflective of the depth to which they are resourced on the Internet.

BUBL Information Service subject tree

<http://bubl.ac.uk/searches/subjects/>

This is a UK-based service to the academic community that is funded by an entity called the Joint Information Services Committee (JISC):

<http://www.jisc.ac.uk/services/index.html>

It was originally developed as a resource for the training and use of librarians. The BUBL Information Service seeks to provide an annotated first stop to available Internet resources in a large number of subject areas. Its *raison d'être* is that the use of a search engine in the first instance results in unfocused information relative to the needs of users. Accordingly, the links provided are arranged in two clusters: annotated guides by subject and non-annotated Internet resources arranged under a much smaller number of headings, and by country. The rationale for the latter is that these non-annotated resources, although providing a less trustworthy route map than the annotated resources, are a better guide than simplistic search queries hurled at Alta Vista or some other search engine.

The subject resources likely to be of interest to social scientists are classified under Ancient and Medieval Worlds, Education, Information Technology, News, Philosophy, and Social Sciences.

The coverage of discipline areas in the social sciences/humanities/arts is extremely limited. Also, with the exception of the Social Sciences subject category in the above list, which links to the Social Science Information Gateway at the University of Bristol discussed in further detail below, all the links are to United States servers.

There is a separate page that allows you to search by country:

<http://bubl.ac.uk/searches/countries/>

Select a link to a particular country and you are directed to a page on a server in that country that provides links to relevant data relating to it. There has been no attempt to tailor the information relating to a particular country to the needs of the UK higher education community. In fact, it does not appear that there are any criteria relating to such needs. So, for instance, the link to India (accessed in March 1998)

<http://www.123india.com/>

includes, in turn, links to sections on Food and Drink, Sports, Travel and Tourism, Humor and Jokes and Personal Pages. Although the rationale underlying the selection of links to non-annotated resources is that they are preferable to basic search engine queries, it is not clear why particular resources have been selected from the many that are available.

Much more useful is what is called the Subject Tree, which can be browsed by subject or by Dewey decimal classification, or explored with the assistance of a search engine. The breadth and depth of coverage is quite impressive. Each resource is annotated, although the annotations are very brief. Despite the breadth of coverage this directory is as much subject to idiosyncrasies of selection as are others. Under History, for example, there is nothing to suggest that BUBL has categorized resources covering warfare. To find references to the Second World War you need to select General History of Western Europe, then General History of Western Europe from 1918, and finally you arrive at four annotations relating to the Holocaust. On the other hand, if you use the query War in the search engine, 36 items are returned, whereas for Warfare there is only one. The items returned do little justice either to this vastly popular and historically significant human pastime, or to the Internet resources currently available on the subject.

The lesson to be learnt is that if you want to track down resources speedily from BUBL you need to use the search engine. To do this efficiently you should master the advanced search syntax. This seems to negate somewhat the objective of providing a resource subject tree to overcome the difficulties associated with employing basic search queries in major search engines such as Alta Vista.

Social Science Information Gateway

<http://www.sosig.bristol.ac.uk>

The Social Science Information Gateway (SOSIG) is funded by the UK Economics and Social Research Council, the Electronic Libraries Program, and the European Commission. The major subject areas covered are listed in Figure 5.7.

- Economics, Development	- Law
- Education	- Management, Accountancy, Business
- Environmental Issues	- Philosophy
- Demography	- Politics - International Relations
- Ethnology, Social Anthropology	- Psychology
- Feminism	- Social Science General - Methodology
- Geography	- Social Welfare - Community, Disability
- Education	- Sociology
- Government, Military Science	- Statistics - Demography

Figure 5.7 *SOSIG main subject areas.*

In their own words, 'SOSIG is an online catalogue of high quality Internet resources' that 'offers users the chance to read descriptions of resources available over the Internet and to access these resources direct. ... each one has been selected and described by a librarian or academic, making this the Internet equivalent of an academic research library for the social sciences.'

The annotations are reasonably informative and a relatively large number of resources are covered. There are, of course, some glaring omissions from the major categories, history being the most obvious. Instead of browsing the entries by subject headings, you can use the search engine which allows for focused queries. For assistance on their formulation you should consult the online help facilities. When the keyword History is employed, 237 entries are returned, indicating that there are plenty of links to history resources, but that you need to seek them through using the search engine.

The resources that are annotated include Web presentations dealing with particular disciplines, topics or themes, mailing lists, organizations, and subject-specific departments in institutions of higher education, including a listing of Social Science departments in the UK,

<http://sosig.esrc.bris.ac.uk/depts.html>

Under some of the main subject headings the resource list returned is rather skimpy and excludes some of the most relevant Web presentations. This is certainly true of the philosophy compilation, which omits reference to the Voice of the Shuttle Philosophy Page, the Marx/Engels Archive, and the Spoon Collective. The total number of resources referenced was 26 using the browse by subject search option (10 December 1997). Using the search engine with the query Philosophy returned 118 entries. This number of entries returns the message 'this is too many to display in full', requiring the user to narrow the search by employing Boolean operators. Although some mailing lists are included in the browse entries, these are not representative of what is available, nor is there any rationale given for those referenced.

The World Wide Web Virtual Library project

<http://vlib.stanford.edu/Overview.html>

Tim Berners-Lee, the originator of the WWW, started up the WWW Virtual Library in 1991 to keep track of discipline-based resources accessible over the Web. For each subject area a maintainer, who may be either an individual or an organization, is responsible for keeping track of resources currently available. The coverage of resources in many fields is broad and the annotations authoritative.

Argus Clearinghouse

<http://www.clearinghouse.net/>

This used to be called the Clearinghouse for Subject-Oriented Resources, and was based at the University of Michigan. Originally its purpose was to provide a rating system for detailed guides of Internet resources arranged by subject. The objective remains the same. The guides are arranged in 12 categories. Those likely to be of primary interest to social scientists are Business and Employment, Government and Law, Humanities, and Social Sciences and Social Issues. The guides are submitted by their compilers, and subsequently rated by the Argus Clearinghouse.

Although each entry under a specific subject category is referred to as a guide, many of them are no more than lists of resources in a particular field of enquiry. The Clearinghouse gives a rating to the guides once a year. Some of the ratings awarded strike me as bizarre. For instance, Leela Balraj's guide on Economics is given a rating of 4, although it is merely a list of economics-related conferences, whereas Bill Goffe's detailed, exhaustive and annotated guide to economics resources merits a 5, the top ranking (November 1997).

Despite such idiosyncrasies, there are some very useful guides here, including Dr T. Matthew Ciolek's on Aboriginal Studies and Richard Kimber's guide to Political Resources at Keele. Given the unevenness of what is available in terms of annotation, and breadth and depth of coverage, there is really no alternative but to browse through the main category lists and select for more detailed exploration those that appear promising. If you are looking for something specific it is quicker to use the search engine.

InterNIC Directory of Directories

<http://ds.internic.net/ds/dsdirofdirs.html>

The InterNIC (National Information Center) Directory of Directories is one of the older subject tree resource guides of the Internet. The list of main categories is not long and the entries in each are neither numerous, reflective of the breadth of Internet resources, evaluated, nor annotated in any great detail. The resources listed can be accessed either through use of the browse facility, or by way of the search engine. Like the Argus Clearinghouse described above, entries in the directory are dependent upon referral by compilers of the resources. It appears that few of these direct their attention any longer to the InterNIC.

5.3 Conclusion

Any one of the aforementioned subject directories could be used to illustrate both the short-term advantages of this form of Internet resource classificatory system, and its tempered imprecision. While glancing down the list gives the reader some idea of the breadth of resources available, it does not make it easy to track down a particular resource. For instance, anyone endeavouring to trace the URL of the Franck Report, 1945, *Report of the Committee on Political and Social Problems, Manhattan Project* (which recommended that the atomic bomb be detonated in a desert or on a barren island, rather than on an inhabited area) would probably encounter considerable difficulty in doing so by navigating through a subject directory. The inclusion of the Stockholm School of Economics in the BUBL entry for economics, and the exclusion of the London School of Economics, must be viewed as somewhat idiosyncratic. The reasons for inclusion and exclusion are nowhere specified.

Subject trees are particularly useful for those who initially have no idea of what they are looking for because they are entirely unfamiliar with the terrain: for instance, those searching for a topic to investigate for a term paper, or a dissertation. Many useful resources that I have located, I have 'stumbled on', as it were, the Franck Report being one example. Such fumbling is expensive in time and unpredictable in its results. The subject tree directory is largely pre-digital in conception. It harnesses the skills of traditional librarianship in a digital medium while neglecting that medium's unique possibilities. The sheer scale of resources currently accessible over the Internet, which is as nothing compared with what the situation will be in five or ten years' time, suggests that the future lies elsewhere. It will focus on the refinement of the searching capabilities of robots, spiders and knowbots, specialized guides to a narrow range of resources and the development of Intelligent Agents, rather than the macro-efforts of directories like Yahoo and BUBL.

CHAPTER 6

Search engines and searches

6.1   Introduction   65
6.2   Basic search query principles   67
6.3   Some search engine sites   70

6.1   Introduction

Search engines are the front-ends of massive databases. Users can key in search strings which when submitted return hyperlinks to records that include matching content. There are thousands of Internet search engines, ranging from those that catalogue files lodged at a particular site to those that regularly process tens of millions of files distributed on servers dispersed across the world. Some search engines target specific types of resource – electronic mail addresses or newsgroup messages – whereas others process files covering a variety of resources. The effective use of search engines requires the acquisition and perfection of specific search skills.

Search engines operate by integrating a combination of software packages, one of which is a database. The database stores information relating to resources (files) that are accessible from servers linked to the Internet. The software programs perform three functions. First, they access files and categorize some or all of the information they contain. Computer programs that perform this function are frequently referred to as 'spiders', 'robots', 'wanderers' or 'worms'. The results of this categorizing process are stored in the database. Secondly, they input user queries to the database. Thirdly, they return search query results, either in the default format for that search engine or, if applicable, in terms of some specification entered by the user.

Search engines can be divided into three types: General, Specialist, and Meta-search. General search engines scan a variety of resources accessible over the Internet. Although they mostly access Web resources, many also survey gopher space and ftp servers; a few also index the contents of newsgroup communications.

Specialist search engines target particular Internet resources. They can be further subdivided into those that monitor a particular type of resource over the Internet, and those that primarily index resources on their own servers. Examples of the first are DejaNews, a search engine that indexes the contents of more than 50,000 newsgroups, and Archie, a search tool that is designed to track down resources held on ftp servers. Examples of search engines dedicated to scanning resources on their own servers are those associated with online newspapers and magazines, or particular Web presentations. *The Washington Post* and *The Times* of London both provide search engines for users to search the files that they make publicly available on their servers. Similarly, the Massachusetts Institute of Technology (MIT) provides a search engine to locate data relating to its Perseus Project on classical texts. Meta-search engines, Metacrawler is one, query a number of search engines simultaneously and collate the results, eliminating duplicate URLs.

A sizeable number of readers are probably already familiar with some of the most popular search engines, particularly Alta Vista, Lycos, Infoseek and HotBot. They are not particularly complicated to use at the most basic level. Key in a word and the search engine returns pages of hits. Unfortunately, the simplicity of the query is often matched inversely by the number of records returned. The most frequently expressed reactions to this dwell darkly on the inadequacy of the search engine and the volume of insubstantial materials on the Internet.

A more adequate explanation is that the query submitted is often less sophisticated than it could be and that more thought could have gone into its composition. For largely understandable reasons there are many computer users who do not trifle with reading manuals or help files. They often pride themselves on 'clicking through'. Although this is a useful and necessary coping strategy when faced with lengthy manuals and badly prepared help files, it frequently proves expensive in time and unproductive in results when trying to locate resources through the use of search engines.

Assume, for example, that you were interested in information relating to functionalism. In particular, you want to compare the approaches to this subject of sociologists and anthropologists. In addition, you would prefer to exclude documents focusing on certain philosophical concerns. The following query syntax, for use with the search engine Alta Vista's Advanced Search interface, should retrieve relevant files if they are available:

<functionalism AND ((Merton AND Parsons) OR (Brown AND Malinowski)) AND NOT epistemolog*>

This query specifies that the documents that are returned should include the term functionalism and also references to both Merton and Parsons, or to both Brown and Malinowski. Further, they must exclude references to epistemology, epistemological or epistemologies. Most readers will probably concur that the probability of stumbling on this query by chance is somewhat remote.

Mastering the search syntax for Alta Vista and other search engines is neither especially complicated nor time consuming. In the following two chapters I outline how to formulate both basic and advanced search queries. The few hours forsaken will be amply repaid in the future, both in time and in the effectiveness of searches. Despite the claims of many software developers and some over-enthusiastic commentators, it is unlikely that some killer application will obviate the need to map the Internet cognitively or to perfect those skills that are required to formulate effective search queries of varying degrees of complexity. That is why information retrieval specialists make a reasonably good living at present and are likely to continue to do so.

6.2 Basic search query principles

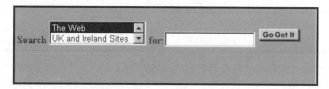

Figure 6.1 *Generic search engine interface.*

Figure 6.1 illustrates an interface similar to that employed by virtually all search engines for basic searches. Once a query is entered in the *for*: text box in Figure 6.1, and the submit *(Go Get It)* button is selected, the search is initiated. A document is returned in due course in which the records of files in the database matching the query are listed. Invariably, the minimal details provided specify the title of the document, its size in bytes, and sometimes the date when the document was compiled, or when it was last entered into the database of the search engine. Figure 6.2 shows some of the records returned for the query <multiplier + economics> submitted to the search engine HotBot on 20 January 1998.

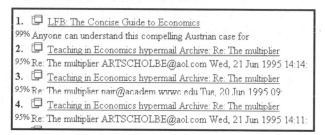

Figure 6.2 *HotBot query/return interface.*

The percentage mark is an indication of the degree to which a record meets the query specified, in terms of the algorithm of the database. As frequently there are many records that meet the initial query specifications, the hits are likely to be listed on a number of separate pages (files). Many search engines permit the user to specify the number of records that will be listed per file as well as particulars concerning how detailed the description of individual records will be. To download a link that appears to be relevant you click on the hypertext link, which will be the title, the URL, or both. If you want to download other records returned in response to the original query, return to the original list and make further selections.

The maintainers of some search engines claim to have processed very large numbers of documents. Alta Vista currently contends that its database processes the complete text of some 31 million files, whereas Lycos contends that its database contains information on more than 51 million URLs. That they contain large numbers of entries is relatively easy to confirm. Entering the word economics in Alta Vista returned 1,197,200 hits, history 4,729,180, politics 710,600, and sociology 283,930 on 2 September 1997. In January 1998, the figures were considerably lower, although still measured in the hundreds of thousands or millions, due to changes introduced by Alta Vista. For most single-word or phrase queries the number of records returned is far too many to sift through if the objective is to locate specific information in as short a time span as possible.

There are a number of factors that you should take into consideration in planning your search.

- The first, and probably most obvious, is to determine what type of information it is that you are looking for. Is it information on a particular concept (e.g. dialectical materialism, post-modernism, historicism, elasticity) or some dataset, such as the current balance of payments situation in European countries, the voting results of the last Israeli election, the rate of population growth in Ruritania or the number of wars fought during the twentieth century? There are many other alternatives, including (1) specific documents (e.g. the International Convention on Political and Civil Rights, the Maastricht Treaty, the Versailles Treaty, the score for Beethoven's Ninth Symphony); (2) names of individuals (e.g. the speaker of the House of Commons, the Master of the Rolls, the commander of EZLN forces in Chiapis during the 1995/96 uprising, Olympic medallists in the marathon); (3) dates; (4) issues (e.g. evaluation of the comparative effectiveness of Keynesian and monetarist policies, human rights violations in Myanmar, political democratization alternatives in former Soviet satellites, the ethical implications and impact of IVF); (5) electronic texts (e.g. electronic magazines or professional journals, works of Karl Marx, Adam Smith's *The Wealth of Nations*, the Code of Hammurabi); or (6) software packages.

- Having decided on the type of information being sought, the next step is to determine what type of Internet resource is likely to incorporate such data. Is it the type of information that would appear in mailing list or newsgroup communications, or is a file likely to be found on an ftp server? Is it the type of data that will feature in Web presentations specializing in the collation or provision of information in a particular subject area? Is the information likely to feature prominently on the agenda of pressure groups, political parties, governments or international organizations? Is it the type of information likely to be published by particular organizations? Population and health statistics are collected and likely to be distributed electronically by the United Nations. Its server is likely to be a good place to start tracking data of this sort relating to particular countries. National economic information will probably be available at the sites of national or central banks.

- The next stage is to decide what type of search engine (general, specialist, meta-search) it is best to employ. A general search engine is frequently best used if you cannot think of a more immediate or proximate source where the information can be located, provided, of course, you know how to access such sources. For instance, if the information can be included under the heading 'topical and current news', it is quite likely that it can be tracked down quickly by accessing appropriate online current news resources. If you are looking for a software package you may track it down more easily by querying a specialist search engine called Archie which was developed for searching ftp servers.

- After you have decided on the type of search engine to employ, it is necessary to select those in that category that are best suited for the particular query that you have. This is where things become somewhat more complicated because the number of search engines available is expanding rapidly. Search engines in any particular category vary along a number of dimensions. Some survey a higher proportion of Internet space than others. Search engines are not all equally up to date. Robots download and process files from Internet sites on a cyclical basis, usually no more frequently than once every 30 days. Many are considerably further behind than this on those sites that they do survey. One very important difference between search engines relates to the types of search query they support. With some, Alta Vista for instance, you can perform relatively complex searches, allowing you to focus in on particular records in an extremely large database.

- Whether you need to use a complex or simple query can only be answered in the context of the information being sought relative to the nature of the database indexed. However, since a search engine that permits complex queries may be as efficient in tracking down files that are easily located with a query that does not include elaborate syntax, your best option is probably to use one that affords maximum flexibility in this respect.

The market in search engines has grown rapidly during the last two years. There are some search pages that list well over 100, including a mixture of general, specialized and meta-search engines. It is clearly the case that users can expend a considerable amount of time establishing their attributes in terms of the dimensions already discussed (size of database, categories of Internet resource indexed, frequency of update, category of file information indexed, speed of operation, search syntax permitted, etc.).

My recommended survival strategy in this context is as follows.

- Become familiar with a maximum of two general search engines, selecting those that have been tried and tested by experienced Internet users.

- Compare the relative efficiency of those that you have selected by submitting the same queries to both and evaluating the search results.

- Use specialist search engines when appropriate, as indicated by my earlier discussion. There is no point scouring the Alta Vista or Lycos databases for information about yesterday's events in Northern Ireland, the Middle East, or anywhere else. Such information is more easily located by using the search engines provided to search through the files of CNN, *The Times*, the BBC or many other news sources available on the Internet (see Chapter 18). To search through Usenet newsgroups, use DejaNews. To locate United Nations documents, first try the search engine provided on its Web pages.

- From time to time monitor Internet sources for current information relating to the performances of search engines. There are always individuals or organizations that are posting information about Internet tools and applications. Conduct a search using the query <"search engines" AND performance> or its functional equivalent, and you are bound to locate a document that provides information on comparative tests carried out. If these indicate that some new search engine is markedly superior to the one that you are using, try it out and see whether you like it and whether it performs for you as well as it is alleged to.

6.3   Some search engine sites

Beaucoup

<http://www.beaucoup.com/engines.html>

Lists more than 800 search engines, classified under categories that include General Search Engines, Multiple (Meta) Search Engines, Geographically Specific, Media, Software, and Email Addresses and Phone Numbers. Not all of these entries are for what I would refer to as search engines, but there are more than enough to keep anyone busy deciding which ones to use.

All-in-One Search Page

<http://www.albany.net/allinone/>

This site lists search engines under various headings (World Wide Web, General Interest, Specialized Interest, Software, etc.) and provides the search query text boxes. In other words you do not have to access the search engine site to submit your query. You can submit it from this site to the search engine of your choice. When you submit the query, you then automatically access the interface of the search engine chosen and the list of results. However, you cannot use all the features of the search engine in your initial query.

CHAPTER 7

Searches: basic

7.1	Introduction	71
7.2	Basic searches	72
7.3	Refining simple searches	77
7.4	Some summary remarks	79

7.1   Introduction

In the discussion that follows I explain how to formulate what I refer to as basic search queries before moving on to outline some refinements to the syntax employed. This search syntax will be sufficient to enable users to locate many items likely to be of interest to them. In the next chapter I discuss the use of advanced search syntax.

The term advanced, as used here, is not employed as synonymous with either complicated or difficult. The term elaborated may have been more appropriate, were the term advanced not employed by some of the organizations that have made search engines available for public use. Two or three hours reading this and the next chapter, experimenting with formulating queries and carrying out some searches, should enable nearly all readers to master the principal elements of advanced syntax usage.

I will focus primarily on illustrating the construction of queries by reference to the Alta Vista search engine in this and the next chapter. I do so for a number of reasons. Nearly all the reports on the comparative performance of search engines indicate that Alta Vista is one of the most efficient. Secondly, Alta Vista indexes the full contents of more than 30 million files. Third, it is extremely fast. Fourth, it allows the use of more complex search syntax than any other search engine with a comparable sized database, although there are few of these. Fifth, with minor adaptations, the search syntax employed by Alta

Vista is transferable to other search engines. You may need to look through the help files of some of them, but having mastered the Alta Vista syntax the conversion process should be relatively easy. Finally, to attempt to cover a variety of search engines would make following the ensuing discussion too complex, as well as time and space consuming. My primary objective is to enable readers to access required information as efficiently as possible. The relatively minute differences between the top search engines are essentially irrelevant to such a goal.

For those new to Internet searching I think that Alta Vista is a good search engine to start with. More experienced users will find that it allows for focused searches and the rapid return of information relating to the queries submitted. The interface is a lot easier to deal with than that of some of the other leading contenders. It has a vast database and it is unlikely that you will not find any records relating to a subject of interest. From these you will frequently find leads to others. If you don't find that the records returned for a particular query are satisfactory, then check out one of the other search engines whose addresses are given near the end of the next chapter. You will find, in any event, that the degree of overlap in the results returned for identical queries submitted to different search engines is very extensive.

Alta Vista has separate interfaces for simple and advanced searches. In this chapter I deal with simple or basic searches. There is no easy answer to the question 'can I make do with simple searches, or must I master advanced searches as well?'. As always with this type of question, it depends. Depends on what? The extent to which you want to use the Internet, the type of document you are searching for in relation to those documents indexed by the databases of the major search engines, the relative costs in time and effort of mastering advanced queries relative to some other alternative for accessing the same information, and more. If you consider that it is unlikely that you will use the Internet frequently in searching for specific information, you can probably make do with simple searches and leave the mastering of more complex queries to a more convenient juncture. Simple searches, if appropriately plotted, should fulfil the immediate requirements of many users. The syntax is quite easy to learn and less easy to forget than that required for advanced queries. If, on the other hand, you want to master what is already a formidable electronic database, a few hours' reading the following chapter as well as this one, and experimenting with searches, is likely to prove well worth the effort.

7.2 Basic searches

When you first access Alta Vista at <http://www.altavista.digital.com> part of the document returned looks like the graphic in Figure 7.1. This is the interface for simple searches.

The Text Query Box is where the search query is entered. You can choose between a search through Web resources or Usenet newsgroups and restrict the search to specific languages in which the documents are written by making appropriate selections from the drop-down menus. It is important to select English if this is the only language that you wish to view documents in, as in many instances this will filter out a substantial number of documents, particularly if your search terms consist of acronyms or URLs. With the expansion of the Web this will become even more important.

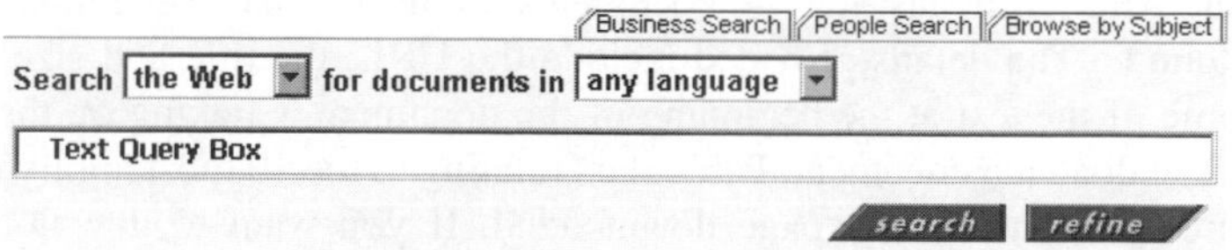

Search | the Web ▼ | for documents in | any language ▼

Text Query Box

search   refine

Figure 7.1   *Alta Vista Simple Search interface.*

The format in which the results of your query are displayed can be changed from the default, which provides detailed information, to compact, by selecting *Preferences* (see Figure 7.2) and checking the appropriate box. Most users will find the default satisfactory. The compact feature provides only information on the title of the document and the first few words of the text.

Alta Vista has recently introduced changes to its search facilities. At the top of the search engine interface there are now three tabs. These allow you to search by subject, search for email addresses *(People Search)*, or search for the addresses of businesses. In most cases, the two latter facilities are useful only if you want to locate information on persons or businesses in the United States and you know the state where the person has an email address facility, or where the business is registered. Generally, most of the address-finding facilities on the Internet are not especially useful for tracing persons resident outside the United States. The *Browse by Subject* facility enables you to use the Alta Vista database as a subject directory. It is quite easy to use but, for reasons discussed in Chapter 5 on subject directories, is less efficient than the submission of adequately formulated search queries for locating information.

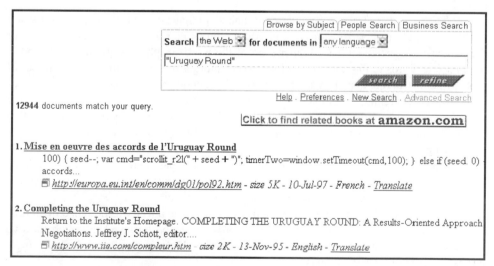

Figure 7.2   *Alta Vista query/return interface example.*

Figure 7.2 shows the document returned when the query "Uruguay Round" was submitted on 21 January 1998 in order to locate the Final Act. The figure at the top left indicates that Alta Vista has 12,944 documents in its database that match the query "Uruguay Round". The details provided include the URL, the title and size of the document and some of the text at the beginning of the document. Clicking on the URL or the title should download the document. Particulars relating to the 10 most highly ranked documents are provided on the first page downloaded. If you want to download additional records you need to scroll to the bottom of the page and click on the graphic. You should note that despite the fact that to the left of the graphic the word *Next* suggests that if you select it additional records will be downloaded, this is not the case. Using the simple search facility permits retrieval of only 200 records. If you want to see more than this you need to use the advanced search interface, particulars of which are given in the next chapter.

There are no limits on the number of items you can scrutinize with the Advanced Search facility. If you use some other search engines, HotBot and Lycos for instance, you will be able to retrieve documents referencing all the hits returned. You should, however, seriously consider whether it is preferable to refine your search, or to scroll through lists referencing thousands of documents, a tedious and tiring activity. Bear in mind, also, that you may have to download quite a few documents to locate the information you are after, as the records returned may only reference documents that have links to the files you are after, rather than to the documents themselves. Thus, for instance, if you submit the query <"Maastricht Treaty">, many of the records returned are likely to point to Web pages that have a link to the Maastricht Treaty, rather than to the treaty itself. Note, however, that by the same token **page titles that may appear to be entirely irrelevant to what you are looking for may include links to information that you are seeking**.

If you have to scroll through more than 200 hits to locate a file relating to a particular query, you probably need to refine it and should be using the Advanced Search feature. You should aim to formulate queries that will return a required file in the top 30 records.

The records returned for a query are ranked so that those entries that are at the top of the list match most satisfactorily your requirements in terms of the relevancy system of the database. A document has a higher score if the words or phrases queried are found in the first few words of the document, close to one another in the document, or a number of times. In constructing a query you should, therefore, endeavour to imagine how the document you are searching for is likely to be set out. In order to increase the probability that what you are seeking to locate is found nearer the top of the list, you can specify that certain words or phrases are included or excluded, as illustrated below.

Conducting basic searches, therefore, is a relatively simple operation. You decide on your query, enter it into the text box, choose the search parameters from those available (Web/Usenet, Languages, Display format – by choosing *Preferences*), and select the submit button. The query can include characters and numbers.

In the example I gave above ("Uruguay Round"), the query was bounded by double inverted commas. This was to ensure that records would be retrieved in which the two words were proximate and occurred in the same order. There is no need to include single words in double inverted commas.

HotBot, <http://www.hotbot.com>, is another very good search engine. It differs from Alta Vista in allowing users to select from quite a wide range of search options through drop-down menus, as well as using complex search queries. Its interface is illustrated in Figure 7.3.

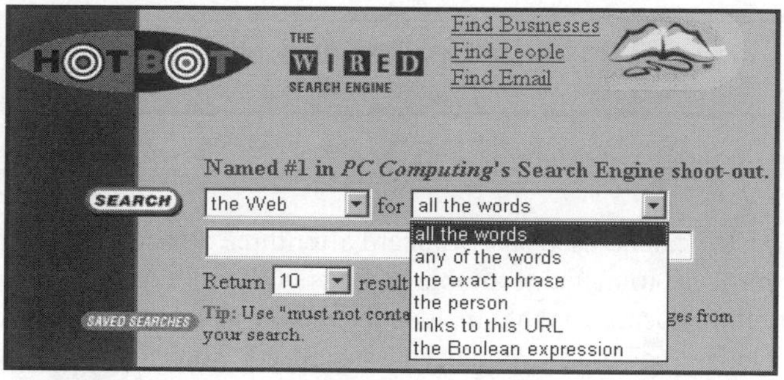

Figure 7.3   *HotBot interface.*

The option *all the words* will return documents that include all the words included in the query regardless of their proximity to each other, so long as they are in the same document. The equivalent selection to inclusion of the phrase in double inverted commas in Alta Vista is the exact phrase. Other options allow you to search for any of the words, words in the title, or a Boolean phrase, a term that will be explained later. You can also restrict the search by date and by continent. If you are searching for resources on North American servers you can restrict the search to a particular organizational domain: org, gov, edu, net, com (see p. 35).

In constructing simple queries for Alta Vista you need to formulate them with the following in mind:

● If you include a string of words in the query, documents will be returned that include one or more of them. The query in Figure 7.4 will return documents that include any combination of these words, that is those that include all three, any combination of two of them, or just any one of them.

Figure 7.4   *OR query.*

● Placing a + sign before a word specifies that the document must include it whereas preceding a word with a – indicates that it should be excluded. The query in Figure 7.5 stipulates that the files returned must include both poverty and unemployment, but must exclude health.

Figure 7.5   *Combined included and excluded query.*

● As noted earlier, a search string that refers to a string of contiguous words should be included in double inverted commas, as in Figure 7.6.

Figure 7.6 *Contiguous words/phrase query.*

- The asterisk * can be used as a wildcard after three adjacent letters if you want the records retrieved to include variable endings of the root query. The query in Figure 7.7 will return documents that include the words social, socialist, socialists, socialism, socialize, socialise, socialized, socialised, sociality, and, of course, any including misspellings after social. Up to five characters can be included after the asterisk, in lower case only.

Figure 7.7 *Wildcard query.*

- Queries in lower case are capitals insensitive. In other words, if you type a word in lower case it will retrieve files that include the word in both upper and lower case. For instance, if you type *holocaust*, files will be returned that include both holocaust and Holocaust. On the other hand, if you capitalize a query the documents retrieved will include only those in which the word is capitalized. If you are searching for files that are likely to include an acronym, include this in preference to its expansion: SEATO rather than South East Asia Treaty Organization.

There are a number of options available for composing simple queries that constrain the search to the retrieval of files with particular titles, files that include links to pages with a specific content in their URL, and to pages with a specific content included in their hyperlinks.

- The queries <title:American Journal of Sociology> and <title:Political Economy> will retrieve files which contain American Journal of Sociology and Political Economy in their titles, respectively. Here the title refers to the html title (see pp. 47–8), not necessarily the opening text title of the file. It is reasonable to assume, and borne out in practice, that academic journals that have Web presentations will include their titles in the html title. The same applies to most organizations. If you want to track down the home pages of the Ford Motor Company, Empress Cars, the United Nations, World Bank, etc., try using title:name as the search query, as in <title:United Nations> and <title:Empress Cars>.

- The query <url:yahoo.com> will retrieve documents in which both yahoo and com appear in its URL. It is reasonable to assume that for many commercial organizations their name will appear in the URL (e.g. Netscape, Microsoft, Demon, Compuserve, etc.). The same applies to other categories of organization, like the United Nations, whose URL, you can reasonably speculate, is likely to include un. Many universities, especially those with short names or known abbreviations, can be tracked in this way. You can increase the probability of locating the information required if you include also the domain entity of the organization. If you want to locate the home page of the University of Bristol, it is reasonable to assume that bristol will be in the title and that as it is an educational institution situated in the UK, its URL will include the letters ac. The query would therefore include <url:bristol.ac>. As educational institutions in the US are signified by edu, the query for the University of Houston would be <url:uh.edu>. There is a moral to this tale: when browsing the Net glance occasionally at the URLs in the address box of the browser. The information that will seep in may prove useful.

- The queries <link:ai.org> or <link:irc.org> will retrieve all documents which include hyperlinks to files which include ai.org or irc.org in their URLs. This would be quite useful if you were interested, for instance, in finding documents likely to be focusing on human rights issues, which frequently would include some references and links to Amnesty International or the International Red Cross. At the same time, the volume of such links is considerable. It is best used when you know that there are unlikely to be many links.

There are additional constraints that can be employed, but those illustrated above strike me as likely to be found most useful. For further information consult the Alta Vista help file.

Alta Vista, as noted earlier, allows for searches of Usenet newsgroup messages as well as of Web documents. I prefer to use DejaNews (see p. 136) for searches of newsgroups as their archives go further back than do those of Alta Vista, and their search options provide information relating to the Usenet history of authors of messages. This is not to say that searching Usenet through Alta Vista is unlikely to turn up information that you may be interested in. The procedure and syntax are virtually identical to that employed for Web searches. The query <Oprah +BSE>, using Search Usenet instead of Search Web, returned the records illustrated in Figure 7.8.

```
1.🖻 L B 08-Jan #Oprah vs. Texas Cattlemen  alt.society.liberali voltai29@geoc
2.🖻 L B 08-Jan Re: #Oprah vs. Texas Cattle  alt.society.liberali Leroy@commiem
3.🖻 L B 08-Jan Re: #Oprah vs. Texas Cattle  alt.society.liberali ricka@praline
4.🖻 L B 09-Jan Re: #Oprah vs. Texas Cattle  alt.society.liberali Leroy@commiem
5.🖻 L B 09-Jan Re: #Oprah vs. Texas Cattle  alt.society.liberali voltai29@geoc
6.🖻 L B 08-Jan Re: #Oprah vs. Texas Cattle  alt.society.liberali ricka@praline
7.🖻 L D 19-Jan Oprah is Sued for a Simple   talk.politics.animal bb_bison@evan
```

Figure 7.8   *Alta Vista Usenet query/return interface.*

As you can see, the first seven messages all dealt with the Oprah Winfrey BSE food defamation issue. The information provided, in compact format, shows the subject of the message, the Usenet newsgroup in which it was discussed (<alt.society.liberali>, etc.), and the address of the person sending the message. Selecting the link will download the message sent.

7.3   Refining simple searches

Recently Alta Vista has implemented feedback facilities that ease somewhat the task of refining queries. These are available for both simple and advanced searches.

I will illustrate the ensuing discussion with an advanced query that I submitted to Alta Vista (13 July 1997), using, of course, the advanced query interface. The syntax will be analysed in the next chapter. The documents that I was interested in concerned war crimes, but I wanted to exclude references to the Bosnian and Rwandan civil wars and genocide in the query, as I was aware that a large number of documents relating to these conflicts were available on the Web. The query I submitted, therefore, was:

<"war crim*" AND NOT (Bosnia OR Serbia OR Yugoslavia OR Rwanda)>

The Advanced Search Interface with the query inserted is illustrated in Figure 7.9.

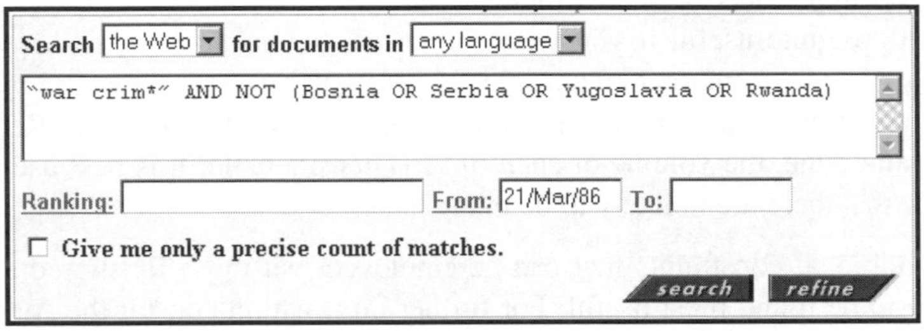

Figure 7.9   *Alta Vista Advanced Search interface.*

The query can be refined further by selecting *refine*, illustrated in the bottom right-hand corner of Figure 7.9. This produces a table with drop-down menus, as illustrated for this particular query in Figure 7.10.

The entries are of concepts or categories that are included in the documents retrieved by the query. The percentage indicates the overall degree of importance of the entry in the document in terms of the relevancy ranking of the database. The higher the percentage the more important the entry. The drop-down menu has two selection choices: *exclude* or *include*. If you select those that are relevant and then the *search* button, Alta Vista will return records that meet the criteria of the original query plus the inclusions and exclusions that you checked in the table.

As an alternative to the table illustrated in Figure 7.10 you can refine the query with the aid of a graphic representation of the tabular refinement. Select the *graph* feature

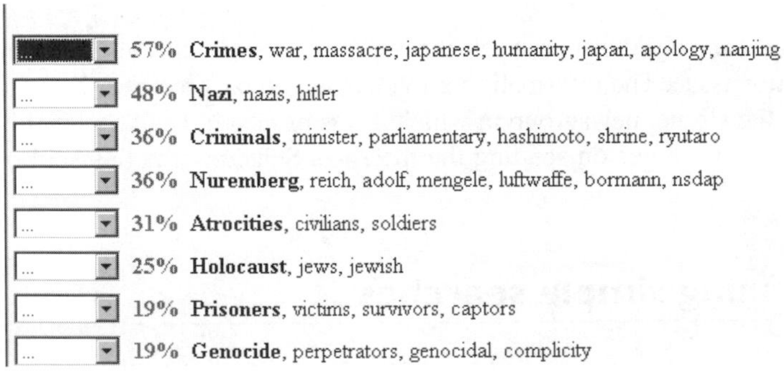

Figure 7.10   *Alta Vista Refined Text query/return interface.*

from the top right-hand corner of the *refine* interface. Figure 7.11 illustrates the graph returned for the query I have been using for illustrative purposes. Selecting any of the entries in Figure 7.11 will open a drop-down menu with sub-entries for the main one. Select those that you want added or removed from the query by clicking once or twice in the boxes provided.

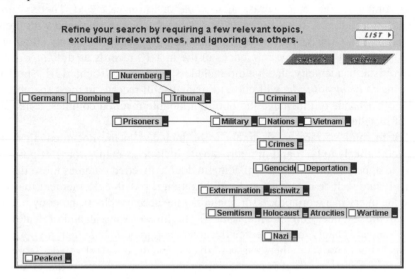

Figure 7.11   *Alta Vista Refined Graphic query/return interface.*

What both the *refine* and the *graph* searches implement is essentially the equivalent of using a + or – associated with a particular word, which will ensure that the word so preceded will be either included or excluded from the documents returned in response to the query submitted. I have not found that using either the table or the graph has been very productive. Although they might be quite useful in suggesting categories that you could use to refine the original search query submitted, the refinement is best undertaken by amending the entry in the text box.

7.4   Some summary remarks

The ability to locate information on the Internet rapidly and accurately is undoubtedly partly a knack, just as is tracking down documents in more traditional archives. In the early days of the Internet a widely publicized and popular pastime for some of those then 'internauting' was an online competition called the Internet Hunt. Ten information retrieval problems would be posed at regular intervals. Those who first submitted the correct answers, indicating how they traced the information, won the game. Partly knack though it may be, there is no question that practice, patience and attention to detail assist in the perfection of search skills.

A careful selection of words and phrases for your search query will cut down on an excessive number of records returned. It may seem obvious, but if your query does not come up with the results you expected, the first thing to do is to check your spelling and typing accuracy. Remember, also, that in the United States numerous words are spelt differently, and that most Web servers are still located there.

Most search engines do not index single or double digit numbers which are not preceded or succeeded by letters, single letters on their own, two-letter words, or some of the more common three-letter words, such as *the* or lower case *and*. There is no point including these, as they will be discarded before the database is accessed with the search string you entered. (Alta Vista is an exception here.) The search string *my kingdom for a horse* returned exactly the same references in the first 10 records as did *kingdom horse*, using Alta Vista. Incidentally, that list did include a reference to Richard III. Similarly the search string *to be or not to be* will not return any useful records in most search engines. If, on the other hand, you included the phrase in double inverted commas, a manageable number of matches will be returned.

Try to think of rare words likely to be included in the document that you are seeking and unlikely to be found in many others. Include as many words as possible that are likely to appear in the document, placing in double inverted commas those that appear successively and include acronyms and capitalization if possible. Remember that you can compose the query in a word processor, including the accents, block and copy it, and then paste it into the text query box in Alta Vista. Try to think of what an author dealing with a particular subject is likely to include in a document and then include that in your query.

It is better to use more than one word to describe the data that you are searching for than it is to use just one. For example, during the 1940s and 1950s the United States government authorized concealed radiation experiments on its population, avowedly to assess the potential impact of atomic warfare on the civilian population. Keying in the word radiation gave rise, predictably, to a large number of hits (100,000) and the first 20 did not include any reference to this subject. On the other hand, "radiation testing" extracted an article with the title US Radiation Testing on Humans, as did <"radiation testing" +humans>.

It is probably preferable to keep your choice of words as simple as possible if alternatives exist. Taking the example just mentioned, substituting the word experimentation for testing did not return the document mentioned already in the first 20 hits.

When constructing queries take into consideration the way in which Web documents are structured and written. The essence of Web documents is not that they are transmitted via computer networks, for other types of files are also transmitted through this medium, but that they are not constrained by sequential presentation and organization. Horizontal movement to linked documents that provide additional or related information is the distinguishing feature of such html files. Accordingly, writers frequently provide an abundance of links to related materials. This means that in attempting to locate information on a particular topic it may be quicker to track down a document discussing a different topic from the one you are interested in, but a topic that is likely to be linked to the one that you are interested in. For example, instead of using <"National Trust"> as your query you could use <"English Heritage"> on the assumption that documents that include the latter phrase are likely to link to those that focus on the former.

After a time you get a feel for the probable returns likely to result from the submission of a particular query, and how these can be altered to locate the information that is required. Thus, the query <"New Federalism"> submitted to Alta Vista in an attempt to track down information relating to Ronald Reagan's programme of shifting power from federal to state level, produced no hits. An entry under <"Ronald Reagan">, on the other hand, produced 30,000, and the sixth of these was a biographical profile that outlined what the term meant. The cluster that includes "Ronald Reagan" is more likely to reference New Federalism than is the Alta Vista database. Likewise, an attempt to track material relating to Stanley Milgram's discussion of obedience, formulated in his monograph *Obedience to Authority: An Experimental View*, by entering *obedience*, returned among the first 20 hits many links to documents concerned with the obedience training of dogs but none relevant to Stanley Milgram. The two records at the top of the list returned in response to the query <"Stanley Milgram"> referred directly to the information required.

CHAPTER 8

Searches: advanced

8.1	Introduction	83
8.2	Boolean operators	84
8.3	Parentheses	86
8.4	Ranking of queries	87
8.5	Sundry matters	88
8.6	Other search engines	88
8.7	Addendum	89

8.1   Introduction

Alta Vista and most other top search engines (HotBot, Lycos and Infoseek) incorporate advanced database search features that allow users to filter records with increased precision. Utilizing these features you may be able to return a relatively short list of records that include the information that you are seeking. In order to access the Advanced Search interface, Figure 8.1, you need to select *Advanced Search* from the Alta Vista home page <http://www.altavista.digital.com> (see Figure 7.2, p. 73).

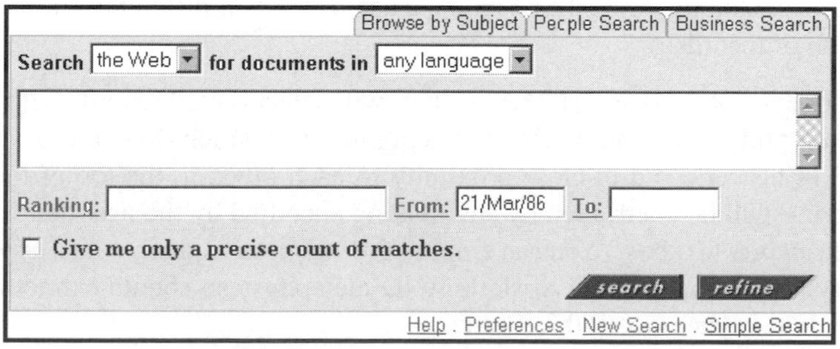

Figure 8.1   *Alta Vista Advanced Search interface.*

The top half of the search engine front-end is similar to that available for simple searches, as discussed in the previous chapter. You can restrict your search to either the Web or Usenet newsgroups, and can select the language of the documents that will be searched. As with the Simple Search front-end, you may browse by subject, or search for electronic mail addresses of persons and information on businesses. The box titled *Ranking* allows you to specify that documents containing selected words that appear in your query, or additional words, will be listed first, that is, ranked highest. This means that of the documents returned in response to your query, those that include the entry in the Ranking box will be at the top of the listing. If you leave this field blank, then the documents returned will be listed in no particular order.

The date boxes allow you to establish the start and end date parameters of the search. The dates refer to those during which the document was most recently revised. This is a somewhat uncertain guide as many Web authors make revisions to documents without revising their date entries, if any were included in the original document. Frequently none are. Some html editors, Microsoft's FrontPage for instance, automatically revise dates when documents are altered.

Alta Vista's advanced searching combines the use of logical operators and expression syntax with a ranking of the resulting output in terms of the user's specifications. The rules for defining words and phrases, and the use of wildcards, accents and capitalization, are virtually identical with those used in simple searches. The principles associated with the deployment of logical operators in searches, as outlined below, are transferable to many other search engines.

Unlike simple searches, advanced searches allow you to view more than 200 of the list of files returned.

8.2 Boolean operators

There are four logical operators that may be employed to constrain searches: AND, OR, NOT and NEAR. They are also frequently referred to as *Boolean operators*, named after the British mathematician George Boole. In Alta Vista they can be used in either upper or lower case.

The use of the operators AND and NOT parallels the use of + and – respectively in simple searches, although the Alta Vista database uses them differently in the context of the extraction of records.

- The query <philosophy AND Aristotle> will select out all records with a reference to both philosophy and Aristotle, placing those in which these terms appear in the title, in headers, and in close proximity to each other, at the top of the list. (This ordering will be overridden by any ranking specified by the user that is inserted in the *Ranking:* text box.) You can employ this operator as many times as you like in a query: <philosophy AND Aristotle AND metaphysics> should extract records that include references to all three terms.

- You can use the operator AND to link a phrase and a concept, or any combination of phrases and concepts. The query <"Karl Marx" AND Critique> should retrieve records that include references to Karl Marx and to his Critique of Political Economy or Critique of the Gotha Programme. You should use "Karl Marx" in preference to just Marx, otherwise you will retrieve a large number of records referencing Groucho Marx, the Marx Brothers, misspellings of Marks and Spencer, etc.

The logical operator AND binds less closely than words juxtaposed in a phrase. The query <"radioactive dust"> will return files in which the two terms appear proximately in succession. The query <radioactive AND dust> will return all files in which the two terms are located, regardless of how proximate they are to each other in the file.

The logical operator NOT is employed to specifically exclude phrases or terms and must be preceded by AND.

- The query <Plato AND NOT Republic> will return all files that include a reference to Plato but which exclude references to Republic. (The query <Plato NOT Republic> is syntactically incorrect; employing it will return an error message.) You can employ this operator more than once in a query, as in <Plato AND NOT Republic AND NOT Laches> which will retrieve all files including the term Plato and excluding references to both Republic and Laches.

- You can employ the operator NOT to link phrases and concepts, or any combination of phrases and concepts. The query <"Karl Marx" AND Critique AND NOT Gotha> should retrieve files that include references to Karl Marx, to Critique, but not to the Critique of the Gotha Programme. Of course if both Critiques are mentioned in the same document it will be referenced.

Whereas queries that employ the operator AND return documents that include all the terms linked by the operator, the operator OR retrieves documents that include either of the concepts or phrases linked by the operator.

- The query <Montgomery OR Alamein> will retrieve records with references to either Montgomery or Alamein, or both. You can use the operator OR to link phrases and concepts, or any combination of phrases and concepts. The query <Wade OR abortion AND "Supreme Court"> should retrieve files that include references to the Supreme Court Judgement in *Roe v. Wade*, or those including references to both Supreme Court and abortion. It should be noted, however, that the order of the results returned will be influenced significantly by the constraining phrases you insert in the *Ranking:* box. If you experiment with the above query and alter the order of the terms, say to <"Supreme Court" AND Wade OR abortion> you will find that the number of file hits returned will be different from the previous version, despite the fact that the syntax and substance are identical. In any event, as explained further on, this query should be formulated with parentheses, <"Supreme Court" AND (Wade or abortion)>, with Wade in the *Ranking:* box.

The operator NEAR is used to retrieve documents when it is probable that certain concepts or phrases, or a combination of the two, are inserted in a document within 10 words or less of each other.

- The term binds to the left, so that <gold NEAR silver> finds those documents in which gold appears within 10 words of silver, whereas <silver near gold> locates documents in which silver appears within 10 words of gold. Compound queries are acceptable: <authoritarianism OR nationalism NEAR sexism> will retrieve documents in which either authoritarianism or nationalism is within 10 words of sexism.

8.3 Parentheses

The above examples of the use of logical operators illustrate that it is possible to create quite complex queries to extract from the database references to records that include sought-after information. As there is no limit on the combination or number of times operators are used in a particular query, working out what the query will extract can become quite confusing. A similar type of confusion can arise in relation to arithmetic or algebraic operations, for instance $7y - 15y \div 3 + 5y * 7$. In the same way as there are rules for ordering operations in arithmetic and algebra, the Alta Vista database algorithm orders logical operations in accordance with specified rules.

Alta Vista evaluates the operators that occur in queries in the following order: NEAR, NOT, AND, OR. This means, for example, that it will perform the search that includes the operator AND before that which includes the operator OR.

- Assume that you are interested in tracing documents that include references to the views of either Karl Marx or Proudhon on poverty. You might construct the query <"Karl Marx" OR Proudhon AND poverty>. Since Alta Vista performs the AND operation first, it will extract all documents in its database referencing both Proudhon and poverty, and then all documents referencing Karl Marx, which is not the information required. What was required was a retrieval of all documents including Karl Marx and poverty, and all those including Proudhon and poverty.

- Matters can get even more complicated with more elaborate queries. If you were seeking documents with information on German or Italian fascism, but excluding nationalism, you could try <fascism NEAR Germany OR Italy AND NOT nationalism>. Working out the order of operations and the sort of information that will be included by the records retrieved at the top of the list is somewhat problematic.

Alta Vista recommends the use of parentheses for elaborate queries. Operations within them are performed before those outside them, as in mathematical or algebraic operations.

- The query <"environmental pollution" AND "water treatment" OR "river management"> will retrieve documents that combine environmental pollution and water treatment or documents that contain references to river management. If the latter two terms are bounded by parentheses, as follows: <"environmental pollution" AND ("water treatment" OR "river management")>, the latter two terms are treated as a unit relative to the other term. Documents retrieved will include environmental pollution and water treatment, or environmental pollution and river management.

- Similarly, the query <fascism NEAR Germany OR Italy AND NOT nationalism> can be simplified to <(Germany OR Italy) NEAR fascism AND NOT nationalism>.

- More than one set of parentheses can be employed to bind a part or parts of a query. For instance, <functionalism AND ((Merton AND Parsons) OR (Durkheim AND Malinowski)) AND NOT epistemolog*> should retrieve documents which include functionalism and either Merton and Parsons or Durkheim and Malinowski, but excluding epistemology, epistemologies or epistemological. Of course, this query would not overlook the inclusion in the same document of references to Merton, Parsons and either Durkheim or Malinowski or both, or to Durkheim and Malinowski and either Merton or Parsons, or both.

The use of parentheses is important for systematic structuring of elaborate queries. As it is relatively easy to confuse the implications of using them in a particular configuration in conjunction with the logical operators, working out the probable impact on a piece of paper often merits pondering as a time-saving device.

8.4   Ranking of queries

The ranking facility, discussed earlier on pages 83–4 and Figure 8.1, enables the user to constrain further the results that will be obtained from a query employing search terms, logical operators and parentheses. If you do not place any terms in the *Ranking:* box, Alta Vista returns the documents retrieved from your query in random order relative to the search terms included. This does not mean that if you submit the query a number of times in succession (having cleared your cache) that they will be in a different order. Documents retrieved are allocated scores on the basis of a scoring algorithm. Documents receive a higher score if the query terms appear in the first few words of the document, in headers and if they appear a number of times, compared to those documents which do not meet these criteria relative to the query. If you submit the query <extroversion OR introversion> some documents with the first term will have a high score and be at the top of the returned list, others have a low score and be displayed at the bottom of the list. The same applies, however, to the other term.

     If you use the ranking facility, you can determine that documents displaying specific terms included in your query are shown at the top of the list. So, to revert to the example above, if you just place extroversion in the *Ranking:* box, all the documents returned containing this term (which will also include some containing introversion if they appear in the same document) will be at the top of the list. You need, however, to be careful in using this facility. It is likely that the query <extroversion OR introversion> will return a significant number of hits (1275 on 2 September 1997). If you place extroversion in the *Ranking:* box, it is unlikely that you will have to scroll through a large number of items and pages before you get to those that include the second term to the exclusion of the first. The solution, in this instance, is to run one query with the first term in the *Ranking:* box and another with the second in it.

     You can also use the ranking facility to narrow down your search further by including in the *Ranking:* box terms that were not used in your original query.

- Assume that you want to trace documents tackling the issue of the relationship between IQ and crime, and you are particularly interested in the mediating role of educational performance. You might construct the following query:

<(IQ OR crime) AND (education* NEAR (performance OR success OR achievement))>

This should retrieve some relevant documents if they are available. You could narrow the search down further to some of the protagonists in this particular dispute by including in the *Ranking:* box one or more of the names <Eysenck, Jensen, Kamin, Burt>.

8.5   Sundry matters

As noted at the beginning of this chapter, wildcards, capitalization and accents can be used in advanced queries along similar lines to those discussed in connection with simple queries in the previous chapter. Similarly, options available for composing simple queries that constrain the search to the retrieval of files with particular titles, files that include links to pages with a specific content in their URL, and pages with specific content included in their hyperlinks, also discussed in the previous chapter (see pp. 76–7), can be entered in as queries in the Advanced Search interface. An important difference is that logical operators and parentheses can be employed in advanced queries. The query <title:WHO OR "World Health Organization"> will retrieve documents with WHO or World Health Organization in the title.

Advanced searches, like simple searches, allow you to refine your query on the basis of the records returned by using the *Refine* feature, as described in the previous chapter (see pp. 78–9). The alternative to using this facility is to look closely at the results that have been returned from your query, modify them accordingly and resubmit. If the first query you submit returns hits that include numerous references to a related subject matter that you are not interested in, you can modify it to exclude appropriate terms or phrases, or include others.

Although I have discussed at reasonable length the most important search features for Alta Vista, there are others that I have omitted. It is, therefore, worth consulting the online help documents available at the Alta Vista site.

8.6   Other search engines

Alta Vista is probably the most widely used general search engine on the Internet, but it is not the only one. Many experienced users prefer to use some of the other top search engines. Although my own preference is for Alta Vista, if I cannot find what I am looking for fairly rapidly using it, I endeavour to replicate the search with others. This is not always easy as no other general search engine allows for such sophisticated filtering as does Alta Vista. Generally, I don't find that the results are in some sense 'superior', but occasionally I get lucky. The reasons for this relate to the different ways in which the same data is filtered, the fact that some sites may be covered by other search engines but not by

Alta Vista, and the recency of information collected by the robots of different search engines. The latter two factors are to some extent interrelated.

The general search engines that you might find useful are listed in Table 8.1.

Table 8.1 *General search engines.*

Name	Address/URL
Alta Vista	http://www.altavista.digital.com
HotBot	http://www.hotbot.com
Excite	http://www.excite.com
Infoseek	http://www.infoseek.com
Lycos	http://www.lycos.com

8.7 Addendum

Since this chapter was completed in February 1998, Alta Vista has changed its basic and advanced searches interfaces.

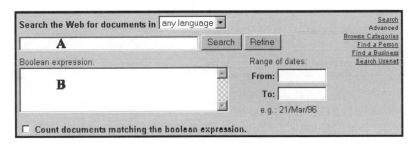

Figure 8.2 *Alta Vista Advanced Search Interface as of February 1998.*

The search query syntax remains unaltered. Your Advanced Search query, Figure 8.2, should now be inserted in text box B whereas the ranking is placed in A. The language and date functions remain the same. The *Count documents matching the boolean expression* feature if checked will inform you how many entries in the database match your query. To obtain more details of the entries uncheck this box. The help files that are now available are not as detailed as those that were provided previously.

PART III

Exchanging views on the Internet

Chapter 9	Locating mailing lists	93
Chapter 10	Mailing list commands and exchanges	103
Chapter 11	Mailing list archives	113
Chapter 12	Reading the news: newsgroups	127

The most prevalent image of the Internet is that of a vast database of useful information that it is relatively easy to access. The warehousing image of the Net is only part of the picture. A significant number of users spend time online less for the opportunity to scour the networks for political constitutions, electronic texts of the classical philosophers or the latest international trade figures, than for the opportunity to interact with and exchange information on shared interests with others. Of course, the two are not mutually exclusive.

Two Internet-linked facilities that are used extensively for such purposes are mailing lists and newsgroups. As the Internet is in all matters quantifiable a moving target, estimates that are produced of the numbers of lists and newsgroups, of subscribers and readers, and of the volume of messages posted, are necessarily underpinned by many assumptions that are beyond substantiation. One major database, Liszt (<http://www.lizst.com>), records more than 71,500 mailing lists, and DejaNews (<http://www.dejanews.com>), a newsgroup database, stores messages exchanged on more than 50,000 of them.

The combined volume of daily postings to mailing lists and newsgroups is very extensive. Archives of past postings are available for many lists, although not for all. Alta Vista archives Usenet information dating from December 1995. DejaNews, a specialist search database for Usenet newsgroups, has stored postings since May 1995, currently claims to store 1 Gb of data daily, and holds more than 300 Gb in its database. (A gigabyte, i.e. 1000 megabytes or 1000 million bytes, is equivalent to about 50,000 pages, since a single-spaced A4 page of 12-point text takes up approximately 20,000 bytes.)

Mailing lists and newsgroups focus on thousands of different subjects. There are lists and newsgroups dealing with every major discipline area of the social sciences. Many focus on specialist fields subsumed under them. So numerous are the lists, and so broad the range of topics dealt with by many, that it is at times difficult to establish where specific categories of information are likely to be posted. The same applies to newsgroups, although these are at least arranged in subject-specific hierarchies. Both mailing lists and newsgroups have much to offer social scientists, as I shall argue in the chapters in Part III. The chapters on mailing lists illustrate how to locate lists that meet particular interests, how to issue basic commands relating to subscribing and managing data inflow, and how to search the vast archives of stored messages. Chapter 12 on newsgroups does the same for this Internet forum.

CHAPTER 9

Locating mailing lists

In technical terms a mailing list is a list of electronic addresses used by a mail exploder (a software application) to forward messages to all those on the list. In common Internet parlance it refers to a group of persons who exchange messages via electronic mail on some theme, or themes, that are usually agreed in advance. Mailing lists are an offshoot and development of ordinary electronic mail.

Electronic mail was the first networked application that was widely deployed. Its widespread use was pioneered by academic staff engaged on research who employed it as a cheap, reliable and fast means of disseminating information and exchanging views. Although electronic mail was extremely important in the development of certain electronic networks and the furthering of academic research in certain fields, it had significant drawbacks when it came to communicating regularly with a large number of persons who shared common interests. Each time someone wishes to post or respond to information it is necessary to send it to everyone who is known to have been a recipient of earlier exchanges. To do so it is necessary to maintain a list of addresses, and to update it regularly if participants no longer wish to receive communications, or prefer to suspend them indefinitely when they are too preoccupied with other matters, or are away.

Managing such an address book can be very time consuming when the number of individuals involved is relatively small; it becomes impossible to arrange efficiently when they are numbered in thousands, yet alone tens of thousands. In 1995, for instance, an email-based tutorial course on the use of the Internet, named Roadmap, included some 90,000 participants. In addition, it is very difficult for those not currently in receipt of communications to find out various matters concerning such networks. What topics do they deal with, how many participants are there, how frequent are the exchanges, how does one join, what arrangements are there for archiving materials, etc.?

These difficulties were overcome with the development of List Management software applications that automate much of the work involved in filtering the flow of information to subscribers to mailing lists. There are a number of different packages available, the most important being LISTSERV, Majordomo, ListProcessor and Mailbase. These software applications automate the subscribing, unsubscribing, forwarding, announcing and archiving operations associated with the management of a mailing list.

To subscribe to a list you send an electronic message that includes the appropriate command to the server where the list management application of the mailing list you are interested in is stored. You are then either placed on the list of subscribers, or asked to confirm receipt of a message from the list administration program prior to being placed on the list. Confirmation of your subscription will be accompanied by information about the list, the procedures for unsubscribing, obtaining access to former and future communications, how to temporarily suspend receipt of communications, and related matters. Usually this is all accomplished in a matter of hours, sometimes in minutes. The exception to this is some moderated lists where the moderator may address further questions to the intending subscriber. Following confirmation that you have been added to the list you will receive copies of all communications that are posted by anyone on the list.

Before subscribing to a list you will need to locate lists that deal with topics that you have an interest in. There are a number of online resources for locating mailing lists. Of the four mentioned below, three are particularly useful and will be reviewed in detail.

Directory of Scholarly and Professional E-Conferences

<http://www.n2h2.com/KOVACS>

A composite of the interface of the Directory of Scholarly and Professional E-Conferences is reproduced in Figure 9.1.

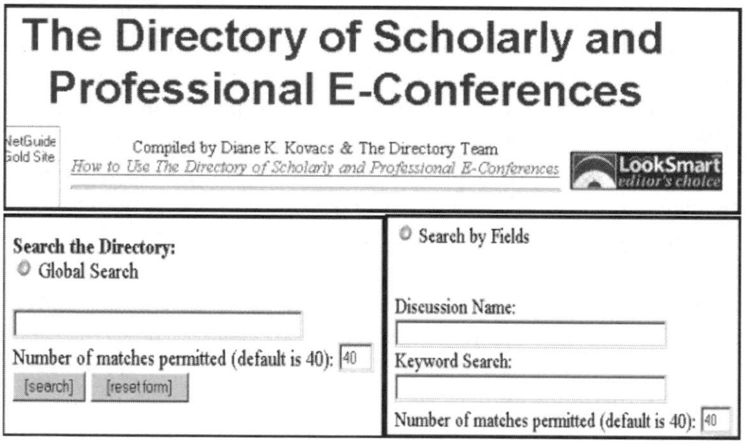

Figure 9.1 *Kovacs interface.*

You can search either by key word (*Search the Directory*) or by the name of the list (*Discussion Name*) if you know it. Key in a term (e.g. Politics or Philosophy) in the *Global Search* and increase the number of matches permitted. The default is 40 but the number of relevant lists is often greater. On 9 February 1998 there were 107 entries under the heading Politics. The reason why you may want to search the directory even if you know the name of the list is that you may wish to obtain information on its address, or other particulars relating to it.

Lower down on the page there is an alphabetical and subject listing of all the mailing lists in the directory. The list is arranged in 56 subject categories, some of which are reproduced in Figure 9.2, which you access by clicking on the *Subject/Category* hyperlink.

17. Ecology and Environmental Studies
18. Economics
19. Education: Computer Assisted Instruction/Educational Technology
20. Education: Developmental Disabilities, Physical Disabilities and ADA (Americans with Disabilities Act)
21. Education: Educational Research (general), Grants and Funding
22. Education: Higher, Adult and Continuing Education
23. Education: Miscellaneous Education, Alumni and Student Groups
24. Education: Primary, Secondary (K-12), Vocational and Technical and Special Education
25. Engineering and Technology General
26. Genealogy and Local History
27. Genetics, General Biology/Biophysics/Biochemistry
28. Geography and Miscellaneous Regional and Individual Country Studies
29. Geology and Paleontology
30. History

Figure 9.2   *Kovacs subject listing.*

If you select the subject listings and then one of the subject categories, or key in a subject descriptor in the directory search form (e.g. politics, sociology, history, etc.), a document is returned that includes all the records in the database that match the query entered. Figure 9.3 reproduces a portion of the listing returned for the category Sociology and Demography.

1. ABSLST-L	13. CESSDA-L
2. ADQ	14. CHILD-MALTREATMENT-RESEARCH-LSU
3. alt.parents-teens	15. CIVILSOC
4. alt.society.anarchy	16. CSOCWORK
5. alt.society.generation-x	17. Cussnet-List
6. ARNOVA-L	18. Daily
7. CAACSALF	19. Demographic-List
8. CAPDU-L	20. DISASTER RESEARCH
9. CASID-L	21. electronic-sociology-L
10. CENSUS-PUBLICATIONS	22. ELIAS-L
11. CENSUS-NEWS	23. H-DEMOG
12. CENSUS-ANALYSIS	24. H-DURKHM

Figure 9.3   *Kovacs subject subheading listing.*

Only the names of matching lists are included in the document. Although you can frequently infer the subject matter from the name (e.g. if you keyed in history, you will infer that H-LAW is a list that deals with the history of law, and H-ECON with economic history), some names do not bring to mind a specific subject matter easily (e.g. ASC-L, SQSP).

When you select a name from a list that is returned in response to your query, say one of those illustrated in Figure 9.3, the document that is returned provides information about it under various headings, as illustrated for two lists shown in Figure 9.4.

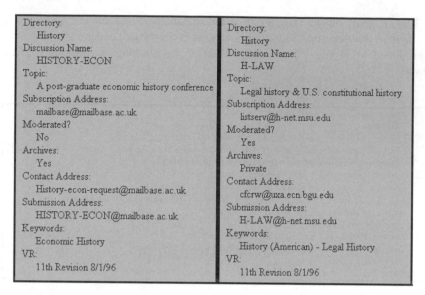

Directory:
    History
Discussion Name:
    HISTORY-ECON
Topic:
    A post-graduate economic history conference
Subscription Address:
    mailbase@mailbase.ac.uk
Moderated?
    No
Archives:
    Yes
Contact Address:
    History-econ-request@mailbase.ac.uk
Submission Address:
    HISTORY-ECON@mailbase.ac.uk
Keywords:
    Economic History
VR:
    11th Revision 8/1/96

Directory:
    History
Discussion Name:
    H-LAW
Topic:
    Legal history & U.S. constitutional history
Subscription Address:
    listserv@h-net.msu.edu
Moderated?
    Yes
Archives:
    Private
Contact Address:
    cfcrw@uxa.ecn.bgu.edu
Submission Address:
    H-LAW@h-net.msu.edu
Keywords:
    History (American) - Legal History
VR:
    11th Revision 8/1/96

Figure 9.4   *Kovacs list particulars.*

The information provided in Figure 9.4 relates to two history lists, one on economics, the other on law. The Discussion Name is the name of the list. The Subscription Address is the *administrative address* of the list. In other words, this is the address of the software application that automates list procedures, such as subscribing and unsubscribing users, processing requests for information, etc. The Submission Address, on the other hand, is the address to which a user should send a posting to the group, either a new one, or a response to that of someone else on the list. It is very important to get the distinction between the two correct. You do not want to send a request to unsubscribe, or for information on the list, to the list itself. This would result in every member on the list receiving your request when they are not in a position to do anything about it. Unfortunately, because some users are not familiar with the distinction, or forget about it, this occurs with some frequency.

> **Send administrative requests to the subscription/administrative address. Send postings to list members to the submission address. The submission address always has the name of the list (e.g. H-LAW, ELIAS-L) preceding the @ character. The administrative address always has the name of the list pro- cessing application before the @ character, as in <listserv@pdu.edu>, or <majordomo@demon.co>. To subscribe to the ARENDT list, you would send the message to <listserv@freelance.com>. To send a message to the list which will be seen by other subscribers, you need to post it to <ARENDT@freelance.com>.**

The information on the list (Figure 9.4) provides schematic details of the subject focus, whether it is moderated or not, whether the list is a public or private one, whether there are archives of postings available and the addresses from which these can be accessed. There is also information on the contact person, variously described as moderator, list owner, coordinator or editor – that is, the human in charge.

The Kovacs directory is an established and respected database of mailing lists and other electronic forums likely to be of interest to members of the academic community. Unfortunately, no information is provided concerning the criteria included in their 'judgement' of scholarship, or about the number of conferences included in the database. In addition, unlike some other Internet mailing list databases, this one does not allow you to subscribe to a list directly from the documents providing details about them.

Liszt

<http://www.liszt.com/>

The interface of the Liszt mailing list directory is illustrated in Figure 9.5.

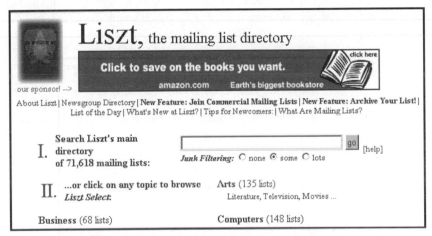

Figure 9.5 *Liszt interface.*

There are two means of selecting lists. Your first option is to choose from what are referred to as Select Lists. These are groups of mailing lists arranged by subject. This is similar in some respects to the way in which the Kovacs directory is arranged, only there are fewer main headings and more subdivisions. Finding a comprehensive listing of mailing lists relating to a subject that you are interested in by using this feature is likely to prove problematic. The main cluster of lists relating to Women, for instance, is found under culture, but the Politics heading includes STOPRAPE. Rather than spend time guessing and searching through main headings, it may be advisable to enter a query in the Search Liszt's main directory form box. This is the second means available for locating lists.

The database supports quite complex queries. Unlike some other search engines the default is subverting searching. This means that if you key in *sex* the database will retrieve records matching asexual, bisexual, heterosexual, homosexual, sexy, sexual and sexuality, if there are matching entries. To restrict the search to sex, include it in double inverted commas, "sex". If two terms are entered, the database uses the default AND. If you enter the words *politics philosophy*, all entries in which both occur will be retrieved. You can also use the logical operator OR, and parentheses for more focused searches. The query <(philosophy or politics) NOT (Adorno or Arendt)> will extract all records in which there are matching entries to philosophy or politics, but which exclude both Adorno and Arendt. If you want the search to match entries of two words that appear in succession, include these in double inverted commas, as in <"mathematical economics">.

Another potentially useful feature of the Liszt database search engine is the Junk Filter (see Figure 9.5). This is designed to filter out records which are unlikely to be of interest by excluding those that contain certain phrases, including *association*, *members* or *course*. The database is compiled by a software program which will net in some URLs/titles which point, for instance, to educational and training courses, tens of thousands of which are marketed on the Internet. The default is set to *medium* filtering. If you select *none* many entries, particularly of the one-word variety, will return many records that will be of no interest. On the other hand, selecting *lots* is likely to strip out some of those that are of interest. In my experience Liszt is a very fast search engine, so the added time required to check on whether you have missed some by choosing the *medium* or *lots* will not be excessive.

Figure 9.6   *Liszt query/return interface.*

Having submitted a query, a document similar to that illustrated in Figure 9.6 is returned. The query to which this document corresponds is for the entry economics. If there are any entries that match the query they are arranged, if appropriate, in three groups. Those in group I are lists that fall under the main categories which appear on the front page (see Figure 9.5, Business, etc.). Group II consists of Liszt Select mailing lists. The difference between this and the more extensive grouping under III, mailing lists, has eluded me. In fact, this arrangement is unnecessarily confusing, for if you want to peruse the records returned for a particular query you need to download additional documents, rather than scroll down one list. In this particular example, the main category Humanities/Economics includes the lists FEMECON-L and POST-KEYNESIAN ECONOMICS. These records are not replicated in group III. Thus, if you scroll down the document returned in response to your query without opening the associated documents under I and II, you will fail to see these entries.

Each list is colour coded. Green signifies that the database contains detailed information on the list, its 'info file', yellow that there is some information available, red that when information was last requested none was available, and white that further information was either not requested or not forthcoming.

---

femecon-l

Feminist Economists Discussion Group
--Send list commands to listserv@bucknell.edu

> femecon-l@bucknell.edu is the Feminist Economists Discussion Group. The list is owned by Jean Shackelford at Bucknell University. Send any questions you have about the list to jshackel@bucknell.edu. Send submissions to femecon-l@bucknell.edu. To subscribe to the list, send a message to listserv@bucknell.edu with the body of your mailgram containing a line like: SUBSCRIBE FEMECON-L your name [more info]

Figure 9.7   *List particulars from Liszt.*

Figure 9.7 illustrates the type of information that is available on some of the lists. If you select list commands, you are provided with details describing how to subscribe, obtain an information file, etc. If your browser is Netscape version 2.0 or above, and configured appropriately (see Chapter 26), selecting *listserv@bucknell.edu* will open a message window with the address inserted. In the body of the message you can now include commands to subscribe, to send the information file, or, if you are already subscribed, to unsubscribe.

CataList

<http://www.lsoft.com/lists/listref.html>

Both the Liszt and Kovacs directories cover mailing lists irrespective of the management software that automates list procedures. CataList, in contrast, provides information only on public LISTSERV mailing lists, that is those in the public domain. Although this may appear somewhat restricted, 79,016 lists were recorded as using this software on 10 February 1998, of which 16,455 were in the public domain delivering more than 20 million messages a day, on 30 July 1997. The majority of academic and professional lists use the LISTSERV system. The search engine available can access lists by name or title. It also enables retrieval of the names of lists that maintain Web-based archives. Generally, the information available is comprehensive, mostly accurate, and returned speedily. In parentheses next to each entry in the list returned are the current numbers of subscribers. Another useful feature is the hyperlink to archives of those lists that maintain them on the Web. If you are in search of academic lists arranged by subject, selecting the title option in the CataList search engine is probably one of the most efficient means of speedily locating appropriate lists.

You can also view lists by host site, by host country, and by the numbers of subscribers. This latter facility is arranged in two categories, lists with more than 1000 subscribers and those with more than 10,000. The information provided is always up to date as it is generated automatically from the databases maintained by LISTSERVs. This information can be useful for various research purposes.

Mailbase

<http://www.mailbase.ac.uk/>

Mailbase was set up in the United Kingdom by the higher education funding bodies to organize mailing lists for the UK higher education sector, and is based at the University of Newcastle. On 10 February 1998 it included 1846 discussion lists and claimed 130,877 subscribers worldwide. The lists are arranged alphabetically.

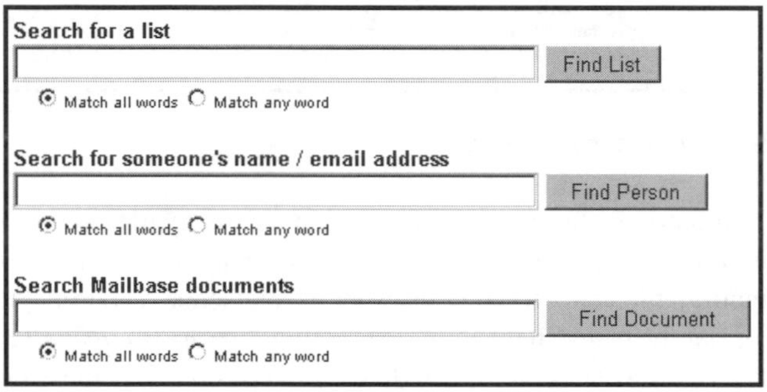

Figure 9.8   *Mailbase interface.*

The search engine, illustrated in Figure 9.8, allows searches for a named list, for information on contributors to Mailbase lists and of their archives of past communications. The *Search for a list* option permits minimal Boolean searches, namely the use of AND/OR. The detailed information provided for each list is very well arranged. It includes details of the subject matter covered, membership, and commands relating to various features of the lists. Of particular value is the hypermail archive of past mailings, arranged by months.

In conclusion, all of the mailing list directories reviewed above are relatively easy to navigate and all of them return sufficiently comprehensive information to allow those accessing them to trace lists that meet the specifications of queries entered. Some, the Kovacs and Liszt directories, provide information on how to subscribe and execute some other commands.

It needs to be emphasized, however, that different databases, whether Internet search engines or those of Usenet newsgroups or mailing lists, employ software applications with different search algorithms. In consequence, although there will be considerable overlap in the records of those which map a substantial portion of Internet space, the fit is not perfect. Thus, for example, Liszt returned 11 lists for the query psychology on 10 February 1998, whereas the Kovacs directory returned 40, CataList 113, and Mailbase 16. My unsurprising recommendation, therefore, is that you refer to more than one database. There are many other Web-based databases of discussion lists. If you need more, use Alta

Vista with the query <"discussion list*"> and then use refining facilities described in Chapter 8. If you use the query <"mail* list*"> you will retrieve references to thousands of mail order and other company lists.

Addresses of mailing list databases
CataList
<http://www.lsoft.com/lists/listref.html>
Kovacs Directory of Scholarly Conferences
<http://n2h2.com/KOVACS>
Liszt
<http://www.liszt.com>
Mailbase
<http://www.mailbase.ac.uk>
Mailing Lists Arranged from A–Z
<http://www.ug.cs.dal.ca/pub/online-dir/internet/mail/mailing-list.html>
Publicly Accessible Mailing Lists
<http://www.NeoSoft.com/internet/puml/index.html>
Tile.Net Lists
<http://www.tile.net/lists>

CHAPTER 10

Mailing list commands and exchanges

10.1	Introduction	103
10.2	Subscribing and unsubscribing to lists	104
10.3	List information	105
10.4	Regulating mail inflow	106
10.5	Contributing to mailing lists	109
10.6	Other mail management/services commands	112

10.1   Introduction

This chapter focuses on some of the details that users need to know concerning the management of mailing lists. Below I will illustrate how to implement some of the more important features of automated list management packages. In the following chapter I will focus on retrieval of information from mailing list archives.

There are a number of widely used list management tools. The three that are most extensively employed are LISTSERV, ListProcessor (ListProc) and Majordomo. The commands that need to be transmitted in mail messages to implement particular features vary in some details, although the underlying principles and some of the commands are similar. I will be focusing on LISTSERV commands as the overwhelming majority of scholarly and professional lists use this mailing list management package. At the end of the chapter I will provide some information on comparable Majordomo and Mailbase commands.

10.2 Subscribing and unsubscribing to lists

In order to subscribe to a list you need to send a command to the computer from which the list is managed, instructing the software package to add your name to its subscribers. It is essential to send the request to the administrative address rather than to the address you would use if you wanted all members on the list to see your communication. The administrative address of the list ADDICT-L is

listserv@kentvm.kent.edu

This can be typed in either lower or upper case. If you want to send a message that would be seen by its subscribers the address would be

ADDICT-L@kentvm.kent.edu

> **The administrative address of the list has the name of the mail package on the extreme left (mailbase, listserv, majordomo). The address for messages to subscribers has the name of the list at the extreme left (ADDICT-L, HOLOCAUS-L, H-POL).**
>
> **All commands to the administrative address are sent in the body of the message. The *Subject:* line in the header should remain empty.**

Having located the list and typed the administrative address in the *To...* form box of your email client, you just type SUBSCRIBE <LISTNAME> in the message body. You can use the abbreviation SUB if you prefer. You should not type anything in the *Subject:* form box. This is illustrated in Figure 10.1.

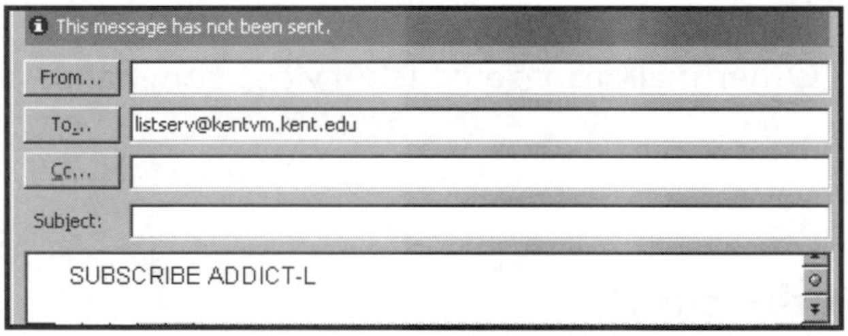

Figure 10.1 *Subscribing address and command.*

In a matter of minutes (or hours) you should receive a message back from the list informing you that you have been added to its subscribers or asking for a confirmation of your request. Either in the same message, or in a message that follows closely on it, you will be provided with information concerning list management and associated commands. You should save this file for future reference, as you are likely to find the information useful for unsubscribing, suspending mail, using archives, and more.

For moderated lists the procedure may be somewhat different. Some lists are closed, that is, not publicly available, or available only to those who meet specified criteria. Others, although public, are moderated. With moderated lists there may be some delay before the application is scrutinized and responded to by the list manager or owner. You will, however, also be sent detailed instructions about administrative matters relating to moderated lists.

To remove yourself from a list, in the body of a message sent to the administrative address type SIGNOFF <LISTNAME>. For the example above, this would be SIGNOFF ADDICT-L. You will be notified that you have been removed from the list.

10.3   List information

You can use the REVIEW command to obtain information about the list. In the body of the message you type REVIEW <listname>, e.g. [REVIEW H-POL]. Although it would seem to be more logical to use this command to obtain information prior to deciding whether to subscribe or not, some lists do not implement the command for non-subscribers or do so only partially. If you send this command to most lists prior to subscribing you will receive a message like: "You are not authorized to review the H-POL list."

The information sent in response to the REVIEW command is divided into two sections. The first, known as the control section, relates to the list itself. It provides details on the subject matter that the list deals with, who is the moderator/list owner, who can join the list, whether it is divided into topics, and whether it is archived, that is, whether all messages sent are kept in a database. The second section, the subscription part, contains a list of all the subscribers to the list, including their names and email addresses, except for those who have specifically requested that this information be withheld, as detailed further below.

The information on subscribers can be useful. You may be looking for someone to review a book or journal, potential delegates to a conference, partners to a research project, information in connection with a research paper, etc. On many lists there are subscribers who never actually send messages, or rarely do so, but who are experts in their field, even though they are only 'lurking'. You might want to exchange personal communications with such subscribers in connection with topics that have been discussed on the list, even though they have decided to refrain from contributing to the general discussion.

You can obtain a list of the subscribers at any time by sending the command

REVIEW <listname> BY NAME, e.g. [REVIEW AAWOMLIT BY NAME]

Subscribers will be listed alphabetically in response to this command, whereas the REVIEW command arranges subscribers by host, that is, by the address of the computer that they are on. If you would like to retrieve a list ordered by host name you send the command

REVIEW <listname> NOHEADER, e.g. [REVIEW H-WOMEN NOHEADER]

A listing of subscribers arranged by country will be returned in response to the command

REVIEW <listname> BY COUNTRY, e.g. [REVIEW AAWOMLIT BY COUNTRY]

Note, however, that all those listed under the heading US are not necessarily resident there. If the Internet Service or Access Provider of the subscriber is registered in the United States, they will appear on the list in the US section even though they may be resident outside the United States.

Many subscribers to lists are not aware of the fact that their email addresses can easily be obtained by others through use of the REVIEW command. Some users may perceive it as undesirable that their electronic address is juxtaposed with an inferred interest, gender or sexual preference. I know of instances where members on a particular list have been recipients of messages with abusive, racist or pornographic content. They have been targeted simply because they were subscribers to specific lists. To avoid this users can employ the CONCEAL command.

To remove your name from the list of subscribers, send the following in the body of the message:

SET <listname> CONCEAL, e.g. [SET EKONLIST CONCEAL]

If subsequently you wish to have your name reinstated on the publicly accessible list of subscribers, send the command

SET <listname> NOCONCEAL, e.g. [SET EKONLIST NOCONCEAL]

The information returned with the REVIEW command relating to the number of subscribers includes details on the number of concealed subscribers, although not their addresses.

LISTSERV packages compile statistical information relating to all lists. The information provided includes details on the names, addresses and number of messages sent by each member to the list. The command required to obtain this data is:

STATS <listname>, e.g. [STATS H-ECON]

Summary: Obtaining and regulating list information

REVIEW <listname> = Send me information about the list.
REVIEW <listname> BY NAME = Send a list of subscribers in alphabetical order.
REVIEW <listname> NOHEADER= Send a list of subscribers arranged by host computer.
REVIEW <listname> BY COUNTRY = Send a list of subscribers arranged by country.
SET <listname> CONCEAL = Do not reveal my address on the list of subscribers.
SET <listname> NOCONCEAL = Reveal my address on the list of subscribers/default.
STATS <listname> = Send me the available statistical information on the list.

10.4 Regulating mail inflow

Some lists give rise to a substantial volume of daily messages during most of the year. By default you will receive messages on a per-sender basis, as the mail server distributes them. For high-volume lists this means that throughout the course of the day there will be inputs to your mailbox from such lists. Some users may find this irritating, particularly if they have configured their mail program to notify them when new messages arrive. In addition, the mailbox can become cluttered very rapidly, particularly after a weekend or a few days away. On the advantages side, receiving individual messages allows you to deal with them variably: delete, print and save to different folders.

If you want to reduce the volume of messages received in your inbox there are a number of things you can do. Some electronic mail clients allow you to filter messages so that they are deposited in folders other than your inbox. This would also allow you to filter from one list into different folders. For instance, the list ACTIV-L deals with human rights, progressive, and peace-related issues. You could arrange for those that include key words such as Mexico, Amnesty International or Bosnia, to be saved separately in named folders while all the rest are deleted.

Another option is to have your messages delivered in the form of a digest. Instead of receiving individual messages, you will receive periodically, usually daily or weekly, one message that includes all mailings sent to the list since the last digest was despatched. The length of the periodic interval varies with the extent of activity on particular lists. This option has the advantage of not cluttering up your mailbox with a large number of messages, and allows you to file away digests for future reference if you do not have time to deal with them as they come in.

The disadvantage is that it reduces the flexibility of control. When you receive individual messages you can frequently establish from the subject heading alone what to do with the message. If it is on a topic that you are not interested in, you can easily delete it. If it covers a topic that you are interested in, but have no time to absorb at present, you can save it to disk or print for later reading. When you receive messages in digest form you have to scroll down what at times can be a very lengthy document, identifying messages of interest. This can be quite tiring and you can easily miss messages that you might be interested in. When you do encounter messages that are of interest, you have to decide what to do with them. To print or save them to disk you would have to block them, copy them to the clipboard, paste them into some other application and then print or save them. It is unlikely that you will want to archive the digest as it will contain many messages that are unlikely to be of any future interest. On the other hand, if you are interested in the range of topics that a list deals with, this might be a good option. Digests are probably particularly useful for those on which the volume of messages is relatively small. On high-volume lists my own experience has been that of filing them away for reading when time became available and then finding that they were outdated or too numerous to cope with by the time I got around to scrutinizing them.

To receive messages in digest form, you send the following in the body of the message to the administrative address:

SET DIGest <listname>, e.g. [SET DIGest ACTIV-L]

There is no need to include anything in the *Subject:* line. The lower-case letters are optional; you do not need to include them. If, having sent such a request, you subsequently decide that you wish to revert to receiving individual messages, the command that needs to be included in the body of the message is

SET MAIL <listname>, e.g. [SET MAIL ACTIV-L]

Managing information from high-volume lists is undoubtedly a problem. On the one hand, the data may be useful. On the other, it is difficult to cognitively process the information, and organizing it is time consuming. An alternative, which cuts down on the quantity of messages and data simultaneously, but which provides the subscriber with the opportunity of reading those messages that they think might be especially relevant, is to obtain an index of the messages sent on the previous day to the list. The information included in an index relating to each message is the name and address of the author, its subject, and the length of the message in lines. You can later send a command requesting that the messages you are interested in seeing be mailed to you. This is particularly useful if you are subscribed to a large-volume list when your particular interests cover only a relatively narrow spectrum of the subjects covered by its subscribers. The command for obtaining an index of list messages is

SET INDEX <listname>, e.g. [SET INDEX MAPOLITICS]

If previously you had been receiving individual messages, or a digest, sending the INDEX command will substitute receipt of an index of messages for either of the other two. If you want to be sent one of the messages on the list, you need to use the following command:

SEND <listname><filename>, e.g. [SEND ADDICT-L 001697]

If you wish later to revert to either individual messages, or a digest, you just send the respective commands to the administrative address.

If you wish to suspend your mail for a period of time, without unsubscribing to the list, the command is

SET NOMail <listname>, e.g. [SET NOMail H-LAW]

To restore mail you send the command

SET MAIL <listname>, e.g. [SET MAIL H-LAW]

Some lists arrange for the list management software to order their communications by topic, 11 topics being the maximum. To establish whether or not the lists you subscribe to have enabled this facility you need to use the REVIEW command discussed above. Having established what these topics are, you can elect to receive only messages relating to topics of your choice. The TOPICS option is available only for the default mode of MAIL. If you have set your options to digest or index mode, you cannot receive information classified by topic.

The topic-related command is

SET <listname> TOPICS: <topic names>

Each topic is separated by a space from the other topics. HUM-MOLGEN, to illustrate, is a list dealing with varied aspects of the Human Genome Project. The topics include NEWS, CALLs, ANNOuncements, LITErature, ETHIcal/social, etc. To receive communications from this list dealing with literature and news, you would need to send the command

SET HUM-MOLGEN TOPICS: LITE ETHI

You can include LITERATURE/LITErature and ETHICAL/ETHIcal in preference if you wish, but this is not necessary.

To add a topic you use the + character, and to remove a topic you employ the − character. To continue with the above example, if you wanted at some stage to drop the topic ETHICAL, and add the topics ANNOUNCEMENTS and CALLS, the appropriate command would be

SET HUM-MOLGEN TOPICS: –ETHI +CALL +ANNO

If you want at some stage to receive all messages, a digest or just an index of communications, you would issue the appropriate command that would supersede the one for topics.

The commands discussed above do not exhaust all those that are available. Some of those relating to mailing list message archives will be discussed in the next chapter. Those referred to above are for the LISTSERV mail management package.

Summary: Regulating mail

SET DIGEST <listname> = Mail forwarded in digest format.
SET INDEX <listname> = Index of mail forwarded.
SET NOMAIL <listname> = No mail until further notice.
SET MAIL <listname> = Send me mail on a per sender message basis.
SET <listname> TOPICS: <topic names> = Send me mail on the topics named.

The DIGEST and INDEX commands supersede and cancel out the MAIL command. Both DIGEST and INDEX commands supersede each other and cancel the MAIL command. NOMAIL cancels all other commands. MAIL supersedes and cancels all other commands.

10.5 Contributing to mailing lists

Being subscribed to a mailing list is an excellent means of keeping abreast of developments in an area of professional or other interest. For many users it is also an easily accessible and inexpensive way of exchanging views with people who they would otherwise be extremely unlikely to meet. Scholars dispersed widely geographically can participate in ongoing exchanges relating to their areas of interest much more readily than they can by attendance at conferences, a luxury that is rarely available to most practitioners and students. Mastering most of the commands should pose few problems to most users. Once you are subscribed to a few key lists, you can forget about most of the commands until you need to suspend mail, unsubscribe or chart new lists.

On many lists you will find that the quality of exchanges is high and that subscribers are careful to limit these exchanges to the subject matter of the list. Some lists, of course, are information lists, rather than forums for exchanges of view. There are, for instance, numerous lists that circulate information about conferences: when, where and on what they are being held. Others circulate book reviews. Some lists discuss topics that require a high degree of expertise to follow. The list ACC PHYS is a pre-print server for Accelerator Physics. Unless you have a degree in physics it is unlikely that you will find much that you will be able to follow readily there. There are, on the other hand, many lists on which most of those with an interest in the social sciences will find postings and articles from well-informed contributors and experts that are more easily followed. In addition to discussing substantive topics, lists are also a forum for informing participants about recently published books, meetings, proposed conferences, joint book or research proposals, and so forth.

When contributing to a list there are a few practices that are worth observing. It is important to ensure that the subject headings you are using in the message headers reflect as accurately as possible their content. Subject headings are important guides that enable readers to decide the significance to them of reading the message. They are also used by some search engines to classify postings under subject headings.

Make sure that your message is being sent to the correct address: to the list if meant for all subscribers, to the administrative address if it is concerned with list management matters. Be careful not to select the *Send* button before you have finished composing the message. It is not possible to retrieve it once sent, and all subscribers will receive an incomplete communication, followed, in all probability, by the completed message and an apology a few minutes later. Keeping up with many lists can be an arduous task without having to deal with too many misadventures.

Before contributing to discussions it is probably best to monitor exchanges for a brief period, gauging what is expected of contributors in terms of subject matter and depth of coverage. Many lists have an associated newsgroup. If there is one you may be able to locate an associated FAQ (Frequently Asked Questions) document that will provide information relating to the topics discussed previously on the list. There are quite a few lists that have either a high turnover or large numbers of additional subscribers per unit of time. Some have both. If a substantial body of new subscribers ask the same questions that their many predecessors have, or provide the same information, this tends to irritate those who are veterans of these exchange markets.

When subscribed to a list you have the option of sending a communication, or a reply, either to the list or to the sender of a message. It is necessary at times to ponder whether a reply should be sent to the former or the latter. Frequently subscribers send messages stating that they have information on X or Y, or that they have read this or that book, or have used this or that piece of equipment or software application, been to this or that conference, etc. If you want to follow this up, it is sometimes preferable to send it to the person concerned rather than clutter up the list with messages like 'Hi Andy/Karen, you said ... Could you please ...' when the probable contents of the reply are unlikely to be of interest to most list members.

Try and keep your messages as concise and to the point as possible if you want other subscribers to follow them up by responding. Most subscribers simply do not have the time to read intensively every communication they receive. It is inevitable that in attempting to cope with such a large quantity of information, many will scan rapidly through those that by their subject line appear to be of some interest. If the point you are making is buried somewhere in 300 lines of closely argued text, few will bother or manage to locate it. You need to market your postings in such a way that others will read and respond to them.

Some of those who complain about the shallowness, pithiness or incompleteness of mailing list communications fail to understand that in this medium the intellectual exchanges of the journal article or the conference presentation are, and need to be, downsized. If you have a copiously detailed argument concerning Bauman's views on modernity, Harré's perspective on the social construction of emotions, or models of the economies of scope, send a brief message outlining the main points in a few lines and attach the more detailed argument as a separate file. If you intend raising a number of separate, albeit somewhat related, issues, consider sending a number of short messages instead of a lengthy and tightly argued communication. The structure of mailing list discourse requires that some consideration be given to the attention span of potential readers.

Keep the formatting as simple as possible. There is a small band of stalwarts who, for unfathomable reasons, prefer to send lengthy messages in capital letters. These are extremely difficult to read, irritate many readers and, consequently, frequently remain undigested. Another category of contribution that I think is well worth avoiding takes the form: 'Hello everyone. I have just joined the list and I thought that I would introduce myself to everyone. I am a student (staff member) at … doing research into/writing a book on …'. If you cannot resist the temptation, make sure that the subject header is entitled Introducing Myself to the List. That way, the rest of us suffering souls can delete it. Far better to wait until such time as you can introduce yourself in the context of posting a contribution to the ongoing subject matter of the list.

You should try to avoid, under all circumstances, getting involved in a pointless exchange of invective. It is unlikely that going down this route will gain any converts and it is more or less guaranteed to arouse the hostility of others. Unless you can pour oil on heated controversies, it is best to sit them out. Equally, if you encounter the message 'how do I unsubscribe/remove myself from the list', restrain yourself; there is no point in sending a communication to the list displaying your proficiency in identifying synonyms of imbecile. If you have that much spare time and energy, send a helpful email to the author of the message detailing how to unsubscribe.

On some lists exchanges do at times get very heated. One of the lists that I subscribed to was REVS (Race and Ethnic Violence Studies). In October 1995 there were heated exchanges relating to the O. J. Simpson trial. A contributor suggested that Nicole Brown Simpson's behaviour could be attributed to her connections with criminal elements. The heated exchanges that ensued arose less from this suggestion than from the use of a common 'anti-woman (sexist) insult' to describe Nicole Brown. Initially an apology was sought from the contributor, but one was not forthcoming. Some subscribers decided to unsubscribe. Personal insults were directed at some of those entering the fray. As the list owner, Alan Spector, was going away for a conference for four days, he postponed the posting of messages from the contributor whose initial communication had initiated this particular spat. This only seemed to fuel further controversy as any act smacking of censorship finds scant support in most Internet forums. The list owner explained his actions by noting that the list should not tolerate sexist remarks any more than it should tolerate 'a neo-Nazi posting a message calling all Jews sub-human or a white racist hurling traditional anti-black insults'. Moreover, he continued, such exchanges laid him, as list owner, open to potential libel suits.

The controversy was calmed by his decision to split the list in two. One part would be moderated; all messages sent to the list henceforth would be scrutinized by moderators. Any deemed offensive would not be posted to the moderated list. The second, to be known as REVS-cafe, would not be moderated. All messages received by the list would be posted there. Individuals who subscribed to REVS-cafe would automatically receive all communications. Those who subscribed to REVS would receive only moderated communications. A neat solution; censorship, inasmuch as it is involved, will be self-imposed.

10.6 Other mail management/services commands

Majordomo

SUBSCRIBE <listname> / UNSUBSCRIBE <listname>

INFO <listname> provides information on the list

WHO <listname> returns a list of addresses of subscribers

INDEX <listname> returns a list of files associated with the list

GET <listname> <filename> returns specified file from specified list

HELP returns a help file

Mailbase

<http://www.mailbase.ac.uk/>

JOIN <listname><firstname><lastname> / LEAVE <listname>

SUSPEND MAIL <listname> / RESUME <listname>

REVIEW <listname> returns a list of addresses of subscribers

CHAPTER 11

Mailing list archives

11.1	Introduction: mailing list archives as a resource	113
11.2	Mailing list archive database commands	115
11.3	Summary and conclusion	124

11.1   Introduction: mailing list archives as a resource

Mailing lists are a useful medium for listening in on communications on particular topics, keeping abreast of developments in particular fields and exchanging views with individuals who have particular interests or areas of expertise. Such considerations do not exhaust the potential usefulness of mailing lists to the social scientist. Past communications on many lists are archived. These can be searched for information on a wide range of matters, factual, conceptual and affective. In addition, mailing lists themselves are interesting subjects of social research respecting their patterns of interaction, online identities, narrative attributes, intensity of communications and characteristics of their participants, to mention a few dimensions.

Mailing lists potentially have three important advantages over more conventional typographical sources of information on many topics. Books and journal articles are frequently published one or more years after they were originally written. This invariably is at some considerable distance from when the original data collection was completed. The interval between completion of writing and publishing on mailing lists is more or less immediate. Commentary on contemporary issues is frequently engaged more or less immediately after they assume prominence on agendas. By the time some of the matters discussed on mailing lists are the subject of printed publications or conference presentations, subscribers to mailing lists have frequently long since discussed them, sometimes in considerable detail.

The second important difference is that mailing list communications do not purport to deal with the 'big idea', the major paradigm shift or the lengthy exegesis on the philosophy of X, Y or Z. If they do, they do so in small chunks. There is, of course, much useful and usable information, many interesting hypotheses and conclusions that never see the printed presses because they are insufficiently bounded by additional material. Mailing lists also afford a reasonably efficient and rapid means of contacting individuals with expertise in particular areas. If you are looking for information on a particular subject, pointers to the research literature or an amplification of views expressed in other contexts, mailing lists can be a very good resource.

Mailing list archives have uses other than the mining of data. Many lists function as organizing and mobilizing platforms for special interest, pressure, support and shared orientation groups. There are a number of lists that focus on progressive social and human rights issues (PSN, REVS, ACTIV-L) whose members are active, partly through these lists, in bringing pressure to bear on governments, organizations or individuals with a view to securing particular ends. Amnesty International works some lists to galvanize support in furtherance of human rights objectives. During the active period of the uprising in Chiapis, Mexico, during 1995 and 1996, there was a lot of activity on some lists aimed at securing support for its leaders and constraining the activities of the Mexican authorities. Subscribers to lists have also been quite effective in campaigning for the rights of illegal migrants in California in response to the passing of Proposition 187 in 1994, and others have been campaigning for the lifting of sanctions against Iraq because of the alleged consequences for the civilian population, particularly children. Subscribers have also successfully exerted pressure against alleged miscarriages of justice, as in the Abu Mumia Jamal case in Pennsylvania. Mobilization of opinion opposed to the Communications and Decency Act was effectively channelled through many mailing lists.

There are other lists that function as support forums for individuals with shared interests, characteristics or preferences. Although their members may infrequently exchange communications that might be classified as 'scholarly', they are very relevant to social scientists who are interested in understanding, explaining and researching issues relating to the dispositions, interests or characteristics of members of such groups. They are also a rich source of 'research' and 'information' leads relating to individuals who do not appear on any lists that can be used for sampling purposes, or where the compilation of such lists can be expensive in both time and resources.

TRNSPLNT (@wuvmd.wustl.edu), for example, is a mailing list for those who have received transplanted organs. The exchanges on this list are archived. The addresses of those who are active participants can be read from the headers of their communications. Those of other subscribers can frequently be downloaded, as they are available to other subscribers. This is potentially useful information for anyone interested in conducting research on the experiences, medical histories, views, and transformations of identity of those who have had organ transplants. At the very least there are bound to be some subscribers who can provide leads to other sources of information and individuals. There are literally hundreds of other mailing lists focusing on medical dysfunctions, sexual dispositions, political identities, leisure pursuits, etc. All are potentially rich sources of varied categories of information for the social scientist. Moreover, their membership is ordinarily drawn from a much wider social and demographic base than the subjects who have been included in more traditional social scientific studies.

11.2   Mailing list archive database commands

> When sending commands to the administrative address of the mailing list the *Subject:* line
> in the mail header should be left blank.

Indexes and files

Unlike newsgroups there is no search engine that can be employed to trawl either current
or past postings to all or even a few mailing lists. To locate lists that are likely to deal with
the issues you are interested in and that also archive their communications, use one of the
mailing list database search facilities reviewed in the previous chapter. You should also
establish whether they maintain Web-based archives. CataList,

<http://www.lsoft.com/lists/list_q.html>

provides information on whether LISTSERV lists have Web archives, although their information is not always accurate on this detail. Generally, Web-based archive search engines
cannot filter queries as powerfully as the database commands described in the remainder
of this chapter.

Having located one or more lists with archives that you think may hold information
on issues you are interested in, the first thing you need to do is to obtain an index of their
files. This is accomplished by sending the following command to the administrative
address of the list in the body of the message:

INDEX <listname>, e.g. [INDEX POWR-L]

(POWR-L is the Psychology of Women Resource List, aimed at sharing information on all
matters relating to the psychology of women.) The mailer will respond with a message
that will take the form of that illustrated in Figures 11.1 and 11.2. The returned document
lists the files that are archived and provides various details concerning each entry.

```
* NOTEBOOK archives for the list
* (Monthly notebook)
*               roc        last-change
*filename filetype  GET PUT -fm lrecl nrecs  date   time  Remarks
*  ____  ____    __ __ __ __ __ __   __   __

 POWR-L  LOG9502  PRV OWN V   165 1881 95/02/28 16:38:43 Started on Tue, 7 Feb 1995
16:10:26 EST
 POWR-L  LOG9503  PRV OWN V    83 5909 95/03/30 06:38:00 Started on Wed, 1 Mar 1995
00:08:25 EST
 POWR-L  LOG9504  PRV OWN V   237 5595 95/04/30 11:26:18 Started on Mon, 3 Apr 1995
05:49:36 EST
 POWR-L  LOG9505  PRV OWN V   109 4210 95/05/31 09:52:46 Started on Mon, 1 May 1995
10:13:58 EDT
```

Figure 11.1   *INDEX query return, top half.*

My objective in what follows is to enable readers to download relevant files and
construct queries so that they will be able to download pertinent information. I will not,
therefore, elaborate on the complete set of LISTSERV database functions. A document
explaining the latter for 'general users' (release 1.5n) takes up 45 A4 pages, and can be

obtained by sending to the administrative address of any LISTSERV the command <Info DATABASE>. You can obtain addresses by accessing CataList.

Taking the first file entry in Figure 11.1 for illustrative purposes, the list name (POWR-L) appears on the extreme left, followed by the file name, which is LOG9502. The period that it applies to is read from the right. In this instance the log is for the second month of 1995. At the extreme right of this file entry it is indicated that the log was started on 7 February. The log for a mailing list includes information on all the messages that were sent for the period indicated. This file will include information on all messages sent between 7 February and 1 March.

The headers for the third and fourth columns in Figure 11.1 are GET and PUT. The row cells under the headers include the abbreviations PRV and OWN respectively. The GET signifies who is entitled to download (get) the file. The PUT specifies who is entitled to make files available on the server for downloading. On this particular list PRV designates list subscribers, as explained elsewhere in the document to which Figure 11.1 relates. Sometimes you will come across the category ANY instead of PRV. That indicates that those files are available to anyone, irrespective of whether they are subscribers to the list.

If you want to receive any of the files indicated you send the command:

GET <listname> <filename>, e.g. [GET POWR-L LOG9505]

It is essential to remember to include the listname in the command as the mailer is likely to handle a large number of different lists. You can request as many files as you want by including a space between filenames.

```
POWR-L WELCOME  ALL OWN V   72   54 95/02/07 07:54:07 POWR-L Welcome Message
CONGRESS TEXT    ALL OWN V   75  559 95/03/17 12:48:10 Congress Information
UNGERAWP TEXT    ALL OWN V   67  773 95/03/17 12:48:19 Unger Address to AWP
UPOWHYDE SYLLABUS ALL OWN V  65  259 95/03/22 09:39:32 Undergrad Psych of Women
Syllabus
GPOWHYDE SYLLABUS ALL OWN V  65  210 95/03/22 09:39:45 Grad Psych of Women Syllabus
GWMSHYDE SYLLABUS ALL OWN V  65  246 95/03/22 09:43:56 Grad Women's Studies Methods
Syllabus
FREUD   TEXT     ALL OWN V   76  413 95/05/05 10:10:04 Gleaves on Freud
CAPLNPMS TEXT    ALL OWN V   78  307 95/05/05 10:09:53 Caplan on PMS
ACAAMEM TEXT     ALL OWN V   80  488 95/05/10 11:35:38 ACAA Letter
SELFHELP TEXT    ALL OWN V   80  510 95/12/29 11:22:36 Harris' List on Emotional
Support
GILLEM  BIBLIO   ALL OWN V   74  164 96/11/06 09:11:03 Gillem Bibliograghic Info
KASHBIB MULTICUL ALL OWN V   80  533 97/05/30 09:21:55 Multicultural Bibliography
```

Figure 11.2   *INDEX query return, bottom half.*

Figure 11.2 shows another portion of the same document illustrated in Figure 11.1. The same interpretative code applies. The second column, filetype, describes what the file is. This could be a syllabus, welcome message, text, bibliography or other category. To download a file you need to send a command to the administrative address including the filename, which is indicated in the extreme left column, and the listname.

GET POWR-L FREUD or GET POWR-L SELFHELP

In Figure 11.2 the first file that is indicated is the welcome message sent to new subscribers, and named POWR-L. The file named FREUD contains various messages that make some reference to Freudian paradigms, interpretation or practice.

To summarize: archives include records of past messages sent to the list. These are usually ordered in logs. The archives also include various files, the numbers and type being indicated in the Index file. To obtain a listing of files and logs you send the Index command **INDEX** *<listname>*. If you want to retrieve a file you send the GET command, **GET** *<listname>* *<filename>*.

Batch database commands

This section will probably strike many readers as being the most difficult in the book. I suggest that you read through it first and then go over it subsequently as a practical exercise. Locate a number of lists that cover the topics that you are interested in, subscribe to them and then send them some of the batch commands illustrated below, substituting for the terms that I have included some that suit the lists you have subscribed to and your interests. I am afraid that at this Rubicon there is no alternative but to move from theoretical to practical activity. You should probably subscribe a day before you undertake this exercise. On some moderated lists it may take a few days before you find that you receive acknowledgement of your membership. This does not apply, of course, to the few lists that do not require subscription to access their files.

For the most part it is likely that you will want to search through the database of archived messages in order to locate specific information, rather than scrutinize files or logs. On a high-volume list even searching the logs for a week can be very time consuming. Database searches can be accomplished by using what is known as a batch command. When you use a batch command you send a database job to a server via email. A database job is a sequence of commands that the server can process in the context of executing a database operation. After the job has been executed the results will be transmitted to you via email.

The syntax for a database job may strike you as being somewhat obtuse. It is not necessary, however, to be overly concerned with the overall purpose of specific lines of syntax other than those that you need to compose yourself. The rest of the syntax, the obtuse component, you just need to copy accurately. There is a standard format to a database job that you need to use, modifying it to include your particular search query. The basic structure of a search request is detailed in the Batch Command Template illustrated in the accompanying box.

Batch command template

// JOB Echo=No
Database Search DD=Rules
// Rules DD *
<command 1>
<command 2>

...
/*
// EOJ

In this database job the only variable components are the line entries designated command 1 and command 2. In other words, when writing out a query you copy all the details of the Batch Command Template exactly as they are, varying only the entries for command 1 and command 2, as discussed below. These latter instruct the LISTSERV to implement your search and do something with the results. The meaning of the rest is not something that you need be overly concerned about, although it is transparent that //JOB signifies the start of the batch command and //EOJ its ending. If you intend to search mailing list archives, type out and save this template and then copy and paste it into your mail message when required, filling in only the details for command 1 and command 2 in accordance with your search requirements.

All this may be somewhat confusing, so before proceeding to discuss how to structure commands 1 and 2 in the above template I will illustrate the procedure with an example. Below is a batch command, which I sent to the list ACTIV-L in order to retrieve details about its holdings of information on human rights in Colombia.

```
// JOB Echo=No
Database Search DD=Rules
//Rules DD *
Search "human rights" and Colombia in ACTIV-L
Index
...
/*
// EOJ
```

If you compare this with the batch command template above, you will observe that it is identical with it, except that for command line 1 there has been substituted Search "human rights" and Colombia in ACTIV-L, and for command line 2 the word Index. Search "human rights" and Colombia in ACTIV-L instructs the LISTSERV to search through its database and extract details on the location of documents including information on both human rights and Colombia. This is the Search command. The command to Index instructs the LISTSERV to provide an index of the findings resulting from the execution of command 1. Command 2, therefore, instructs the database to do something with the output of the Search command, namely, to index it. The product of this database job will be a file whose details are similar to those illustrated in Figures 11.1 and 11.2.

There is, unfortunately, an additional minor complication. There are different releases of the LISTSERV mail management package. The batch database job commands referred to below are used for versions 1.8b or earlier. For these you need to include the above template, varying only the command lines 1 and 2 to meet your requirements when you send a database query, as illustrated in the batch command template above. For releases 1.8c and later you only need to send command 1 in the body of your message. In other words the obtuse syntax (e.g. // JOB Echo=No) above and below the command lines does not need to be included. Similarly, having received information relating to your query in the form of a listing of files that match it and now wishing to request that some of those files be sent to you, which is the substance of command 2, you do not need to include the syntax above and below it. To establish which version a list is using, send a message with the command RELEASE in the body of the message to the administrative address of the list, leaving the *Subject:* line empty.

The Search command

The Search command is the first one that you use when you begin a database search and is positioned where command 1 appears in the batch command template illustrated above. All the other commands that can be issued are executed in relation to or upon the findings of a Search command.

The Search command has two components, which are referred to as the search rules and the optional rules. The term search rules is basically another term for search syntax. The term optional rules is applied to the syntax linking variables you can employ to constrain the search that you are conducting. In other words, the optional rules are appended to the search query and are employed to make it more focused. Before expanding on this, and to help in clarifying the distinction, look at the Search commands below, all of which would be included as command 1 in the batch command template above.

Search "cocaine poisoning" in ADDICT-L

Search "cocaine poisoning" in ADDICT-L where subject contains (treatment or death)

Search "cocaine poisoning" in ADDICT-L where subject contains (treatment or death) FROM July 96 to Aug 97

In the first query the command requests a search for the term cocaine poisoning in the database of the list ADDICT-L. Search "cocaine poisoning" constitutes the search rules component. ADDICT-L is the database optional rules component. In the second query, the search rules content remains the same but I have added the constraint where subject contains (treatment or death). This requests that the search select out those records where the phrase cocaine poisoning occurs, but only where either of the terms treatment or death appears in the *Subject:* line entry of the message header as well. This appendage to the search rules, where subject contains (treatment or death), falls under the heading of keyword optional rules. The third query confines the search to a time band. This is referred to as the date optional rules component of the search command.

The simplest search string consists of a single word: e.g. GATT, Paris, Rousseau, punishment, etc. Frequently you will want to narrow the search further. If you are searching a list that focuses on psychoanalytic thought, the search string Reich might land a large number of files dealing with varying aspects of Reich's work and life. Your specific interest might, however, be with his notion of the social psychology of authoritarian regimes. To locate such documents you need to employ search syntax in the search rules that is similar to that described earlier in connection with advanced searches using the Alta Vista search engine (Chapter 8). This could take the form

Search 'Wilhelm Reich' AND ("race theory" OR "organi*ed mysticism") in PSYCHOANALYTIC-STUDIES

You can employ the logical operators AND, OR and NOT, double inverted commas for phrases, and parentheses, as illustrated in the following example:

Search oceans AND ("toxic waste" OR nuclear) NOT "uranium isotope" in ENVINF-L

You can make the query as complex as you like to narrow the focus of your search. When working out how to formulate your query, remember that operations in parentheses are performed prior to those outside them, as in arithmetic and algebraic operations.

The default rule for a string of words not included in double inverted commas is Boolean AND. In other words, if you include the query *repressed memory syndrome*, documents including all of these words will usually be identified. They will not, however, necessarily be sequentially proximate in the documents retrieved. If you want to retrieve documents in which the words appear in the same order and juxtaposed, you need to bound them with double inverted commas, as in "repressed memory syndrome".

Unless a search string is bounded by double inverted commas, a query including it will extract records that include it irrespective of case. If the search string is BSE, the records retrieved will include, if available, not only those that include BSE, but also bse, Bse, bSe, and other variants. In addition, the LISTSERV database functions do not require that query terms be surrounded by blanks. Thus, records that included absent, absent-minded, absentee, and similar, will also be retrieved. If you want to restrict your query to a specific search string then it should be included in double inverted commas to cut down on the numbers of records returned.

The optional rules

The optional rules component enables researchers to constrain their search queries by date, keywords, and a database list, consisting of one or more named databases (mailing lists).

Date rules   Dates can be specified using alternative date rules:

SINCE (e.g. SINCE JULY 1995)

FROM (e.g. FROM JULY 1996 TO APRIL 1997)

UNTIL (e.g. UNTIL MAY 1993)

A query might, therefore, take the following forms:

Search "potato famine" in H-ALBION SINCE FEB 97

Search "frustration aggression" AND (hypothesis OR theory) in AGGRESS FROM JAN 1996 TO AUG 1997

Dates may be specified in a number of alternative formats:

TODAY
yy (96)
mm (04)
<dd><-->month name<-><yy> (17-06-97)
mm/yy (04/95)
yy/mm/dd (97/04/17)
yy-mm-dd (97-04-17)

By default, if you specify the month without a date (e.g. July) the records retrieved will include all those between 00:59:59, 30 June, and 00:59:59, 31 July.

Keyword rules   The second component of optional rules is keyword rules. The term has its origins in the fact that all messages to mailing lists have some common parameters.

They all have a list name, subject and sender information and a message header and body. They were all sent at a specific time on a particular date, are entered into the database at a particular time, etc. These parameters can be utilized in the context of database organization. The words designating these attributes are referred to as keywords. The format of keyword rules is:

WHERE/WITH keyword-expression

The keyword expressions that are likely to be of primary interest to most users are SUBJECT and SENDER. The former refers to the entry in the subject line of the message header, and SENDER refers to the author of the message. FROM can be employed as a substitute for SENDER. The format of search commands that include keyword rules is illustrated in the examples in Figure 11.3.

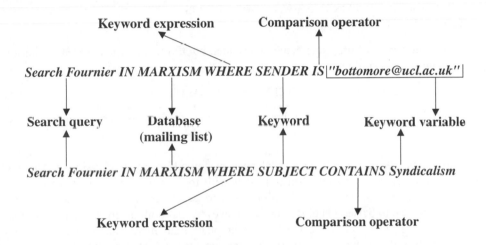

Figure 11.3 *Components of Search query commands.*

The terms IS and CONTAINS are referred to as comparison operators for WHERE/WITH clauses. The complete list of comparison operators is displayed in the accompanying box.

Comparison operators	
=	IS
< >	IS NOT
>	CONTAINS
<	DOES NOT CONTAIN
>=	SOUNDS LIKE
<=	DOES NOT SOUND LIKE

The operators that are included on the same line are synonymous. The operator IS indicates identity (as in SENDER IS [identical to] "j-crow@ucla.edu"). Conversely, IS NOT signifies absence of congruence. The mathematical symbols apply only in expressions relating to numerical entities. CONTAINS/DOES NOT CONTAIN are homologous with includes/excludes. The last two operators SOUNDS LIKE/DOES NOT SOUND LIKE are employed for database searches in which you are uncertain of the precise spelling of the search or optional rule variables.

The syntax that can be employed in the formulation of the search rules component of the query can also be used in the optional rules segment of the search command. That is, you can employ Boolean operators, parentheses, double inverted commas and a number of keywords. You could, for instance, formulate a search command like the following:

Search "A Monetary History of the United States" in EKONLIST
WHERE Subject CONTAINS "review of" and SENDER IS
((Smith or Jones) NOT Hutton)

If you were uncertain of the exact name of a sender, but thought that it sounded similar to something else, you could try:

Search Fournier in MARXISM WITH SENDER SOUNDS LIKE Johns

This should retrieve records with Johns, Jones, Johnston, Johnson, and similar, if they appear in the database.

Database lists At last we have arrived back at something relatively simple. Having composed the search query and constrained it with the optional rules, it is, of course, necessary to specify the databases (mailing lists) to be searched. You can specify more than one database to be searched. Remember, however, that both databases must have the same address. That is, the same LISTSERV or other mail management package must manage them both on the same server. You can establish which lists are managed at a particular address by sending the command *List* to the administrative address. CataList,

<http://www.lsoft.com/lists/list_q.html>

provides a link which informs you of all the lists that are included on the LISTSERV of any list you select.

Having established the databases available you can compose the query to include all those you consider likely to be relevant. A query could take the following form:

Search <query> in <mailing list name 1> <mailing list name 2>
<other optional rules>

Having got this far you will no doubt appreciate that although the search procedure appears somewhat involved, it is also quite powerful in that you can refine your search to focus closely on a combination of topics/authors/time periods that interest you.

Final note The whole of the Search command must appear on the same line. If you start a new line before the end of the query you must insert a – character before pressing the Enter/Return key. In the Summary shown in the accompanying box there is a dash after

RIOT-L. It is best, therefore, to let the text word-wrap and to press the Return key only when you want to begin a new line of search syntax.

Summary of search query procedures (Command 1 in batch query template)

1. Copy the batch command template reproduced below to the body of the message.
2. Compile your search query, taking into consideration the various factors discussed in Chapters 6–8.
3. Enter the name of the list you want to search on and decide on other variables which form part of the *optional rules* that you want to employ.

When you have completed all that, the database job should have the following form:

// JOB Echo=No
Database Search DD=R
// Rules DD *
Search Query, e.g.
[SEARCH "police brutality" AND Los Angeles IN RIOT-L –
SINCE 1995 WHERE SUBJECT CONTAINS 'Clinton']
<command 2>
...
/*
// EOJ

Output commands

As you can see in the example given in the box, the standard batch database job includes two commands, the first being the Search command just discussed. The second command relates to what you want done with the results obtained from submitting the Search command. There are two options here, INDEX and PRINT/GETPOST.

Ordinarily, when you send your first batch database job you will want to have returned a list of all the files that include references to your query. If the mailing list is being managed by LISTSERV release 1.8c or above, you will automatically be sent a list of the files that correspond with the search command submitted without having to do anything further. If the LISTSERV is release 1.8b or earlier, you substitute INDEX for command 2 in the batch database job template. To establish which version a list is using, send a message with the command RELEASE in the body of the message to the administrative address of the list, leaving the *Subject:* line empty. The batch database job will now take the following form:

    // JOB Echo=No
    Database Search DD=Rules
    // Rules DD *
    Search "cocaine addiction" in Addict-L FROM FEB 1997
    Index
    ...
    /*
    // EOJ

The file returned in response to the above database job is illustrated in Figure 11.4.

```
Subject:   Output of your job "SD-STEIN"


The DATABASE command has not yet been ported to this environment.

Unknown command - "RULES". Try HELP.

-> 9 matches.

Item #  Date   Time  Recs  Subject
_____  ____   ____  ____

016997 97/02/20 20:14  29   Special treatment for cocaine "addiction?"
017017 97/02/21 06:22  59   Re: Special treatment for cocaine "addiction?"
017032 97/02/21 08:19  42   Re: Special treatment for cocaine "addiction?"
017133 97/02/22 10:52  58   Re: Special treatment for cocaine "addiction?"
017154 97/02/22 12:08  57   Re: Special treatment for cocaine "addiction?"
017508 97/03/01 10:57  80   Re: Special treatment for cocaine "addiction?"
017517 97/03/01 12:29 104   Re: Special treatment for cocaine "addiction?"
018173 97/03/08 12:21 114   Re: Special treatment for cocaine "addiction?"
019244 97/04/09 18:30 253   Re: Top 10 Myths in Alcoholism
```

Figure 11.4   *Batch database job query return.*

In addition to details relating to the file, further on in the document there will be a few lines from the start of each message, which may give you some idea of its relevance to your query. You now need to select which of the postings you want to look at. This is done using the PRINT or other command as may be specified in the document that is returned. Further down in the file that was illustrated in Figure 11.1, p. 115, it is specified that to retrieve a file, the GETPOST command with the filename should be used. The command will take the form:

GETPOST ADDICT-L 016997 017017

If some of the file numbers are consecutive and you wish to see all those that fall within a range, you can use the following syntax:

GETPOST ADDICT-L 016997-017009

If the file returned does not specify how to request particular documents, and the GETPOST command results in an error message being returned, then you should use the PRINT command, which is inserted as command 2 in the batch database job template. Taking the above example again, the syntax would take the following form:

```
// JOB Echo=No
Database Search DD=Rules
// Rules DD *
Search "cocaine addiction" in Addict-L FROM FEB 1997
PRINT 016997 017017
...
/*
// EOJ
```

11.3   Summary and conclusion

The database search functions of mailing list management packages are extremely powerful. It is true that the more intricate your search requirements, the more complicated the composition of an appropriate search command is likely to be. It is not necessary, however, to jump in initially at the deep end. Frequently the information required can probably be retrieved with a relatively simple query to an appropriate list, involving a word or a phrase, perhaps with date and/or subject constraints. A limited amount of practice with simple to moderately complex search commands will provide the necessary experience to experiment with more elaborate searches when required.

It is, in any event, a mistake to accept uncritically some of the hype about the Web, namely, that it is just a question of click and go. No social scientist with experience in library-based or field research should expect that online research using databases running to hundreds of millions of megabytes of data will be either simple or problem free. Mailing list database features, on the other hand, do have the advantage of being extremely rapid in returning results once you acquire the requisite skills. The time required to acquire these is not extensive.

Those who do persevere should consult some of the online documents on database functions that are available from servers using LISTSERV and other mailing packages. My discussion above has not been exhaustive of the commands that are available.

Finally, it is worth noting that there are an increasing number of lists that maintain Web-based archives. This means that instead of having to master rather arcane syntax, you access the URL of the mailing list archive and then use the search engine provided to select out messages that match your query. Simplicity, alas, is not everything. First, only a small proportion of mailing lists currently maintain Web-based archives (12 out of 134 history, 16/151 women, 1/35 economics LISTSERV lists, 25 February 1998). Secondly, the search facilities are frequently not as sophisticated as archives that employ the electronic mail database functions. Thirdly, often you cannot establish whether the list has a Web-based archive before subscribing. Although CataList claims to indicate for LIST-SERV-based mailing lists whether the archives are Web based or not, its data is not always accurate.

CHAPTER 12

Reading the news: newsgroups

12.1	Introduction	127
12.2	Newsgroups and Usenet	128
12.3	Configuring the newsreader settings	130
12.4	Netscape newsreader interface	132
12.5	Accessing discussion groups	133
12.6	Reading the news	134
12.7	Posting messages	135
12.8	Newsgroup archives	136
12.9	Graphics and software programs	141
12.10	Commercial newsreaders	142

12.1   Introduction

Internet newsgroups, frequently referred to as Usenet (USENET) newsgroups, Usenet News, or just Usenet, are all terms employed to refer to a framework of electronic discussion forums arranged in subject and other hierarchies. Many of the comments that I have made already in connection with the usefulness of mailing lists apply in equal measure to newsgroups. They are, as Keeler and Miller (1997) point out, 'one of the best places online to get the most recent information or advice on a staggering array of topics'.

As with mailing lists, you generally need to subscribe to a specific newsgroup in order to read communications posted to it. Unlike mailing lists you do not subscribe to newsgroups as such. Instead, you indicate to the organization through which you link to the Internet and which is prepared to feed you messages sent to newsgroups, that you wish to subscribe to particular discussion groups from all those that the organization subscribes to.

If you have access to newsgroups through your organization or Internet Service Provider, you will be able to subscribe to them and read and post messages if you also have access to a software application called a newsreader. This is a dedicated application for reading discussion group messages. The Netscape and Microsoft browsers, versions 3.0 and above, have built-in newsreaders. Earlier versions of Netscape also had built-in newsreaders. Internet Service and Access Providers frequently provide their subscribers with a software suite that includes a dedicated newsreader as well as a browser that incorporates this facility. These dedicated newsreaders frequently include additional features that are not included in newsreaders that are part of the browser suite of applications. It is also possible to read the messages of newsgroups without a newsreader at some Web sites through facilities that will be discussed later (Section 12.8). Newsreaders provide faster and greater functionality than browsing communications over the Web.

There are many different proprietary brands of newsreader available. In this chapter I discuss in detail only the newsreader associated with the Netscape browser, with occasional comments on the Internet Explorer newsreader. If you follow the discussion of the procedures associated with the Netscape newsreader, you should find it relatively easy to apply these to the Internet Explorer equivalent.

12.2   Newsgroups and Usenet

There are thousands of newsgroups arranged in a number of hierarchies. Demon Internet, a UK-based Internet Access Provider, listed 25,702 discussion groups that were available to its subscribers on 30 November 1997. In January 1998, DejaNews, an organization that archives newsgroup messages, and which is discussed in detail later, included communications posted to 50,000 newsgroups. Because there are so many, the volume of disk space required to archive discussion group exchanges over a substantial interval is very large. Consequently, many organizations that subscribe to a newsgroup feed hold only a few days' postings of a selection of newsgroups.

Although the term Usenet newsgroup suggests that all or a sizeable number of newsgroups constitute some kind of network, this is not the case. The term denotes the assemblage of messages arranged into groupings that can be accessed by means of protocols that carry discussion group data. A newsgroup with a designated name, for instance alt.soc, alt.chile, or biz.books.technical, is an assemblage of messages that are deposited in a directory whose contents are differentiated from others by their subject matter. The software that carries discussion group traffic allows users to access all messages that deal with the same subject, as defined by the subject line in the message header, in the temporal order in which responses to a particular message were sent. This is called threading.

Figure 12.1 displays a portion of the newsgroup alt.politics.economics, 25 November 1997, in the Netscape Communicator 4.04 newsreader. The spool-like icon to the left of the message subject line indicates that the message is part of a thread. The thread can be expanded by selecting the + to the right of it, or by double clicking on the spool icon. This will reveal the postings that are responses to that and subsequent messages. Displayed in Figure 12.1 are a number of messages that follow on from the initial message on False Advertising on Global Warming, and the associated messages on Global Warming. Most newsreaders have menu or mouse button options that enable the user to select Next in Thread or Previous in Thread so that you can follow a particular theme from the beginning to the end. It is not possible to do this on a mailing list, as many messages may intervene between the first one on Subject X, and the responses to it. Newsgroup server software arranges materials posted to newsgroups in such a way that you can follow threaded exchanges. Threading allows readers to follow sequentially the development of a discussion on a particular topic, facilitates the selection of subjects to read, and shortens the length of the list that needs to be scrolled through. In earlier versions of the Netscape newsreader the thread is expanded or contracted by the + and – characters, as illustrated in Figure 12.5 below.

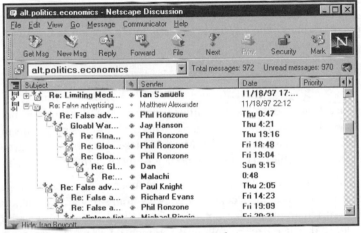

Figure 12.1 *Newsgroup messages in browser window.*

Newsgroups are arranged in a number of different hierarchies. The primary newsgroup hierarchy is divided into six main sections.

- **comp** Includes newsgroups dealing with computing-related issues. Probably the most active newsgroups with a very high volume of messages in many. There were 884 groups in the Demon Internet newsfeed on 25 November 1997, including:

    comp.compression

    comp.infosystems.intranet

- **sci** Newsgroups focusing on the sciences. Many deal with highly complex technical and theoretical issues. There were 203 groups in the Demon Internet newsfeed on 25 November 1997, including:

    sci.archaeology

    sci.chemistry

- **talk** A mixed bag of discussion groups covering a very wide variety of topics. There were 28 groups in the Demon Internet newsfeed on 25 November 1997, including:

talk.abortion

talk.politics (13 groups)

- **news**   Considered to be one of the most important of the discussion group hierarchies. Newsgroups in this category include information about Internet-related developments, including those concerning newsgroups. There were 29 groups in the Demon Internet newsfeed on 25 November 1997, including:

    news.admin.censorship

    news.groups

- **rec**   These discussion groups focus on recreational activities. There were 680 groups in the Demon Internet newsfeed on 25 November 1997, including:

    rec.antiques

    rec.music (95 groups)

- **misc**   A residual category that includes groups that are not slotted in under one of the other headings. There were 131 groups in the Demon Internet newsfeed on 25 November 1997, including:

    misc.forsale

    misc.writing.screenplays

There are many thousands of additional newsgroups that are not included in the above categories. There were, for instance, 695 Microsoft discussion groups in the Demon Internet newsfeed on 25 November 1997. Many of these other discussion groups are classified under other hierarchies. The most important of these currently are probably:

- **alt**   This hierarchy includes a very large number of discussion groups. alt stands for alternative, this being a collection of newsgroups that are not subject to some of the formal requirements that obtain in the main newsgroup hierarchy relating to procedures that need to be followed for inclusion in the categories mentioned above. There were 7429 groups in this category in the Demon Internet newsfeed on 25 November 1997. They cover all of the topics discussed in the main hierarchy, and many more besides.

- **clari**   An abbreviation of ClariNet. This is a commercial service that provides information under a large number of headings derived from various sources, including Reuters and United Press International. As the service is provided on payment of subscription, not all Internet Service Providers or organizations carry it. Demon Internet carried 971 of these groups on 25 November 1997.

- **biz**   Discussion groups centred on business-related issues.

12.3   Configuring the newsreader settings

If you connect to the Internet through an Internet Service or Access Provider, or have access to the Internet through a university or college, it is likely that you will have access to a newsfeed, a server that provides you with access to newsgroups. To read news from a newsfeed you will also need a newsreader. To configure the newsreader for Netscape versions 3.X, first open the newsreader by choosing *Netscape News* from the *Window* menu. This will bring up the newsreader interface. You can now close down Netscape if you want to. From the *Options* menu in the newsreader select *Mail and News Preferences* and then the *Servers* tab. A dialog box corresponding in part to Figure 12.2 will appear.

```
News
    News (NNTP) Server:    news.demon.co.uk
    News RC Directory:     D:\Netscape Gold\News
    Get                    100    Messages at a Time (Max 3500)
```

Figure 12.2   *Netscape newsgroup configuration dialog box.*

Insert the address of the News (NNTP) Server. You may need to obtain this from your system administrator or from your Internet Service or Access Provider. It is also possible that this has already been set by the system administrator, or configured by default in the software provided by an Internet Service or Access Provider.

The *News RC* directory includes information on the groups that you have subscribed to as well as other details concerning your handling of newsgroups. By default this is usually the News subdirectory of the Netscape directory. You can, however, set this to any directory of your choice. You should also complete details relating to your identity by selecting the *Identity* tab on the Mail and News Preferences dialog box reached from the Options menu. This will cause a screen corresponding to Figure 12.3 to appear in which you should complete the appropriate details.

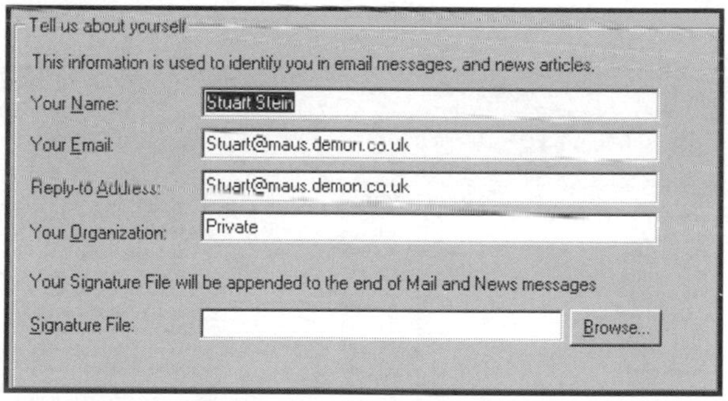

```
Tell us about yourself
    This information is used to identify you in email messages, and news articles.
    Your Name:          Stuart Stein
    Your Email:         Stuart@maus.demon.co.uk
    Reply-to Address:   Stuart@maus.demon.co.uk
    Your Organization:  Private

    Your Signature File will be appended to the end of Mail and News messages
    Signature File:                                        Browse...
```

Figure 12.3   *Netscape identity details.*

In Netscape Communicator, the latest browser version from Netscape, you need to access the screen in which you set the configuration settings for the news server by selecting *Preferences* from the Edit menu, and then *Groups Server*. In Internet Explorer, version 3.X, you bring up the newsreader by selecting *Read News* from the *Go* menu. To configure the server settings for Internet Explorer select *Options* from the News menu, and then the *Server* tab, as illustrated in Figure 12.4. Select the *Add* button and then fill in the address of the newsfeed server.

Figure 12.4   *Internet Explorer configuration dialog boxes.*

12.4   Netscape newsreader interface

The main data window of the newsreader interface, Netscape version 3.X, is divided into three sections, as illustrated in Figure 12.5. The top left-hand pane, *News Server*, displays the names of newsgroups. The top right-hand pane displays message headers. The bottom pane displays the content of messages.

To read and post messages to discussion groups using the Netscape newsreader you need to:

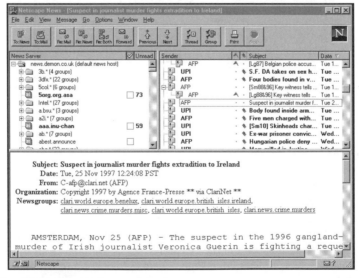

Figure 12.5   *Netscape newsgroup interface.*

- Identify newsgroups likely to be of interest by downloading a list of those available on your newsfeed server.
- Subscribe to groups.
- Read messages.
- Respond to messages or post messages on new topcs.

12.5   Accessing discussion groups

In order to establish which newsgroups are currently available through your newsfeed you should download the complete list of newsgroups that is currently available. This is done by selecting *Show All Newsgroups* from the *Options* menu on the newsreader interface whilst you have an open connection to your newsfeed, as illustrated in Figure 12.6. If you are accessing newsgroups from an Internet Access Provider you need to be online before you can download a current listing.

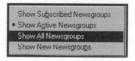

Figure 12.6   *Display newsgroup options.*

Having done so, a file listing all the newsgroups that can be subscribed to will be downloaded. This could be a large file that will take some time to download on a slow connection. To give you some idea of its potential size, that of the Demon Internet list of newsgroups was 1.6 MB on 30 November 1997. A list of the newsgroups will appear in the top left pane of the newsreader interface, as illustrated in Figure 12.7.

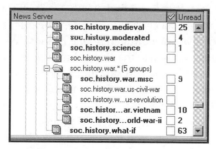

Figure 12.7   *Subscribing to newsgroups interface.*

You should now scan the list to locate groups to subscribe to. Newsgroups can be located more easily than scrolling down the list by entering a subject area in the Search for Group dialog box. You will need to expand some of the folders in the list (e.g. soc.history.war in Figure 12.7) as there are many newsgroups associated with each of the main or top level groups mentioned above, such as talk, sci, soc, as well as those in other hierarchies. The figures to the right of the check box indicate the number of messages for the group on the newsfeed server that you have not yet read, which, in the first instance, will be equivalent to all the messages. Having identified the groups that you wish to explore, subscribe by placing a check in the box to the right of the name of the newsgroup. If you subsequently wish to unsubscribe remove the check.

After you have checked those groups you are interested in viewing, choose *Show Subscribed Groups* from the *Options* menu. In the top left window you will now see the groups that you have checked. (There is also an option named Show Active Groups which displays a list of those groups that have messages on the server. I am assuming that in the first instance you will not subscribe to groups for which there are no messages.)

12.6   Reading the news

The Netscape newsreader will download unread messages for a discussion group if you select it from those listed in the News Server panel by double clicking on its name. (It will also select these from the overall list of newsgroups if you selected *Show All News-groups*.) As far as reading messages is concerned, you may want to adopt a different procedure depending on whether you are connected permanently to the Internet through a network during a session, or you connect through an Internet Access Provider. If you are on a network which has a newsfeed the downloading of a message is more or less instanta-neous. You just have to click on headers of messages that you are interested in reading which are displayed in the top right-hand panel. Each time you see a header of interest and select it, Netscape establishes a connection with the server, downloads the message into the message content panel, and closes the connection to the newsfeed.

If you are connecting via a modem or ISDN to an Internet Access Provider's news-feed, you may want to close the connection to save on charges whilst you scroll through the listing of message headers. In some newsgroups you may find that there are thousands of messages accessible if the newsfeed system administrator has decided to archive these for an extended period for some or all newsgroups. Having closed down your connection, scroll down the list of headers. When you find one that you are interested in reading, *flag it* by selecting the *Message* menu and choosing *Flag Message*. This puts a little red flag next to the message. When you have gone through all the headers, or as many as you are inter-ested in, reconnect. You can now select the flagged messages for downloading. From the *Go* menu choose *First Flagged*. This will download the first message flagged. To down-load successive flagged messages, from the *Go* menu select *Next Flagged* repeatedly until you have gone through them all. You can now disconnect. As long as you do not close down the newsreader or select another subscribed group, the messages downloaded will remain in virtual memory and can be read by selecting the flagged messages. You can also save the message to disk by selecting *Save As...* from the file menu.

The message headers of all unread messages are emboldened. Once you have down-loaded a message it changes to regular font. The newsreader has additional features to facil-itate movement between messages. These are accessible from the *Go* menu and include moving to the first unread, next unread, previous unread, next and previous messages.

You can search for messages with particular content in the subject heading by selecting the *Find* command from the *Edit* menu. The search will be conducted on all message headers in the folder that is currently open, that is, the newsgroup messages or message headers that are in the top right document window. You can also employ this feature to search for an entry in the body of an open message.

After you have dealt with all the messages that were of interest, you may want to mark all the messages in that newsgroup as having been read. Doing so will ensure that you will not have to go through those headers again when you next connect if they are still held on the server. You do this by choosing *Mark Newsgroup Read* from the *Message* menu. Once you have done this with respect to all the newsgroups that you are subscribed to, you can then configure the newsreader to *Show Only Unread Messages* by selecting this option from the *Options* menu. When you connect subsequently, if you select a newsgroup from the list of subscribed newsgroups only new messages will be downloaded. You can at any time revert to *Show All Messages*. Equally, you can at any time use the *Mark Newsgroup Read* feature.

12.7   Posting messages

To respond to messages using the browser newsreader you need to ensure that your mail settings have been configured properly (see Chapter 26).

There are three ways of replying to a message. In each case highlight the message header or ensure that the message body is in the active window.

1.   Send a reply to the sender. Select the button *Re:Mail* on the toolbar, or choose *Post Mail* from the *Message* menu. A standard email message window will appear. Complete and post

2.   Send a reply to the newsgroup. On the toolbar select the button *Re:News*. Alternatively, select *Mail Reply* from the *Message* menu. Many newsgroup messages are cross-posted to different discussion groups. The reply will be sent to all those that appear in the Newsgroups line of the message header.

3.   Send a reply both to the sender and to the Newsgroup(s). Choose the *Re:Both* button on the toolbar, or *Post* and *Mail Reply* from the *Message* menu. You might select this option if you wanted to ensure that the message is likely to be seen by the author of the communication that you are responding to.

In many electronic mail and newsreader applications it is standard practice that the default reply message includes the text of the original message, in the format displayed in Figure 12.8.

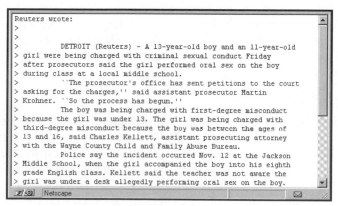

Figure 12.8   *Newsgroup message format.*

The logic of this is compelling. Many of those accessing the reply will probably not have seen the original. At the same time, for those who did, this format tends to be somewhat irritating. You can, of course, block and delete the previous message, which would mean either that some readers will not understand what you are discussing, or you will need to write a longer message to ensure that new readers understand the context. The optimum solution is one that maximizes comprehension and minimizes length.

If you want to initiate a new thread, that is start a discussion around a new subject heading, select the *To:News* button from the toolbar, or select *New News Message* from the *File* menu. This opens up a standard email window with the name of the newsgroup in the *To:* box.

The Netscape newsreader has many additional features that cannot be covered here. The above schematic coverage of some of the basic operations should suffice to enable you to subscribe to groups, read messages and respond to them. You can, of course, save messages and copy sections of them to some other application in the same way that you carry out such operations in other software applications. The newsreader associated with Internet Explorer 3.02 has some features that the Netscape newsreader does not have. One of these that might be of some interest is the ability to read discussion group messages without the need to subscribe to them. The IE newsreader help file explains the basic operations quite clearly.

12.8   Newsgroup archives

The daily volume of exchanges in more than 50,000 newsgroups is so vast that few organizations can afford the disk space to archive postings. Past messages of some newsgroups are archived. You can establish their location, frequently on ftp servers, either from the FAQ of the newsgroup (see p. 157–8) or by submitting a query to a search engine. The query that is functionally equivalent to <newsgroup* AND archive*> in Alta Vista advanced searches should net some of these. However you package your query, you will have to filter out a substantial number of references to other archives, including those of mailing lists, historical documents, etc. If you are searching for archives of a particular newsgroup, employ a query such as <newsgroup name AND archive*>, such as <"news.answers" AND archive*> in Alta Vista Advanced Search with archives in the *Ranking* box. This query returned 11,995 records on 11 February 1998, with the archives of this newsgroup as the first in the list.

By far the easiest way to locate information that has been posted to many newsgroups is to access these through DejaNews at

<http://www.dejanews.com>

This is the only important Internet database of newsgroup messages. In December 1997 DejaNews was archiving the messages of 50,000 newsgroups. Its database included more than 300 gigabytes (one gigabyte is equal to 1000 megabytes) of data, which was being augmented by an additional gigabyte every day. The database search engine is extremely fast and includes some useful features.

You can conduct a number of different types of search with DejaNews, including quick searches, power searches and searches using a search filter, etc.

Quick search

Quick Search

Type a specific **question** or **topic**:

[   ] [Find]

Find messages in the [standard ▾] archive

Example: year 2000 problem

Figure 12.9 *DejaNews basic search interface.*

To conduct a quick search, type a query in the search box provided, illustrated in Figure 12.9. This can be a single word or a phrase. By default the database search on the latter will be carried out as if you had requested that records should be returned that include all of the words entered in the query. You can elect to search either the standard, the complete, the job or the adult archive from the drop-down menu. *Find messages in the standard archive* excludes postings relating to employment and adult themes. The complete archive includes them. If your search is restricted to either job or adult postings, the records returned will focus exclusively on these subjects respectively.

Part of the document returned in response to the query <Goldhagen> is illustrated in Figure 12.10.

Matches **21-40** of exactly **325** for search: [Goldhagen] [Find]

```
     Date    Scr      Subject                  Newsgroup           Author
21. 98/01/30 022 Re: Die Massenmörder        de.soc.politik.deutsc Manfred Koch
22. 98/01/30 022 aol                    #4/9 alt.support.ex-cult.s Bhaskari
23. 98/01/30 022 Re: Phillips & oOck. Let#1/2 alt.revisionism      smock
24. 98/01/29 022 Re: Holocaust          #6/6 alt.revisionism      Hitler's Sacred Te
```

Figure 12.10 *DejaNews query/return interface.*

The details provided include the date, the subject of the communication, the newsgroup that it was posted to, and the author of the communication. In many newsgroup communications the authors, for various reasons, adopt an alias, as some of those who posted the messages illustrated in Figure 12.10 have done. If you select the Subject line, the message itself will be downloaded. The format of the message header and the icons above it are illustrated in Figure 12.11.

Article 38 of exactly 325 Text Only⬛ Help

Previous Next   Current View   Author Post
Article Article Results Thread Profile Message

```
Subject:      Goldhagen& Germans-again
From:         fvj@world.std.com (Septimus)
Date:         1998/01/10
Message-ID:   <EMKz82.1Er@world.std.com>
Newsgroups:   soc.culture.jewish
[More Headers]
```

Figure 12.11 *DejaNews navigation and information options.*

The *Previous Article* and *Next Article* buttons download the previous and next article respectively that appear in the list of records returned in response to your original query. *Current Results* reloads the last page of records that you examined. The *View Thread* button lists, with hyperlinks, other messages in the same thread, that is, those dealing with the same subject matter as defined in the subject line of the communications. Selecting the *Author Profile* button can access the profile of the author of the communication. The query that I chose to illustrate the use of DejaNews above is the name of the author of one of the most controversial non-revisionist books dealing with the Holocaust, Daniel Goldhagen, who wrote *Hitler's Willing Executioners*. Various issues relating to this work have been debated heatedly in exchanges in certain newsgroups and on some mailing lists. The author profile facility in DejaNews provides some useful information that may allow users to form their own conclusions respecting the authority of the communication in particular instances. The profile of the author of the message whose header is illustrated in Figure 12.10 is illustrated in Figure 12.12.

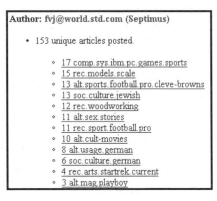

Figure 12.12   *DejaNews author messaging preface.*

Power search

With quick searches the archive that is trawled for matches to a query is the default, current, archive. This includes messages posted in the previous 30 days. If you want to conduct a search on newsgroup postings that extend back further than this, some to March 1995, you need to conduct a power search. Power searches also allow you to focus queries by employing Boolean logical operators. (see p. 84).

The search string/query is entered in the *Search for:* box illustrated in Figure 12.13. As the queries permitted are virtually identical with many of those described for Alta Vista, you may want to review this material (see Chapter 8). The Help page, which can be selected immediately above the *Find* button, is clearly and concisely written and should be consulted. The *Archive:* options are identical to those described already for quick searches.

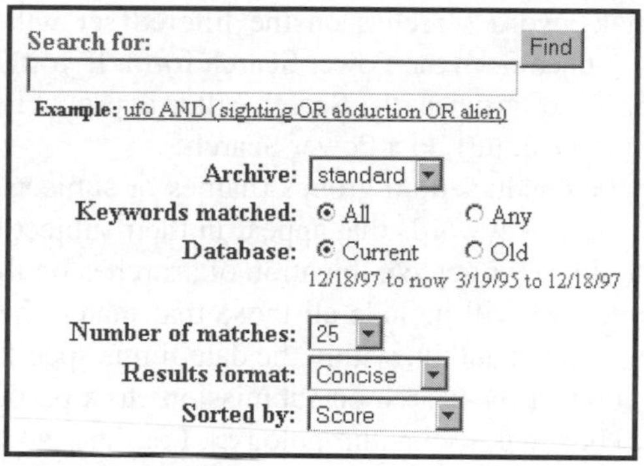

Figure 12.13 *DejaNews power search interface.*

If you do not want to employ Boolean logical operators, you can enter a number of words in the *Search for:* box and then check one of the *Keywords matched:* options. Select the *Database:* option in line with your preference for recent postings, or all those included in the database archive. The *Number of matches* specifies the number of records returned per page downloaded. If the number of records in the database that match your query is larger than this, there is a link at the bottom of the page that if selected will download the next file of records returned.

You can elect to have the information on matches provided in lesser or greater detail by selecting the *Concise/Detailed* option on the *Results format:* drop-down menu. This menu also allows you to situate the posting in the context of those on the same subject that preceded or succeeded it if you select *Threaded*. Finally, results can be sorted by score, those that match your query best being at the top of the list, by date, author, newsgroup, and subject.

Search filter

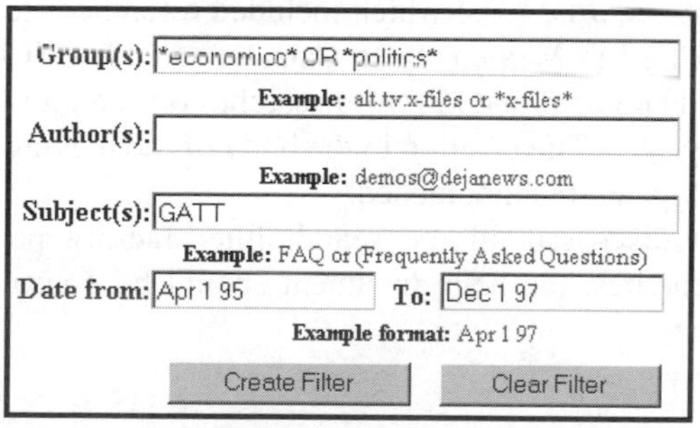

Figure 12.14 *DejaNews search filter dialog box.*

The search filter interface, illustrated in Figure 12.14, enables users to conduct further searches on the records returned with a search filter query. Until you clear the filter the set of records retrieved in response to your query will remain active. You can, therefore, conduct as many searches as you like on these records. As noted in the help file, 'this means that subsequent keyword searches on the filtered set will be much faster than entering all your terms at once from the Power Search form. If you'd like to search several times on an unchanging set of articles, the Search Filter is probably the way to go. But if it's just a one- or two-shot deal, just do a Power Search!'.

The search may be conducted on groups (names or subjects appearing in names), author(s) of communications, keywords that appear in their subject lines, all of which can be restricted by the date fields, or any combination of searches on these fields. You should note that the records returned will include all those that match the newsgroups selected and/or the subject for a selected author, within the date limits specified.

If you want to conduct the search on submissions to a particular newsgroup, type its name in the *Group(s)* box, e.g. <sci.anthropology>. For the search to be performed on a number of groups, combine them by using AND e.g. <soc.politics.marxism AND soc.rights.human>. To include in the search all groups that include psychology in their name, for instance, the query should take the form <*psychology*>.

If you know the email address of an author you can restrict your searches to messages they posted, either to all the newsgroups included in the DejaNews database, or to those included in the *Group(s)* filter. If you only know the email name, but not the remainder of the address, you can use the wildcard facility, as in <name@*>. If you do not know the precise login name, try tracking it down through a search engine, the Web page of an organization that the individual works for, or by using a keyword search in DejaNews using a query that covers the type of topic this individual is likely to cover in discussion group postings.

The *Subject(s)* filter refers to keywords that appear in the subject line of the message, not those that appear in the body of the message. You can use Boolean logical operators to narrow down the search.

The query illustrated in Figure 12.14 searches for records that are included in discussion groups that have economics or politics in their names, include a reference to GATT in their subject line, and were posted between 1 April 1995 and 1 December 1997. In this instance I was interested in tracking down information comparing the perceived impact of the GATT agreement on NAFTA and the EU, and the members of the former. The query returned 118 records, 73 of which included references to NAFTA, three to the European Union or EU, 22 to Mexico, 13 to Canada, and 51 to (United States OR USA OR America). It should be noted that keyword searches on search filters are conducted on the contents of the messages. The position in the body of the message where the keywords included in the query appear are emboldened.

As I have not discussed all the search filter facility possibilities enabling a narrowing down of searches, the help document should be consulted. This is accessed from the search filter page.

Browse

Instead of reading discussion group news through a newsreader, you can browse the news-groups archived by DejaNews by selecting the *Browse Groups* option from its home page. This feature is only available for messages posted in the previous 30 days. You can either enter the name(s) of the newsgroup(s), e.g. <sci.psychology>, or browse one of the hierarchies included under *Popular Top Level Groups*, as illustrated in Figure 12.15. The groups are arranged in a directory tree, and you move down the tree by selecting the subgroupings you are interested in until you arrive at the messages themselves.

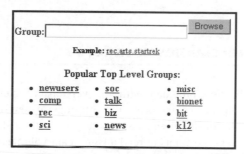

Figure 12.15   *DejaNews subject browse interface.*

Interest Finder

Finally, if you select *Interest Finder* from the home page and enter a term or combination of terms in the search box, the database will return a listing of newsgroups that discuss the terms entered. When I entered the term econometrics, the records returned included sci.econ.research (99%), misc.jobs.resumes (93%) and sci.stat.consult (17%). The percentages are a rating of the frequency with which the term or query is discussed in the group specified.

To sum up, DejaNews is an extremely impressive database engine and archive. In many respects it is much more impressive in the speed of its operation and the variety of search facilities available than many other Internet search engines. The messages database included in DejaNews includes an enormous volume of substantive information on an incredibly wide variety of subjects. It is also a database of expertise and links to individuals and materials relevant to research on virtually every subject matter that social scientists discuss, teach about and research.

12.9   Graphics and software programs

In some newsgroups you will find that there is an extensive volume of postings that include attached graphic images, photographs or software programs. To be transmitted across the Internet using the protocols employed by discussion groups, it is necessary to convert (code) the graphic images or photographs into a form of ASCII text. For the user to see the graphic image or photograph it is necessary to decode it once it has been received. The Netscape newsreader will do this automatically, displaying the image in the content pane. You can explore how this works by taking a look at some of the newsgroups in the alt.binaries hierarchy, for instance alt.binaries.clip-art and alt.binaries.photography.

The computer-oriented hierarchies frequently include software programs as attachments. These are often in compressed format and require decompressing software such as WinZip or pkunzip. For further information see Chapter 26.

12.10 Commercial newsreaders

The newsreading application provided with the versions of Netscape available until recently is perfectly adequate for exploring the offerings of newsgroups. It should also prove more than adequate for those who want to keep up with postings to relatively low-volume groups. The reader who wants to read a significant volume of newsgroup communications should, if possible, upgrade to Netscape Communicator. Its newsreader is far superior to that of the versions that I have been considering in this chapter. One of its major advantages is that it has an offline browsing facility. This enables the user to download all the messages in particular groups and read them offline.

There are a number of very good commercial newsreaders available that incorporate extremely useful features for the serious discussion group reader/participant. As these are quite easy to access, install and use and are very inexpensive in terms of the features they deliver, the small financial outlay will be returned with interest in terms of enhanced functionality. There are two that I would particularly recommend:

- OUI (Offline Usenet Interface), from Peak to Peak Services and Development, Inc., which is downloadable from

    <http://www.peaktopeak.com/>

    The cost at the beginning of December 1997 was only $30 for electronic delivery.

- Agent, from Forte, Inc., which is downloadable from

    <http://www.forteinc.com/forte/>

    The cost at the beginning of December 1997 was $29 for electronic delivery.

PART IV

Social Science subject resources

Chapter 13   General reference resources   147
Chapter 14   Electronic texts and reviews   159
Chapter 15   Data archives   165
Chapter 16   Statistical resources   177
Chapter 17   Social Science funding   185
Chapter 18   Current news online   189
Chapter 19   History resources   201
Chapter 20   Human rights resources   217
Chapter 21   Philosophy, sociology and psychology   225
Chapter 22   Political Science and government resources   243
Chapter 23   European Union resources   259
Chapter 24   Resources for economists   267

In previous chapters I reviewed a number of sources of information accessible from Internet-linked hosts, namely mailing lists, discussion groups and subject directories. In reviewing subject directories and search engines I discussed two of the most common means used to locate information on the Internet.

Although thus equipped it is possible to tap vast databases of materials, these search tools are not always the most efficient means of finding required information, or of keeping abreast of the resources available online that are relevant to particular interests. Familiarization with the Internet takes time. Not everyone will want to launch immediately into mastering and experimenting with search engine query syntax. Whilst mailing list archives are a source of much useful subject-specific information, and a research resource in their own right, the procedures for extracting past communications that meet specified requirements are far from being intuitively self-evident. The same applies, although to a lesser degree, to discussion group exchanges.

The objective of subject directories is to collate resources so that those accessing them can locate quickly materials that fall within a particular field of enquiry, interest or topic. They tend to be relatively crude instruments because of the sheer volume and range of the resources that they are attempting to chart. These are being added to, moved, altered and deleted with a frequency that few resource compilers, if any, can cope with. As the volume of Internet resources continues to expand, the gap between that portion of Internet space that subject directories map reliably and the volume of resources available is likely to grow.

Search engines, on the other hand, are likely to reduce this gap and extend the efficiency of their database filtering features. One of the reasons for this is that most users of the Internet employ search engines to track down data. It is estimated that about 70% of Internet files are accessed from hyperlinks downloaded following a search. This makes search engines attractive to advertisers. As electronic commerce expands during the next few years the numbers using the Internet will continue to increase significantly. So too will the numbers of those accessing search engines, making them even more attractive to advertisers, thereby increasing the revenues available for storing more information and increasing the functionality of Internet data retrieval systems.

Despite their speed of operation, breadth of Internet resource coverage and sophisticated data processing features, placing *total* reliance on search engines is likely to prove unsatisfactory for a number of reasons.

- Resorting to a search engine to locate even clearly defined information is not always an efficient use of time. It may be very difficult to formulate a query that will not throw up hundreds of records irrelevant to your search.

- The information processed by search engines is frequently dated. Resources that have only recently been added may not be processed for months, sometimes many months. As some users are primarily interested in whether resources that they failed to locate previously have subsequently become available, using a search engine may not be the best means of establishing this.

- Locating resources through the use of search engines is a very abstract kind of procedure. If you have only limited knowledge concerning the range and type of resources that are currently online in a subject field that you are investigating, you may needlessly waste time trying to locate data that is not available.

Most Social Science students and academic staff who will use Internet resources for teaching, locating information or research, are likely to be interested primarily in data that falls within the boundaries of relatively circumscribed subject areas. The economist or student of economics will rarely be interested in resources relating to anthropology or social psychology. Their principal interest is likely to be in finding information relevant to their own disciplinary interests. One of the best ways of doing this is to monitor resources available in particular subject areas by accessing those sites that specialize in compiling links to such resources, or providing them. Sometimes the same sites do both.

Web authors who compile links to resources in particular discipline areas, or who make such resources available, are generally subject specialists who are familiar with the interests of practitioners in their own field. They generally have a reasonably good idea of what resources their colleagues and students are likely to find useful. This does not mean, of course, that all are equally expert, or that professional qualifications in a field of enquiry guarantee the provision of access to high-quality resources. There are many non-specialists in this sense who have made available exceptionally useful resources.

In the chapters that follow I review Web-based resources that are available in particular Social Science disciplines as well as some that may be of use to social scientists regardless of their particular areas of expertise or interests. A few caveats are in order at this point.

- It should be apparent from what I have said already that it is impossible to provide an annotated listing of resources in all Social Science fields of expertise. There are simply too many of these. It would require a separate volume, or volumes, to do so.

- I have endeavoured to include Web presentations that I consider make available useful resources not found elsewhere, and those that provide a substantial body of resources or a comprehensive listing of links to materials, all in specific subject areas. My focus has been disproportionately on main sites, those that already provide substantial added value in materials or a relatively comprehensive listing of resources. These are sites that I consider are less likely to disappear suddenly without trace.

- The volume and quality of electronic resources currently available from Internet-linked servers vary by discipline. At present there are many more resources online that most specialists would subsume under the heading history, than resources that would be included under the category sociology. Many of the most important treatises of pre-twentieth and early twentieth century philosophers are available in electronic format. With the exception of the works of Marx and Engels, this does not apply to works of the founders of sociology, at least to those available in English. Whilst copyright considerations may explain the absence of electronic texts of middle to late twentieth century sociologists, it does not account for the dearth of late nineteenth or early twentieth century works.

- Although all the hyperlinks to the resources that are listed in the following chapters have been checked as late as possible within the constraints of the publication timetable, it is inevitable that a few will lead to barren results when you endeavour to access them. Some of these will simply have moved elsewhere on the same server, or to a different server within the same organization. Others will have moved with their compilers. The information provided in the chapters on Internet addresses (Chapter 3) and search engines (Chapter 6) should assist you in locating them if they are still available.

CHAPTER 13

General reference resources

13.1   General reference desks   147
13.2   Biographical resources   149
13.3   Encyclopedias   153
13.4   Country and geographic resources   153
13.5   Language resources: dictionaries, thesauri, etc.   155
13.6   Articles and printed books   156
13.7   Miscellaneous   157

Webster's International Dictionary defines a reference work as a 'book (dictionary, encyclopedia, atlas) intended primarily for consultation rather than for consecutive reading'. I shall allow myself some licence here, as one social scientist's reference work may very well be another's source of consecutive reading.

13.1   General reference desks

These are sites that collate links to large collections of reference resources available on the Internet. Although the sections below are by no means exhaustive, they include some of the sites providing comprehensive listings.

My Virtual Reference Desk: Facts on File

<http://www.refdesk.com/index.html>

Anyone who is looking for a site with a comprehensive and systematically organized collection of reference resources need look no further. The My Facts Page lists resources under 23 categories, including Atlas/Maps, Biography, Dictionaries, Electronic Texts, Encyclopedias, Subject Topics (e.g. Government, Law), Libraries and Science. The list of resources under each is extensive.

The Dictionaries and Language Resources Page had 218 entries on 2 February 1998. The ARTFL (American and French Research on the Treasury of the French Language) Project has a database of 150 million words written in French. There are links to a large number of specialist dictionaries, including the American Sign Language Basic Dictionary, Dictionary of Cell Biology, Dictionary of Scientific Quotations, HTML (the markup language in which Web pages are written) Dictionary, Jargon File, Rhyming Dictionary, Unix and Internet Dictionary, and a Poker Dictionary.

The listing of language dictionaries includes English–German/German–English, Estonian–English/English–Estonian, Hungarian–English/English–Hungarian, English–Italian/Italian–English, Norwegian Dictionary, Finnish–English/English–Finnish. A separate section provides links to Thesauri and Quotations.

You will find links to map resources in the section titled Atlas & Geographic Information Resources which currently has 70 entries for map collections. Other main sections worth mentioning are Electronic Text Information Resources, Phone Book and Area Code Resources, Postal Information Resources, Time and Date Resources, and World Religion Resources.

The above-mentioned resources and main category headings by no means exhaust this massive collation.

Caltech General Reference Page

<http://library.caltech.edu/reference/default.htm>

This is a useful and manageable set of links to various reference resources. There are links to language resources (including a hypertext Webster dictionary), encyclopedias, maps of the USA, an articles database, sources of current news reports, geographic resources, maps of different parts of the world, electronic texts, Internet search engines, information sources about individuals (telephone numbers) and areas (zip codes), and medical and weather information, among many others.

Ready Reference Collection of The Internet Public Library

<http://www.ipl.org/ref/RR/static/ref0000.html>

This page includes links to almanacs, biographies, census data, encyclopedias, geographical information, quotations and addresses. The lists under each category are far less comprehensive than those referenced above, but useful nonetheless.

The above general reference desks should provide for the most immediate reference needs of Social Science students and academic staff. Below I list links that will access reference resources subsumed under categories that I assume are those likely to be most frequently sought. I have not included links to reference-type resources relating to specific subject matters, or to sources of information on current news as these are covered elsewhere.

13.2   Biographical resources

In addition to references to individuals found in some of the encyclopedias mentioned in the relevant section below, there are a number of online biographical resources.

Notable Citizens of Planet Earth

<http://www.s9.com/biography/>

This resource contains some 19,000 entries. The information recorded against each name tends towards the minimalist end of the continuum of biographical reference materials. Each record provides information on dates of birth and death, country of origin/residence, major achievements and positions held. To access information on a particular individual you have to key in the surname/first name (optional) in a search engine. As an example, the reference for Margaret Thatcher returned the following:

> "Thatcher, Margaret Hilda (nee Roberts; the Iron Lady) Brit. polit.; leader of Conservative Party 1975–1990; Brit. prime min. 1979–1990; wrote memoirs "10 Downing Street" 1994, "The Path to Power" 1995_1925--"

The information in some cases is quite sparse. The entry for the American monetarist economist, Milton Friedman, returned the following:

> "Friedman, Milton US economist; NP Econ. 1976_1912-- "

The Cambridge Biographical Encyclopedia

<http://www.biography.com/find/find.html>

The entries are considerably more detailed and professionally written than those in Notable Citizens of Planet Earth. There are entries for 20,000 individuals. For comparative purposes, here is the entry for Milton Friedman:

> Friedman, Milton
>
> Male. Pronunciation: [freedman]. (1912--)
>
> Economist, born in New York City. He studied at Chicago and New York universities, and after eight years at the National Bureau of Economic Research (1937--45) became professor of economics at Chicago (1946--83). A leading monetarist, his work includes the permanent income theory of consumption, and the role of money in determining events, particularly the US Great Depression. His ideas have been influential with a number of right-wing governments. He was awarded the Nobel Prize for Economics in 1976.

The database entries are cross-referenced; records returned include links to a list of others significantly associated with the main entry. The entry for Adolf Hitler, for example, returns links to the biographical entries for Eva Braun, Rudolf Hess, Paul Hindenburg, Erwin Rommel, and others. The cross-referencing is somewhat imperfect as it tends to be unidirectional in terms of assessed significance of the person whose record entry has been retrieved. Thus from the entry for Hitler there are links to Himmler and Göering, but not vice versa.

Yahoo search engine

<http://www.yahoo.com>

Instead of searching through a bibliographical dictionary or encyclopedia for information on individuals, it is possible to use one of the search engines in order to track down the information. Yahoo references a substantial proportion of Web space and is worth resorting to if you require more substantial and diverse information than that available from biographical dictionaries, or if you cannot find in those sources even basic information on some individual.

There are two ways of locating biographical information. One is to enter the surname of the individual you are tracing in the search engine. Alternatively, you can select one of the subject categories and work your way down the hyperlink tree until you find the category People. If, for example, you want to find biographical materials relating to individuals of 'historical significance' you would go down the link hierarchy Arts and Humanities/ Humanities/ History/ People. If you wanted to locate material on physicists the route would be Science/ Physics/ Physicists.

Although for many entries you will, in all probability, locate more material by using a search engine or subject directory, the downside is information overload, and lack of detailed specification of what is contained in the document references (links) that are returned by the database search engine.

In addition to the general biographical encyclopedias referred to above, there are a number of specialist presentations dealing with particular categories of expertise, participant or gender. The list below is not exhaustive.

The Complete List of Popes

<http://www.knight.org/advent/Popes/ppindx.htm>

This is an excellent resource for those interested in ecclesiastical history or issues influenced by it. The Popes are listed in chronological order. The articles on some are very extensive. That on St Peter, the first Pope, is 56K. In some instances the articles provided at this Web site are excerpts from the full-length article. Select the link provided to download the complete version, available via Telnet. Some of the proposed articles have not yet been placed online. The endnotes include references to numerous authorities, and there are links to many speeches made by the pontiffs.

The Catholic Encyclopedia

<http://www.sni.net/advent/cathen/cathen.htm>

Although this is not, strictly speaking, a biographical reference resource, it necessarily covers all persons who have figured prominently in the history of the Catholic Church. Even this, however, is too limited a description of its scope as it includes extensive articles on other religious denominations. In addition to links to articles on the Popes you will find substantial information on non-Catholic religious persons and denominations. It is also worth noting that the encyclopedia contains articles on certain philosophical issues. There

are reasonably extended discussions of the works of philosophers of particular signifi-
cance in the development of church doctrines, including Immanuel Kant and René
Descartes. There are also articles on conceptual and philosophical issues. The entry for
Dialectics, for instance, includes a discussion of the theological, Platonic, Aristotelian,
Kantian and Hegelian variants.

The Catholic Encyclopedia is a 15-volume work covering a broad range of topics,
secular and religious, from a Catholic perspective. The version being used for this project
was published in 1913. This edition is being used for copyright reasons, although those in
charge of the present project maintain that in many respects the scholarship of this edition
is superior to that of its successors.

Distinguished Women of Past and Present

<http://www.netsrq.com/~dbois/index.html>

Compiled by Danuta Bois who was motivated by the fact that her schooling left her with
the 'impression that women did not contribute much of significance to our civilization,
other than as carctakers of their families'. The biographies are arranged both by subject
and alphabetically. There are links to related sites.

NOEMA: The Collaborative Bibliography of Women in Philosophy

<http://billyboy.ius.indiana.edu/womeninphilosophy/womeninphilo.html>

The database holds bibliographical details on the contributions of 5000 women in
aesthetics, epistemology, ethics, logic, metaphysics, history of philosophy, and the philosophies of mind, science, art and related subjects. It can be searched by author, title,
keywords and publication date. The search engine is rather slow and the list of authors
takes some time to download. There are no hyperlinks from the entries on that list to associated records so you need to determine whether there is an entry in the database for the
person and then use the search engine to return the associated records.

Women in American History by Encyclopaedia Britannica

<http://women.eb.com>

The best starting point is by way of selecting *Articles*. This lists entries in alphabetical
order. The biographical information is relatively detailed and well presented. Where
appropriate there are links to other entries in the database. Under *Recommended Reading*
there is an extensive, up-to-date and briefly annotated bibliography on women and their
role in American history.

Gale Celebrates Women's History

<http://www.thomson.com/gale/cwh/cwhset.html>

Web presentation by Gale Research, which includes biographies of more than 60 publicly esteemed women.

Bjorn's Guide to Philosophy

<http://www.knuten.liu.se/~bjoch509/>

This guide to philosophy includes one section on philosophers. Entries provide some biographical information, data on papers and monographs that they have published, articles about them, graphic images, bibliographies and details about professional journals that focus on their philosophy and related issues.

History of Science, Medicine and Technology Dictionary

<http://www.asap.unimelb.edu.au/hstm/hstm_bio.htm>

This dictionary includes useful articles on esteemed scholars and practitioners in the fields of science, medicine and technology. The information can be retrieved by entering a name in the search engine, or by browsing the alphabetical index. The information available on particular individuals is of variable breadth and depth, reflecting the degree to which others have loaded relevant resources over the Internet.

Biographies of the American Presidents

<http://www.grolier.com/presidents/ea/prescont.html>

This is part of Grolier's excellent Web presentation on American presidents and the presidency. There are biographies of all US presidents drawn from two sources: Encyclopedia Americana, and Academic American Encyclopedia. The articles are comprehensive with cross-referencing to many other themes relating to the presidency and American politics. Also available on this server are biographies of the vice presidents of the United States. Various materials relating to the presidency can be accessed directly from the home page of the presentation, including a listing of the electoral vote for the presidency, both that of the Electoral College and the popular vote, since the first presidential election.

US Civil War Generals

<http://funnelweb.utcc.utk.edu/~hoemann/generals.html>

Arranged alphabetically in two major categories, Union and Confederate. The information has been gleaned from a number of sources: 'Ezra Warner's comprehensive works Generals in Gray and Generals in Blue, the Historical Times Illustrated Encyclopedia of the Civil War, Mark Boatner's Civil War Dictionary, and the Historical Register and Dictionary of the United States Army 1789–1903'. The more prominent the general is considered to be the more detailed the information provided.

13.3   Encyclopedias

Free Internet Encyclopedia

<http://clever.net/cam/encyclopedia.html>

This encyclopedia is divided into two sections, paralleling the structure adopted earlier by the Encyclopaedia Britannica, a Macro- and Microreference, although the Britannica used the suffix -paedia. The macroreference categories are those of broad headings of knowledge: Education, Employment, Biology, etc. The microreference consists of entries that are subsumed under the broader macropedia headings. Both are listed in an alphabetical index. Select the letter, and then a subject in the document that is returned.

The information available from this source under different entries varies substantially in terms of both quantity and quality.

Encyclopaedia Britannica

<http://www.eb.com:80/>

In terms of breadth and depth of coverage there is no other online resource that can equal the Britannica. Unfortunately it is only available on subscription, individual or institutional. The individual subscription costs (8 February 1998) $8.50 a month, or $85 a year. Institutional subscriptions depend on the number of prospective users. There is usually a seven-day free trial offer available.

The Encyclopedia Mythica

<http://www.pantheon.org/mythica/>

An encyclopedia on mythology, folklore and mysticism. Contains hundreds of definitions of gods and goddesses, supernatural beings and legendary creatures and monsters from all over the world. There are currently (8 February 1998) 4000 articles online. The entries are categorized under mythologies (Chinese, Egyptian, Etruscan, Greek, Haitian, Japanese, Latvian, Mayan, Native American, Norse, Persian, Polynesian, Roman, Welsh, and other) and Folklore (e.g. Greek Heroic Legend, Occult and Mysticism). Although probably not a resource likely to be used frequently by most social scientists, this is a very well organized and presented Web resource. A bibliography of sources used is provided.

13.4   Country and geographic resources

The World Factbook 1997

<http://www.odci.gov/cia/publications/factbook/index.html>

<http://www.globalserve.net/~nac/wfb-all.html>

This is the electronic edition of an annual publication compiled by the United States Central Intelligence Agency. It is largely descriptive in orientation. A linked document explains the methodology adopted. There is an entry for each country, which provides quite extensive information relating to their economic, political and institutional circumstances. You will find here a listing of the major political institutions of the country, basic demographic information, names of members of the government, the major political parties, etc. Also included are various economic statistics, a brief listing of current international disputes the country is involved in, information on its defence forces and expenditure, data on its infrastructure and much else besides. This is a very good resource for basic information about specific countries.

This publication appears annually. It is available at numerous sites on the Internet, and editions going back a number of years can be located by using a search engine. These are useful for comparative purposes. Use <title:"World Factbook"> as a starting query.

The Commonwealth Yearbook 1998

<http://www.tcol.co.uk/cyb1.htm>

Provided by the Commonwealth Secretariat, this site provides details about the Commonwealth and its members. Entries on the Commonwealth include information on its history, major declarations, communiqués and summits, the role of its secretariat, and major events in the Commonwealth calendar. Of particular interest is likely to be the country-specific information. This provides outline details relating to demography, geography, communications, transport, macroeconomics and finance, physical economy, history, the legal system, the constitutional structure and topical recent events.

Date and Time Gateway

<http://www.bsdi.com/date>

Gives the date and Greenwich Mean Time at the moment of access. Select any other country, or US time zone by city, and it returns the date and time at that location at the time that the query was entered.

Country Maps from W3 Servers in Europe

<http://www.tue.nl/europe/>

The document consists of a table and a graphic representing the countries of Europe. Select a country and a document is returned with links to information under a diversity of headings relating to that country. The breadth and depth of coverage is a function of the amount of information that has been uploaded onto Web servers, and the degree to which links to it have been included on these pages, which, of course, varies. The French entry provides a map of France divided into regions. You select a region, and then a department within the region. This will list the WWW servers for the department and information about them. The data provided gives you some idea about the type of information that you can expect to find loaded on that server. This is a useful means of tracking down information. The only drawback, of course, is that you need to be fluent in the languages of the countries concerned.

The Perry-Castañeda Library Map Collection

<http://www.lib.utexas.edu/Libs/PCL/Map_collection/Map_collection.html>

The University of Texas at Austin has made this collection of maps available. There are more than 230,000 maps in the collection, of which some 1500 are currently available online. There is no copyright on these maps. Many have been produced by the United States Central Intelligence Agency. In addition to country maps, there are maps of cities, historical maps and political maps, as well as ethnolinguistic and administrative ones.

13.5   Language resources: dictionaries, thesauri, etc.

There is an extensive collection of language resources accessible over the Internet. The search string <dictionar*> returned 174,207 records from the database of the Alta Vista search engine (8 February 1998), although, of course, this does not mean that there are 174,207 online dictionaries. Below I list some links to significant language resources.

Hypertext Webster Interface Dictionary and Thesaurus

<http://c.gp.cs.cmu.edu:5103/prog/webster>

When you key in a word a number of hypertext interpretations are returned. You can follow these hypertext links for further elaboration on the original entry you made if the returned interpretations are inadequate relative to your query. There is also a link to a thesaurus. If you misspell the word, the server may offer a list of close matches as alternatives. If you know the prefix, but are uncertain of the rest, you can use the wildcard *. Thus, for instance, if you are checking for the correct meaning of munifecence, but are uncertain about the ending after munif and do not wish to spend too much time on the various possibilities, you can enter munif* and locate the correct spelling from the list returned. For other uses of this resource, please read the online accompanying instructions.

The Logos Dictionary

<http://www.logos.it:80/query.html>

This Italian-based project translates an input word in one language into words in other languages. At present the database has 7,105,435 entries (8 February 1998). Although it is unreasonable to expect miracles, particularly when the input is not contextualized, it does work for many queries.

Dictionaries, thesauri and acronyms from Purdue University Library Service

<http://thorplus.lib.purdue.edu/reference/dict.html>

In addition to a link to the Webster dictionary referred to above, there are a variety of other language dictionaries at this site, including French, German, Estonian, Japanese, Russian and Slovene to English dictionaries. Also available are some acronym and technical dictionaries.

The Free On-Line Dictionary of Computing

<http://wombat.doc.ic.ac.uk/foldoc/contents.html>

'FOLDOC is a searchable dictionary of acronyms, jargon, programming languages, tools, architecture, operating systems, networking, theory, conventions, standards, mathematics, telecomms, electronics, institutions, companies, projects, products, history, in fact anything to do with computing. ...The dictionary started in 1985 and now contains 11,000 definitions totaling more than four megabytes (8 February 1998). Entries are cross-referenced to each other and to related resources elsewhere on the net. It services around 5000 queries per day.' Not the easiest to use format, but given its scope and erudition, there are few good reasons for complaint. Compiled by Denis Howe whilst a computing graduate student at Imperial College, London.

Explain Acronym Dictionary

<http://www.ihi.aber.ac.uk/cgi-bin/explain>

The database has some 22,000 records. You key in the acronym and the expansion is displayed. There are also links to other acronym dictionaries which you can access from the same page for an expansion of your search string. Very fast and comprehensive.

Dictionary of International Trade and Business

<http://pacific.commerce.ubc.ca/ditb>

Resource based at the University of British Columbia. This is an 'experimental' hypertext dictionary that covers the fields of international trade, international business, international financial economics and general macroeconomics. Currently about 2000 terms are defined. There are 4000 hyperlinks to resources relevant to these subjects.

13.6 Articles and printed books

UnCover

<http://uncweb.carl.org/>

UnCover is an online article delivery system. For a fee it will fax within 24 hours any article that is in its database. Although the articles themselves may be more expensive than if acquired through the UK interlibrary loan scheme, for most academic staff and students the usefulness of UnCover resides in its massive database which can be searched freely by author, subject or title. The database includes records, dating from 1988, on more than 7,000,000 articles in English published in 17,000 multidisciplinary journals, 4000 additional records being added daily. The search can be queried by keyword, author and title and can be narrowed by using Boolean logical operators.

If you query the database by keyword or author, the first screen of records provides brief hypertext details of the author and title. If you select the title the document downloaded includes the title, the journal and the cost of purchasing the article through UnCover. If from this you select the journal title (or the button table of contents), the document downloaded includes links to all the pages of contents of the journal in the UnCover database. On the other hand, if you select the author, the document downloaded will list all the articles in the database authored or co-authored by the individual concerned.

UnCover also has a subject title database that lists all the journals subsumed under specific subject headings. Some of these files are quite large.

Another very useful service offered by UnCover which should be of interest to many teaching and research staff in the social sciences is called Reveal. For a fee of $25 per annum UnCover will deliver via electronic mail the tables of contents of up to 50 journals of choice, as well as the output of 25 search strategies to be run against new articles added to the database on a weekly basis.

Amazon Books

<http://www.amazon.com>

Amazon Books is one of the largest bookstore chains in the world, if not the largest. It includes 2.5 million records in its database. You can search for books by title, keyword, subject, ISBN or author with the search engine provided. There are reviews from various publications (e.g. New York Review of Books, Kirkus) linked to many of the entries. Books can be ordered and paid for online, at substantial discounts. Shipping to the UK takes about six weeks, packaging costing $5.95. This is a very useful resource for tracking down books by subject area. The search engine is very fast.

13.7 Miscellaneous

The news.answers archive

<http://www.cs.ruu.nl/cgi-bin/faqwais>

This is an archive of Frequently Asked Questions (FAQ) that are posted to one of the Usenet newsgroups, news.answers. This is a newsgroup that is a repository for a list of

FAQs which are posted from other Usenet newsgroups. Confused? Well, here comes the technical bit.

As noted before, there are thousands of these discussion forums arranged in a number of hierarchies that focus on anything from abseiling to zoology. As there are no fixed membership or entry requirements, individuals who have not followed the exchanges for an extended period of time may request information on matters that have been extensively discussed in the past. The 'veterans' alighted upon the idea of organizing a list of Frequently Asked Questions so that the same questions would not be asked repeatedly by new entrants or the inattentive. New participants are expected to read these and thereby avoid posting 'silly' or 'well-worn' questions that have been answered umpteen times in the past.

The Frequently Asked Questions files of some of these groups contain a substantial volume of potentially useful information. In order to access information in the search engine provided, you enter a search word, phrase or complex query and the database will retrieve those records in which your search word, etc., appears. They are ranked in descending order of compatibility – as interpreted in accordance with the search engine algorithm – with the query you submitted. The score 1000 signifies maximum compatibility.

You do have to exercise some judgement in going down the list in order to establish whether it is probable that a particular newsgroup is likely to discuss the issues you are inquiring about. Thus, if your quest is for information about Max Weber, no purpose is likely to be served by selecting the FAQ of alt.painting.

Oxford University's FAQs server

<http://www.lib.ox.ac.uk/search/search_faqs.html>

This is another site for Usenet newsgroups FAQs, described above.

CHAPTER 14

Electronic texts and reviews

Electronic texts, referred to also as e-texts or etexts, is a term that refers to the digital equivalent of printed materials accessible from Internet servers, namely books, journals, newsletters and documents. Some of these are digital reproductions of printed items. Many thousands of classic texts in philosophy, history, social philosophy and political science have been painstakingly typed, scanned and edited into digital format. Others have no printed equivalent.

Below I list some electronic text resources. Some of the references are to large collections in particular subject areas, or to compilations of links, others to more general collections. In addition to collections I also list some individual items that I think may be of some interest and which do not fit conveniently under other chapter headings. Some resources that could be classified under the heading of electronic texts are referenced in chapters that focus on particular discipline areas. Others that are included here could have been referenced in these chapters. As the parameters of the term electronic text are somewhat vague, a degree of imprecision is unavoidable.

Anthropoetics: The Electronic Journal of Generative Anthropology

<http://www.humnet.ucla.edu/humnet/anthropoetics/home.html>

'The ordinary hypothesis of GA is that human language begins as an aborted gesture of appropriation representing – and thereby renouncing as sacred – an object of potential mimetic rivalry.' It publishes articles directly relevant to GA, 'fundamental anthropology' based on the mimetic theory of desire, and work that reflects fundamentally on the human. There are five issues online, including Special Issues on Religion and René Girard. Articles are evaluated for publication by an editorial board.

ARACHNION: a Journal of Ancient Literature and History on the Web

<http://www.cisi.unito.it/arachne/arachne.html>

Four issues online, the latest being May 1996. Articles are written in either English or Italian. Articles are evaluated for publication by an editorial board.

Australian Humanities Review

<http://www.lamp.ac.uk/ahr/>

Eight issues online, the latest being November 1997.

Boston Book Review

<http://www.bookwire.com/bbr/bbr-home.html>

Electronic version of the print edition. The sections that are likely to be of most interest to social scientists are History, Politics, Polemics and book reviews. Back issues of reviews are available. The electronic edition includes only extracts from the printed version.

Carrie: A Full-Text Electronic Library

<http://www.ukans.edu/carrie/carrie_main.html>

Provided by the University of Kansas, this is a compilation of links to electronic texts available on the Web, only some of which are stored on the University of Kansas server. There was no help file or search engine when last examined. The Reference link lists only a few reference tools. The Stacks, on the other hand, consists of a very large collection of resources arranged by language, most of which are in English. The subject matter is diverse. It includes histories of American Civil War regiments, Abbot Thomas's translation of Kant's *Fundamental Principles of the Metaphysics of Morals*, Pascal's *The Provincial Letters*, and US governmental reports on various issues. Many of the links are to individual works that feature in some of the larger collections of etexts on the Internet, particularly those of CMU, MIT and Virginia Tech.

A separate section, the Documents Room, collates links to collections of documents on the Catholic Church, the United Nations, European Documents and United States historical documents. The European Documents link is to a collection by Brigham Young University entitled EuroDocs: Primary Historical Documents from Western Europe, which is particularly comprehensive and is arranged by period and era.

CIC Electronic Journal Collection

<http://ejournals.cic.net/>

The Committee on Institutional Cooperation, a consortium of 11 American universities, manages this resource. The 'collection aims to be an authoritative source of electronic research and academic serial publications – incorporating all freely distributed scholarly electronic journals available online'. The collection can be browsed by subject or author, or searched by keyword, title or subject. Main subject areas include Arts and Humanities,

Education, Environmental Science, Nature, Government, History, Social Science, and Society and Culture. The number of journals in each category is not large, reflecting the current online situation.

Classic Electronic Texts

<gopher://gopher.vt.edu:10010/10/33 >

Managed at Virginia Tech., this lists classic texts by author. Access is generally fast. Some of the files are large. Indicative works include Adam Smith's *The Wealth of Nations*, Charles Darwin's *The Descent of Man* and *On the Origin of Species*, David Hume's *An Enquiry Concerning Human Understanding*, and Friedrich Nietzsche's *Thus Spake Zarathustra*.

Classics Archive

<http://classics.mit.edu/titles.d.html>

The Internet Classics Archive is managed at MIT. This is an outstanding resource that includes over 400 Greek and Latin texts and commentaries. It includes many of the major works by Aristotle, Plato, Cicero, Hippocrates, Homer, Livy, Tacitus, Plutarch and Virgil. The works of 48 authors were available online in mid-February 1998. Many of the files are large. The History of the Peloponnesian Wars is 1.1 Mb, although the chapters can be downloaded separately if preferred. There is also a compilation of links to other classics and electronic text resources that is worth exploring.

E-Journal

<http://www.edoc.com/ejournal/>

This is the World Wide Web Virtual Library listing of electronic journals. Journals are listed under Academic and Reviewed Journals, College or University, Newsletters, Magazines and Newspapers, and Political. There is also a search engine. Journals in the Academic and Reviewed Journals category are subdivided into Scientific and Humanities, in each of which there are three subdivisions, these being Peer Reviewed, Non-Peer Reviewed, and Student Reviewed.

Electronic Journals Database

<http://biblio.kbsi.re.kr/yellow/index.html>

This resource indexes and provides links to the home pages of more than 9600 of the world's leading journals. From these you can establish whether they have materials in electronic format. By January 1998 the database had indexed 1300 in Arts and Humanities, 3100 in the Social Sciences, and 5200 in Science. In each category you can search by alphabetical title, use a search engine that queries by title, publisher and ISBN, or use the subject index. For each journal the information provided includes the title, publisher, and details of whether the table of contents is provided, or the full text of articles, the frequency of publication and whether abstracts are available.

H-Net reviews

<http://www.h-net.msu.edu/reviews/>

This site provides access to reviews of recently published books that have been posted to the member discussion groups of Humanities Net. These reviews are commissioned by 140 specialists who edit the H-Net discussion lists. They are assisted by more than 600 scholars who are members of international boards. This is a very useful resource that is well arranged and kept up to date.

You can access reviews with the aid of a search engine which accepts queries by author, ISBN, title, publisher, reviewer's name, date of review, and Library of Congress subject. Alternatively, you can browse through recent reviews arranged by any of the criteria just mentioned.

Instead of accessing the Web site you can request that reviews are delivered to you by electronic mail.

The Internet Public Library

<http://ipl.si.umich.edu/col/>

This directory includes 7651 titles that can be searched by author, by title, by Dewey Subject Classification or with the assistance of a search engine. To take some examples more or less at random, the entry for Immanuel Kant includes the full texts of 10 works, including *Critique of Pure Reason* and *Critique of Practical Reason*, that for Shakespeare includes 55 works, and there are five by Booker T. Washington.

John Labovitz's E-Zine list

<http://www.meer.net/~johnl/e-zine-list/index.html>

'For those … not acquainted with the zine world, "zine" is short for either "fanzine" or "magazine," depending on your point of view. Zines are generally produced by one person or a small group of people, done often for fun or personal reasons, and tend to be irreverent, bizarre, and/or esoteric. Zines are not "mainstream" publications – they generally do not contain advertisements (except, sometimes, advertisements for other zines), are not targeted towards a mass audience, and are generally not produced to make a profit.'

There are 1700 listed. They can be searched by keyword or by title.

The Law and Politics Book Review

<http://www.unt.edu/lpbr/>

The Law and Courts section of the American Political Science Association sponsors this resource. The reviews are arranged alphabetically by author. More books on law tend to be reviewed than those on politics. Like the H-Net book reviews, you can subscribe for free and have them delivered by electronic mail. The reviews are frequently more detailed than those that you would find in refereed journals, appear sooner after publication and are of high quality.

NYBooks

<http://nybooks.com>

This page provides access to presentations by *n. b. (New Books)*, the *New York Review of Books* and *Granta*. *New Books* includes reviews of recently published books. Its archives date from October 1997. The *New York Review of Books* section includes a selection of articles published in each current issue. Their article archives date from mid-January 1998. *Granta* provides information only on the contents of its latest issue.

Penn Library Electronic Journal Index

<http://www.library.upenn.edu/resources/ej/>

The electronic journals are arranged by subject. Many of the journals in this well-arranged compilation are restricted to University of Pennsylvania students. There are many others that are available freely online.

The Perseus Project: an Evolving Digital Library

<http://www.perseus.tufts.edu/indexPlain.html>

This is another outstanding Web presentation, managed by Tufts University. It provides a variety of resources on the ancient world, including an historical overview, a large number of primary texts, essays, pictorial representations of artefacts, maps, etc. The primary texts can be browsed in translation or in Greek. There are a variety of tools available for studying the texts that are arranged alphabetically by author and for each of which a brief biography is available. There is extensive cross-referencing through hypertext. Some may think that this has been somewhat overdone, as in some sentences you may find hyperlinks to four or more files, or positions in the file.

Project Gutenberg

<http://promo.net/pg/index.html>

Project Gutenberg is one of the most widely known and respected Web projects. Michael Hart has managed it from its early beginnings in 1971. He concluded that 'the greatest value created by computers would not be computing, but would be the storage, retrieval, and searching of what was stored in our libraries'. Hart's goal is to provide as many etexts as possible in a format that virtually any computer user can read, regardless of the operating system or word processor that they may be using.

The Marx/Engels archive

<http://csf.colorado.edu/psn/marx/>

Access to electronic versions of many of the writings of Marx and Engels, arranged in chronological order. Most of the major works are already online and others are being added regularly. The search engine will search through all 40,000 pages of the printed text in electronic format to track down specific search queries.

CHAPTER 15

Data archives

In the context of the present chapter I use the term data archive to refer to resources that collate information relating to substantial numbers of datasets and studies in the social sciences.

The Data Archive

<http://155.245.254.47>

This used to be referred to as the ESRC Data Archive. It stores the largest collection of 'computer-readable data in the social sciences and humanities in the United Kingdom'. Funded jointly by the Economic and Social Science Research Council, the Joint Information Systems Committee and the University of Essex, it currently archives more than 7000 datasets. In most instances these datasets were originally collected for studies the results of which have been published. They are now made available for secondary research purposes, including re-evaluations of the findings of the primary studies.

The holdings fall into three broad categories:

- Datasets produced under the auspices of central and local government or public bodies such as the National Health Service. These include major national social surveys such as the General Household and Family Expenditure surveys, and data collected for administrative purposes, such as National Health Service Patient Re-registrations.

- Datasets produced by academic researchers. Many of these investigations were fully or partly publicly funded, a condition of the funding being that the datasets be deposited with the Data Archive, which is a national resource centre.

- Datasets made available through reciprocal arrangements with other data archives. These include those of the International Consortium for Political and Social Research (ICPSR), based at the University of Michigan, and European-based data archives, made available through the Council for European Social Science Data Archives.

Although many of the datasets are available to academic users without charge, this is not uniformly the case:

'The Archive's users are primarily in the academic sector but commercial users are catered for when the data depositor is willing to allow them access. The Archive's charging policy zero rates academic usage (provided that the research is not externally funded by any organisation other than the ESRC) charging only for the cost of materials [the medium of data transmission, e.g., floppy disks or CD-ROM]. Royalty fees are not normally due for such usage although there are some exceptions to this rule. When the proposed research has received external funding, however, Archive administrative fees are imposed. These differ according to whether the funder is a charity, a non-profit organisation or commercial. The Archive may, in addition, collect royalties on behalf of the data owner.'

The Data Archive uses a standard cataloguing format so that information can be easily exchanged with other data archives. The idea behind this is that in the not too distant future those accessing any major data archive accessible over the Internet will be able to search through all linked data archives with the use of what is called a WAIS (Wide Area Information System) search engine. In a similar manner it will be possible to search through all the major publicly accessible online library catalogues in one sweep, as it were.

Particulars relating to datasets and requests for access to them are executed online through a resource called BIRON, an acronym for Bibliographical Information Retrieval On-line.

BIRON

<http://155.245.254.46/cgi-bin/biron>

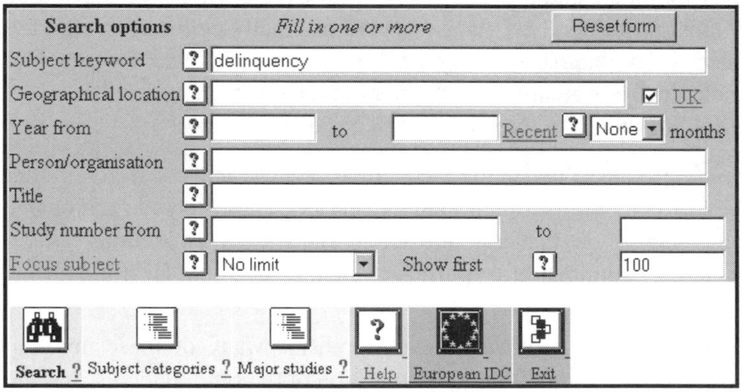

Figure 15.1 *BIRON entry interface.*

Although the Data Archive describes the BIRON interface illustrated in Figure 15.1 as simple and intuitive to use, these are both adjectives that are bandied around by Web designers and search engine developers rather loosely. You will need to spend some time reading the various help files to familiarize yourself with the wide-ranging features of the BIRON system.

I will illustrate the query procedures with reference to a search for investigations of delinquency, restricting the search to UK studies, but entering no date restrictions. To do so I entered delinquency as the *Subject keyword*, Figure 15.1. Note that next to text boxes there are question marks. When you select a question mark information is returned relating to how the search engine uses that particular variable in querying the database. The entry under Subject keywords, for example, is 'Subject keywords may consist of a single word, e.g. elections or a phrase, e.g. political allegiance'. Having entered your query variables, select *Search* at bottom left. The file returned in response to my query is illustrated in Figure 15.2.

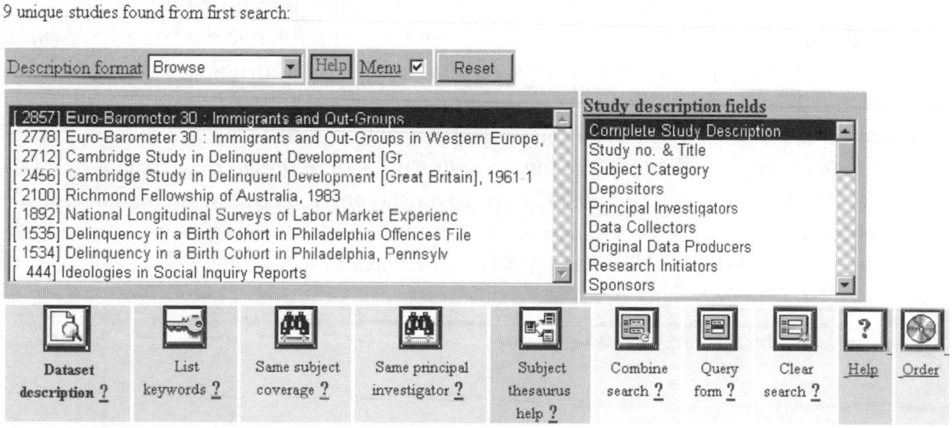

9 unique studies found from first search:

Figure 15.2   *BIRON query/return interface.*

The total number of studies falling under the keyword delinquency is noted as nine. You can now highlight any of these studies that you are interested in and obtain details under any of the entries listed in the drop-down menu box to the right. The Complete Study Description returns information that includes particulars that fall under all the other headings in this box. This includes an abstract, details about the sampling universe and procedures, time period, etc. The information is well organized and carefully described. If you do not want to read the information online you can select to have it sent to your electronic mail address by choosing that entry from the Description Format drop-down menu box, and have this sent in alternative formats. This is a useful feature if you want to look at details relating to a number of studies; you can highlight each in turn and then use the electronic mail delivery feature so that you can peruse them when convenient.

To receive datasets you need to complete a very detailed online form. If you do not have an open connection it is worth disconnecting, completing the form and then reconnecting to send it. Additionally, 'recipients of data are normally required to sign undertakings to the effect that they will not attempt to identify individuals when carrying out analyses. Where names of individuals do appear in the data supplied, for instance the names of politicians as the subject of questions about political preferences in political polls or elite studies, users are advised of the data protection legislation which applies to the analysis of these data.' The online information specifies that the request is ordinarily handled within 28 days. It is, however, somewhat irritating to find that you can obtain access to some datasets without all this bureaucratic overseeing, particularly when some of them can be obtained more easily from ICPSR or other online data archives.

The original query can be focused by various means, including the two methods described below.

1.   From the button bar on the interface returned in response to the original query, Figure 15.2, select *Subject thesaurus help?*. This returns an interface and button bars as illustrated in Figure 15.3. In the box at the top left are terms that are associated with the original keyword query delinquency, these being either narrower terms in relation to the database thesaurus, or related terms, or both. If you select either *Include narrower level terms* (nt), *Include all related terms* (rt), or *Substitute single term*, you can extend the query to focus on the original term and one of these. To do so with the option *Substitute single term*, you need to highlight the term of your choice. If you then select the button *Extend using?* and one of the menu choices available in the button *with <no.> from previous search* (AND, OR, NOT), the search will be extended to cover the previous query, delinquency in the present example, with the additional term(s) selected, using one of the logical operators AND, OR, NOT (see p. 84). So, for example, if you

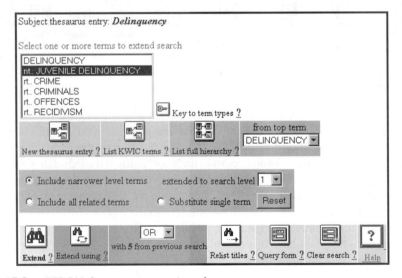

Figure 15.3   *BIRON thesaurus query interface.*

- checked *Substitute single term*
- highlighted CRIME in Figure 15.3
- made a selection from the drop-down menu on the button *with <no.> from previous search* (the number in this example being 5)
- chose the button *Extend using?*

the database will be queried for UK-based studies that include

- delinquency AND crime,
- delinquency OR crime, or
- delinquency NOT crime

depending on the choice you made on the drop-down menu included in the *with <no.> from previous search* button drop-down menu.

2.   Alternatively select the button *Combine search?*, Figure 15.2. The interface with your original query will appear, but with a different toolbar below it, which is illustrated in Figure 15.4.

Figure 15.4   *BIRON combine search toolbar.*

If you delete the keyword subject entry that you originally inserted, substitute another and then select *Combine?*, the search engine will query the database for all entries that include the original term or terms along with those just inserted, employing the logical operator AND. So, to continue the previous example, I substituted administration of justice for delinquency. Whereas five studies were found for delinquency focused on the UK, only one was found that combined that query with the string administration of justice.

As is probably clear from the above discussion, the searching procedures are neither simple nor intuitive. I do not mean this entirely critically, as the search facilities are elaborate, making it relatively easy to extract relevant information, and the help files are, for the most part, clearly written. Do not expect, however, to be able to maximize the data extraction possibilities without experimentation and a reading of the help files. I suspect also that there are some imperfections in the working of the search engine, as dissimilar search options using the same queries return similar results.

ESRC Qualitative Data Archive Centre

<http://www.essex.ac.uk/qualidata/>

This archive was established by the ESRC with a view to preserving primary qualitative data so that it could be employed subsequently in secondary research. A pilot study conducted in 1991 revealed that over 90% of qualitative data was either already destroyed or at risk in researchers' homes or offices. The QUALIDATA Centre was established at the University of Essex with a view to remedying this situation.

This is not a repository archive, but a database that keeps track of the location of archived qualitative data. Information on the location of qualitative data can be accessed by means of the QUALICAT search engine at

<http://www.essex.ac.uk/qualidata/data/catinput.htm>

Searches can be carried out on title, subject category, primary discipline, investigator, sponsor, contents or keywords and can be focused by dates of fieldwork and geographical location. The information returned includes a short abstract and where the data is located.

Arts and Humanities Data Service

<http://ahds.ac.uk/>

Funded by the Joint Information Systems Committee of the UK's Higher Education Funding Councils, the mission of AHDS is 'to collect, describe, and preserve the electronic resources which result from research and teaching in the humanities. It will encourage scholarly use of its collections and make information about them available through an on-line catalogue.'

The efforts of AHDS are coordinated through a number of Service Providers that focus on the collection, cataloguing and distribution of digital resources in subject-specific areas. The main subject areas that are of relevance to the present volume are history, and literary, linguistic and other textual studies. Its primary services to users are:

- free or at-cost access to all services for the academic community
- expert guidance on the creation and scholarly use of digital materials
- professional cataloguing and documentation of digital resources
- expert information on resource availability and usefulness.

The History Data Service

<http://hds.essex.ac.uk/homepage.stm>

This archive is located at and integrated with The Data Archive at the University of Essex. Their holdings currently amount to some 400 datasets in the following areas:

- European State Finance across a broad time period
- Manuscript Census Records
- Community history
- Aggregate statistics for the 19th and 20th centuries
- Political history
- Historical Geographic Information System for Great Britain
- Economic history
- Mortality and disease.

The holdings are accessed via the BIRON online catalogue described earlier. Information on recent additions to the collection can be accessed from

<http://hds.essex.ac.uk/scripts/releases.idc>

which provides details on the study number, the title and an abstract describing the dataset.

CESSDA IDC

<http://155.245.254.48/Cessda/IDC/>

This is an integrated search engine that you can use to search the specified catalogues of the data holdings of archives held in France, Denmark, the UK, Norway, Sweden, Israel, the Netherlands, Hungary, Germany, Australia and the USA. There are also direct links to each of the catalogues included. The idea is that you enter the query variables in the search engine interface illustrated in Figure 15.5, check all those catalogues that you want the engine to query and then submit the query.

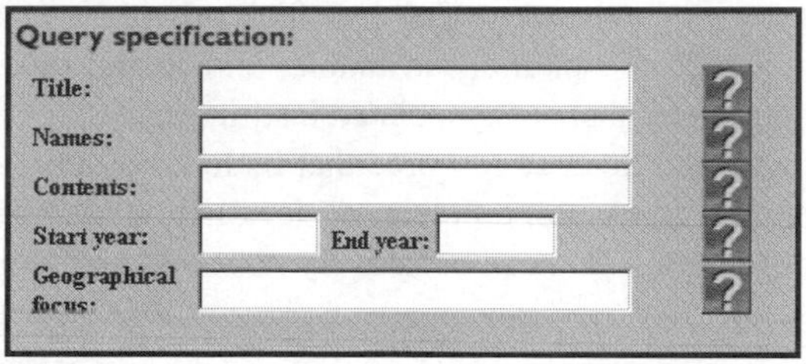

Figure 15.5   *CESSDA IDC query interface.*

Because this search engine integrates catalogues from different countries and the information that they record on particular holdings differs in certain respects, the searching facilities are not as powerful as you will find if you link to individual catalogues. It is, however, useful for a broad first sweep. The most useful search field is likely to be *Contents* which 'contains the text of abstracts describing the studies and in some cases keywords for identifying research. Abstracts are freeform. Keywords may be controlled but differ from archive to archive.' The results that are returned are scored so that those that approximate your query best in terms of the database algorithm have the highest score and appear at the top of the list. The details specify the title of the study, the data archive where it is located, the type of data and the size of the abstract. The abstract is downloaded when you select the hyperlink if you select *Verbose List: Yes*. If you select *No*, only the title is returned.

Inter-University Consortium for Political and Social Research (ICPSR)

<http://www.icpsr.umich.edu/>

Established in 1962 at the University of Michigan, the ICPSR is a non-profit institutional membership-based organization that has the largest holdings of computer-based research and instructional data in the Social Sciences in the world. Their holdings 'cover a broad range of disciplines, including political science, sociology, demography, economics, history, education, gerontology, criminal justice, public health, foreign policy, and law'. Although the datasets are only available to individuals who are associated with member institutions, the abstracts, codebooks and other documentation are publicly accessible for many studies in the collection.

The holdings can be searched by broad subject area, of which there are currently 18, which include International Systems, Legal Systems, Economic Behavior and Attitudes, Mass Political Behavior and Attitudes, and Conflict, Aggression and Violence. Some of these are further subdivided. Alternatively, the database can be searched by Title, PI (Principal Investigator) or Study Number, or queried with the aid of a search engine.

The files that are returned are displayed in tabular form and provide information on the Study Title, the Principal Investigator and the Study Number. There are also links to the Abstracts (AB) and the Data (DA). The AB files provide information under a large number of headings. These include the date added, the date updated, a summary of the principal aims and methods of the study, the extent and nature of the data, the time period the study covers, data source, data format, the sampling method and universe, and the appropriate format for citing the study. The DA files provide access to codebooks and other documentation, which are publicly available, and to the raw data, which is only available to those who are members of associated institutions.

This is a major Social Science resource that includes a very large volume of datasets. There are no lengthy forms to complete, no legalistic undertakings to sign, and no waiting for weeks until the raw data can be actively reviewed and worked.

National Archive of Computerized Data on Ageing

<http://www.icpsr.umich.edu/NACDA/>

This archive is housed at the ICPSR and is the largest US collection of computerized data on ageing. It is arranged in much the same manner as the ICPSR archive described above. The data collections are ordered under six topic headings: demographic, social, economic, psychological, physical, and health characteristics of older adults. Although many of the studies originate with US agencies and investigators and have a US sampling universe, there are also some studies that have been carried out by United Nations organs and on samples of other nationals.

Having reviewed the contents of some of the files under topic headings to obtain an overview of the type of data that is available, it is advisable to use the search engine as not all the studies are detailed in the topic listings. For each study there is a detailed abstract, and access to codebooks and other documents is publicly available. Access to raw data is restricted to users associated with member institutions of ICPSR. There are also links from this site to other archives and sites that focus on ageing-related issues.

British Library for Development Studies (BLDS) Bibliographic Database

<http://www.ids.ac.uk/blds/blds.html>

This is a very well-organized and useful source of information on both hardcopy and Web resources relating to developing countries and development studies. Managed by the Institute of Development Studies at the University of Sussex since 1966, the IDS has collected an impressive volume of materials on developing countries and development. 'The collection currently comprises some 250,000 monograph items and approximately 8000 serial titles with over 25,000 further documents added each year. Collection policy encompasses literature, in English and other European languages, relating to economic and social development, both rural and urban, while specific areas of subject interest include: health, education, communication, industrial development, debt and adjustment, population studies, gender and development, the environment, participatory appraisal, human rights, good government and democratization.' It now also collates information on resources accessible over the Internet and provides links to many full-text documents that can be downloaded.

There are two main entry points to the collection. One is through ELDIS (Electronic Development and Environment Information System) accessible from the home page, whose URL is

<http://www.ids.ac.uk/eldis/eldis.html>

You can choose either to use the search engine or to access records from the 60 or so subject guides. If the data is available online this is indicated. Alternatively, the BLDS Catalogue and Journal Article database can be accessed directly at

<http://nt1.ids.ac.uk/dbases/bldsdb0.htm>

This provides for both simple and focused searches.

EURYBASE: The European Community Database on Education

<http://www.eurydice.org/Eurybase/files/dossier.htm>

This is a very well-arranged and useful database of information on the educational systems of member states of the European Union, provided by EURYDICE, the Information Network on Education in Europe. The information is detailed, covers all levels of education and is arranged by country. Details are provided on the cultural, political and economic background of each country and the European dimension in education. For each country there is a bibliography of official reports, a glossary of terms, and a listing of relevant legislation and institutions.

National Archive of Criminal Justice Data

<http://www.icpsr.umich.edu/NACJD/>

This archive was established in 1978 under the auspices of ICPSR and the Bureau of Justice Statistics of the US Department of Justice. The archive provides access to compu terized datasets relating to crime and the criminal justice system. Access to the raw data is not restricted to users who are associated with member institutions of the ICPSR. It is arranged in much the same manner as the ICPSR and NACDA archives described earlier.

Studies are arranged under 11 subject headings: attitude surveys, community studies, corrections, court case processing, courts, criminal justice system, crime and delinquency, official statistics, police, victimization and drugs, and alcohol and crime. As noted in connection with other ICPSR archives, it is advisable to use the search engine to locate studies in areas of interest. Although many of the datasets originate with agencies associated with the US criminal justice system, there are also many that have been deposited by academic researchers. These include those by Reiss on police–citizen transactions, Monkonnen on Police Departments, Arrests and Crime in the United States, 1860–1920, and the study by Gelles and Straus on Physical Violence in American Families, all of which are very well-known studies. There are many others that are equally well respected.

Crime & Justice Electronic Data Abstracts

<http://www.ojp.usdoj.gov/bjs/dtdata.htm>

Provided by the Bureau of Justice Statistics division of the US Department of Justice. The abstracts consist of data from a variety of sources that have been aggregated into spreadsheets 'to facilitate use with analytical software'. The raw data originates from a variety of sources, including FBI statistics, the Uniform Crime Reports, Bureau of Justice statistical programmes and the Bureau of the Census. The data is arranged both by topic (crime and arrest, criminal justice, and demographic) and by jurisdiction (federal, state, county and city). The files are in .wkl format, a format that can be read by most spreadsheet, statistical and word-processing applications.

Social Science Data Libraries and Data Archives

<http://dpls.dacc.wisc.edu/datalib.html#map>

A list of links to data archives in the United States and elsewhere provided by the University of Wisconsin. There are access restrictions on some of the datasets at the archives listed, but there are many others on which there are none. Some datasets are supplied only on payment of fees.

Social Science Data Extraction Sites on the Net

<http://sun3.lib.uci.edu/~dtsang/ext.htm>

The University of California main library resource. Extraction sites 'permit one to select variables and output data in different forms, including tabular, rectangular file (accessible via FTP) or map format. Sites linked include: County and City Data Books, 1988 & 1994; County Business Patterns, 1977–1994; General Social Survey, 1972–1994; Historical, Demographic, Economic, and Social Data for the United States, 1790–1860; National Income and Product Accounts; Penn World Tables; Regional Economic Information System, 1969–1993; State Personal Income, 1969–1995; Uniform Crime Reports, 1990–1993; World Bank's Social Indicators of Development, 1994 and Trends in Developing Economies; U.S. Government Extraction Sites such as: CIESIN Demographic Data Viewer; Foreign Labor Statistics; International Data Base; U.S. Bureau of Labor Statistics, including its Economy at a Glance; U.S. Census Data Extraction System (DES); U.S. Census Summary Statistics; World Crime Survey Data; World Tables of Economic and Social Indicators.'

The State of the Nation's Cities: a Comprehensive Database on American Cities and Suburbs

<http://policy.rutgers.edu/cupr/SoNC.htm>

This database was produced originally in 1996 by the Center for Urban Policy Research at Rutgers University for the US Department of Housing and Urban Development, and has most recently been updated in January 1998. It provides a comprehensive database on 77 US cities and suburbs, including more than 3000 variables. The database can be downloaded in a variety of formats, including those suited for use with Excel and SPSS (Statistical Package for Social Sciences). The spreadsheet includes 77 columns and 3000 rows. Detailed instructions relating to operating system platform and downloading are provided.

CHAPTER 16

Statistical resources

There is an enormous volume of statistical information accessible from Internet sources. Some of this is detailed in sections dealing with particular subject areas. Thus, for example, information relating to certain aspects of crime and the criminal justice system, particularly in the United States, can be found in the datasets included in the National Archive of Criminal Justice Data mentioned in the previous chapter, p. 173. Other information can be accessed through exploring some of the resources mentioned in Chapter 18 on Current News Online. One of the fastest means of finding statistical data is to use a search engine. In order to find information on the number of executions by country, for example, I used the query

<executions AND statistics AND (countries OR states)>

in Alta Vista Advanced Search, with statistics in the *Ranking* box. This returned 2371 documents, the first of which was an Amnesty International report for 1997 which included information on executions by continent.

The Research Road

<http://trochim.human.cornell.edu/kb/kbroad.htm>

William M. K. Trochim, Professor of Policy Analysis and Management at Cornell University, has authored this presentation. It consists of three main parts and their subsections: Introduction to Research; Sampling, Measurement & Design; and Data Analysis. Topics covered include 'variables, hypotheses, research problem formulation, levels of measurement, reliability and validity, survey research and questionnaires, research design, statistical power, and various types of statistics and statistical analysis' (Scout Report). This is an excellent introductory guide to research methods which is very clearly written and helpfully illustrated. You can move to particular topics through the table of contents page at

<http://trochim.human.cornell.edu/kb/content1.htm>

or explore the subject by way of an image map which includes sections on The Problem, Measure, Sample, Design, Analyze, and Conclude, this being an alternative route to that of proceeding sequentially through the table of contents. Before starting you should briefly read the instructions/guide on all four of the main route maps: Knowledge Base Home Page, Table of Contents, Dual Path Research, and The Research Road. An excellent demonstration of the pedagogic opportunities presented by html.

Introductory Statistics: Concepts, Models and Applications

<http://www.psychstat.smsu.edu/introbook/sbk00m.htm>

or

<http://www.psychstat.smsu.edu>

This Web text has been written by David W. Stockburger of Southwest Missouri State University. It is a very well-written text that covers most of the subject matter included in introductory undergraduate statistics courses. There are plenty of examples and the detailed and clear explanations should make it easy for most students to progress through the work. It includes a large quantity of graphics, and some files may take some time to download. It is also a presentation that relies on frames. The links to other major Web resources, both explanatory and data, are extremely useful. In sum, this is an excellent resource.

SurfStat Australia

<http://surfstat.newcastle.edu.au/surfstat/main/surfstat-main.html>

This is an excellent introduction to statistics by Dr Keith Dear of the University of Newcastle, Australia. It is divided into five sections: Summarizing and Presenting Data; Producing Data; Variation and Probability; Statistical Inference; and Control Charts. It is clearly written and accompanied by numerous graphs, illustrations and examples. Some of the chapters have progress checks where you receive feedback to answers given to questions, and there are also some exercises along with answers. This is an extremely useful introduction to basic statistical concepts and applications.

Agricultural World Census Program

<http://www.fao.org/waicent/faoinfo/agricult/census/wcahome.htm>

Under the auspices of the Food and Agricultural Organization of the United Nations, this is a programme aimed at encouraging countries to carry out an agricultural census during every decade. The results of the census carried out in the years 1986–1995 for some 60 countries are currently online. The online publication, Conducting Agricultural Censuses and Surveys, discusses various methodological issues relating to the conduct of agricultural censuses and surveys.

AQUASTAT

<http://www.fao.org/waicent/faoinfo/agricult/AGL/AGLW/AQUASTAT/AQUASTAT.HTM>

AQUASTAT is an information system on water in agriculture and rural development, organized under the auspices of the United Nations. It produces country profiles on water resources development with an emphasis on irrigation and drainage.

'Each country profile describes the situation regarding water resources and use in the country, with special attention to the water resources, irrigation and drainage sub-sectors. Its aim is to emphasize the particularities of each country, as well as the problems encountered in rural water management and irrigation.'

There is a general summary of the water resource situation for both Africa and the Near East. For each country there is a profile of its water resource situation which provides information on its geography and population, climate and water resources, irrigation and drainage development, institutional environment, trends in water resource management, bibliographic information and tables of relevant data. This is a very well-organized resource.

Census and You

<http://www.census.gov/prod/www/abs/msgen.html>

A monthly newsletter from the US Census Bureau that includes articles summarizing newly issued findings, reports and data files. 'The principal emphasis is on demographic, social, housing, and economic data for states and smaller areas.' It also publishes key economic indicators (such as housing starts, retail sales, and the Consumer Price Index). Files are available in .pdf format.

Data Ferret (Federal Electronic Research Review and Extraction Tool)

<http://ferret.bls.census.gov/cgi-bin/ferret>

'This joint project of the U.S. Commerce Department's Census Bureau and the Department of Labor's Bureau of Labor Statistics (BLS) enables users to access and manipulate large demographic and economic data sets. It is designed to aid not only sophisticated researchers, but also reporters, students, government policy-makers or amateur statisticians. The CPS is a survey of about 50,000 households that the Census Bureau conducts for BLS, which is used to produce BLS' estimates of employment and unemployment. It also includes periodic supplements covering a range of topics, such as income and poverty, health insurance coverage and school enrollment. These are published by the Census Bureau. The SIPP, a Census Bureau survey of about 37,000 households, collects data monthly on sources of income and participation in government-assistance programs, as well as on various aspects of economic well-being. Among the current and future data topics that will be accessible through FERRET are: employment, health care, education, race and ethnicity, health insurance, housing, income and poverty, aging and marriage, and family. FERRET allows users to quickly locate current and historical information from these sources, get tabulations for specific information they need, make comparisons between different data sets, create simple tables and download large amounts of data to desktop and larger computers for custom reports.' (Review by SSDC UC San Diego/ Social Science Data on the Net)

FAOSTAT

<http://apps.fao.org/>

This is the address for the United Nations Food and Agricultural Organization's online statistical databases. They contain over one million time-series records covering international statistics under a number of headings. Those likely to be found most useful by social scientists include Production, Trade, Food Balance Sheets, Food Aid Shipments, and Population.

This is a very useful and efficiently arranged resource. By default the data is presented in a table. If you want to compare a number of countries, or access data on more than one item or element, or years covered, hold down the Ctrl key when you highlight successive variables. Read the associated help files for information on how to configure your spreadsheet application so that the data is opened directly in it.

EUROSTAT

<http://europa.eu.int/en/comm/eurostat/serven/home.htm>

This is the site of the Statistical Office of the European Communities. There is hardly any online statistical information other than some basic statistics relating to transport, energy, population, etc., most of which would be of use mainly for primary school pupils. However, there is plentiful information about their printed and other format products that can be accessed for hard cash.

FEDSTATS

<http://www.fedstats.gov/>

This is the main gateway to statistical series published by the US federal government. This is another very well-organized resource. If you select the heading Agencies you are presented with a framed presentation. In one of the frames are listed all the agencies represented on the Interagency Council on Statistical Policy, that is, agencies whose statistical series are collated by FEDSTATS. If you choose an agency, say the Bureau of Labor Statistics, in another frame there are details of what that agency provides statistics on, whilst in the third frame there are links to major statistical series produced by the agency. The information is available in graph and tabular formats. There is a non-frame version of the Web presentation available.

Instead of locating series via agencies this can be approached via Programs. The series are arranged under 14 fields, including agriculture, crime, labor, economic, energy and environment. There is also a collection of regional statistical series. Although most of these provide data relating to the separate states of the Union there are others that provide international comparisons.

IDB Population Pyramids

<http://www.census.gov/ipc/www/idbpyr.html>

The US Census Bureau has made this series available. You select a country from the list provided, decide whether you want to view the output for the default years of 1997, 2025 and 2050, or whether you wish to choose years for comparison yourself. When you submit the query the demographic graphs of the projections for the years chosen are downloaded, the variables included being gender and age band. The year variables range from 1987 to 2050.

Infonation

<http://www.un.org/Pubs/CyberSchoolBus/infonation/e_infonation.htm>

Provided by the United Nations and using statistics collected by its Statistics Division, this is a two-step database. In the first step you choose a list of countries, the maximum being seven, from a listing of all countries arranged by continent. You select by placing a check in the box next to the country's name. When you have done that you select the button *Data Menu*. This downloads a list of variables arranged under four headings: Geography, Economy, Population, and Social Indicators. You choose up to four of these and then select the button *View Info*. The variables you chose are presented in tabular form cross-referenced in relation to the countries you selected in the first phase. So, for example, you can select up to seven countries and cross reference these with information on their geographical area, GDP per capita, infant mortality rate and adult illiteracy.

International Data Base

<http://www.census.gov/ftp/pub/ipc/www/idbnew.html>

The US Census Bureau provides this resource. It is a computerized data bank containing statistical tables of demographic and socio-economic data for all countries of the world. The major data series available include population by age and sex, vital rates, infant mortality and life tables, fertility, migration, marital status, family planning, ethnicity, religion and language, literacy, labour force, employment and income, and households. Data series are available from 1950 to the present with projections to 2050, relating to all countries of the world. The data has been sourced from the United Nations, national statistics offices and United Nations specialized agencies.

Office of National Statistics

<http://www.emap.com/ons97/>

This is the central UK statistical collecting agency. It was formed in 1996 by a merger of the Central Statistical Office and the Office of Population Censuses and Surveys and is a government department and executive agency. Its objective is 'to meet a widely perceived need for greater coherence and compatibility in Government Statistics, for improved presentation and for easier public access'.

In line with European traditions there is little online data available from this site, other than a few token tables, nothing that really merits the click of a mouse. Like most European ventures on the Internet the site is essentially a marketing window for agency products. There is an online Guide to Official Statistics, which you can browse by category (e.g., education or employment) that provides some basic information on what statistics are collected. You can also browse the ONS Databank at

<http://www.emap.com/cso/databank/>

where details of the cost and the special software necessary to run the datasets can be found.

Statistical Abstract of the United States

<http://www.census.gov/prod/www/abs/cc97stab.html>

Data is ordered in 31 sections and arranged in more than 1500 tables. The data is available only in .pdf format.

National Statistical Offices/International Statistical Organizations

<http://www.stat.fi/sf/tilulkoe.html>

A listing of national statistical offices by country from Statistics Finland. This is a very useful resource as many of these offices provide extensive statistical information relating to their countries. For instance, the Israeli Central Bureau of Statistics provides online the Statistical Abstract of Israel, in English. This includes statistical series under 27 headings. Also available is the Monthly Bulletin of Statistics. Of course, not all statistics provided by national statistics offices are in English. Separate mention should be made of the link to statistics on Finland at the home page of Statistics Finland,

<http://www.stat.fi/sf/home.html>

as these, obviously, do not appear in the list.

Further down the list there are links to the statistical divisions of various international organizations. These include the International Monetary Fund, the Interstate Statistical Committee of the Commonwealth of Independent States, the OECD, the World Trade Organization, various United Nations agencies, and the World Bank.

Statistical Links

<http://www.cbs.nl/eng/link/index.htm>

A listing of links to major sources of statistical information by international organization and country arranged by continent from a Netherlands site.

Statistics on the Web

<http://maddog.fammed.wisc.edu/~helberg/statistics.html>

This is a major compilation of links to statistical resources maintained by Clay Helberg. The resources are arranged under the following categories: Professional Organizations, Institutes and Consulting Groups, Educational Resources (Web Courses and Online Textbooks), Publications and Publishers, Software-oriented Pages, Mailing Lists and Discussion Groups, Other Lists of Links, and Statisticians and Other Statistical People. This is a very useful compilation.

StatLib

<http://lib.stat.cmu.edu/>

At this site, managed by the Carnegie Mellon University Statistics Department, you can obtain information on statistical software and datasets and access to them. The datasets include some that have appeared in printed materials. Generally, this site is likely to be of use mainly to those with significant statistical expertise.

United Nations Population Information Network

<http://www.undp.org/popin/popin.htm>

This site provides access to a very extensive volume of information relating to population issues. This includes links to the documentation for the UN Commission on Population and Development and all the documentation relating to the Conference on Population and Development that was held in Cairo in 1994. There are links here to many other sources of information on all matters related to population development and growth. See in particular the very detailed report by the United Nations Population Fund (UNFPA) on The State of the World Population, available in English and French. This is a very detailed report at

<http://www.unfpa.org/swp96.html>

Its separate chapters deal with The Urban Potential, Conditions of Life in Urban Areas (Urban Poverty, Health, Reproductive Health, Education) (62K), Urban Population Dynamics: the Processes of Urban Growth (17K), and Sources of City Growth (Natural Increase, Migration) (23K), with conclusions, appendixes, extended notes on a variety of issues (definitions of poverty, urban compared with rural poverty, urban violence, etc.), charts, graphs, tables and technical notes. There are also links to very extensive bibliographical resources on population-related matters. A recent addition is a paper from the Population Division of the Department of Economic and Social Affairs of the United Nations Secretariat, which argues that the world population will stabilize at approximately 11 billion in the year 2150. Any reader who wants to locate information about population issues anywhere in the world should make this one of their sites of orientation.

University of Michigan Documents Center Statistical Resources on the Web

<http://www.lib.umich.edu/libhome/Documents.center/stats.html>

An excellent gateway to a very large number of statistical datasets on the Web. The categories under which they are subsumed include Business and Industry, Consumers, Demographics, Environment, Foreign Economics, Health, Military, Sociology, and Transportation.

World Population Information

<http://www.census.gov/ipc/www/world.html>

Information on the world population from the US Census Bureau. The information includes an annual World Population Profile, a World Population Clock, World Vital Events per Time Unit, World Population Estimates 1950 to 2050, historical estimates of world population from different sources for years up to 1950 and a link to an International Data Base on population. This latter is a computerized data bank containing statistical tables of demographic and socio-economic data for all countries of the world.

World Resources 1996–97

<http://www.wri.org/wri/wr-96-97/index.html>

'World Resources 1996–97 is an authoritative primary reference volume on global environmental and natural resource conditions and trends for the United Nations, World Bank, and related international organizations. It is widely used by scientists, students, and nongovernmental organizations. As a printed book, it runs to 384 pages, including 162 pages of data tables covering 150 countries. The full text of this volume is available on this web site, but to make it easier to use and to find the information that you need, the text has been separated into short sections linked to subtitles in the table of contents. Figures are linked to the appropriate section of the text. Data tables can be viewed in their entirety using Adobe Acrobat viewer software.' The chapters are in html, the data in .pdf.

CHAPTER 17

Social Science funding

Most of the important funding bodies, whether governmental or charitable, have a Web presence. Invariably you can obtain information from their sites on the grants that are available. In some instances you can submit applications electronically. Below I list only a few. Many others can be found by employing a search engine. It may also be useful to explore the resources I mention later in connection with monitoring additions to Web based resources, pages 310–11. Past issues, which in most cases can be trawled with the aid of a search engine, include resources relating to funding, for both students and research projects.

Economic and Social Research Council (ESRC)

<http://www.esrc.ac.uk/home.html>

The ESRC is the largest and main funding agency in the UK for research and postgraduate training in the social and economic sciences. Detailed information is provided on the grants available under various headings, including amounts and submission deadlines. Latest News Reports and the Social Science Newsletter provide information on recent activities and projects. You can also locate information on particular projects funded by the ESRC from its REGARD database at

<http://www.regard.ac.uk/>

A Guide to European Funding Opportunities for UK Social Science

<http://www.lboro.ac.uk/departments/eu/esrclh.html>

The European Research Centre at Loughborough University and the Economic and Social Research Council have made this resource available. Detailed information is provided in the form of Information Sheets relating to funding opportunities available for social scientific research and social scientists, primarily through the European Commission. There is a general introduction and information on fund provision through different Commission frameworks (FPIV and FPV), as well as on specific programmes. The latter include Targeted Socio-Economic Research (TSER), Training and Mobility of Researchers (TMR), European Co-operation in the field of Scientific and Technical Research (COST) and DG Discretionary Funds. Another sheet provides information on the Jean Monnet Awards: 'The Jean Monnet scheme on European integration is aimed at facilitating the introduction of new teaching activities in European integration in universities. Grants fund the creation of chairs, the setting up of new permanent courses in European integration and new European modules, and a limited number of research projects in European integration.' In addition, there is information on non-EC European funding from various sources, including the European Parliament, the Council of Europe, the European Science Foundation and the British Council's Intra-European Awards.

CORDIS

<http://www.cordis.lu/>

CORDIS is the Community Research and Development Information Service of the European Commission, providing information on EU research and exploitation possibilities.

> 'CORDIS provides information on all research and technological development activities in the EU through a complete collection of databases. The objective is to disseminate information on R&D to the widest audience possible with complete, up-to-date, and easily accessible data helping research projects across borders.
>
> The service features, among many other functions, a listing of thousands of European companies that want partners to develop or exploit technologies and know-how.
>
> If looking for a partner, if needing to know opening/closing dates and the content of the Commission's Calls for Proposals, looking up projects, finding EU decisions on research – simply get in touch with CORDIS.' (The European Union website).

There are 10 databases that can be explored. These provide information on all aspects of EU research, training and development activities, including current calls for proposals and tenders, potential partners in projects, details of projects and on publications relating to such activities. Anyone interested in obtaining EU funding under these headings should consult these databases.

Leverhulme Trust

<http://www.leverhulme.org.uk/index.html>

Details are available on the various types of grant that are available, to both individuals and institutions. No information is provided on application submission deadlines. Addresses and phone numbers are available and you can send an electronic mail request to obtain further information.

Joseph Rowntree Charitable Trust

<http://www.jrct.org.uk/>

There is detailed information on the subject areas that are covered, which are poverty and economic justice, handling conflict and promoting peaceful alternatives, democratic process, racial justice, corporate responsibility and Quaker and other religious concerns. Information is provided on deadlines and guidance on the completion of an application form, how it will be dealt with, etc. There is also a list of recent grants that have been awarded which should provide some guidance on the type of project that falls within the frame of reference of the Trust and appeals to the trustees.

UK Fundraising

<http://www.fundraising.co.uk/>

This site has a wealth of information relating all aspects of fundraising. Although its primary focus is not that of raising funds for scholarly research or the financing of education courses, you will find here information that is relevant to these things as well. There are separate sections on Education and on Grants and Funding.

National Lottery Charities Board

<http://www.nlcb.org.uk/>

The Foundation Center

<http://fdncenter.org/>

The Foundation is a US-based organization that is 'an independent nonprofit information clearinghouse established in 1956. The Center's mission is to foster public understanding of the foundation field by collecting, organizing, analyzing, and disseminating information on foundations, corporate giving, and related subjects. The audiences that call on the Center's resources include grantseekers, grantmakers, researchers, policymakers, the media, and the general public.'

CHAPTER 18

Current news online

18.1	Introduction	189
18.2	General electronic newspaper resources	190
18.3	Newspapers and agencies	193
18.4	Television and radio news	197

18.1   Introduction

There is no other delivery platform to rival the Internet in terms of the range, volume, geographical spread and immediacy of news coverage that is easily and freely available. No library could afford the acquisition of as many hardcopy equivalents of electronic newspapers, Usenet newsgroups and electronic magazines, nor afford the costs of ordering and archiving such a volume of materials. If you are interested in knowing what is on today's agenda of the General Assembly of the United Nations or the European Parliament or Commission, what the weather is in Tokyo or the level of the Hang Seng, what are the television and radio schedules in Toronto, or what political news is breaking in Damascus or Pretoria, it is frequently much easier to locate such information from Internet sources than from any other.

Internet news coverage is, with some exceptions, free, immediately accessible, and occasionally archived over extended periods. In addition to volume and recency, a major advantage of Internet news sources is that they are more likely to provide consistent coverage of events or issues arising in particular localities, and to follow them through in successive editions, than are hardcopy newspapers, or radio or television newscasts. Current news reports frequently have links to earlier information on the same topic, or other relevant topics covered by the same source. Following developments in countries or localities other than those that you are currently situated in is virtually impossible through national newspapers or other media, unless these are deemed to be particularly newsworthy. Events in western Poland, Slovakia and eastern Germany may be discussed at length when these lands are about to be submerged under floodwaters, but as soon as the waters subside news coverage of the area ebbs as well. Hardcopy, radio and television coverage, for economic reasons, is directed at audience attention, not consistent monitoring of information falling under particular headings. Although this is true also of Internet news sources to a degree, it is much less so. The economics and marketing of Internet news publishing are quite different from those of hardcopy newspapers, radio and television.

There are many issue areas covered extensively in Internet resources that are not as comprehensively covered in other media, or at all. Electronic newsletters and bulletin boards cover a wide range of subjects. Some fields are covered by so many of these and in such detail that the problem is less one of finding information than of keeping it at arm's length. Nonetheless, if your interests cover the latest shareware, daily law developments in California, the decisions of the Courts of Appeal in English-speaking jurisdictions, political issues in South Africa, and many others, somewhere on the Net you may very well find regularly updated information of relevance.

The resources referred to below should provide most users with an adequate enough baseline from which to track down news sources of potential interest. If you require sources of information relating to a particular country, locality or topic that do not feature in these links, use a search engine such as Alta Vista. If you require current news information about the Czech Republic try

<Czech AND (news*agency OR newspaper*)>

with Alta Vista advanced search. If you know the name of a hardcopy paper published in a particular locality, enter that, in double inverted commas if more than one word. This will usually bring up a link to the electronic version if it is available. Another strategy that usually works is to enter the name of the locality or country. This will frequently bring up links to pages that include hyperlinks to local news resources.

18.2   General electronic newspaper resources

You should probably bookmark more than one of the resources listed below, as even those with the most comprehensive compilations of links do not exhaust the field.

Asia Related News Site

<http://www.asiawww.com/misc/news.htm>

Links to a large number of news resources relating to countries in Asia. Separate sections on China, Indonesia, Japan, Korea, Malaysia, Nepal, Pakistan, Philippines, Singapore, Sri Lanka, and Turkey.

Ecola's Newsstand

<http://www.ecola.com/news/press/>

This Web page includes links to numerous newspapers, ordered by continent and then country. Select a country and you are presented with a list of online newspapers. Alternatively, you can use the search engine if you know the name of the publication. There is a separate section on magazines, arranged by major and minor topic areas – Art and Entertainment (Architecture/Design, Fashion, … Television/Radio), Business (Employment, Finance, … Transportation), … Travel. These can also be searched by country. A separate section takes in computer publications. This is a very comprehensive and reliable source that is invariably easy to access, and fast.

e.journal

<http://www.edoc.com/ejournal>

Part of the World Wide Web Virtual Library Project. It covers magazines, newspapers, academic and reviewed journals and email newsletters. The newspapers are arranged in alphabetical order in one long list.

Internet Newspapers

<http://www.voyager.co.nz/~vag118/news.html>

Links to online newspapers are arranged by continent and country in tabular form. The information is very well organized, although the number of newspapers included under each country entry is not as extensive as it is at some other sites. On the other hand, it does list some countries which others do not.

Mario's Cyberspace Station: Online News Worldwide

<http://mprofaca.cro.net/mainmenu.html>

This site is maintained by Mario Profaca, a Croatian journalist who also maintains an excellent page on war and war crimes, with particular emphasis on the conflict in Bosnia–Herzegovina. This page collates links to news arranged by country in alphabetical order. Accordingly, the links for each country cover other news media such as press agencies and television, as well as other WWW resources linked to that country. The pages are very well organized and in many instances extremely comprehensive, sometimes to the point of being overwhelming. The site does tend to be difficult to access at times due to its reliance on all the latest in animation, Java, and audio files. You may find it difficult to get back to a previous document through the use of the back button, and have to resort to the History list. As Mario is forever changing things around, the news section may have another URL by the time you access the above address. It will, however, be somewhere on the site.

My Virtual Newspaper

<http://www.refdesk.com/paper.html>

This site probably collates links to more sources of news on the Internet than does any other. The links are to all sources of news, not just newspapers. Newspaper links are arranged in a separate section, organized by continent, then, on separate pages, by country. The entries for the United States are arranged by state. The list for England includes, in addition to the main national newspapers online (*Financial Times*, *The Guardian*, *The Observer* and *The Times*), the *Chorley Citizen*, *Blackburn Citizen*, *Lancashire Evening News*, *Socialist Worker* and *South Bucks Star*. There are also links to press agencies and radio and television resources. A very comprehensive site that should fulfil the average user's needs more than adequately.

Web News Index

<http://207.87.128.102/cgi-bin/all.cgi>

This is a search engine/spider which links to current news articles from press agencies currently online (Reuters, Press Agency, Associated Press, etc.). It checks the news headlines, and links to the information every 15 minutes, so you cannot get more up-to-date on what is being reported by the major news agencies internationally than by accessing this resource. As the resource maintainers note: 'by allowing you to search multiple news providers at one point you can find out what everyone is reporting, not just the news service you happen to belong to or prefer. You will also be able to find alternate sources for your news. Finally you get access to more news than you would any other way.' To locate news information on a particular topic, enter a query in the search engine provided. The Web News Index is an extremely valuable resource for up-to-the-minute information on current events in all categories.

Yahoo News and Media

<http://www.yahoo.com/News/>

The compilation of links here is massive. Under the heading Full Coverage,

<http://headlines.yahoo.com/Full_Coverage/>

there are links to hundreds of files on issues featuring in the news on the day of access. There are links to other resources relating to the news item if these are available. For instance, on 7 February 1998, the main story was the impending confrontation between the US/UK axis and Iraq. In addition to reports from the major news agencies, the BBC, ABC and CNN, there were also links to UN Security Council resolutions, audio news reports, and to related Web sites, including Jane's World Iraq Armed Forces Analysis.

Primary newspapers are divided into two main subdivisions, Countries and United States. In the Countries section there were links to 1298 newspapers on 7 February 1998, whereas the United States page included links to 1394.

Some others

The Omnivore, <http://way.net/omnivore/>
The Virtual Daily News, <http://www.pilot.infi.net/~opfer/daily.htm>
World News Index, <http://www.stack.nl/~haroldkl/index.html>

18.3   Newspapers and agencies

In the list below I have excluded newspapers that are primarily oriented toward reporting on business and economic issues. For links to such resources, see Chapter 24 on economics resources.

Amnesty International News Releases

<http://www.amnesty.org/news/index.html>

Included here are the latest information/news briefings from the foremost international human rights organization. The archive of news releases extends back to July 1995. This is a valuable source of information for specialists in this field.

AfricaNews Online

<http://www.africanews.org/>

One-stop link to news sources on African affairs. Coverage is arranged by country, region and topic (Arts and Entertainment, Business and Finance, Science and Health, and Sports). There are also various background documents available with particular emphasis on United States/Africa relations. In addition to the regional and countrywide news coverage, news stories are available from the Panafrican News Agency. Using the search engine provided you can access their archives, dating from April 1997.

Greek News Agencies

<http://www.hri.org/news/greek/>

This is a Web presentation that is part of the Hellenic Resources Network. It provides links to various sources of information relating to Greece, including both newspapers and news agencies. Among the latter are the Macedonian Press Agency, Reuters and The Associated Press. Some of the materials are in English.

Kyodo News

<http://home.kyodo.co.jp/>

Kyodo News is a Japanese news agency that provides political and business news relating to Japan. In addition to the daily news summary, there is a weekly summary of the main news, Japan Weekly, which is archived from 15 March 1996.

Mexican News Archives

<http://lib.nmsu.edu/subject/bord/mxarch.html>

There are many links to current and archived news reports on Mexico, from both official and other sources. Extensive archives of news relating to EZLN and the Chiapis uprising are available.

Press Agency NewsCentre

<http://www.pa.press.net/news/>

Hourly updates of news from the London-based Press Agency. The reports tend to be rather short. You can also download an audio version, prepared three times a day. Headlines from the major English tabloids and broadsheets are also available.

Reuters News Summary via Yahoo

<http://www.yahoo.com/headlines/./news/summary.html>

This is a very good source for current news reports. The page that loads initially tends to focus on US affairs, but there are button links at the top and bottom to other categories. In addition to headline news, more detailed reports are available, as well as links to earlier and related stories. Reports are archived for a week.

RFE/RL Newsline on the Web

<http://www.rferl.org/newsline/index.html>

Radio Free Europe/Radio Liberty provides daily reports on developments in Eastern Europe, Russia, the Caucasus and Central Asia, drawing on some 600 correspondents and 19 broadcast services. News is divided into four main sections: Russia, Transcaucasia and Central Asia, Central and Eastern Europe, and Southeastern Europe. Archives are available from April 1997. Instead of accessing the reports on the Web you can subscribe to the daily reports through their mailing list. In the body of an email message type

<subscribe RFERL-L your first name your last name>

and send it to

<listserv@listserv.buffalo.edu>

The Christian Science Monitor

<http://www.csmonitor.com/>

The *Christian Science Monitor*, established in 1909, is a daily newspaper published from Monday to Friday inclusive. It also monitors radio programmes and newscasts broadcast in the US by stations affiliated with Public Radio International, as well as foreign short-wave broadcasts. Audio files can be downloaded. The newspaper, although published by a religious organization, is not a religious newspaper. It publishes only one article on a religious topic per day.

The CSM provides detailed analysis of US and international affairs. Coverage of US politics is extensive. In addition to the high quality of reporting for which the *Christian Science Monitor* is renowned, this site has links to its extensive archives which are available online. These extend back as far as 1980 and a search engine retrieves articles relating to queries rapidly. As far as I am aware, there is no freely available source of archived news going back that far anywhere else on the Internet. It covered the Balkan crisis in depth, and as of 4 August 1997 it had 3005 documents online linked to the query Bosnia, and 694 to Rwanda; "European Union" returned 3339 documents. The search engine supports Boolean searches and has a user-friendly help file linked to its page.

The Jerusalem Post

<http://www.jpost.com/>

Reports tend to focus primarily on Israeli internal and political affairs, as well as the wider geo-politics of the Middle East. The reports are not particularly detailed. They also tend to be slanted towards presentations of factual details and opinions that are clearly designed to legitimate whatever policies the Israeli authorities are pursuing in the context of the ongoing conflict with the Palestinian population.

Times Newspapers Ltd

<http://www.sunday-times.co.uk/>

This home page gives you access to *The Times*, the *Sunday Times*, the *Times Literary Supplement,* the *Times Educational Supplement*, and the *Times Higher Education Supplement*. The publishers claim to now provide in electronic format 'virtually the complete content of the printed editions', uploading more than 10,000 pages a month. If you have not registered before, you are required to do so. There is no fee. Once you have registered you can then proceed to access the publication of your choice. When you access the site subsequently, it is not necessary to go through the registration procedure again; just type in your user-id and password. Be sure to write this down somewhere so that you do not need to re-register.

The presentation of *The Times* is well organized and reports on various subjects are easily accessible. There is an index that lists all the reports in the current edition. In addition, news coverage is divided into a number of categories: Arts, British News, World News, Features, Opinion, Business, Court Page, Obituaries, Sport, and Weather. Back issues of the Internet edition are archived, covering all editions from January 1996. To access these you need to select *library*, which is just below the banner.

You can search in the current edition, browse previous editions of the *Sunday Times* or *The Times*, or search through the archives of all Times Newspapers since January 1996. You can restrict your search to a particular topic (e.g. Art or Finance) or to a particular newspaper. The electronic *Sunday Times* is produced along similar lines to its daily counterpart.

The Times Higher Education Supplement/Internet Supplement, unlike *The Times* and *Sunday Times*, does not provide full article coverage. The various sections, such as Home News and International News, provide only brief summaries of items that appear in the hardcopy edition, with the page numbers on which they appear. The Interview section, on the other hand, provides a full list of the occupational vacancy advertisements that appeared in the original edition, as well as archives of earlier editions. Subscribers to the printed edition can access the complete paper in electronic format.

The Sydney Morning Herald

<http://www.smh.com.au/>

Australian and world news, with particular emphasis on information relating to Asia and the Far East. Archives go back to April 1996.

Time Daily

<http://www.pathfinder.com/@@cASSDgcAHvMvlUma/time/daily/>

US and world news from *Time* magazine. The articles are linked to other reports from their archives. The archives are a valuable source of information on current affairs, and appear to go back at least one year. The search engine allows you to decide whether the search should be confined to *Time Daily*, or take in the whole stable of Pathfinder publications, which include *Time* magazine. In any event, the archives hold numerous articles on current issues of national and international concern. Searches will also retrieve access to documents as well as audio and graphic materials. The keyword Rabin returned 140 records in *Time Daily*, and 441 in Pathfinder publications, whereas for John Major the figures were 96 and 341, reflecting, no doubt, the significance of that 'special relationship'. Where appropriate, records returned include links to associated treaties, protocols, etc. There is so much material at this site that the problem is not one of tracking down materials, but of sifting through them without being overwhelmed.

Time Magazine

<http://www.pathfinder.com/@@YlXWUAcAJPNsPb32/time/magazine/index.html>

The Internet edition of the weekly current affairs magazine, probably the most widely read English magazine in the world. Although not the complete hardcopy version, it includes the more important features and articles. These tend to be reasonably informative and well researched and written. It is particularly good on American affairs, and its sports coverage is relatively comprehensive, although slanted towards a focus on the US, as it is in many other categories. Nonetheless, for an overview of important political and business stories breaking globally, this is a reasonably good resource. Materials are archived, for which see the commentary above under Time Daily.

United Nations News

<http://www.un.org/News/>

The United Nations News home page. Includes information about the daily meetings at the UN, previous daily journals, brief press summaries, press releases, and recent and past daily briefings.

USIA: Daily Washington File

<http://www.usia.gov/products/washfile.htm>

The home page of the United States Information Agency. The information provided is extensive. The Washington File includes US government official texts, policy statements and interpretive material, features, and byline articles prepared daily by the United States Information Agency. Contents are organized in a variety of ways. All new items are placed simultaneously in Latest Items in English for 48 hours, under at least one topical or geographical heading for two weeks and then in the archive section for permanent retention. A limited number of items in this section are translated into Spanish, French, Russian and Arabic.

Washington Post

<http://www.washingtonpost.com>

Daily coverage of US and international affairs, with primary emphasis on the former. There is an extensive volume of information included in the *Today's Paper* file. In addition, there are sections on politics, sports, business, editorials and opinions. You can also search the text of the past two weeks of the *Post*'s articles, for which there is no fee. The fee for earlier articles is either $2.95 or $1.50 depending on the time of day when you access them. The archives extend back to 1986.

18.4   Television and radio news

Below I list some sources of television and radio news. As far as television news is concerned, the information is in the form of text scripts of the news that was broadcast. For radio broadcasts there are frequently available both text and audio files. These may at times be quite large and take some time to download. To play these files your PC must have a sound card and have the appropriate plug-ins or applications, as audio files come in a variety of formats. For further information about plug-ins and helper applications, see Chapter 26.

ABC Audio News

<http://www.prognet.com/contentp/abc.html>

News is presented at 15 minutes past the hour. There are sound archives going back to the beginning of 1996 covering general news and sport.

BBC television and radio schedules

<http://www.bbc.co.uk/>

Radio and television schedules are provided for a nine-day period forward, including the day of access. There are also a few real audio files of the programme On the Record, being interviews with leading politicians, and considerably more text transcripts at

<http://www.bbc.co.uk/otr/frames/interviewsf.html>

The news available is presented under UK, World, Business, Sci/Tech, Sport, and Despatches. There is also a world summary in audio format. There is a lot of useful information on current events at this site and the graphics tend to be superior to those found at many other news sites. There do not appear to be any archives.

CNN Interactive

<http://cnn.com/>

Headline news from around the world. This is an excellent source for current news. The stories are sufficiently detailed, and there are links to related stories, as well as to relevant related sites. News from at least two days prior to the day of access is immediately accessible. In addition to text materials online there are also audio and video files that can be played online, or downloaded.

CNN holds extensive archives on its server that can be accessed through use of the search engine provided,

http://cnn.com/SEARCH/

The query <Iraq> yielded 1093 results on 7 February 1998. Results are ordered by date. Another excellent resource.

The MIT List of Radio Stations on the Internet

<http://wmbr.mit.edu/stations/list.html>

Provides links to radio stations worldwide, divided into US (and then by state), Canada, Australia, Europe, and Other International. On 7 February 1998 it listed more than 4000 stations available on the Net.

Voice of America Reports/Daily

<http://www.voa.gov/english/welcome.html>

Voice of America newscasts can be listened to in Real Audio, providing you have a sound card and the Real Audio plug-in or player, both of which are available at no cost. The newscasts are updated hourly. Also available are the World Report and VOA today. The text versions are available for the previous seven days at

<http://www.voa.gov/english/gopher.html>

VOA Internet Audio

<http://www.voa.gov/programs/audio/audio.html>

VOA audio files of selected newscasts from the previous three days are available in a variety of languages, including English, Chinese (Cantonese and Mandarin), Hindi, Farsi, Ukrainian, Russian, Korean, Czech and Slovak. You need to select the format most suitable for your computer platform and software.

CHAPTER 19

History resources

19.1	General history	201
19.2	Ancient history	206
19.3	Medieval history	208
19.4	Eighteenth century history	209
19.5	American history	209
19.6	Twentieth century history	212

The volume and range of history resources that are stored on Internet-linked servers has grown extensively over the past two years. A few sites are making available a substantial volume of digitized primary materials in specialist fields, particularly in ancient and medieval studies and twentieth century history. There is understandably a strong resource base relating to many facets of American history, particularly the Civil War. Documents and Web presentations relating to the First and Second World Wars are especially numerous.

19.1   General history

Index of Resources for Historians

<http://history.cc.ukans.edu/history/index.html>

Compiled at the University of Kansas, this is probably the most comprehensive listing of historical resources available on the Internet. Its extensiveness and variety can be gauged simply from its size, which on 22 February 1998 ran to 265 Kb and included 2500 connections. There are no annotations, just hyperlinks to the resources that are referenced. The listing, which its compilers do not claim is exhaustive, is arranged by subject and country. There are, however, too many resources that are referenced that are unlikely to be of interest to those searching for strictly 'historical' materials, such as the Rough Guide and the Comprehensive Weather Server.

Horus' Web Links to History Resources

<http://www.ucr.edu/h-gig/horuslinks.html>

Presented by the University of California, Riverside Department of History. This is another massive collation of links to history resources, better arranged, to my mind, than the Index of Resources for Historians described immediately above. It is a framed presentation. The collated links are organized under six sections: Histories of Specific Countries, Times and Places, Areas of History, On-Line Services About History, Web Tools, and an Alphabetical Listing of Link Collections. There are no annotations in this presentation.

History Learning Resources

<http://www.warwick.ac.uk/fac/arts/History/teaching>

There is a large volume of history resources accessible from this page, targeted principally on the requirements of those undertaking undergraduate history courses. They are arranged in three sections. The first focuses on *The French Revolution 1787–1789*, the second on *European History Since 1750*, whilst the third deals with a variety of subjects arranged under the heading *TLTP History Courseware Consortium*. The presentational modes are radically different despite the fact that they are all directed at the same category of student.

The *French Revolution 1787–1789* includes an essay by Professor Gwynne Lewis on *The People and the French Revolution*. There is also a chronology of events, a very useful glossary, and an extensive bibliography arranged by topic. I assume that these have also been made available by Professor Lewis, although this is not documented.

The *European History Since 1750* section provides online some primary texts related to a number of seminars that, presumably, are part of a module delivered at Warwick. The seminar topics include *European Imperialism, Japan, Marxism in Context* and *The Revolt Against Reason*.

By far the most sophisticated presentations appear in the third section. These presentations, which range over a variety of topics, including *The 18th Century English Town, Social Aspects of Industrialisation, Mass Politics and the Revolutions of 1848, Enfranchising Women* and *Major Themes in Women's History*, are all by-products of the Teaching and Learning Technology Programme which has been funded by the UK Higher Education Funding Councils. Each of the presentations is very detailed, providing links to resources referred to in the text, including bibliographies, statistical tables, maps, graphics, primary materials, chronologies, etc. There is a large volume of useful information included in these presentations. It would, however, have been more useful if the various tables, primary source materials, indexes, chronologies, etc., had been indexed adequately so that those who were not interested in reading an electronic book could access them more immediately.

Texts and Documents

<http://history.hanover.edu/texts.html>

Compiled by the Department of History of Hanover College, this listing references digital copies of primary texts and secondary sources covering all historical periods and geo-cultural regions. The primary goal of their Web presentation is to make primary texts available to students and faculties for use in classes.

Documents and resources cover economic, political, scientific, diplomatic, military, social and cultural developments, where available. The documents relating to the entry for Europe are divided by period into ancient (to 500 AD), medieval (500–1500), early modern (1500–1789) and modern (1789–). In the section on the Roman Republic there are links to the writings of Cicero, Julius Caesar, Polybius and Titus Lucretius. In the Greek History section there are links to the writings of Herodotus, Livy, Plutarch, Polybius, Thucydides and Xenophon.

There is a large volume of materials relating to European religious history, including pages on the Crusades, the Papacy, the Protestant Reformation and the Catholic Reformation. The Theology page compiles links to the writings of influential religious thinkers and activists, including Baxter, Boehme, Calvin, Fox, Pascal and Wesley. The pages on the Reformation include links to secondary resources as well as primary ones.

To summarize, there is a vast amount of information and links to primary and secondary resources collated at this site. Where the files are on external servers this is indicated. Although the resources are well organized, the time required to locate specified documents would be reduced considerably if a search engine were available. Moreover, although there are pages relating to Africa, the Middle East, and India and South Asia, there are few, if any resources, linked to these pages.

Historical Text Archive

<http://www.msstate.edu/Archives/History/index.html>

This archive is housed at Mississippi State University. It is an extensive collection of links to history resources arranged by region, topical history (African–American, Native American, Afrigeneas, genealogy, women, war, teaching, journals, and a residual general category), and resources (addresses, archives, directories, history servers, bibliographies, databases, departments, reviews, and photos and maps). Most of the resources are located on other servers.

The Oxford Text Archive

<http://sable.ox.ac.uk/ota/>

This archive currently holds about 2000 documents in electronic format and includes 'electronic versions of literary works by many major authors in Greek, Latin, English and a dozen or more other languages'. Obtaining access to these documents is not as simple as from some other sources, and you might be advised to check whether the text that you are interested in is available elsewhere. The coding associated with a book determines whether you can download it from an ftp site immediately, whether is only available to Oxford University students or if you need to complete a form and then send it to the archive. In some instances permission will have to be obtained from the copyright holder. In many instances you will have to pay charges for the materials.

EuroDocs

<http://library.byu.edu/~rdh/eurodocs/>

EuroDocs is subtitled 'Primary Historical Documents from Western Europe – Selected Transcriptions, Fascimiles and Translations'. This is a service provided by Brigham Young University. There are documents relating to Medieval and Renaissance Europe, to Europe as a Supernational Region and to specific countries.

History Reviews On-Line

<http://www.depauw.edu/~dtrinkle/hrol.html>

An electronic journal that reviews books in all fields of history, managed by an editorial board at Depauw University. It is issued three times a year. Back issues dating from 1995 can be accessed. The graphic takes some time to download so you might want to select *Current Issue* or *Past Issues* instead of waiting for this 3D effort.

The American Academy of Research Historians of Medieval Spain

<http://kuhttp.cc.ukans.edu/kansas/aarhms/mainpage.html>

Primary and secondary sources relating to the medieval history of the Iberian Peninsula. There are links to various bibliographies, to a listing of doctoral dissertations from Spanish universities post-1974, and to library catalogues (e.g. Institute of Medieval Mediterranean Spain, Biblioteca Nacional), as well as to some manuscripts and images.

Christian Classics Ethereal Library

<http://ccel.wheaton.edu/>

A large collection of classic Christian books in electronic format. The largest single compendium is the 38 volumes of *The Early Church Fathers*, being writings covering the first 800 years of the Church. It is divided into three series. Some portions, primarily of bibliographic significance, have been omitted from the electronic edition (prefaces, footnotes, indices). The volumes are available in a variety of formats, including many which have been subdivided into html files.

The other available texts are divided into fiction/non-fiction. The non-fiction section ranges widely over various religious or religious commentary texts. It includes writings of Aquinas, Augustine, Benedict, Bunyan, Calvin, Dante, Fox, Luther and Wesley. The fiction section is still small, but includes Chesterton, Dostoevsky and Tolstoy. This collection is being added to continuously.

History of Germany: Primary Documents

<http://library.byu.edu/~rdh/eurodocs/germany.html>

Compiled by Richard Hacken, Brigham Young University, and arranged by period, topic and names. It includes documents relating to the impact of the Germans on the end of the Classical world and materials on the early Germanic kingdoms, Frederick II and after, the Protestant Reformation, the Weimar Republic, fascism, the Second World War and the Holocaust.

Kaiserreich, 1817–1918

<http://h-net2.msu.edu/~german/gtext/nazi/>

Translations from the H-GERMAN mailing list. A somewhat mixed bag, including Bismarck's speech of 28 January 1886 concerning the Polish question, Hitler on antisemitism in Vienna, Hitler's first antisemitic writing, Wilhelm II's speech to new army recruits in 1891, and *Die Internationale* (1881). There is a separate section dealing with the Nazi period.

War, Peace and Security Guide

<http://www.cfcsc.dnd.ca/links/index.html>

Prepared by the Information Resource Center of the Canadian Forces College, this is an excellent collection of resources on military history. The resources are arranged by period (ancient, medieval, 1500–1700, 1700–1900, and 20th century), by subject (general, aviation, technology and weapons, naval history, and military museums and institutes) and in terms of wars arranged in chronological order. The links in all categories are comprehensive. The Military Museums and Institutes page is a compilation arranged by country of organizations with a military history component accessible over the Web. Information is available on contemporary conflicts, arranged by country.

Center of Military History

<http://www.army.mil/cmh-pg/>

A useful collection of official documents relating to the activities of the United States Army. In addition to resources relating to the world wars, there are files on the Korean War, the invasion of Panama, the Gulf War, the Spanish–American War, the War of Independence and the Civil War. There are also some bibliographies, those of the American War of Independence being particularly extensive. This is a very useful site that is making accessible a substantial volume of primary and secondary resources.

History Departments around the World

<http://chnm.gmu.edu/history/departments/research/depts.html>

Institute of Historical Research Bibliographies

<http://ihr.sas.ac.uk/cwis/aahcbib.html>

Bibliographies of works on history published in the UK each year. Those for 1993, 1994 and 1995 are currently available. Also available are bibliographies for 1994 covering books and articles published elsewhere in the world on UK and Irish history.

UK Historians

<http://ihr.sas.ac.uk/ihr/info3.html>

Information on UK historians from the Institute of Historical Research. Arranged alphabetically, by universities, by research interests, by teaching interests and by PhD supervision.

Historical Research for Higher Degrees in the UK

<http://ihr.sas.ac.uk/publications/link5.asc.html>

Compiled by the Institute of Historical Research. 'Work by nearly 3,000 students preparing for higher degrees on historical topics is listed under chronological and topographical headings in THESES IN PROGRESS issued annually and based on information received from all the universities of the United Kingdom. THESES COMPLETED describes over 500 historical theses completed and approved in the previous calendar year, with indexes of authors and subjects.'

19.2   Ancient history

Worlds of Late Antiquity

<http://ccat.sas.upenn.edu/jod/wola.html>

Collates resources relating to Augustine, Boethius, Cassiodorus, Erasmus, Gregory the Great and others. There is a short bibliography There are various texts of Augustine, including *Confessiones*, both the Latin and the English translation, *De musica* and *De dialectica,* and various essays and commentaries.

Late Antiquity in the Mediterranean

<http://www.unipissing.ca/department/history/orb/lt-atest.htm>

A guide to online resources produced by Professor S. Muhlberger. It includes a very extensive overview of late antiquity by Muhlberger, three essays by Hugh Elton on the Roman military, online bibliographies, teaching resources, historical atlas of late antiquity and links to centres for the study of late antiquity.

De Imperatoribus Romanis

<http://www.salve.edu/~dimaiom/impindex.html>

Short biographical essays of all the Roman emperors is the objective. The essays already written have been peer reviewed. Many of the biographies remain to be written.

Guide to Early Church Documents

<http://www.iclnet.org/pub/resources/christian-history.html>

Provided by ICLNet (Institute for Christian Leadership Net), categories include New Testament canonical information, writings of the apostolic fathers (e.g. first and second epistles of Clement to the Corinthians, the Shepherd of Hermas, the Martyrdom of Polycarp), patristic texts (e.g. the writings of Tetrullian, Cyprian and Augustine), Creeds and Canons, and later texts (the *Summa Theologiae* and Gregory of Nyassa).

The Anglo-Saxon Chronicle

<http://sunsite.berkeley.edu/OMACL/Anglo/>

This is the digitized version translated by the Revd James Ingram (London, 1823) with additional readings from the translation of Dr J.A. Giles (London, 1847). The text of this edition is based on that published as *The Anglo-Saxon Chronicle* (Everyman Press, London, 1912).

De re militari Information Server

<http://www.e-hawk.com/deremil/index.html>

This Web presentation focuses on classical and medieval military issues. The substantial volume of primary resources accessible via the home page include Sun Tzu's *On the Art of War, De Bello Gallico* by Julius Caesar, Herodotus' *History,* and the *History of the Peloponnesian Wars* by Thucydides. The subjects of the bibliographies include shipbuilding, the Roman army, Roman Lines, castles, the Crusades, the Knights of the Teutonic Order and others.

19.3 Medieval history

ORB

<http://orb.rhodes.edu/>

On-Line Text Materials for Medieval Studies is a cooperative project among medieval historians to provide online primary and other sources for medieval studies. The resources available are located on servers designated by the contributors, the ORB pages acting as an index, reference shelf, or library to facilitate ease of use by those wishing to access these resources.

The primary index is divided into early medieval (antecedents and then to 1000), high medieval (1000–1300), late Middle Ages (1300–1500) and religion and culture.

There is a significant volume of primary materials, including Dante's works, Old English literature, texts and translations, maps, and images of works of art. There is a collection of bibliographies, some of which are quite extensive, e.g. Albertus Magnus (53 Kb), Castles (270 Kb), Crusades (34 Kb), Order of St John of the Hospital (74 Kb), Roman History (101 Kb), etc.

This is an excellent site and there are pointers to many of the most important medieval resources on the Internet.

The Labyrinth

<http://www.georgetown.edu/labyrinth/labyrinth-home.html>

This site is sponsored by Georgetown University. The resources are organized by texts (Latin, Old English, Middle English, French, Italian, German and Spanish) and by subject areas. The subject areas include National Cultures (Anglo-Saxon, Germany, Iberia, Scandinavia), International Culture (Art and Architecture, Philosophy and Theology, Sciences, etc.) and Special Topics (including Arthurian Studies, Heraldry, and Medieval Women), pedagogical resources, online bibliographies from various hosts, discussion lists, electronic journals, and links to other online medieval resources.

The above is just a brief outline description. There are links to a very large volume of resources from this site, including electronic versions of many original texts, scholarly articles and bibliographies, dictionaries, current news on conferences, electronic forums, etc.

The Internet Medieval Sourcebook

<http://www.fordham.edu/halsall/sbook.html>

This is part of the ORB project. It aims to provide electronic texts useful for classroom work, which means that most of them are about three pages long. At the moment, the texts available focus on elite governmental, legal, religious and economic concerns.

The sourcebook is divided into two sections. The first consists of extracts from texts. The second consists of the full texts, or links to them. The sourcebook is compiled by Paul Halsall who relies extensively on P.J. Geary's *Readings in Medieval History* and Brian Tierney's *The Middle Ages, Volume I: Sources of Medieval History*. This is another excellent resource that is regularly augmented and well organized.

NetSERF

<http://www.cua.edu/www/hist/netserf/home.htm>

Sponsored by the Department of History at the Catholic University of America, this site provides a very extensive, well-organized and useful compilation of links to medieval resources on the Web. Resources available include articles, a list of associations and organizations, bibliographies, notices on conferences and seminars, teaching materials, a listing of discussion lists, newsgroups and journals.

19.4   Eighteenth century history

Eighteenth-Century Studies

<http://english-www.hss.cmu.edu/18th/>

This collection archives works of the eighteenth century from the perspectives of literary and cultural studies. Novels, plays, memoirs, treatises and poems of the period are kept here (in some cases, influential texts from before 1700 or after 1800 as well), along with modern criticism. The resources are arranged alphabetically.

Eighteenth-Century

<http://www.english.upenn.edu/~jlynch/18th/history.html>

Compiled by Jack Lynch, this is organized into sections on British history, American history and European history. A useful compilation of links to resources generally located elsewhere.

19.5   American history

American Memory

<http://rs6.loc.gov/ammem/ammemhome.html>

This is part of the American National Digital Library project. The objective is to digitize materials currently found in public and private library collections. Although still in its early phase, there are already a significant number of documents available online. With such a vast collection of different types of documents and images, locating required items, or establishing what is available, is likely to be a prime concern. Although the materials already online are well organized, locating particular items is not easy, and in many instances it was not clear whether the documents were currently in digital format, or whether this was just planned for the future.

Some of the categories under which the documents are collated are Afro-American Perspectives, The Evolution of the Conservation Movement, American Life Histories, Votes for Women, and Documents from the Continental Congress and the Constitutional Convention 1774–1789. There are a number of broadside collections as well.

Voices from the Dust Bowl

<http://lcweb2.loc.gov/ammem/afctshtml/tshome.html>

This is part of the *American Memory Web* series presented by the US Library of Congress. It focuses on 'documenting the everyday life of *Farm Security Administration* (FSA) migrant work camps in central California in 1940 and 1941'. The presentation puts online the ethnographic collection of Charles L. Todd and Robert Sonkin. Todd's interest was in the folk music and balladry, whereas Sonkin's passion was focused on linguistics and American speech formations. The collection consists of audio recordings, photographs, manuscript materials and 'ephemera generated during two separate documentation trips supported by the Archive of American Folk Song'.

There are 18 hours of audio materials available online, graphic images, field notes, recording logs and news clippings. There is also a brief historical overview of migrant camp experiences with links to materials in the collection which illustrate its substance.

This is an excellent Web project in terms of both content and presentation and demonstrates the way in which the Internet can make available to anyone resources that previously were accessible only to the professional historian, or the very dedicated and reasonably financially resourced non-professional.

Anti-Saloon League Home Page

<http://www.wpl.lib.oh.us:80/AntiSaloon>

Although as a pressure group the Anti-Saloon League's influence waned with the repeal of the 18th Amendment in 1933, it has had a lasting impact on American political and social culture. Without its crusading successes organized crime is unlikely to have evolved into the territorially based structures that wielded such substantial political influence on city, state and union politics in the four decades that followed repeal. This presentation provides an outline of its activities and influence, with links to associated resources, including some biographies of leaders of the movement, related organizations and a bibliography. Unfortunately, the bibliography omits some of the better social and sociological histories of the movement, including Andrew Sinclair's *Prohibition* and Joseph Gusfield's *Symbolic Crusade*.

Historical Documents

<http://www.law.uoknor.edu/ushist.html>

The University of Oklahoma Law Center provides access to a collection of American historical documents dating from the seventeenth century to the present. Among the oldest are the Virginia Charters, the Mayflower Compact and the Charter of Massachusetts Bay. The eighteenth century collection is much larger and includes a wide variety of documents, among which are the Articles of Confederation, the Declaration of Independence, the First State of the Union Address, the Fugitive Slave Act, the works of Benjamin Franklin and the papers of George Washington. In addition to the inaugural addresses of the Presidents, the nineteenth century collection includes a range of documents relating to the Civil War. Those of the twentieth century include the declarations of war and surrender documents with Germany and Japan, the North Atlantic Treaty, the Truman Doctrine, the Treaty on the Non-Proliferation of Nuclear Weapons and the Civil Rights Act of 1991. The collection is being added to regularly.

The Rare Map Collection of the Hargrett Library

<http://www.libs.uga.edu/darchive/hargrett/maps/maps.html>,

The University of Georgia has made available 20% of its library in digital form on the Web. The Library's collection extends to some 800 historical maps, including some of those produced by early cartographers such as Sebastian Munster and William Blaeu. Those available online are maps of the New World, Colonial America, Revolutionary America, the Civil War and Transportation. There are also historical maps of Georgia, including city maps and seaports on the Atlantic coast. The maps are quite large, generally between 150 and 500 Kb.

American Civil War Home Page

<http://sunsite.utk.edu/civil-war/>

This the main gateway to Civil War Internet resources. Its main subdivisions are general resources (timelines, overviews, etc.); the secession crisis and before; graphic images; letters, diaries and other documentary records; modern histories, FAQs and bibliographies; state/local studies; specific battles; rosters of combatants and regimental histories; miscellaneous military information; and links to other sites with information on the Civil War.

In nearly all sections there is a very extensive compilation of resources, including many primary sources in electronic format (Lincoln documents from Pierpont Morgan's Library, inaugural addresses of Lincoln and Davis, Gettysburg Address, Emancipation Proclamation, Constitution of the Confederate States of America). Personal documents include war letters and diaries, Ritland's *The Civil War History*, and narratives of the life of Frederick Douglas. As many of the files referenced are part of other Web presentations on the Civil War, this site should cross-reference to most available on the Web.

Causes of the Civil War

<http://members.aol.com/jfepperson/causes.html>

The aim of this site, managed by Jim Epperson, is to provide links to as many primary documents as possible relating to the period from the secession crisis to the end of the Civil War. With few exceptions, entire documents are available, although for especially long ones there are both full and short versions on offer. The document categories are party platforms, secession documents, state and local resolutions and correspondence, compromise proposals, political speeches, and correspondence and editorial commentary. This is a useful collection of primary documents.

Inaugural Addresses of the Presidents of the United States

<http://www.cc.columbia.edu/acis/bartleby/inaugural/index.html>

The Vietnam War History Page

<http://www.bev.net/computer/htmlhelp/vietnam.html>

The Vietnam War History Page focuses on the political and military conflicts over Vietnam, 1945–1975. It is a project of Dr Ron Nurse and students at Virginia Tech University. There are links to various resources available over the Web relating to the war, to Vietnam and the Vietnamese. Some of the resources do not fall, strictly speaking, into the category 'historical'. The opening page is very heavy on graphics and may take some time to download.

19.6   Twentieth century history

World War I Document Archive

<http://www.lib.byu.edu/~rdh/wwi/>

This is a useful and impressive collection of documents, treaties, articles, reports, commentaries and miscellany. Its aim is to put online an archive of primary documents relating to the First World War. Participants in the World War I Military History List (WWI-L) have undertaken the work.

It is divided into seven sections. The first, Conventions, Treaties, & Official Papers, provides access to important international instruments relating to the war, including the Hague Conventions, Treaty of London, Peace Treaty of Brest–Litovsk, Peace Treaty of Versailles, and the League of Nations Protocol for the Pacific Settlement of International Disputes. The Documents by Year section links to some of the more important papers, speeches and commentaries relating to the war or to an understanding of the historical background. The pre-1914 section includes the Triple Alliance Articles (in French, with an

English translation), the Schlieffen Plan, Hay's First Open Door Notes and reports on various crises and affairs. The post-1918 section includes the Versailles Treaty and the Bryce Report on alleged German atrocities.

This is an excellent resource. There is a very large collection of primary documents available, in addition to which there are bibliographies, biographies, memoirs, timelines, accounts of battles, articles on a variety of subjects and links to other sites. The only drawbacks relate to the difficulty of finding particular files due to the absence of a search engine and the fact that some files are placed in sections in which you would not ordinarily expect to find them.

The First World War Chronology

<http://www.earth.nwu.edu/people/tom/wwi.chron.html>

Detailed chronology based on official documents, from the outbreak of the war to the signing of the Treaty of Versailles.

Stone and Stone Second World War Books

<http://www.sonic.net/~bstone/bookinfo.html>

Provides very extensive bibliographical information on the Second World War with links to other sites. There are also some reviews of recent additions to the literature in this field. The bibliographical database contains thousands of listings and is probably the largest such database on the Web. The database can be searched by either author or title.

This is an important and useful bibliographic resource for those interested in printed materials on military matters. There are also some links to other sites dealing with military issues.

World War II Resources

<http://omni.cc.purdue.edu/~pha/master.html>

Undertaken by volunteers who have scanned in thousands of pages of documents, with a view to ensuring that perusing them will not be confined to librarians and scholars, this presentation includes many important documents relating to the antecedents of the war, as well as some relating to its course. They include the British War Blue Book, the French Yellow Book, Nazi–Soviet Relations (1938–1939), Pearl Harbor Attack Hearings, and many others.

World War II: A Selected List of References

<gopher://marvel.loc.gov:70/00/.ftppub/reference.guides/WWII.bib>

Compiled by Jon Simon and Albert E. Smith of the Library of Congress. They note that in 1992 the Library of Congress computer catalogue included 50,000 works on the subject.

'We have identified the most useful reference tools – bibliographies, dictionaries, chronologies, histories, and documentary sources – in the Library of Congress that pertain to the war and United States involvement. However, this bibliography is not intended to be comprehensive. Although it was prepared using the Library's collections, we have selected titles with an eye toward availability. Almost all the reference sources are in English and have been published or reprinted within the last ten years.' (Dated 1992)

World War II Timeline

<http://ac.acusd.edu/History/WW2Timeline/start.html>

Created by the Department of History at the University of South Dakota, this timeline is chronologically and then topic based. Because it is a mixture of the two (you choose a year, and then a topic), it does not give an overall chronological picture of the war. In addition, some of the chronologies are too schematic. Nonetheless, there are some useful topic-based chronologies, including Hitler and the Final Solution, Nazi Concentration Camps 1933–1945, Barbarossa, the Atomic Bomb and the Destruction of Japan, and the Spanish Civil War.

United States Strategic Bombing Survey: Summary Report (Pacific), July 1946

<http://www.anesi.com/ussbs01.htm>

'The United States Strategic Bombing Survey was established by the Secretary of War on 3 November 1944, pursuant to a directive from the late President Roosevelt. It was established for the purpose of conducting an impartial and expert study of the effects of our aerial attack on Germany, to be used in connection with air attacks on Japan and to establish a basis for evaluating air power as an instrument of military strategy, for planning the future development of the United States armed forces, and for determining future economic policies with respect to the national defense. A summary report and some 200 supporting reports containing the findings of the Survey in Germany have been published. On 15 August 1945, President Truman requested the Survey to conduct a similar study of the effects of all types of air attack in the war against Japan.'

Imperial Japanese Navy Page

<http://www.skypoint.com/members/jbp/kaigun.htm>

This is one of the best Web presentations on the Second World War. Compiled by naval historian Allyn Nevitt, it provides an extensive volume of information on various aspects relating to the naval war in the Pacific. The presentation is also very well designed, with either hypertext or image map links to the battles. There are articles written by others on particular battles, comparisons of the military armamentarium of the United States and Japanese navies, and very detailed information on various classes of naval vessels. The presentation is a model of what a value-added hypertext presentation can and should be.

U-Web: The U-boat War 1939–1945

<http://rvik.ismennt.is/~gummihe/uboats/u-boats.htm>

This is an excellent presentation compiled by Guamondur Helgason on submarine warfare, albeit focusing exclusively on the German fleet. Its two primary sections are on the boats and the men. The U-boat Index provides information on all 1154 German submarines, plus 14 foreign-built submarines that were pressed into action. The presentation provides tabulated information on every one of these vessels, including details of when commissioned, type, patrol history, tonnage sank, commander, and fate. Technical and other information is provided about each submarine type. Another section gives biographical details of submarine commanders, 54 as of 21 April 1997. There is a glossary of terms and a bibliography of books in English and German.

The presentation is very well organized and referenced, although some historians may baulk at the suggestion that German U-boats fought hard but fair considering the situation, and at the suggestion that Dönitz shouldered no responsibility for warfare waged by the Third Reich, at sea or elewhere.

Atomic Bomb: Decision

<http://www.peak.org/~danneng/decision/decision.html>

Lists documents relating to the decision to employ atomic weapons in the war in the Pacific. These include the Minutes of the Target Committee, the Franck Report, which recommended that the weapon be demonstrated in the desert or on an uninhabited island, various petitions, eyewitness accounts, the official bombing order, and excerpts from Truman's radio broadcast.

CHAPTER 20

Human rights resources

20.1	Introduction	217
20.2	Treaties, declarations and other instruments	218
20.3	General resource sites	218
20.4	Human rights in particular countries	219
20.5	The United Nations and human rights	222

20.1   Introduction

The Internet provides a large volume of data likely to be of interest to those with a concern for human rights related issues, whether academic or activist. Amnesty International is one among a few organizations that are using the Internet as another means of developing awareness of human rights issues and extending the numbers supporting the various campaigns it promotes. Many individuals use the Internet as a means of promoting support for specific causes or for safeguarding the human rights of particular individuals.

There is a large volume of primary materials available on the Internet. It is no longer necessary to enter a library or open a book in order to access any international legislative instruments on human rights. They can all be downloaded from numerous Internet-linked sites. Many international reports relating to human rights are available online, as are reports of United Nations human rights rapporteurs. The decisions of United Nations human rights organs, of judicial tribunals and of commissions of inquiry are also stored on publicly accessible Internet-linked servers. It is also probably a lot easier to find out what is on the international human rights agenda from Internet sources than it is from printed materials.

20.2   Treaties, declarations and other instruments

It is possible to find at a number of different sites many of the major international conventions and declarations relating to human rights. Many sites that focus on the compilation of lists of law resources include links to servers from which these can be downloaded. Below is a listing of some sites that include links to the various international conventions, proclamations and declarations of primary importance.

- Amnesty International Human Rights Standards

    <http://www.ncf.carleton.ca/freeport/social.services/amnesty/menu>

- The US House of Representatives Internet Law Library Civil Liberties and Civil Rights: General

    <http://law.house.gov/93.htm>

- The US House of Representatives Internet Law Library Treaties and International Law

    <http://law.house.gov/89.htm>

- Multilaterals Project at the Fletcher School of Law and Diplomacy

    <http://www.tufts.edu/departments/fletcher/multi/humanRights.html>

20.3   General resource sites

There are a number of sites that provide an extensive compilation of links to human rights resources. Many of these also have numerous documents stored on their servers.

University of Minnesota Human Rights Library

<http://www.umn.edu/humanrts/links/alphalinks.html>

This site probably has the most comprehensive and systematically arranged set of links to human rights resources on the Internet. When I last printed out the list of resources in November 1997 it filled 15 single-spaced A4 pages. Anyone in search of human rights related materials would most probably find something useful included in this extensive listing of resources.

Although comprehensive, bordering on the exhaustive, the list is not annotated. It is not always easy, therefore, to gauge the quality of the resources that are referenced. There has been a tendency on the part of the compilers to reference all agencies in a particular organization, whether or not they are likely to store on their servers relevant human rights information. Thus, all UN organs are referenced regardless of whether they have a primary interest in human rights related issues.

Human Rights Web

<http://www.hrweb.org/>

The Human Rights Web includes some useful, albeit brief, introductory materials for those new to human rights issues. In addition to *An Introduction to the Human Rights Movement* (which does not say very much), there is a document named *A Short History of the Human Rights Movement* and links to major UN treaties on human rights. There is also a useful summary of some of the main provisions of the most important of these.

The list of human rights related resources at this site is much smaller than on the University of Minnesota human rights Web pages. They are organized under a manageable number of headings, including newsgroups and mailing lists. There are also links to the most important international human rights NGOs as well as some of the most useful human rights Web presentations.

Martin Hogan's Human Rights Page

<http://www.intac.com/PubService/human_rights/>

Hogan references a wide range of resources relating to human rights and related issues, although these are not very systematically ordered.

20.4   Human rights in particular countries

There is a significant amount of information on human rights in particular countries that can be accessed from Internet-linked servers. Some of this has been specifically compiled to illustrate human rights issues in a specific region or country, whereas other materials are available as a by-product of other considerations, particularly news gathering.

US State Department Country Human Rights Reports

<http://www.state.gov/www/global/human_rights/hrp_reports_mainhp.html>

<http://www.state.gov/www/global/human_rights/1997_hrp_report/97hrp_report_toc.html>

The first URL includes links to reports from 1993 to 1997, inclusive. The second has links to the 1997 reports. My experience has been that these reports are regularly moved to different directories or servers. If you cannot locate them using the above URLs you should have little difficulty tracking them with the assistance of a search engine.

These reports are one of the most useful sources of information on human rights practices in various parts of the world. Published annually by the United States Department of State, they describe in considerable detail human rights practices in most member states of the UN. The origin of these reports lies in the linking of financial assistance provided by the US to other countries to their human rights record.

Some of the countries with very poor human rights records are among the closest allies of the United States, including Israel, Saudi Arabia and Kuwait. It might be suspected, therefore, that these reports would not be very factual. However, a reading of the reports relating to the countries mentioned indicates no lack of willingness to critically review their human rights practices. Detailed information on the methods that have been employed in the collection of data used to compile the reports is provided. The above comments should not be construed as indicating that the reports are in some absolute sense reliable and objective.

Country Area Study Books

<http://lcweb2.loc.gov/frd/cs/cshome.html>

Strictly speaking this is not a human rights resource. The books included in this series have been prepared by the Federal Research Division of the Library of Congress and have been sponsored by the United States Department of the Army. Each book provides extensive information on a particular country. At the time of writing (17 February 1998), the series contained 85 studies.

> 'Most books in the series deal with a particular foreign country, describing and analyzing its political, economic, social, and national security systems and institutions, and examining the interrelationships of those systems and the ways they are shaped by cultural factors.
>
> A multidisciplinary team of social scientists writes each study. The authors seek to provide a basic understanding of the observed society, striving for a dynamic rather than a static portrayal. Particular attention is devoted to the people who make up the society, their origins, dominant beliefs and values, their common interests and the issues on which they are divided, the nature and extent of their involvement with national institutions, and their attitudes toward each other and toward their social system and political order.'

As these works include detailed information about particular countries, they are quite useful for placing human rights policies in a broader social, political, economic and historical context. The country area study on Israel, for instance, includes useful information relating to the 1982 invasion of Lebanon and the subsequent massacres that occurred in the Sabra and Shattila camps, as well as the uprising in the occupied territories known as the Intifada. For those not familiar with the history of the country, its division into ethnic groups, the military situation, etc., this is a useful online guide. Similarly, the study on El Salvador provides detailed information relating to the civil conflict, the guerrilla movement and human rights related issues.

US Department of Justice Reports

<http://www.umn.edu/humanrts/ins/inservie.htm>

More limited in scope than the two previous resources, these reports are written by the United States Department of Justice Immigration and Naturalization Service Asylum Resource Information Center. They are drawn up to provide information on certain countries because of the potential implications of the human rights situation in them on the seeking of asylum in the United States. The conflict in the former Yugoslavia during the first half of the 1990s, for instance, led to the displacement of some two million persons. The countries reported on include Somalia, Sudan, Turkmenistan, Bulgaria, Liberia, Russia and Haiti. Some of the reports are quite lengthy. The one on Peru, for instance, is 498 Kb.

Amnesty International Publications: AI External Country Reports

<http://www.amnesty.org/ailib/aipub/index.html>

The reports are arranged by year and by continent. There are a large number of reports on particular themes (e.g. the death penalty, children and women) as well as on human rights issues relating to particular countries. There are also files of AI's submissions to various UN committees on particular subjects. Amnesty International has a well-deserved reputation for wide-ranging research into human rights violations worldwide. Their extensive network of investigators and contacts gives the organizations virtually unrivalled access to data on human rights issues in most countries. The reports that are available at this site provide an extensive volume of data on some general human rights issues, as well as on human rights conditions in particular countries and on some specific topics, such as the death penalty and the human rights situations of women and children.

Amnesty International annual reports should also be consulted. The URL for 1997 is

<http://www.amnesty.org/ailib/aireport/ar97/index.html>

For earlier annual reports substitute the appropriate digit for 7 in this URL. The report is available in Italian and Swedish as well as English.

Derechos: Human Rights Around the World

<http://www.derechos.org/human-rights/world.html>

Derechos means rights in Spanish. This site provides excellent resources on human rights, arranged by region. The resources are more extensive for some countries than for others. On some territories, however, they are excellent. A very good example is the presentation on Human Rights in Israel, the Occupied Territories and the Palestinian Authority,

<http://www.derechos.org/human-rights/mena/iot.html>

Human Rights Watch Reports

<http://www.drugtext.nl/hrw/research/nations.html>

This is the URL for the main index. The reports are arranged by country. Some of the reports, particularly those for later years, have extensive summaries, or include the introduction and recommendations.

20.5   The United Nations and human rights

United Nations bodies produce a veritable mountain of documents that touch to some degree upon human rights related issues. Whether the substantive topics are economic development, population monitoring and control, food and agriculture, education and science, children, peace keeping, or specifically human rights, many United Nations organs report on topics, sponsor activities and investigations and promote policies that have a bearing on human rights issues in specific contexts. All of this is documented at some length and an increasing amount of the associated hardcopy paperwork is being made available in electronic format. It is likely that in the immediate future the extent of electronically accessible documentation will increase substantially.

United Nations home page

<http://www.un.org>

From the United Nations home page there is a direct link to that part of the UN presentation dealing with human rights, which I will detail below. There is also general information about the UN, its proceedings, organizational structure, membership, etc., all of which can be accessed from the link About the UN. This document links to information about the principal organs of the UN, to documents such as the UN Charter, the Universal Declaration of Human Rights, and data on the history of the United Nations.

The link to UN Databases provides access to a large number of documents in certain areas. Refworld includes hundreds of documents developed by the UNHCR Centre for Documentation and Research. This is subdivided into legal information, country information, maps, news, searches and indexes, and UNHCR information. ReliefWeb provides information on humanitarian relief efforts of the United Nations and other organizations and includes archived materials. There is also a database of United Nations treaties.

The section on UN Documents includes a United Nations: Documentation Research Guide 'designed for researchers and information professionals new to United Nations documentation. It provides an overview of the various types of documents and publications issued by the Organization (e.g. reports, resolutions, meeting records, sales publications, press releases) and gives guidance as to where to find them in either electronic or paper format and how to work with them. More in-depth coverage is available in United Nations documentation: a brief guide, published in six languages.'

UNHCR (United Nations High Commission for Refugees)

<http://www.unicc.org/unhcr/>

The home page of the United Nations High Commission for Refugees links to a substantial and varied collection of documents focusing on national, regional and international refugee issues and situations. These documents explain the role of the UNHCR, the criteria for deciding who refugees are and the relevant international instruments, as well as providing broad statistical information on the number of refugees worldwide. Details concerning the refugee situation in particular countries can be gleaned from The World Country Index.

In addition to reports, of which there are a large number that are best retrieved by using the search engine, there are documents that provide up-to-date news on world, regional and country-specific issues. There are also articles dealing with refugee issues that have appeared in periodical publications of the UNHCR. Under the heading News there is a link to Briefing Notes that are released twice a week, Repatriation Information Reports, Press Releases, and information on Recent Publications. Also of some interest is a collection of articles listed on the ISSUES page that appeared in UNHCR publications, including the magazine *Refugees*. These range over historical and contemporary issues relating to the problems and regulation of refugee crises in various parts of the world.

OHCHR (Office of the High Commissioner for Human Rights)

<http://www.unhchr.ch/>

This is the focal point of United Nations online materials and information relating to human rights issues. A good starting point is the Organizational Structure link,

<http://www.unhchr.ch/hrostr.htm>

which provides an organizational chart of the various United Nations organs and agencies with responsibilities in the field of human rights. There is an image map showing the component parts and the relations between them. This should prove useful for those wanting to obtain a basic understanding of the rather complex United Nations human rights regulatory apparatus. If you select part of the map representing a particular body or agency, a file is downloaded which provides basic information about it, including its responsibilities in the field of human rights. This is also a useful entry point to finding documents relating to the activities of sub-committees and commissions, such as the Sub-Commission on the Prevention of Discrimination and the Protection of Minorities, and the Commission on the Status of Women.

There is also a detailed listing of the programmes that the OHCHR is engaged in, a chronology of events, links to information about particular human rights issues (minorities, indigenous peoples, racism and racial discrimination, etc.) which links to documentation, international human rights legislation, and the like. There is a separate section on treaties that provides online access to all the United Nations treaties concerned with human rights and related issues, as well as the various Geneva conventions dealing with armed conflicts.

The file entitled Documents,

<http://www.unhchr.ch/html/otherdoc.htm>

links to United Nations human rights documents arranged by originating body: the General Assembly, Economic and Social Council, Commission on Human Rights, and Sub-Commission on the Prevention of Discrimination and the Protection of Minorities. These link to lists of files embracing resolutions and decisions of these organs. There is an extensive amount of information relating to human rights issues from these pages. However, you should use the search engine as well, as there are many that deal with human rights related issues that do not appear to be linked to from these pages. As the United Nations presentation is so vast, the information that you obtain tends to vary according to the path that you take through it.

There is, of course, considerably more human rights material available on the Internet under each of the above headings than I have been able to record here. There are also many other headings that I have not touched upon. More information can be found on the Web pages that I edit,

<http://www.uwe.ac.uk/facults/ess/htm/docs/hrtsres.htm>

by following up the links listed above, and by using a search engine.

CHAPTER 21

Philosophy, sociology and psychology

21.1	Introduction	225
21.2	General resource sites	226
21.3	Journals	230
21.4	Mailing lists	234
21.5	Miscellaneous	234
21.6	Subject areas	235
21.7	Texts, bibliographies and thinkers	238

21.1   Introduction

I have included in this chapter an annotated listing of resources that many other social scientists would classify under the separate headings of philosophy, critical theory, cultural theory, political philosophy, sociology and sociological theory, and psychology. My reasons are largely pragmatic. The Web resources in some of these subject areas are not yet plentiful. Various reasons can be advanced to account for this but here is not the place to analyse this question. Let me illustrate briefly with reference to sociology and psychology. Although there are many resources on the Web that are relevant to sociologists, there are few that would meet Durkheim's strictures of sociological *sui generis*. Sociology is largely a twentieth-century discipline whose intellectual artefacts are covered by copyright laws. In addition, with the exception of left-leaning sociologists, and there appear to be few of them putting their heads above the parapets these days, there have not been many who have enthusiastically embraced electronic communication platforms. Thus, even those nineteenth-century masterpieces that are not covered by copyright laws have not found a pathway through the scanner or word processor on to the Web.

As for psychology, much the same appears to apply. In many subdiscipline areas the corpus consists of thousands of experimental findings woven together occasionally through many loosely articulated theoretical frameworks. There are some areas, generally at the more conceptual end of the continuum, at the philosophy/psychology interface, where there is an interesting body of work available on the Web, particularly in relation to issues surrounding body, mind and consciousness. This does not mean, of course, that there are not a large number of links that you will come across if you resort to the search engine. I have, however, refrained from referencing files or Web presentations that appear to include very little of substance. A number of Web pages, for example, include links to Sigmund Freud and the *Freud Archives* at

<http://plaza.interport.net/nypsan/freudarc.html>

often accompanied by lavish praise. There is, however, little information of much use there, certainly not in relation to the voluminous printed biographies available in virtually every academic library or the corpus of his writings. Another equally good example is PREP – the Psychology Preprint Server at

<http://www.ccsnet.com/prep/>

While the idea is excellent, few preprints are currently archived. I have tried to refrain from referencing resources that I think most social scientists will not find very useful.

I have not included references to individual thinkers largely, but not solely, for reasons of space. You will be able to link to such resources readily enough through the sites mentioned in the next section or by using a search engine.

21.2   General resource sites

Many of the sites listed in this section provide information on mailing lists, newsgroups, electronic texts, thinkers, associations and departments specializing in philosophy, sociology or psychology.

Bjorn's Guide to Philosophy

<http://www.knuten.liu.se/~bjoch509>

Considered by many other compilers of philosophy resources to be qualitatively one of the best. It provides, however, access to only a limited volume of resources. Arranged around philosophers, 27 at present, there is a short biographical entry, a listing of major works and links to other sites. There are also resource entries under journals, mailing lists and philosophy departments.

Chad Hansen's Home Page

<http://hkusuc.hku.hk/philodep/ch/>

Chad Hansen is Professor of Philosophy at the University of Hong Kong; his primary interests are Chinese philosophy and classical Chinese theories of language and mind. There are a few articles of an introductory nature that may be of some interest to those seeking a brief and coherent introduction to aspects of Chinese classical philosophy.

CTI Centre for Psychology

<http://www.york.ac.uk/inst/ctipsych/web/MainMenu.html>

Very few resources listed here other than links to other departments, a directory of CTI software, notices of open days and workshops and links to other CTI centres, where, for the most part, you will find a similar dearth of major activity.

Cultural Studies and Critical Theory

<http://eng.hss.cmu.edu/theory/>

'Cultural Studies draws from the fields of anthropology, sociology, gender studies, feminism, literary criticism, history and psychoanalysis in order to discuss contemporary texts and cultural practices.'

This page, from the renowned English Server at Carnegie Mellon, provides a substantial number of links to resources in this field, including electronic journals, newsgroup and other resource pages. A useful entry point.

Dead Sociologists Index

<http://diogenes.baylor.edu/WWWproviders/Larry_Ridener/DSS/INDEX.HTML>

Presented by Larry Ridener of Baylor College, this provides basic information on central sociological thinkers. Those currently included are Comte, Martineua, Marx, Spencer, Durkheim, Simmel, Veblen, Addams, Cooley, Park, Mead, Thomas, Dubois, Pareto and Sorokin. The information relating to each scholar is divided into three sections: the person, which consists primarily of personal and intellectual biographical information; a summary of ideas; and the original work. The main problem with the presentation is that the middle section, the summary of ideas, consists of lengthy sections from Lewis Coser's work of 1977. The final section, the original work, which comprises links to primary source materials, is rather skimpy.

Guide to Philosophy on the Internet

<http://www.earlham.edu/suber/philinks.htm>

Prepared by Peter Suber, Philosophy Department, Earlham College, this is a very extensive listing of resources which is available in one large file. Those that are considered by the compiler to be particularly useful are starred. The annotations, if any, are very brief. To give you some idea of the number of entries, under the heading of Philosophers and Philosophies there were 196, none of which were starred (16 March 1998). Of course this list includes the names of many that would be claimed by sociological theorists (Adorno, Foucault, Marx, Derrida, etc.). Other major headings include guides, journals, etexts, mailing lists and bibliographies. I would recommend this site as the first port of call. If you cannot find a philosophy resource through the network of links originating here, it may not be available.

Humanities Hub

<http://www.gu.edu.au/cgi-bin/g-code?/gwis/hub/qa/hub.home.html>

Managed by the Faculty of Arts, Griffiths University, Australia, this is a large and well-organized compilation of annotated links to resources in the humanities and social sciences. The subject areas covered likely to be of primary interest to social scientists are cultural studies, European studies, gender studies, government and governments, history, philosophy, political economy, research sociology and women.

Infomine

<http://lib-www.ucr.edu/rivera/>

Social science, humanities and general reference resources from the University of California. The compilation is arranged alphabetically by subject. The annotations are limited. The total number of entries is extremely large and somewhat overwhelming, although the number under the headings of discipline areas referenced in this chapter, sociology and psychology for instance, was small. There is a search engine.

Internet Crossroads in the Social Sciences

<http://dpls.dacc.wisc.edu/internet-table.html>

Maintained as part of the Data Program Library Service of the University of Wisconsin, this is divided into two main sections. Information Services refers to social science gateways, subject guides, home pages of data producers, and textual resources. Data Services refers to Web sites that provide access to numeric data via the Internet, or provide descriptive information about a particular dataset. Information and data resources are available under seven subject categories: General, Economic/Labor, Education, Geographic/Historical, Health, Political, and Sociological/Demographic. These are further subdivided into US Government and Non-Government, and International Government and Non-Government. Although some of the resources are quite useful, a few of course being widely known and used, the volume of resources annotated or linked to is small.

Philosophy in Cyberspace

<http://www.monash.edu.au/~dey/phil/home.htm>

This is an extensive annotated guide to philosophy resources available on the Internet.

Psychology Web Archive

<http://swix.ch/clan/ks/CPSP1.htm>

This is a compilation of links to Internet resources on some psychology subdisciplines. It does not include materials dealing with parapsychology, artificial intelligence, psychophysiology, neurosciences and psychobiological themes. It does include materials relating to environmental, ecological, health and community issues, and those classified under social psychology, social cognition, persuasion, psychology of attitudes, psychoanalysis, psychotherapy and clinical psychology.

A significant number of the resources, particularly those pointing to papers, are located in Germany, Austria and Switzerland. The number of online articles in English that fall within the mainstream of social psychology discourse is very limited.

SocioSite

<http://www.pscw.uva.nl/sociosite/>

This is a Dutch site that links to sociological resources. The headings include sociologists, sociology departments, sociology courses, associations, mailing lists and newsletters. However, there is not much of substance that the various links lead to, reflecting the rather paltry volume of online sociological resources available. The Sociologists page (Dead and Very Much Alive) provides links to excerpts from the writings of a significant number of prominent sociologists. Unfortunately, these constitute to all intents and purposes, random selections of a few pages here and there, likely to give rise to frustration more than anything else. Similarly, the journals page is not confined to online journals.

SocioWeb

<http://www.socioweb.com/~markbl/socioweb/>

Similar in many respects to SocioSite.

Stanford Encyclopedia of Philosophy

<http://plato.stanford.edu/contents.html>

This is an excellent resource in the making under the editorial guidance of Edward N. Zalta. The entries are well written and authoritative. Although, as yet, there are not many available, these few are worth consulting. Look, for instance, at those for Hegel and

Kierkegaard. There are, of course, extensive bibliographical references where appropriate. Information pertaining to particular entries will be modified in the light of new scholarship.

University of Chicago Philosophy Project

<**http://csmaclab-www.uchicago.edu/philosophyProject/philos.html**>

Offers a number of forums for discussion of philosophical issues. Designed primarily for the university's student/staff body, the quality and scope of the papers should be of interest to a wider audience. Each discussion forum includes some lengthy papers and sequential commentaries. Participation is at the discretion of the moderator.

Voice of the Shuttle Philosophy Page

<**http://humanitas.ucsb.edu/shuttle/philo.html**>

This is a very large listing of resources compiled by Alan Liu at the University of California, Santa Barbara. Resources are classified by subject area, those most likely to be found useful by social scientists being arranged under General Humanities Resources, Anthropology, Area and Regional Studies, Cultural Studies, History, Philosophy and Women's Studies, Gender Studies, and Queer Theory.

21.3 Journals

The Electronic Journal of Analytic Philosophy

<**http://tarski.phil.indiana.edu/ejap/**>

Published by the Philosophy Department at Indiana University, which has been publishing online since 1993. The articles are available for downloading in hypertext, .txt and .pdf format. The spring 1996 issue focused on Existential Phenomenology and Cognitive Science.

CTHEORY

<**http://www.ctheory.com/**>

This is 'an international journal of theory, technology and culture. Articles, interviews, and key book reviews in contemporary discourse are published weekly as well as theorisations of major "event-scenes" in the mediascape.' This electronic journal appears to be a major outlet for Jean Baudrillard's online contributions, his having authored 10 of the 42 articles published to date.

Electronic Journal of Sociology

<http://www.sociology.org/>

Online since 1995, this journal is peer reviewed and published three times a year. Topics discussed in the 1997 issues included Hate on the Net, Researching Serial Murder, and Rereading Lyotard.

Electronic Journals in Psychology

<http://www.cycor.ca/Psych/jours.htm>

A listing of journals in psychology, which should be interpreted to mean journals with at least some psychology content, however limited. The list is very lengthy (129 Kb). It does have the merit of specifying whether the journal articles are online and whether abstracts and/or tables of contents are provided.

Ends and Means

<http://www.abdn.ac.uk/~phl002/techno.htm>

A newsletter issued twice a year, April and October, by the University of Aberdeen's Centre for Philosophy, Technology and Society. Currently there are online articles on the philosophy of science and the philosophy of mind, and one on the implications of the Internet.

Ex-Nihilo

<http://uts.cc.utexas.edu/~bbarnes/Contents.html>

An online journal produced by undergraduate students at the University of Texas at Austin:

'Material ranges from analytic to continental philosophy, from the religious to the scientific. Submissions covered the spectrum from essays to poetry. Plato wrote dialogues, Sartre plays, Camus novels, and Parmenides poetry.'

Mind and Behavior

<http://kramer.ume.maine.edu/~jmb/welcome.html>

An interdisciplinary journal devoted to exploring the relations between mind and behaviour. All abstracts of journal articles since the first issue in 1980 are online.

Psyche

<http://psyche.cs.monash.edu.au/>

A site maintained by Patrick Wilken at Monash University, Australia, this features access to the journal *Psyche* and the mailing list PSYCHE-D. The journal is concerned with the interdisciplinary exploration of the nature of consciousness and its relation to the brain. Disciplines of primary relevance are cognitive science, philosophy, psychology, artificial intelligence, physics and nueroscience. Published by MIT Press. Volume 2 includes symposia on Implicit Learning, Quantum Theory and Consciousness, Synethesia, and Roger Penrose's *Shadows of the Mind*. The first volume's symposium was on Contrastive Analysis.

The mailing list PSYCHE-D is a focus for the discussion of issues relating to consciousness. The archives are accessible from this location and there are instructions for subscribing.

Psycholoquy

<http://www.cogsci.soton.ac.uk/psycholoquy>

This is a peer-reviewed electronic journal, sponsored by the American Psychological Association. It publishes articles and commentary relating to cognitive science, neuroscience, behavioural biology, artificial intelligence, linguistics and philosophy. The search engine can be used to query by subject, author and date. Archived for the years 1990–1996, it is widely considered to be one of the most useful and prestigious online sources of current information and commentary on the subjects that fall within its frame of reference. It also publishes multiple reviews of books.

There is a *Psycholoquy* mailing list in which all the communications are included. To subscribe, send an email to listserv@pucc.bitnet, or listserv@pucc.princeton.edu, leaving the subject line blank, and including in the body of the message sub psyc Firstname Lastname.

The Stanford Electronic Humanities Review

<http://shr.stanford.edu/shreview/>

This is the online version of the hardcopy edition. It usually includes a very good collection of articles and is worth bookmarking. A recent edition had as its theme The Cultural and Technological Incubations of Fascism. Earlier issues focused on Contested Politics and Constructions of the Mind: Artificial Intelligence and the Mind.

Social Research Update

<http://www.soc.surrey.ac.uk/sru/Sru.html>

Published by the Department of Sociology at the University of Surrey four times a year. Its mission is to bring information on new methods of doing research arising from developments in information technology to the attention of social scientists.

'New developments in information technology enable complex analyses to be carried out on a personal computer. Laptop computers and computer assisted telephone interviewing change fundamentally the way in which surveys are done. New statistical techniques are being developed which are better suited to the kinds of data which social researchers generally deal with. New approaches to qualitative data raise new theoretical and ethical problems.'

The Qualitative Report

<http://www.nova.edu/ssss/QR/index.html>

'*The Qualitative Report* (ISSN 1052-0147) is a peer reviewed, online journal dedicated to writing and discussion of and about qualitative and critical inquiry. *The Qualitative Report* serves as a forum and sounding board for researchers, scholars, practitioners, and other reflective-minded individuals who are passionate about ideas, methods, and analyses permeating qualitative and critical study.'

Online since 1990. Back issues are available.

Undercurrent

<http://darkwing.uoregon.edu/~heroux/home.html>

'Published from the University of Oregon. This is a free e-journal for analysis of the currents beneath current events. UNDERCURRENT is published three times per year, and seeks to provide interdisciplinary analysis of the present in an accessible format. We seek to publish analysis of the present from diverse intellectual perspectives – feminist, historical, ethnological, sociological, literary, political, semiotic, philosophical, cultural studies, and so forth. We seek applied analysis rather than theory.'

Given this breadth of focus, the articles published to date range over a wide variety of issues. They have included an article by Warren Sproule of the Sociology Department of the University of Tasmania on Virtual Battlefields: Informatics, 'Irreality', and the Sociology of War; an article by Chris MacNeil on The Paradox of Liberalism versus Illiberalism: The British Middle Class Portrayed in 1980s Popular Culture; and a review of Sander L. Gilman's On Jewish Identity and Contemporary German Culture.

US Department of Housing and Urban Development: Publications

<http://www.huduser.org/publications/periodicals/>

'The US Department of Housing and Urban Development offers the full text of two of its periodical publications. Cityscape: A Journal of Policy Development and Research, published three times per year, is an in depth publication that summarizes research on housing issues. Past issues are available in Adobe Acrobat (.pdf) format and early issues are single compressed (.exe) .pdfs. US Housing Market Conditions is a quarterly publication that contains national and regional housing information, as well as historical data tables.'(Scout Report, Vol. 4, No. 33, December 1997)

Nine issues of Cityscape are online, dating from August 1994.

21.4 Mailing lists

Mailing lists dealing with the subject matters referenced in this chapter can be accessed by the methods discussed in Chapter 9. There is, however, one collection of philosophy mailing lists worth mentioning separately.

The Spoon Collective

<http://jefferson.village.virginia.edu/~spoons/index2.html>

Hosted by the Institute for Advanced Technology in the Humanities at the University of Virginia, this is a series of lists on philosophical topics arranged by philosopher and subject. They include Foucault, Deleuze-Guattari, Frankfurt School, French Feminism, a number of Marxist themes, Habermas, and Film Theory. There is an excellent guide under each heading on how to subscribe, order postings by digest and how to access the archives.

21.5 Miscellaneous

The Gallup Organization

<http://www.gallup.com/>

Links to monthly archives of reports on surveys carried out. There is a search engine that will return a list of links to documents in the database that match the keyword entries, i.e., documents relating to Gallup surveys that include information relating to the search string.

Philosophy Departments

<http://www.rpi.edu/~cearls/phil.departments.html>

Compiled by Sean Cearley, this lists philosophy departments by country, with a separate page on various research projects:

<http://www.rpi.edu/~cearls/proj-dept.html>

Both lists are useful for tracking down philosophy resources and individuals on the Internet. Although some philosophy departments mount major Web sites, many others have a presence on the Web and upload useful resources. You can track down some of these by using some of the general lists on philosophy resources, but many will fall through these macro listings because the volume of resources being provided is low.

SIByl

<http://www.gamma.rug.nl/sibyl.html>

SIByl, the Software Information Bank of iec ProGAMMA, contains comprehensive information on computer applications for the social and behavioural sciences. Its purpose is to prevent the duplication of programming efforts by providing scientists with a library of existing (special purpose) software. Both submitting a program description to and retrieving information from SIByl are free of charge. Each entry includes a functional description, technical and data requirements, prices, availability of manual and interface, literature references, and purchase addresses.

WEDA (Worldwide Email Directory of Anthropologists)

<http://wings.buffalo.edu/academic/department/anthropology/WEDA/>

A project established to aid communication between scholars of anthropology around the world. 'Anthropologists' is taken to include physical, earth and social scientists, as well as their colleagues in the humanities. As of 7 November 1997, WEDA contained information on 1554 institutions and 4085 individuals!

21.6 Subject areas

Institute for Information Technology (Artificial Intelligence)

<http://ai.iit.nrc.ca/ai_top.html>

A Canadian organization, this provides information on the Canadian Society for Computational Studies of Intelligence and links to resources on the Internet on artificial intelligence. The subject list of resources relating to AI accessible through links from this site is extensive, and ranges through Agents, Chaos, Complex and Nonlinear Systems, Fuzzy Logic, Games and AI, History and AI, and Philosophy of AI, to the Turing Test. The AI resources list is also lengthy. This includes AI archives, bibliographics, conferences, companies, employment opportunities, journals, newsgroups and repositories and resources lists. In sum, this is quite a good starting point for locating AI Internet resources.

Index of Cognitive and Psychological Sciences on the Internet

<http://dawww.essex.ac.uk/~roehl/PsycIndex/>

Provided by Ruediger Oehlmann at the University of Essex, this is directed at those with research interests in these fields. The primary sections provide information on current academic programmes, worldwide, organizations (always a useful place to locate resources), conferences, a listing of relevant online journals and magazines, a lengthy compilation of discussion lists and a listing of Usenet newsgroups. The newsgroups include sections on cognitive science, artificial intelligence and robotics (a large number), philosophy (few) and psychology. The listing of journals and magazines does not always indicate whether full text articles are online. Associated resources accessible through these pages include a list of publishers, links to software applications and a page on announcements. In sum, this is a very useful resource for those interested in pursuing issues relating to cognitive science and psychology.

Toward a Science of Consciousness

<http://www.merlin.com.au/brain_proj>

Referred to usually as The Brain Project, this is largely the work of Stephen Jones. It is a by-product of, and based upon, the conference *Toward a Science of Consciousness*, held at Tuscon, Arizona, during 6–13 April 1996. The first thing to be said about this Web presentation is that it is very well organized, extensively and well illustrated, clearly written, and informative in respect of its subject matter. It should be a very useful starting point for those interested in this subject. It is divided into a number of major parts. The first consists of major topics discussed at the conference forums: Philosophical Issues; Neuro Anatomy and Neuro Physiology; Quantum Mechanics; Neural Nets and Artificial Intelligence; and Cybernetics, Organization and Complexity. The section on Philosophical Issues behind Ordinary Consciousness is divided into two parts: pre-twentieth and twentieth century.

A separate section provides background notes on historical ideas of the brain and the mind. In sum, this is an excellent hypertext project that utilizes well the potentialities of a Web presentation while doing so judiciously.

Contemporary Philosophy of Mind

<http://ling.ucsc.edu/~chalmers/biblio.html>

An annotated bibliography compiled by David Chalmers, Professor of Philosophy, University of California, Santa Cruz. It includes references to recent work in the philosophy of mind, the philosophy of cognitive science and the philosophy of artificial intelligence. There are 2395 entries classified under five headings, each of which is further divided by topic and subtopic. Many of the entries are annotated with a brief summary.

Resources on the Philosophy of Mind, Consciousness, AI and Philosophy

<http://ling.ucsc.edu/~chalmers/>

This is the home page of David Chalmers, mentioned above, from the University of California, Santa Cruz. Author of *The Conscious Mind: In Search of a Fundamental Theory*, Professor Chalmers' primary interests are centred on the philosophy of mind and the related issues of AI and cognitive science. At his site are links to some of the papers that he has written on these subjects, commentaries delivered at conferences, Usenet postings, and a list of resources elsewhere on the Internet dealing with these and other philosophical subjects. This is a good place to keep up with some of the developments available over the Internet in this field.

Centre for Applied Ethics

<http://www.ethics.ubc.ca/phil.sources.html>

From the University of British Columbia's Centre for Applied Ethics. The applied ethical issues referenced here include biomedicine and health care, business, information technology, the environment, the media, professional ethics, and science and technology.

Ethical Updates

<http://pwa.acusd.edu/~hinman/applied.html>

Professor Lawrence Hinman, author of *Contemporary Moral Issues: Diversity and Consensus* (Prentice-Hall, 1996), maintains a Web presentation on applied Ethics Updates. This is an annotated bibliography of resources available on applied ethical topics. Generally, it is divided into online resources, a survey of some of the more important philosophical works on the topic, which is further subdivided, variously, into popular literature, articles, anthologies, etc. The topics covered include abortion, reproductive technologies, euthanasia and decisions at the end of life, punishment and the death penalty, race and ethnicity, gender and sexism, sexual orientation and gay rights, poverty and welfare, world hunger, animal rights and environmental issues. This is a well-maintained and useful resource.

WWW Virtual Library for the History of Science

<http://www.asap.unimelb.edu.au/hstm/hstm_alphabetical.htm>

A large selection of links to resources associated with the history of science, technology and medicine. Includes a sizeable range of links to biographical materials on men and women of science, technology and medicine.

Psychiatry On-Line

<http://www.cityscape.co.uk/users/ad88/psych.htm>

This is a UK-based venture by Priory Lodge Education. Although described as a journal, the site does not confine itself to the delivery of lengthy learned articles. It is more a combination of bulletin board and journal dealing with issues relating to psychiatry. The dominant disciplinary orientation tends towards the medical–pharmacological/social policy cluster on the continuum. It covers a range of psychiatric specialisms, including affective disorders, neurotic disorders, schizophrenia, substance abuse, sexual disorders and personality issues, as well as psychopharmacology, psychotherapy, forensic psychiatry and epidemiology and public health issues. In addition to articles there is a news section that provides brief reports on topical issues. Materials are archived by subject matter. The journal is peer reviewed and there are links to other psychiatric resources online. A useful resource for brief discussion of topical issues as well as more in-depth coverage of persistent issues.

Academic Info on Religion

<http://www.academicinfo.net/religindex.html>

This is a very large compilation of resources. The Meta-Listings and General Pages focus on links to other major resources, academic departments of religion, Societies and Associations, Libraries, Mythology, Religous Tolerance, Alternative Spirituality and New Religious Movements. There are sections on Women and Religion, Art and Religion, and then on various religions: Eastern, Western, and Religions of the Americas. This is a very large undertaking and should link into most of the important resources on the Net dealing with religions and religious issues.

Urban Planning 1794–1918

<http://www.library.cornell.edu/Reps/DOCS/homepage.htm>

Provided by Professor J.W. Reps, Professor Emeritus, Cornell University.

> 'These documents are primary source material for the study of how urban planning developed up to the end of World War I. They include statements about techniques, principles, theories, and practice by those who helped to create a new professional specialization. This new field of city planning grew out of the land-based professions of architecture, engineering, surveying, and landscape architecture, as well as from the work of economists, social workers, lawyers, public health specialists, and municipal administrators. Some essays describe or illustrate an ideal physical pattern for cities. Several survey broadly the state of planning at the time of writing. A number use a single city as an example of how improvements should be made. Others discuss legal issues of land use regulations. A topical bibliography provides more than a dozen headings, and alphabetical and chronological bibliographies guide you to authors and time periods. Each entry is a link to the document. An internal key word search engine lists all documents in which a chosen word or phrase appears. The collected documents are equivalent to a 600-page book, but bibliographies and key word searches make it easy to find selections you need.'

An introduction to the anthology is provided. The subject hierarchy is divided into 15 sections. In each section there is a list of articles/books. The articles are scanned in and there is an entry that provides information on the author. An excellent resource.

21.7   Texts, bibliographies and thinkers

Anthropological Index Online

<http://lucy.ukc.ac.uk/cgi-bin/uncgi/Search_AI/search_bib_ai/anthind>

This is the Anthropological Index to Current Periodicals in the Museum of Mankind, which incorporates the former Royal Anthropological Institute Library. You can search from 1970 to 1993, by individual years, or for the whole period. There is also some limited data available relating to the 1960s. Searching terms include subject, author, title and journal. These search terms can be focused by continent, region and subject area. In searching, only the abbreviations should be used in the Journal dialog box. The records return particulars on the periodical in which the article relating to the query appeared.

Annual Review of Sociology Online

<http://198.94.213.3/soc/home.htm>

Abstracts of articles that have appeared in the *Annual Review of Sociology* since 1985, with full text articles since 1993. You can browse the tables of contents of the volumes from 1984 and then move to the abstracts. Articles published since 1993 can be downloaded in Adobe .pdf format at a cost of $5 each.

Clearinghouse for Asian Studies and Social Sciences Subject-oriented Bibliographies

<http://coombs.anu.edu.au/CoombswebPages/BiblioClear.html#S>

A long list of bibliographies on Asian studies and social science subject areas. There were 166 bibliographies, arranged alphabetically, on 12 March 1998. The subject range is broad and some of the files are large.

The Noam Chomsky Archive

<http://www.worldmedia.com/archive/>

A substantial collection of articles and interviews. In January 1998 there were more than 10 Mb of text and 7 Mb of audio files on the server. Some of Chomsky's books are available in electronic format as well.

Bibliography of Books and Articles on Consciousness in Philosophy, Cognitive Science, and Neuroscience

<http://mind.phil.vt.edu/assc/biblio.html>

The bibliography covers the period 1970–1996 and has been compiled by Thomas Metzinger and David Chalmers. It is subdivided into 12 subsections. A printed version is available, although not through bookstores. The drawback, however, is that the bibliography is password protected. To gain access you need to become a member of the Association for the Scientific Study of Consciousness, full membership of which costs $20 p.a. Membership carries a subscription to the journals *Psyche* and *Consciousness and Cognition*.

Contemporary Philosophy, Critical Theory and Postmodern Thought

<gopher://oasis.cudenver.edu/h0/UCD/dept/edu/IT/ryder/itc_data/postmodern.html>

This extensive listing is provided by the School of Education at the University of Denver, Colorado. It is subdivided into Resources, Readings (etexts) and People. The writers include Barthes, Baudrillard, Foucault, Derrida, Habermas, Lacan and Lyotard. Some of the resources in this section are just typescripts of interviews; others are brief biographical sketches.

Indexes, Abstracts, Bibliographies, and Table of Contents

<http://info.lib.uh.edu/indexes/indexes.html>

'This site focuses on research-oriented, Internet-based indexes, abstracts, bibliographies, and tables of contents that will help people locate journal, magazine, and newspaper articles; research papers; preprints; proceedings and transactions; book chapters; and similar materials.'

The subjects covered are history, philosophy, sociology, psychology, political science, gender studies, education, business/economics, and 'SocScience Multidisciplinary'. Some of the bibliographies linked to from this site are very large. The Jourlit/Bookrev Databases of the American Psychoanalytic Association, for instance, is a searchable index of almost 30,000 journal articles, books and book reviews in psychoanalysis that dates back to 1920. The Bibliography on Social and Economic Development compiled by Richard J. Estes, School of Social Work, University of Pennsylvania, lists over 1750 journal articles, books, book chapters, reports and similar materials relating to social development, economic development, social work, social welfare and related areas.

This is an extremely useful resource that is well worth browsing through.

The International Philosophical Preprint Exchange

<http://cogsci.l.chiba-u.ac.jp/IPPE.html>

This resource is provided by the Department of Philosophy at Chiba with the assistance of an international working group. The service provides facilities for philosophers to deposit papers prior to their publication in scholarly journals. Abstracts of all articles are available. The articles can be downloaded in a number of formats.

The articles are classified in terms of the American Philosophical Association's categories. Instructions on how to submit papers are available from the main page.

There is also some information here on journals in some fields of philosophy, on books and on conferences.

International Directory of Online Philosophy Papers

<http://hkusuc.hku.hk/philodep/directory/>

Joe Lau of the Department of Philosophy, University of Hong Kong, hosts this presentation. The objective is to provide an easy way of tracking down philosophy-related papers which are dispersed over the Web. The search engine database records can be queried by topic area (e.g. metaphysics, consciousness, philosophy of mind), keyword, or a combination of the two. At present it is probably best to use the topic directory and keyword, rather than the author keyword, due to the limited number in the database. There are no articles loaded on this server.

The Internet Classics Archive

<http://classics.mit.edu/home.html>

Located at MIT, this is a searchable collection of over 400 classical Greek and Roman texts in English translation. These include works by Aristotle, Plato, Hippocrates, Herodotus, Thucydides and Virgil. As many of the texts are lengthy, they are subdivided into sections to speed up download times. The translations are by various authorities, including Benjamin Jowett and R.D. Ross. Some texts have extensive reader commentaries associated with them.

Person, Self, Personal Identity, Self-Consciousness, Self-Knowledge

<http://www.canisius.edu/~gallaghr/pi.html>

Compiled by Shaun Gallagher. Although not exhaustive, it is lengthy (132 Kb) and includes references to recently published materials.

Philosophy Texts

<http://english-www.hss.cmu.edu/philosophy/>

Philosophy electronic text page on the English Server at Carnegie Mellon. It has a large number of entries. The most comprehensive collections are those of Aristotle, Plato, Hume, Kant, Marx and Nietzsche.

The Wellek Library Lecturer Bibliographies

<http://sun3.lib.uci.edu/indiv/scctr/Wellek/index.html>

This collection of bibliographies is sponsored by the Critical Theory Institute at the University of California, Irvine, and is based around the annual Wellek lectures. Annually, leading scholars defend their theses in a series of three lectures. Although the lectures themselves do not appear to be available online, Dr Yeghiayan has compiled extensive bibliographies relating to the published works and interviews of many of those who have delivered these lectures. Included among these scholars are Edward Said, Jacques Derrida, Natalie Zemon Davis and Jean-François Lyotard. The search engine can be used to access materials directly.

CHAPTER 22

Political Science and government resources

22.1	Introduction	243
22.2	General resource sites	244
22.3	Country politics (non-UK)	249
22.4	Country politics (UK)	252
22.5	Elections	255
22.6	Subject areas	256
22.7	Texts	257

22.1   Introduction

There is a wide range of resources likely to be of interest to political scientists available from publicly accessible Internet sources. In addition to those referenced in the present chapter, you should consult Chapters 14, 18 and 23 on Electronic texts, Current news online and European Union resources respectively. The archives of CNN, *Christian Science Monitor*, *The Times*, Pathfinder publications (which publishes *Time* magazine) and others should be consulted for reportage on contemporary political affairs. Chapter 14 should be consulted for electronic versions of the classic works of political philosophers and political scientists. Chapter 21 should also be consulted, particularly Section 21.2 on General resource sites. Many of these sites include links to electronic versions of works in political philosophy and government. Finally, in the present chapter, some of the sites listed in Section 22.3 under Country politics (non-UK) include links to political resources in many countries, particularly those focusing on US politics.

22.2 General resource sites

Address Directory for Politicians of the World

<http://www.trytel.com/~aberdeen/>

Claims to list the mailing addresses for every nation's leaders and provincial governors. The phone, fax, email and Web sites are added when available.

International Constitutional Law

<http://www.uni-wuerzburg.de/law/index.html>

This is an excellent source of information on constitutional law matters provided by the University of Würzburg. It is arranged by country and provides access to all relevant constitutional law documents, to legislative and judicial institutions of the country if available, and to a few country-specific sites or newsgroups. There is also a brief résumé of background factors and the course of constitutional developments.

International Political Science Association Guide to General Politics Resources

<http://midir.ucd.ie/~coakleyj/genpols.html>

This is a collation of resources that are generally found on other servers. It includes links to political science associations and departments. The Political Science subfields are categorized under Method and Theory, Political Thinkers and Ideas, Governmental and Administrative Institutions, Political Processes, International Relations, and National Area Studies. There are also links to newspapers and journals, although not many political science periodicals are available in electronic format.

International Relations Data

<http://garnet.acns.fsu.edu/~phensel/intldata.html#conflict>

A large collection of links to datasets on international relations compiled by Paul R. Hensel, Department of Political Science, Florida State University. Arranged under General International Relations Data, International Conflict and Cooperation Data, International Economic Data, International Social Data, International Political Data, and International Environmental Data. Many of the files need to be downloaded to view them. There is a separate file with links to US Economic, Political and Social Data at

<http://garnet.acns.fsu.edu/~phensel/usdata.html#usecon>

Inter-Parliamentary Union

<http://www.ipu.org/>

Established in 1889, the IPU works to encourage the introduction of representative democracy worldwide and currently has a membership of more than 100 national legislatures. In addition to information on the structure, membership and organization of the IPU, the PARLINE database has entries providing information on the legislative chambers of each country. To access the details for any country just key in its name. Alternatively, you can search by region. The information provided is well arranged, giving brief details of the electoral system, names of state and legislative functionaries, percentage of women members of the legislature, term, addresses, particulars on eligibility of voters, candidacy requirements, background and outcome of the last elections with the names of the parties, the number of seats gained and the percentage of the vote. All this information is very clearly presented.

Another extremely useful facility at this site is the PARLIT database. This provides bibliographic information dating from 1992. The information is not confined just to matters relating to electoral procedures, legislation, outcomes and similar. The publications referenced cover a very broad range of topics that relate to political governance in all countries of the world. The search engine itself is extremely easy to use and permits very focused queries through the use of drop-down menus. You can, for example, choose to search by all languages, or by one of the 29 languages in which the publications included in the database are published.

Louisiana State University Political Resources

<http://www.lsu.edu/guests/poli/public_html/index.html>

A very large collection of useful links, the main categories of which are American Politics, the Constitution Page, Foreign, Comparative and International, Political Documents, Political Theory, Political Parties and Interest Groups, and Research Resources in Political Science. Each of these pages includes a large number of links.

The Constitution Page provides links to the constitution of every country in the world, in addition to a large number of links to the US Constitution, annotations of it, and various documents dealing with amendments to it. The Foreign and International Materials Resources List is an extremely lengthy list of links to resources on international relations, non-US political systems, international law, international organizations, and country- or regionally-specific political science resource materials

Online Resource Guide to Political Inquiry

<http://alcor.concordia.ca/~dartnel/>

Produced by Dr Michael Dartnell, Department of Political Science, Concordia University, Montréal. This is a very comprehensive and well-organized listing of resources under headings which include British Politics, Irish Politics, Canadian Politics, Environmental Politics, Central and East European Politics, Scottish and Welsh Politics, Political Theory, and Terrorism. There are far too many resources referenced from this site to annotate adequately here. The site is, however, well worth looking at. In my opinion its coverage of resources relating to British and Irish politics is excellent

Political Resources on the Net

<http://www.agora.stm.it/politic/>

Arranged by country. The range and comprehensiveness of resources accessible for a particular country are a function of what has been made available in each. An attempt has been made to subsume the information under a number of common category headings. These include election results, political parties, constitutional and related documents, and links to government servers for particular administrative bodies (ministries, agencies, embassies). For some countries there are separate pages for politics and parties (which includes information on elections and constitutional laws), organizations, and government.

This is an extremely useful resource linking to a substantial volume of information relating to the politics, government and administration of many countries. Frequently there are also links from pages dealing with specific countries to resources outside the politics/government category. Much of the information relating to particular countries is not in English.

Political Science Resources (1)

<http://www.psr.keele.ac.uk/>

Arranged by Richard Kimber, University of Keele. This is the most comprehensive listing of resources for political scientists in the UK.

The links are arranged first by topic and then by country. The main headings are Area Studies, British Politics, Official Websites (links to government agencies, parliaments, etc.), Information About Governments (primarily named membership), Elections, Constitutions, Political Parties, Manifestos, Political Theory, Political Thought, Local Government, and International Relations. Each of the pages to which one of these main headings is linked is divided into two parts. The first consists of a short list of general resources relating to the topic, if applicable, and then information relating to that topic for particular countries, arranged alphabetically.

The Political Thought page links to Web materials focusing on the work of particular writers, including Marx, Engels, J.S. Mill, Nietzsche, Plato, Hume, Locke, Russell and Chomsky. The range of materials accessible from the Political Theory page is somewhat restricted, game theory being somewhat disproportionately represented in a relatively short listing.

The British Politics page collates links to resources on government bodies, legislative institutions, elections and their results, political parties, MPs and MEPs, local and regional government bodies, and the like.

Although this presentation pulls together a substantial number of links to various resources relating to political science and politics, as the major UK politics site it is somewhat disappointing. Nearly all of these links are found elsewhere on the Web, frequently arranged more systematically. The data relating to particular countries is sometimes out of date or not representative of the scope of information that is available relating to them on Internet hosts. Especially disappointing is the fact that the resources are for the most part not annotated and there are few, if any, resources that are original to this site.

Political Science Resources (2)

<http://php.indiana.edu/~rmtucker/data.html>

Compiled by Daniel Tsang, Social Science Bibliographer at the University of California. This lengthy list focuses primarily on United States politics and political institutions. There are, however, sections on Canadian Politics and on Comparative and World Politics.

Political Science Resources on the Web

<http://www.lib.umich.edu/libhome/Documents.center/polisci.html>

Links to political science resources from the University of Michigan under a variety of headings.

The Political Scientist's Guide to the Internet

<http://www.trincoll.edu/~pols/guide/home.html>

Arranged by Peter Adams at Trinity College. It includes an article written by Adams on the subject of 'Why it is Important for Political Scientists to Use Internet Resources'. There is a compilation of links to political science resources under five headings: federal and state US government resources, political research, issues and people, and international affairs. The political research page includes links to major political science departments (mainly American), libraries, research institutions and documents. The documents page is not particularly comprehensive. A useful site with a manageable set of links.

Richard Tucker's Data Page

<http://php.indiana.edu/~rmtucker/data.html>

Includes links to datasets on Conflict, Cooperation, Aggression and Violence, Regime Attributes and Social Indicators, and Electoral Politics. There are also links to other important data archives.

Roberto Ortíz de Zárate's Political Datasets

<http://web.jet.es/ziaorarr/welcome2.htm>

The dataset on Political Leaders 1945–1998 is arranged by country and provides information on the names and terms of offices of heads of government and/or state and other leading members of the executive branch of government. The categories included in this listing tend to vary. So, for example, the entry for Israel provides details on ministers of foreign affairs and defence and leaders of the Likud and Mapai parties. The entry for Canada, on the other hand, provides information only on the Prime Ministers. There is also a chronological listing, available since 1996, which charts on a monthly basis major changes in leadership positions.

The European Governments (1945–1998) dataset 'provides brief descriptions of European governments since 1990, detailing prime minister, ruling term, cabinet composition and date of the general elections held'. The first African Rulers Quick Table gives details of what happened to those rulers of African countries who assumed head of government or state positions immediately after the granting of independence. There is also a dataset of rulers who died in violent circumstances since 1945.

Rulers

<http://www.geocities.com/Athens/1058/rulers.html>

'This site contains lists of heads of state and heads of government (and, in certain cases, *de facto* leaders which don't occupy either of those formal positions) of all currently existing countries and territories. Also included are the subdivisions of some countries (the links are at the bottom of the respective country entries), as well as some international organizations. Foreign ministers of all countries are listed separately.'

The entries are arranged alphabetically for both countries and foreign ministers. There is also a listing of the membership of major international associations, namely the Arab League, the Association of Southeast Asian Nations, the Commonwealth, EU, OAU, OAS and UN. There is a monthly chronology that goes back to January 1996. This gives brief details, arranged by country, on changes in leadership. It includes information on substate level entities (e.g. Montenegro) and on major ministerial changes in addition to those of heads of state or government and ministers of foreign affairs.

University Politics Departments from the Political Studies Association, UK

<http://www.lgu.ac.uk/psa/depts.html>

Divided into UK, USA, and Rest of the World. Sometimes you can find links to other politics resources from departmental pages. Usually it is quicker to use a search engine. Primarily useful for scrutinizing courses being offered, addresses of faculties, working papers and bibliographies.

Web Sites on National Parliaments

<http://www.soc.umn.edu/~sssmith/Parliaments.html>

Maintained by Professor Steven Smith of the Political Science Department at the University of Minnesota. Links are provided to the home pages of national parliaments and to international and regional parliamentary institutions. Although the information provided relating to legislatures varies in terms of its comprehensiveness, this is a useful resource from which it is possible to link to information, not only about the legislature, but also about other aspects of the political systems of the countries concerned. Despite the fact that in some instances the information is nearly entirely in the language of the country concerned, there are frequently parallel presentations in English, or at least some documents of relevance.

For many of the countries there is information on the electoral system, procedures of the legislature constitutional documents, committees of the legislature (frequently with membership and party representation), lists of members, links to pages which provide information about the government, the occupants of particular ministerial positions, and similar.

This is a very useful resource.

22.3   Country politics (non-UK)

The Australian Politics Resource

<http://www.adfa.oz.au/~adm/politics/politics.html>

An excellent presentation on Australian politics by David Moss. It includes sections on topical events, political parties (with links to the home pages of a very lengthy list), Internet newsgroups and Australian newspapers online, some articles on political matters, Australian laws and treaties, Hansard (the official record of proceedings of the federal and state parliaments) and political issues. Among the latter are included environmental issues, the republic issue, the flag, gun, euthanasia and aboriginal issues.

Malcolm Farnsworth's Politics Resources

<http://www.netspace.net.au/~malcolm/>

The presentation covers Australian, American and British politics. The section on British politics is not up to the very high standards of the Australian and American sections which are very well arranged and provide useful information on a wide range of topics. There is a hypertext version of the Australian Constitution, information on the High Court and its justices, links to the High Court Bulletin and to transcripts of cases heard before it. Under all headings there is useful historical information.

Political Database of the Americas

<http://www.georgetown.edu/LatAmerPolitical/home.html>

'The database provides documentary and statistical political information on Latin America, including constitutions, electoral laws, legislative and executive branch information and election data.' This is a very well-organized resource. The information under some headings is taken from other sources. Whilst a substantial body of the information is in English there are some files, such as constitutions, where English translations are not yet available. Similarly, information on the Judicial Branches is not available for all countries listed.

Foreign Governments

<http://www.library.nwu.edu/govpub/idtf/foreign.html>

Links to the home pages of government offices, political, legislative and other central institutions arranged by country, where available. There are also links to sources of statistical information for many entries in the list.

OMRINet (Eastern Europe and the Russian Federation)

<http://www.omri.cz/>

The Open Media Research Institute, formerly part of the Soros group, published information on current events in Central and Eastern Europe and in the former Soviet Union until 28 March 1997. It was then restructured. It was at the time the most extensive and detailed source of information on the Internet on current affairs in this region. It has been operating from Prague since June 1994. Electronic reports began appearing in January 1995; they are archived and are still available despite the fact that it has ceased operating.

The reports provided information under four headings: OMRI Daily Digest, Russian Regional Report, Pursuing Balkan Peace, and OMRI Analytical Briefs. The daily digest consisted of short or paragraph-length reports about important current developments in four main regions: Russia, Transcaucasia and Central Asia, Central and Eastern Europe, and south-east Europe. The Russian Regional Report provided weekly updates on political and social developments in the 89 regions of the Russian Federation. Pursuing Balkan Peace monitored events in the former Yugoslavia and the implementation of the Dayton accords. The Analytical Briefs appeared at less regular intervals but were considerably more detailed than either the Daily Digest or Russian Regional Reports on particular topics. Search engines are available to locate information in any of the reports.

The collation and reporting of information on the topics and countries covered by OMRINet have now been taken over by Radio Free Europe/Radio Liberty, particulars of which are given below.

Radio Free Europe/Radio Liberty

<http://www.rferl/org/>

This site is an excellent source of information on current affairs in Russia, Transcaucasia and Central Asia, and south-east Europe. In addition to the information that is available in text files, it is possible to listen to audio broadcasts in 20 languages, the schedules for which are provided. Broadcasts in many are online 24 hours a day. The Newsline link provides daily coverage on breaking news, which you can subscribe to by sending a message to

<listserv@listserv.acsu.buffalo.edu>

placing in the body of the message the line

subscribe RFERL-L <first name> <last name>

There is also a Weekday Magazine which provides more detailed reports, and a section called Special Reports. There are archives dating from April 1997 when OMRINet ceased operations.

Guide to Irish Politics Resources

<http://www.ucd.ie/~politics/irpols.html>

Compiled by the Political Science Department, University College Dublin. Provides links to politics departments in the Republic, in Northern Ireland, Britain and the United States. Available online are documents relating to the conflict in the North, including the Mitchell Report, the Downing Street Declaration, the IRA statement ending the ceasefire in February 1996, and others. Other useful resources are links to Northern Ireland Election Results since 1970 and bibliographies on Irish nationalism and British and Irish legal history.

In sum, a good launching pad for access to Internet resources on Northern Ireland and Eire.

Documents on Mexican Politics

<http://daisy.uwaterloo.ca/~alopez-o/polind.html>

A large collection of documents, mainly articles, relating to contemporary Mexican politics, arranged by Alex López-Ortiz. Some of these, the minority, consist of excerpts. Arranged in sections that include On Democracy, On Freedom of the Press, Analysis on Political Parties, NAFTA, On the Economy, About Chiapis and the EZLN, Government Documents, Reference Documents and Opinion/Research Articles. Some of these are in Spanish. This is a large and useful collection.

FedWorld Information Network

<http://www.fedworld.gov/>

This search engine is designed to provide links to United States federal government information, which is available on Web servers through this information network. There are tens of thousands of files currently available, and more are being uploaded all the time. There is also an index that lists all of the files available from their library on the FedWorld Information Network.

National Political Index

<http://www.politicalindex.com/>

'The National Political index is a web site which provides an index of substantive political information for voters, political activists, political consultants, lobbyists, politicians, academicians, and media editors with a wide range of products, information, services, simulations, games, and polling in an interactive communications environment.' It is a non-profit and non-partisan organization that is registered as a charity. At present they claim to index 3500 political Web sites and to add an additional 50 a week and they index 200 departments of political science.

The information is focused entirely on Americn politics on which it provides useful information. The page on Contacting Elected Federal Officials provides very extensive information on senators and representatives, alphabetically and by state, details relating to senate committees and the legislative process. There is also detailed information on state and local officials, on federal, state and local candidates, and links to federal agencies and political science departments in the United States.

The Jefferson Project

<http://www.voxpop.org/jefferson/>

Links to resources and information relating to American politics. If you want to find links to the home pages of the various political parties in the United States, including those that you rarely hear of, such as the Communist and Reform parties, this is a good place to look. Although the recipient of some Web-type awards, this site is somewhat overrated, in my opinion.

US Government and Politics

<http://www.clark.net/pub/lschank/web/gov.html#contents>

Compiled by Larry Schankman who has written a large number of guides to Internet resources in a number of subject areas. This is a very large collection of links with brief annotations to resources dealing with all facets of US government and politics. Although the title suggests a restriction to US politics, there are plenty of links and files focusing on international and country-specific issues. The page on International and Area Studies provides links to data relating to specific countries, arranged alphabetically by continent, region and country. This resource is so massive that if you were to follow up every link it would probably take a few days.

22.4   Country politics (UK)

BOPCAS (British Official Publication Current Awareness Service)

<http://www.soton.ac.uk/~bopcas/>

This a database of official UK publications provided by the University of Southampton. The database consists of summary information, not the full text. This generally includes the title, date of publication, ISBN, series, publisher, number of pages and price. These can be searched by subject (Defence, Economy, Education, Environment, Europe, Health, Law, Science and Technology, Statistics and Transport) combined with date. There is a search engine that permits gross and refined searching. As of 27 February 1998 the databank held 8400 references.

Government Information Service

<http://www.open.gov.uk/>

A very well-organized site that provides access to UK government-related online resources. This includes health authorities, commissions of inquiry, government departments, government laboratories, police services, agencies (CSA, OFWAT, OFSTED, etc.), museums, etc. It is not clear how comprehensive the coverage is in each category, but the alphabetical listing is lengthy.

There are a number of alternative means of locating particular entities. The Organisational Index lists the resources alphabetically. The Functional Index lists them alphabetically by main subject category, whereas the Public Services Directory provides a graphical representation of the same with fewer categories. Also of interest is the What's New on GIS which should be explored for its daily addition to government-related online resources, including reports, departmental briefings and notices, datasets, etc. There is also a search engine that is fast and relatively easy to use.

In sum, an excellent resource which should be a first choice starting point for finding UK government-related resources. It could, however, do with a separate listing of the main government departments and some more cross-referencing under some headings.

UK Houses of Parliament

<http://www.parliament.uk/>

The United Kingdom Parliament's home page, giving access to both the Commons and Lords Web presentations (see below).

House of Commons

<http://www.parliament.uk/commons/HSECOM.HTM>

A very well-organized and speedy service. You will find here a considerable volume of information relating to the current legislative activities of the House, its committees, proceedings, membership, members' non-parliamentary interests and their conclusions as expressed in reports. All the important publications relating to Commons deliberations are available online. These include a daily summary agenda and order of business, questions arranged by day, the complete text of all the public bills before the House, Hansard (the daily record of proceedings in the chamber), the full text of Standing Committee debates on bills, and reports of the Standing Committees.

There is also a substantial volume of information relating to individual members, the political party groupings, membership of the government and the opposition, membership of Standing Committees and information on by-elections. To get to this information you need to select the link to Information about the House of Commons and Members of Parliament, and then List of Members, Ministers and Committees. If you then select Members of Parliament and their Responsibilities, you obtain an alphabetical listing of all MPs which provides information on their constituency and their membership of committees, if any. The link to Her Majesty's Government provides information on members of the cabinet, ministers by department of state and an alphabetical listing of members of the government. There is also information available on the opposition and other parties.

Also available is the Register of Members' Interests (select the link to Other House of Commons Papers from the home page) and links to all the Standing Committees. From these you can establish the committee's membership and also access their reports. The Factsheets provide information on various aspects of the proceedings of the House. They are accessed from the Information about the House of Commons and Members of Parliament page. They are in .pdf format so you will need to download them and have an Adobe viewer to read them.

House of Lords

<http://www.parliament.the-stationery-office.co.uk/pa/ld/ldhome.htm>

The information available parallels in large measure that which is provided through the House of Commons Web presentation. The daily proceedings, standing orders, public bills and Select Committee reports are all accessible. There is also a guide to the proceedings of the Lords.

The House of Lords judgements have been available online since 14 November 1996 and can be downloaded by selecting the link to Judicial Business. There are files available that provide details on its judicial role.

UK Politics: The British Politics Home Page

<http://www.ukpol.co.uk/>

Sponsored by the London political bookshop Politico's and compiled by Julian White, this presentation collates links to a substantial volume of information relating to varied aspects of UK politics.

The Constituency Profiles, which is subdivided by region, provides information on the candidates who stood at the last general election. To obtain details on the votes cast for each one you need to select the link to the constituency. There is a search engine that enables you to trace your MP by keying in your post code. For some constituencies there is also information on votes cast in earlier elections. The Councils file provides access to the Web pages of all councils in the UK that are available. There is also information here on newsgroups that discuss UK politics, political and electoral news, a twentieth-century time-line of British politics and a listing of members of the Cabinet since 1945 by administration.

This is a useful site for schematic information about British politics.

Politics Links [UK]

<http://users.ox.ac.uk/~kebl0613/poli.html>

Made available by the Oxford Union Fabian Society, this provides links to Green Party, Labour Party, Trade Union, and Christianity and Socialism resources. There is also a list of the electronic addresses of those MPs and MEPs who are online. The Constituency

Links page provides access to the Web pages of Labour Party constituencies and some MPs who have them. The Campaigning Groups page provides links to some activist groups, including Urban 75, CND and Gingerbread.

22.5   Elections

The Electoral Web Sites

<http://www.agora.stm.it/elections/election.htm>

This excellent presentation is edited by W.P.C.G. Derksen. It provides information on the outcome of elections and related issues for all independent countries of the world, both member and non-member states of the United Nations, autonomous overseas dependencies and entities which are recognized by international organizations but 'not generally recognized' (such as Palestine and Western Sahara). For each country there is information on the size of its area and population, the names of the head of government and head of state, and the dates of presidential elections (first and second round where applicable) with the names of the parties' candidates and the percentage votes. For legislative chambers information is provided on the total number of seats for each house and the percentage vote and the number of seats obtained by each party.

You can also subscribe to the monthly electronic mail newsletter *Info on Elections Around the World* by sending a message to

<majordomo@mlist.stm.it>

with the instruction subscribe infoelect in the body of the message. There is no need to include anything in the subject line.

Election Notes

<http://www.klipsan.com/elecnews.htm>

Provided by Klipsan Press, this is a daily newsletter on election-related issues occurring all over the world. There are links to local and other media reports providing information on the stories reported on. Back issues of the newsletter from 1996 are available. There is also a list of elections due to take place during 1998/99, including presidential, parliamentary, regional, local and other elections in various parts of the world. Similar documents are available for 1996 and 1997.

Elections Today

<http://www.ifes.org/newsletter/eltodind.htm>

This is a publication of the International Foundation for Election Systems, which 'brings up-to-date information on election administration techniques, principles, and notable innovations to election administrators worldwide. It includes a comprehensive calendar of upcoming elections and selected election results.' Published four times a year, all the issues for 1996 are online, with two for 1995 and a few others from earlier years. The articles range over a wide variety of issues and countries. The latest edition had a special section on electoral issues relating to persons with special needs, as well as articles on Assembling a Computerized Voting System in Brazil and The Role of NGOs in the Election Process in Bosnia and Herzegovina. This is a useful source of information on a variety of election-related issues.

Parties and Elections in Europe

<http://www-public.rz.uni-duesseldorf.de/~nordsiew/indexe.html>

Edited by Wolfram Nordsieck, this is a very well-arranged and useful site that provides information on European Union elections, elections in European countries, and elections in Germany, in many cases since 1945/46. The information on German federal elections includes a file on elections from 1949 to 1990, one on German Reich elections during 1919–1933, one on the 1990 GDR elections and another on the federal elections of 1990 and 1994. In addition there are details of the federal state elections in eastern Germany for the years 1990, 1994 and 1996.

The EU page provides information on the number of seats for each of the political groupings from 1979 to 1994, with the percentage vote for each available for 1994. There is also information on the membership of each political grouping.

The entries for separate European countries provide information on votes cast for each party for the last two elections, information on the head of state/prime minister, number of seats in the legislature and its term. There are also files for many countries on electoral results since 1946.

22.6   Subject areas

Anarchy for Anybody

<http://www.radio4all.org/anarchy/>

A page of links to various matters relating to anarchism. Among the subtopics included are Anarchist Ethics, Anarchist FAQ (frequently asked questions about anarchism), and Famous Anarchists. There are links to other anarchism sites.

Contemporary Conflicts

<http://www.cfcsc.dnd.ca/links/wars/index.html>

The Canadian Forces College, Department of National Defense, Canada, provides this resource. Thirty-three countries were listed at the end of February 1998. Nearly all the conflicts are internal ones, including those in Chechnya, Cyprus, East Timor, Kashmir,

Liberia, Somalia and Sri Lanka. For each country there are links to resources that provide information relating to the conflict and the country. The quantity and quality of resources is variable. Predictably, the more 'fashionable' the conflicts are in the 'West', the more resources there are available relating to them. For example, the resources relating to East Timor, Myanmar, Bosnia, the Middle East and Rwanda contrast favourably in terms of volume with those available on the Algerian conflict. Nonetheless, this is a very useful resource.

Political Methodology Working Papers

<**http://wizard.ucr.edu/polmeth/polmeth.html#WORKING_PAPERS**>

Working and conference papers submitted to the Political Methodology Society and the Political Methodology Section of the American Political Science Association (APSA). The working papers date from 1995 and there are a substantial number of them. The abstracts are available online. The full papers need to be downloaded and are generally in postscript format. The help files provide information on downloading the papers, on decompressing utilities and on viewing and printing files in this format, the software for which can be downloaded from this site as well.

Political Science Statistical Resources on the Web

<**http://www.lib.umich.edu/libhome/Documents.center/stpolisc.html**>

A very large collection of links to political science datasets from the University of Michigan Documents Center, divided into Comprehensive Sources, Campaign Finances, Elections, Public Opinion, Military, and Human Rights.

22.7 Texts

Journals and Online Journals

<**http://www.apsanet.org/~theory/**>

From the American Political Science Association site, a list of links to the home pages of journals in political theory and philosophy. Most of them provide only tables of contents or abstracts online.

Marx' and Engels' Writings

<**http://eserver.org/marx/**>

A collection of the writings of Marx and Engels from the English Server at Carnegie Mellon. The texts available and ease of use should be compared with the Marx/Engels Archive referenced in Chapter 14. There is a search engine associated with every text.

Political Theory Texts from Carnegie Mellon

<http://english-www.hss.cmu.edu/Govt/Theory.html>

Various texts grouped under the heading Political Theory from the English Server at Carnegie Mellon. There are some useful texts collected here, including Machiavelli's *The Prince*, Hobbes' *Leviathan*, Locke's *Concerning Toleration* and his *Second Essay on Government*, Lenin's *State and Revolution* and Trotsky's *Fascism and How to Fight It*, as well as more contemporary articles by André Gunder Frank, Ted Goertzel and others.

CHAPTER 23

European Union resources

23.1   Institutions   259
23.2   Policies   263
23.3   Publications and documents   263
23.4   Other European Union resources   266

Main EU URLs

Entry page all languages *<http://europa.eu.int>*
English language entry page *<http://europa.eu.int/index-en.htm>*
Institutions home page *<http://europa.eu.int/inst-en.htm>*
European Parliament *<http://europa.eu.int/inst-en.htm#commission>*
European Commission *<http://europa.eu.int/en/comm.html>*
Directory of the European Commission *<http://europa.eu.int/en/comm/dgserv.html>*
European Court of Justice *<http://europa.eu.int/cj/index.htm>*
Search engine *<http://europa.eu.int/geninfo/query-en.htm>*

The EU Web presentation is organized around two main foci, institutions and policies.

23.1   Institutions

<http://europa.eu.int/inst-en.htm>

The institutions of the EU that are likely to be of primary interest to Social Science students and staff are the European Parliament, the European Commission and the European Court of Justice. The Directory of the European Commission, which encompasses all of the separate directorates of the EU, is under the direct line management of the European Commission and will be discussed in that context.

Generally, there is a lot of information available on European Union Web servers, although some of it is not as easy to locate as it could be. If you select the link to Institutions a file with the title Institutions of the European Union is downloaded. This provides outline details relating to the functions, powers and responsibilities of each organizational entity of the EU (e.g. Parliament, Commission, Court of Auditors) and links to their home pages. These home pages are relatively informative and the details should suffice to give those not familiar with the EU and its institutional structure a broad overview of how it operates and what the functions of its constituent organs are. In addition to the information that is available from the pages of each organ, there is a useful document called A General Overview of the Institutions of the European Union,

<http://europa.eu.int/en/comm/opoce/brocint/gb/default.html>

that also links indirectly to the home pages of the separate organizational entities. This is a good place to start from to develop familiarity with the organizational structure of the EU.

The European Parliament

<http://www.europarl.eu.int/sg/tree/en/default.htm>

There is a considerable volume of information on the organization, functions and responsibilities of the EP *vis-à-vis* other organs of the EU. The file Overview of the European Parliament has an introductory section that provides information on the member states of the EU (including maps), details relating to community institutions and bodies, and an outline of the aims of the EU. The sections on Powers and Responsibilities, and on Organisation and Operation, provide details on its workings and relations with other EU organs.

The Members of the European Parliament file gives details of members ordered by country. For each member there is information on their political grouping, committee membership or other function, telephone and fax number, and some biographical information, although this tends towards minimalism. Information on members is also available by political grouping, and by name querying of a search engine. Information on the political groupings of the EUP is more extensive for some groupings than for others.

The Activities document provides information on plenary meetings, Parliamentary committees, temporary committees and the conciliation committee, and has a calendar of meetings and a section on parliamentary questions. The document on Parliamentary Committees provides an overview in tabular form of the various committees and subcommittees of the EUP and their responsibilities. Information on both is provided in lengthy documents that you have to scroll down to find the committee or subcommittee of interest. Details on responsibilities are schematic. You can establish the membership of the committees but as yet there are no copies of reports or recommendations produced by them. The hearings and/or summaries of debates of some committees are available online. Establishing which are available and then downloading them requires a lot of mouse work.

Parliamentary questions are accessible by Official Journal (OJ) number, by MEP and by political grouping as well as some other categories. There is also an Oral questions section.

The largest volume of information available is on the Plenary Sessions. There are two agendas, one for the sessions held at Strasbourg and another for those conducted in Brussels. Reports are available under a number of different headings, including the name of the rapporteur (changeable and unlikely to be known by many), by committee responsible, by word in title, by speaker and by various EUP cataloguing numbers. Unfortunately reports are not available by subject matter or by title, or in html format if they were published before 1 January 1997. As reports cannot be searched for by date, finding those that are available online is an unnecessarily lengthy business. In fact this mechanism of providing access to information can only be described as pretty hopeless.

Minutes of Plenary Sessions can only be accessed by date. They are available from 16 December 1994. This, however, is also not particularly useful in the absence of a search engine that accommodates complex queries with logical operators. Although a search can be conducted on word in title, presumably of the debate, this is not especially helpful as, for example, transport-related issues can be raised in a wide variety of different plenary contexts, not only those with transport in the title. The above applies as well to the Official Journal. The search engine permits queries by series, OJ number, or date of publication. Moreover, the contents of the Journal are not publicly available online, just the table of contents.

The European Commission

<http://europa.eu.int/en/comm.html>

The home page of the European Commission provides links to files that include information on its work programme, its organization, aims and objectives, profiles of the commissioners, particulars on the separate Directorates, official documents and a guide on how to access Commission documents. The files that are likely to prove of most interest to social scientists are those providing links to the various Directorates and the one on Official Documents.

The home page of The Directorates-General and Services,

<http://europa.eu.int/en/comm/dgserv.html>

provides details on the functions and responsibilities of the Secretariat-General, the Inspectorate-General, the Legal Service, the Statistical Office, the Informatics Directorate and the Directorates-General of the European Commission.

If you are looking for information relating to particular policy areas (agriculture, transport, development, information technology, etc.) this is probably the best place to start from in the EU Web presentation. Taking DGVI, Agriculture, as an illustration, it provides information on its aims, press releases, publications and documents, key speeches of the Commissioner responsible, and information relating to its main areas of activity, which include agricultural markets, agricultural research and genetic resources, rural development and quality policy.

Here too, however, don't rely on your intuition for finding information under particular headings. You might think that information relating to BSE would appear under the heading of Quality Policy, or at least that it would include a link to where such information was located. You would be wrong. Links to some information, a meagre volume in relation to the amount of paper and ink that it has consumed, are located under Veterinary Questions. On the other hand, if you enter the query BSE in the search engine, a link to which is not provided on most of the EU Web pages, 1397 documents matched the query on 16 February 1998, some of which emanated from DGVI.

Although the Directorates-General have overall responsibility for overseeing EU grant-aided programmes, there is no file that collates links to such programmes. In fact it is quite difficult to find some of these. The SOCRATES programme, for instance, falls under the jurisdiction of DGXXII, Education, Training and Youth. However, there is no direct link to this from its home page. Those accessing it are expected to fathom intuitively that the place to look would be under EURYDICE, the Information Network on Education in Europe, although the acronym is not expanded. Sure enough, in you march through the link to EURYDICE, which is via a link page, and you stumble on information relating to the SOCRATES programme. Similar difficulties will be experienced in tracking down other grant programmes. If you enter SOCRATES as your query in the search engine you will net more than 1690 documents. Trying to narrow this with the query <SOCRATES, programme> increased the number of documents on 16 February 1998 to 283,390! Obviously the search engine does not use the logical operator AND.

The Official Documents page,

<http://europa.eu.int/comm/off/index-en.htm>

of the European Commission links to Work Programmes/Action Plans, Reports (not many), and Green and White Papers. Green Papers are documents that are presented for public discussion and debate, whereas White Papers are those that present 'a detailed and debated policy, both for discussion and political decision'.

Although among the links on the Official Documents page there is one entitled Grants and Loans from the European Commission,

<http://europa.eu.int/comm/sg/aides/en/cover.htm>

there is no information relating to grants or loans. It does include, on the other hand, general information relating to the European budget.

The European Court of Justice

<http://europa.eu.int/cj/en/index.htm>

This page provides details of the workings of the court, its membership, diary of sittings, publications, press releases and recent case law. The latter is likely to prove to be of the most interest in the long run. In order to access cases your browser needs to be Java enabled. Cases can be accessed with the aid of a search engine which queries by case number, date, names of parties, field (agriculture, community budget, etc., for which there is a drop-down menu to choose from) and words in the text. Alternatively, you can list case number, date and names of parties.

23.2 Policies

<http://europa.eu.int/pol/index-en.htm>

This section provides information on European Union policies under four headings: Economic and Social Area, The Role of the Union in the World, Justice and Home Affairs, and Financing Community Activities. Although various links are provided from pages dealing with specific subject areas, most of this is more conveniently accessed from the pages of specific Directorates-General, mentioned in the previous section.

23.3 Publications and documents

Some documents have already been referred to in connection with the files available from the European Commission home page (see p. 261). There does not appear to be a central collating page for documentation. Pages relating to the separate Institutions and Directorates-General provide some access to publications, but not systematically, as I indicated earlier in connection with publications relating to BSE, Directorate-General VI, Agriculture. The alternative is to resort to the use of the search engine. This does not allow for very focused queries and throws up thousands of records under many headings.

Below are listed some access points to documents and databases. As far as most documents are concerned you have to pay a charge per page, usually 0.5 ecu. In some instances there is also an unspecified subscription fee. All in all, it is not very easy to find particular documents due to the absence of any coherent overall guidance and the numerous access points to different categories of document and database.

Access to Commission Documents: A Citizen's Guide

<http://europa.eu.int/comm/sg/citguide/en/citgu.htm>

This is accessed from the European Commission's home page. Its contents are too detailed to present here. Many of the documents are not available without cost. There is no link from this page to even the important treaties of the European Union. These are accessible from a page with the title The abc of the European Union – Citizenship

<http://europa.eu.int/abc-en.htm>

From this page you can download the Treaty Establishing the European Union, the Single European Act (1987) and the Maastricht and Amsterdam Treaties.

EUR-OP

<http://eur-op.eu.int/indexen.htm>

This is the major source of information on EU documents. It is responsible for publication of the *Official Journal of the European Communities* and, on average, some 6000 monographs and 110 periodicals each year, currently in 11 languages. Although it is the official policy of the Commission to make the policies of the Community more transparent by making documentation more readily available, the fact of the matter is that very few documents are freely available online. On 3 March 1998, out of 72,000 documents 2887 were available freely online. My impression from a number of searches that I carried out, was that these tend to be very short documents with the occasional lengthier report.

The European Commission: Official Documents

<http://www.europa.eu.int/comm/off/index_en.htm>

Available here, without charge, are Work Programmes, Action Plans and Guidelines, both for the current year and for 1996 and 1997. For 1998 these include guidelines on the introduction of the Euro and current economic policies. This is also an access point for Green and White Papers and for the *Bulletin of the European Union.* The latter is published 10 times a year and reports on the activities of the Commission and other Community institutions and includes links to some associated documentation. Bulletins for 1996 and 1997 are available. The Reports category includes a small number dating from 1995 and 1996.

One of the most useful documents available here is Grants and Loans from the European Union, a lengthy tome made available at the behest of the European Parliament and now presented as a 'product of the new information policy and the new openness towards the European citizen as voter'. It is divided into various sections and provides extensive details on grants and loans relating to different domains. The section entitled A People's Europe includes information on education, training and youth programmes.

Official Documents

<http://www.europa.eu.int/abc/off/index_en.htm>

The Treaties link provides access to some of the European Union treaties, including the treaties establishing the European Atomic Energy and the Coal and Steel Communities, the Maastricht Treaty and the Treaty of Rome. There are also links to Other Treaties and Instruments, Other Instruments, and Resolutions and Declarations. From the titles you can probably deduce that coherence has not been the uppermost consideration in collating this data. Another important series of documents available from this page is the consolidated texts of legislation in force.

ECLAS: The European Commission Library Catalogue

<http://europa.eu.int/eclas>

ECLAS is a bibliographic database consisting of some 172,000 completed catalogue records in the domain of European affairs; about 7000 new records are added annually. About 20 Directorates-General manage and catalogue their departmental collections in ECLAS.

In order to access the database you need to register, for which there is no charge. You will then be sent a user-id by electronic mail, usually within minutes. If at any time you do not login for more than a month you will be automatically deleted and need to reregister.

You can search by author, title, subject, or a combination of the three. You can restrict your search by data, language and document type (all, audio cassette, video, map, country study, etc.). The files retrieved will list a maximum of 200 entries that match your search criteria, the default listing being 20 titles per page. If you select any of the entries, details relating to the publication are provided, including a brief description. If these are available on the Web the link is provided so that you can download them. The database is well organized although at times somewhat slow to return information.

CELEX

<http://europa.eu.int/celex/celex-en.html>

'CELEX is a comprehensive and authoritative information source on European Community law. It offers multilingual, full text coverage of a wide range of legal acts including the founding treaties, binding and non-binding legislation, opinions and resolutions issued by the EU Institutions and consultative bodies and the case law of the European Court of Justice. Sophisticated cross-referencing features hypertext links to subsequent modifying acts, earlier acts and to national legislation implementing Community directives. CELEX is an essential information source for legal professionals, consultancies, European information relays and administrations as well as decision makers and researchers worldwide.'

There is an unspecified subscription charge and a charge per page. Information on how to subscribe is, of course, provided on this page.

SCADplus Database

<http://europa.eu.int/scad/>

SCAD is a bibliographical database containing references to more than 250,000 publications relating to various aspects of the European Community, and is divided into four sectors:

- Sector A: Community legislation
- Sector B: Official publications
- Sector C: Articles from periodicals
- Sector D: Opinions from the two sides of industry.

A special 'News update' section provides information on a selection of the most recent documents on the activities of the European Union. A table gives details of the date of the latest update and references to the most recent Official Journals in the database. The database is produced in MISTRAL language and is divided into 18 fields. You can search on the number of a regulation, decision, directive, COM document, Official Journal, or European Parliament report. You may also search by domain (agriculture, industry, etc.), sector, words in the title or text, year of publication, language, author, keywords, or periodical title. The keyword search is only available at present in French. There are no materials available online.

From the entry page select the language you want to view the presentation in, then either Search on No., or General Search. This is an extremely useful resource and is, understandably, in heavy demand so you may find difficulty accessing it at certain times of the day. From the information returned in response to a query, if you select text details a detailed abstract seems to be available in addition to all the necessary information relating to the publication.

23.4   Other European Union resources

Eurhistar Database

<http://www.iue.it/LIB/Welcome.html>

These are the online historical archives of the European Community. The documents are housed and catalogued by the European University Institute. Materials are released in accordance with the customary 30-year closure rule on official documents. The archive seeks to acquire papers by politicians and others useful for the study of the history of the European Communities. At present some 'oral archives' are being processed. Not many of those documents that have catalogue entries can be accessed online.

Harvard Jean Monnet Working Paper Series

<http://www.law.harvard.edu/Programs/JeanMonnet/jmpapers.html>

Papers dating from 1995 submitted under the auspices of the Jean Monnet initiative, Harvard Law School. 'Under the Jean Monnet Project, the European Commission supports university initiatives aimed at creating teaching activities in European integration. … In 1995 a Jean Monnet Chair was established by the European Union at Harvard.' As of 17 February 1998 some 40 papers were available online.

A Glossary of the European Communities and European Union

<http://www.abdn.ac.uk/~pol028/sources/europe.htm>

Alphabetically arranged and provided by Professor Derek Urwin of the Department of Politics and International Relations at the University of Aberdeen, this provides information on Acronyms, Initiatives, Institutions, Policies, Programmes, and Terms. The entries under each item are short. The file itself is large, 215 Kb. A very useful resource.

CHAPTER 24

Resources for economists

24.1	Mailing lists and newsgroups	267
24.2	Current economic news	268
24.3	Journals and working papers	271
24.4	Guides and lists	273
24.5	Multiple topic sites	274
24.6	Specialized topic sites	277
24.7	Miscellaneous	282

24.1   Mailing lists and newsgroups

There are a considerable number of mailing lists dealing with economics, financial and business matters. As with printed journals, they range from those dealing with very specific sub-areas of economics, to those that are more general in nature. In earlier chapters I provided detailed information on how to locate the names, subject matter and addresses of relevant lists, as well as how to subscribe, unsubscribe, etc. Bill Goffe's Resources for Economists on the Internet,

<**http://netec.mcc.ac.uk/~adnetec/EconFAQ/EconFAQ.html**>

which is a very comprehensive guide to resources in economics, has a section on mailing lists dealing with subjects likely to be of interest to economists. The LISTSERV economics mailing lists that were most heavily subscribed to, with the number of subscribers as of 7 February 1998, were as follows:

- AGECON-L@UMDD.BITNET
  Agricultural Economics Discussion List (325 subscribers)
- ECNAGING@LISTSERV.SYR.EDU
  Economics and demography of ageing, ageing policy (361 subscribers)
- EKONLIST@CC1.KULEUVEN.AC.BE
  Ekonomika mailing list (2065 subscribers)
- RESECON@LSV.UKY.EDU
  Land & Resource Economics Network (863 subscribers)
- SIRFF-L@SIVM.SI.EDU
  Ecology and Economics Seminar Series (357 subscribers)

The two most prominent discussion groups are sci.econ and sci.econ.research. The communications of the latter are archived at

<ftp://sunsite.unc.edu/pub/academic/economics/sci.econ.research/>

24.2 Current economic news

Up-to-the-minute economic news can be obtained from general Internet news sources (Chapter 18) and from sources that specialize in providing information of particular interest to practising economists and business. Press agencies and online television news services like CNN provide up-to-the-minute headline news, as do Voice of America and other radio sources on the Internet.

CNN Financial Net (CNNfn)

<http://cnnfn.com/hotstories/>

CNN Financial Net provides relatively comprehensive financial news on a daily basis. The home page relates the top stories of the day and links to other CNNfn resources. It provides news covering the US and other stock markets, making available up-to-the-minute information on each of the major indexes. US indexes are updated throughout market hours. The world markets page follows major exchanges in Asia, Australia, Europe and North America. There is also extensive information on currencies, interest rates and commodity prices.

    CNNfn reports are archived back to 1995, providing an abundance of information on breaking economic, financial and commercial issues. The search engine retrieves records rapidly and has a focused search facility. Thus, if your search string is European Union you can conduct subsequently a search on the records retrieved, focusing the query, for example, on Germany.

Handbook of International Economic Statistics 1997 – CIA

<http://www.odci.gov/cia/publications/hies97/toc.htm>

Published by the US Central Intelligence Agency, the handbook 'provides basic world-wide statistics for comparing the economic performance of major countries and regions. In general, the data in the *Handbook* are for 1970, 1980, and individual years in the period 1990–96. Data for the presented countries have been adjusted, where necessary, to achieve comparability and therefore may differ from data presented in original sources. Footnotes have been used liberally to give definitions, exceptions, and methodology.' Additional information on methodology can be found at

<http://www.odci.gov/cia/publications/hies97>

The headings under which the contents are arranged include aggregative trends, OECD country trends, energy, agriculture, and foreign trade and aid. There is a separate heading for the independent republics of the former Soviet Union.

STAT-USA/Internet

<http://www.stat-usa.gov/>

This is a useful source for current economic information, providing extensive daily information on varied aspects of US and global business. This is now a fee-based service, an individual user licence costing $150 per annum or $50 per quarter. The Newsletter is free. In addition to a page on Daily Economic News, information is arranged by subject, divided into Export and International Trade, Domestic Economic News and Statistical Series, and Business Leads and Procurement Opportunities.

Financial Times (London)

<http://www.ft.com:80/>

The *Financial Times* is available free of charge although you do have to register. This is not an electronic equivalent of the printed edition. A valuable feature of the site is the search engine that allows you to track down reports on particular topics by entering an appropriate search string. Reports are archived for a period of 30 days. Information on how to employ the search engine is provided.

Wall Street Journal

<http://www.wsj.com/>

The *Wall Street Journal* is currently available on subscription, at $49 per annum. A limited number of features are available to non-subscribers. If you register and provide your credit card details you can try the online facilities for a period of two weeks free of charge. Subscription entitles users to search through the 100,000-file database. The major subsections are Market Place, Money, Sports, and Personal Journal. The important subdivisions include World Wide, Asia, Europe, Economy, Politics and Policy, Leisure and Arts, Editorial, and Weather.

The Economist

<http://www.economist.com/>

The online version of the *Economist* magazine, published weekly in the United Kingdom, offers selected articles from the printed edition. An annual subscription to the Web edition costs $49.

Fortune magazine

<http://www.pathfinder.com/@@W5a82gcAd*lX7r3M/fortune/index.html>

This provides more comprehensive coverage than the free online *Economist* and its archives extend back to the beginning of 1996. Part of the Pathfinder stable, you can confine your archival search to *Fortune* or extend it to all Pathfinder magazines.

There are many electronic editions of other financial newspapers and magazines that can be easily accessed. Below are listed a small selection. To locate others, use Alta Vista (advanced search) or another search engine with variations on the following:

<(business OR econom*) AND (news OR newsletter OR daily OR world OR weekly) AND [region/country]>

- Belgium: Financieel-Economische Tijd (in Dutch)

    <http://www.tijd.be/tijd/>

- Ecuador: El Comercio (in Spanish)

    <http://www.elcomercio.com/>

- Mexico: El Economista (in Spanish)

    <http://www.economista.com.mx/>

- Singapore: Business Times

    <http://www.asia1.com.sg/biztimes/>

- Sweden: Veckans Affärer (in Swedish)

    <http://www.va.se/>

Banks that publish on the Web are also useful sources of current economic and financial data.

Bank of America

<http://www.bankamerica.com/>

This a particularly useful stopping point for information on the United States economy, as well as reports on global economic and financial matters. Its coverage includes various reports and indicators relating to the US and OECD economies. Of particular interest are the Weekly International and US Economic Briefings, which reference market highlights

(Forex, Money, Bonds), upcoming data and events, and forthcoming economic indicators for the US and other OECD economies. It also features information relating to interest and currency rates. Other reports of interest include the Monthly Survey of Wall Street Economists' predictions concerning the state of the US economy, and special reports on a variety of subjects.

News Watch

<http://www.bmo.com/fcfunds/forms/fb5/fb5.html>

This service relies on information provided by the Bank of Montreal at <http://www.bmo.com/> and some mutual funds companies. It provides daily updated accounts of current market and economic data, with particular focus on the Canadian economy.

BankWeb

<http://www.bankweb.com/>

A comprehensive list of banks with pages on the Web is available at the above site, arranged by geographical region and country. On 5 February 1998 their list included links to 734 banks outside the United States. State national bank sites are worth looking at as they sometimes have online the latest reports relating to their economies.

Financial Information Link Library

<http://www.mbnet.mb.ca:80/~russell/>

This presentation includes more than 400 links to worldwide sources of financial information, including banks, stock exchanges and commodity services, and is arranged by country. Many of the links provide up-to-date information relating to a variety of economic indicators, policies and programmes, on a country or regional basis.

24.3 Journals and working papers

There are very few economics journals being published online at present and even fewer that are available without charge. The main one that falls into the latter category is B>Quest,

<http://www.westga.edu/~bquest/1997/index.html>

which focuses on applied topics in business and economics, published by the School of Business, West Georgia College.

Working papers in economics are in much greater supply on the Internet than refereed economics journals.

Networks and publishers' lists

Social Science Research Network

   <http://www.ssrn.com/>

This is the parent network of the Financial Economics Network (FEN), the Legal Scholarship Network (LSN) and the Economics Research Network (ERN). It has available online 10 downloadable papers dealing with the subject matter covered by each of these networks. These papers are in .pdf format and require an Adobe Acrobat viewer to read.

ECONbase

   <http://www.elsevier.nl/inca/homepage/sae/econbase/>

This database includes records of 8500 refereed articles published in the 36 economics and finance journals published by Elsevier North-Holland. Access to abstracts and the table of contents is now freely available. You can also order online a sample issue.

Blackwell's

   <http://www.ilrt.bris.ac.uk/ctiecon/blackeai.htm>

This provides a similar service to ECONbase although without the detailed abstracts available from Elsevier North-Holland. The database is at present restricted to published articles included in their journals during 1993 and 1994.

General databases

Although there are not many economics journals that are freely available on the Internet at present, there is no dearth of information relating to printed journals. The information available usually includes data concerning subscription rates, primary academic focus, publication details, submission of manuscript details, and readership. Many of the journals also include abstracts of contents; some include abstracts of past issues.

WebEc

   <http://netec.mcc.ac.uk/%7eadnetec/WebEc/journals.html>

Provides the most comprehensive listing of economics journals in print.

BibEc

   <http://netec.mcc.ac.uk/BibEc.html>

This is part of NetEc, which is discussed in greater detail below. It is a massive bibliographic database of printed working papers in economics. In February 1998 there were 44,451 records drawn from 472 series. If you select the link for a particular series and then a year and volume, the record provides information on the title, the authors, key words, and the length of the publication.

WoPEc

<http://netec.mcc.ac.uk/WoPEc.html>

This a database of working papers in economics in electronic format that can be downloaded in a variety of formats from Internet sources. In February 1998 the database held information on 6569 documents in 322 series.

Reports

IMF Staff Country Reports

<http://www.imf.org/external/pubs/CAT/scr.cfm>

Reports are available for various countries for 1998 and a few for 1997. They are available in .pdf format and many are quite large, being greater than 1 Mb. If you do not have the Adobe viewer you can download it from this site as well.

24.4 Guides and lists

Although there are various Web pages that allude to the availability of guides to economics resources on the Web, there is only one that is both comprehensive and sufficiently annotated to merit the designation guide. This is Bill Goffe's Resources for Economists on the Internet,

<http://netec.mcc.ac.uk/EconFAQ.html>

This guide is revised a number of times a year. The resources annotated in the May 1997 edition were classified under 44 headings, and can be downloaded from a number of additional sites:

<http://econwpa.wustl.edu/EconFAQ/EconFAQ.html> (Missouri)

<http://COBA.SHSU.edu/EconFAQ/EconFAQ.html> (Texas)

<http://www.econ.nyu.edu/EconFAQ/EconFAQ.html> (New York)

All of these sites have a search engine that enables you to enter a search string that will point you to those parts of the guide where the query is referenced. You can obtain the guide by electronic mail if you address a message to

Majordomo@wuecon.wustl.edu

and in the body of the message you type

subscribe rfe-all

The list can also be obtained through ftp. Any economist who wants to keep abreast of economics resources accessible on the Internet will probably benefit from scrutinizing this document periodically.

Many so-called guides include links to general Internet resources (e.g. search engines) and overlap to varying degrees with related guides. Among the best that I have found is the LEAD (Leadership for Development and Trade) Guide to Sources of Trade Information,

> **<http://www.lead.org/Trade.html>**

This provides a useful compilation of links to resources dealing with international trade, the most important being that of the International Trade Law Monitor at the University of Tromsø,

> **<http://ra.irv.uit.no/trade_law/>**

This site provides a comprehensive and well-organized series of links to various resources relating to international trade, as well as international trading law.

Among subject directory lists of economics resources, the most useful are those retrievable from Yahoo,

> **<http://www.yahoo.com/Business/>**

where economics is a subcategory of business, and the World Internet Directory,

> **<http://www.tradenet.it:80/links/arsocu/economics.html>**

24.5   Multiple topic sites

At some point 'guides' to resources that appear in hypertext format on the Web merge imperceptibly into what Goffe refers to as multiple and single-subject economic sites. Although I retain the distinction here between lists and sites, from the perspective of the user the distinction is somewhat obtuse.

NetEc

> **<http://netec.mcc.ac.uk/NetEc.html>**

NetEc is the most important network of economics resources currently on the Web. Originally located at the Manchester Computing Centre, the site is mirrored at Washington University St Louis. The network is subdivided into a number of specialist networks, the most important being:

- BibEc/

  > **<http://netec.mcc.ac.uk/BibEc.html>**

  A database of information on printed working papers in economics.

- WoPEc/

  <http://netec.mcc.ac.uk/WoPEc.html>

  A database of electronic working papers in Economics.

The first two components were dealt with earlier in the section on journals and working papers.

CodEc

<http://netec.mcc.ac.uk/CodEc.html>

Provides links to computer software resources that are likely to be of interest to economists and econometricians.

> 'CodEc provides source code for several programming languages (currently in C, C++ and Fortran) as well as programs written in some of the econometrical and statistical software used in Economics (for example Gauss, Rats and Shazam). CodEc also has programs for computer algebra systems (Mathematica) and executable binaries for DOS or Windows. More CodEc information is available as WWW hypertext, in PostScript for GhostView or for printing and in dvi format for xdvi or other dvi drivers.'

HoPEc

<http://netec.mcc.ac.uk/HoPEc.html>

Provides links to the home pages of economists. These give varying details about their areas of interest but also include links to online papers that can be downloaded. The index is arranged alphabetically by author and the papers are classified in terms of the Journal of Economic Literature Classification System. In February 1998 the database included information on 325 authors.

WebEc

<http://netec.mcc.ac.uk/WebEc.html>

Part of the WWW Virtual Library project, this is essentially a subject directory for economics resources. Subjects are classified under economics subdisciplines. The associated document lists links to a very substantial range of economics resources and is the most comprehensive collation of economics-related links currently available on the Internet. These resources are listed by specialism area and include those on Economics and Teaching, Methodology and History of Economic Thought, Quantitative Methods, Public Economics, Law and Economics, Economic Systems, Agriculture and Natural Resources, Regional Economics, and Economics of Networks. Each of these main categories is further subdivided. The collection of links is obviously too large to describe here. This is a very substantial resource that is well worth bookmarking and checking back with periodically. There is also a search engine that can be queried across all NetEc subnetworks.

FINWeb

<http://www.finweb.com>

This Financial Economics WWW Server aims to list Internet resources providing substantive information concerning economics and finance-related topics and is a major collation of links to such resources. Although it includes far fewer links than WebEc, it contains a significant number of useful ones, some of which, of course, overlap with those accessible from other networks and link pages. Resources accessible from FINWeb are briefly annotated. The main categories under which the links are subsumed are:

- Electronic publishing
- Working papers
- Databases
- Other finance and economics WWW servers.

The search engine can be queried for local searches.

VIBES (Virtual International Business and Economic Sources)

<http://www.uncc.edu/lis/library/reference/intbus/vibehome.htm>

Compiled by Jeanie M. Welch who is an International Business Subject Specialist at the University of North Carolina at Charlotte. Some indication of the comprehensiveness, coverage and arrangement of links is the award to this home page of the Dunn and Bradstreet 1996 Online Championship. Although the primary theme of the topics around which the links are organized is that of international business, there are many links to information and data series of interest to economists specializing in other fields of the discipline. The links to other sites are arranged in three categories:

1. Comprehensive, being sites that deal with topics that are not restricted to one part of the world. The subject matters included in this section are Agricultural Products, Banking and Finance (also includes taxation), Business and Marketing, Country Information (General), Country Information (Economic), Foreign Exchange Rates, Foreign Stock Markets, International Trade Law and Intellectual Property (patents, trademarks, copyright), Metapages (home pages with several international links), Petroleum and Energy, Trade Issues and Statistics – United States, and Trade Issues and Statistics – General.

2. Regional, being sites devoted to one particular region. Those included in VIBES are Africa, Asia–Pacific, Eastern Europe, Western Europe, Latin America, NAFTA, and Middle East.

3. National, being sites devoted to one particular country. As with regional data, the breadth of coverage, and the specific subjects and data series accessible for each country, is variable.

24.6   Specialized topic sites

There are a significant number of sites that collate links relating to economics subdisciplines. Goffe's guide,

> **<http://netec.mcc.ac.uk/EconFAQ.html>**

lists some of the most important, as does WebEc,

> **<http://netec.mcc.ac.uk/WebEc.html>**

I shall restrict my own review to comments and references to some of those sites that are particularly comprehensive in their coverage, and/or that list other specialized single-subject economics resources sites. Anyone interested in topics that I have not included should find little difficulty tracing relevant sites, either from the resources mentioned above or by using a search engine.

Agricultural economics

The Agricultural Economics Virtual Library

> **<http://www.ttu.edu:80/~aecovl/>**

This is maintained by Jason Beddow at Texas Tech University. Its objective is to provide a starting point for those interested in this subject. The page provides an extensive collection of links to various resources, including journals, agricultural mailing lists and newsgroups, agricultural markets, agricultural associations, international documents and agreements (for example, those relating to GATT and NAFTA), links to departments of agricultural economics in colleges and universities, agricultural trade datasets, agricultural statistics of various countries and statistics of the United Nations Food and Agricultural Organization, to mention just some of the major resource categories.

Asian economies

What Caused Asia's Economic and Currency Crisis and Its Global Contagion?

> **<http://www.stern.nyu.edu/~nroubini/asia/AsiaHomepage.html>**

Professor Nouriel Roubini of the Stern School of Business, New York University, has arranged this presentation. It provides access to a comprehensive volume of resources relating to the Asian economic crisis. In addition to basic readings, there are links to hundreds of articles bearing in some way on this issue, including statements by Michel Camdessus, Alan Greenspan and Robert Rubin, and articles by many economists. There is also an extensive collection of articles from the heavyweight financial press, analyses by the IMF and World Bank, and country-specific reports. In short, if you wanted to arrange a short course on the Asian crisis, or write an extended essay or dissertation on the subject, you could probably get away with just reading the materials on this site and the associated links.

Banking

The Center for Banking Studies

   <http://www.uncc.edu/colleges/business/cbs/>

Based at the University of Charlotte, North Carolina, this presentation provides links to other banks on the Internet, to banking and finance research and statistics links, and to bank regulatory agencies. There is also information at this site on the Stanford Bank Game, a software package that simulates the operations of a commercial bank.

Mark Bernkopf's Central Banking Resource Center

   <http://adams.patriot.net/~bernkopf/index-nf.html>

This site provides easy access to a list of central banks, multilateral financial institutions, and ministries of finance arranged by country. There is a page that links to numerous articles on central banking history, a listing of bankers' institutes, central banking research departments, and more. In sum, if you require information relating to central banking, or links to central banks and ministries of finance, this is probably the best place on the Net to start from.

Economic growth resources

Economic Growth Resources

   <http://www.nuff.ox.ac.uk/Economics/Growth/>

Compiled by Jonathan Temple, this is arranged under Data Sets, Growth/Development Links, Journal of Economic Growth, Journals, Key References, Literature Surveys and Books, Mailing Lists, Researchers with Home Pages, Working Papers, and World Bank Economic Growth Project.

   This is a very useful compilation with a considerable amount of information relating to Web and printed materials dealing with issues of economic growth. The section on datasets includes links to the Interactive Penn World Tables, version 5.6, based on the work of Summers and Heston which appeared originally in the *Quarterly Journal of Economics*, 1991. It currently comprises data for 152 countries and 29 subjects. If you key in the name of the country, or countries, and select one or more from the 29 subjects (variables), which include real GDP per capita and population, investment share of GDP, you can retrieve from the database the statistical series for the country/variables for the years 1950–1992.

   There are other datasets on political instability and growth, annual production and cost data for 450 manufacturing industries from 1958 to 1991 and links to World Bank datasets, which are dealt with below. The page on Key References provides bibliographies relating to theories of economic growth, including the Augmented Solow Model, convergence theoretical, cross-section and other approaches, social capability and growth, and others.

World Bank's Web presentation on Economic Growth Research

<http://www.worldbank.org/html/prdmg/grthweb/growth_t.htm>

Provides links to published articles, working papers, and datasets. The published articles are drawn from various sources, including the *American Economic Review* and the *Quarterly Journal of Economics*, as well as IMF and World Bank publications. Although some of the datasets linked to the articles can be downloaded, most of the articles cannot. The working papers, on the other hand, can be obtained by sending an email request. There is a separate listing of the individual datasets that can be downloaded. These are large files and relate to research published between 1993 and 1997.

The economics of networks

Internet Site for the Economics of Networks

<http://raven.stern.nyu.edu/networks/site.html/>

Nicholas Economides maintains this resource on the server of the Stern Business School at New York University. In addition to the text of his Economics of Networks, there are documents and research papers dealing with various issues which he subsumes under the heading 'economics of networks'. These networks include the Internet, telephone, fax, transport and financial networks. The two main categories of papers available are on network compatibility and related issues, and financial networks and electronic trading. All the articles are written by the very prolific Nicholas Economides, sometimes with the collaboration of others, originally published in such journals as the *American Economic Review, Journal of Industrial Economics, European Economic Review* and *European Journal of Political Economy.* There is also an interactive bibliography on network economics.

The Economics of the Internet

<http://www.sims.berkeley.edu/resources/infoecon/>

This site is maintained by Hal Varian, currently Dean of the School of Information Management and Systems at the University of California at Berkeley, the full title of the Web presentation being The Economics of the Internet, Information Goods, Intellectual Property and Related Issues. Although this includes a section on Network Economics, it is much broader in scope than the presentation of Nicholas Economides. There are separate sections on Commerce, Electronic Publishing, Intellectual Property, Pricing, Policy and Law, and Security, Privacy and Encryption.

The section on Network Economics has links to papers of the Internet Economics Workshop, held at MIT. These include an introduction to the economics of the Internet, a series of papers on the economics of digital networks, papers on Internet resource allocation and pricing models, requirements for pricing Internet services, network interconnection, Internet economics, and more besides.

Game theory and experimental economics

Game Theory and Experimental Economics

<http://www.pitt.edu/~alroth/alroth.html>

Maintained by Al Roth, this resource provides extensive links to resources on these subjects. The first part of the page includes links to numerous articles on the subject of game theory and experimental economics authored either by Roth alone, or by Roth and associates. Also available are bibliographies on two-sided matching, learning in games, minimax trees, and the table of contents of *The Handbook of Experimental Economics* edited by John H. Kagel and Al Roth, as well as the very extensive bibliography (1995) on bargaining experiments and related papers which is included in that volume. There are links to other centres where economists specialize in experimental economics and game theory.

John Van Huyck's Web: Games Theory and Experimental Economics

<http://econlab10.tamu.edu/JVH_gtee/index.htm>

Health economics

Health Economics Research Group (HERG)

<http://http1.brunel.ac.uk:8080/departments/herg/home.html>

Based at Brunel University, Middlesex. In addition to links to various resources and sites on health economics, there is a listing of HERG Research and Discussion Papers, some of which can be downloaded.

Patti Peeple's Guide to Health Economics, Medical and Pharmacy Resources

<http://www.exit109.com/~zaweb/pjp>

This presentation collates links to a wide variety of resources. The Pharmacy section provides links to resources on drugs that should satisfy the needs of anyone who needs to know anything about pharmaceutical substances. The page on Medical Libraries is useful for those wishing to track down bibliographic resources on health economics, including links to more than 130 sites.

Among the databases linked to is the California Health Data Base Inventory which contains information on over 125 databases currently maintained by 10 Health and Welfare Agency departments or programmes. It is available in printed form and in a software program that allows anyone with a personal computer running DOS to sort and search for information in the inventory. The software program can be downloaded from this site. Also listed are various health-related associations, most of them American.

International trade

There are extensive resources relating to international trade dispersed over numerous sites on the Internet.

The International Trade Law Monitor

<http://itl.irv.uit.no/trade_law/>

Provided by the University of Tromsø, there is comprehensive online information on matters relating to international trade law, procedure, conciliation, programmes and institutions. Although this site is primarily concerned with regional and international agreements relating to trade, it also includes valuable pointers to other sites with resources relating to international trade.

The best way to navigate the site is probably through the subject index. Selecting a category provides links to the text of the relevant treaties, conventions, model laws, rules and other relevant trade instruments. The site is very well organized and kept up to date with developments and proposals in this field. There are also search engines for particular instruments, enabling users to search, for instance, through the GATT/Uruguay Round (1994) text for queried information. The documents accessible from this site can be downloaded in various formats, and often in different languages. This is the oldest site on the Net dealing with issues relating to international trade and one that provides some very valuable resources that are competently arranged.

Macroeconomics

Quantitative Macroeconomics and Real Business Cycles

<http://www.cr.uqam.ca/nobel/r14160/rbc/>

Christian Zimmerman, of the University of Québec at Montreal, collates materials relating to the home pages of economists working in these fields, where you can find papers and data series that can be downloaded. For instance, John Hassler, of the Institute for International Economic Studies at the University of Stockholm, includes on his home page at

<http://www.iies.su.se/data/home/hasslerj/homepage.htm>

various articles, a dataset on Swedish macro data covering the years 1861–1988, and comprehensive lecture notes on differential equations, dynamic opitimization in continuous time, consumption and investment under uncertainty, asset pricing, and real business cycles. Not all the sites listed in the directory of macroeconomists with home pages are equally fulsome. Zimmerman includes a directory that provides email and Web addresses of some 78 macroeconomists worldwide, listing their institutional addresses and specific interests. The Papers Online page provides links to Web pages where papers in macroeconomics and real business cycle theory can be downloaded.

24.7 Miscellaneous

OECD Observer

<http://www.oecd.org/publications/observer/index.htm>

In six issues a year the *OECD Observer* provides commentary on major international political and economic developments. These are now available in .pdf format. The subject areas include agriculture and fisheries, development, economies in transition, economic commerce, economy, education, and science and technology. There is an index to the various issues. Also available from this page is *OECD in Figures*, which provides the equivalent of 60 hardcopy pages of statistical data under headings that include capital, investment, agriculture, industry and services.

OECD Policy Brief

<http://www.oecd.org/publications/Pol_brief>

Briefing papers from the OECD on various topics. The briefs are descriptive rather than analytical. Additional information on the topics covered (e.g. electronic commerce, Multilateral Agreement on Investment) can be accessed from the tables of links and addresses provided.

PART V

Closure

Chapter 25   **Ancilliary computing skills**   285
Chapter 26   **Additional techniques, applications and resources**   297

The information provided in Chapter 25 is primarily directed at readers who are relatively new to working in a Windows environment and computing. My experience is, however, that some of the sections, notably those on the use of the File Manager and on Saving Files, could beneficially be read by a wider audience than this. Many staff and students frequently do not make efficient use of the software applications that they have available, and expend efforts all too frequently on repeating work due to the loss of data. Much data is needlessly lost due to a failure to take simple precautions or to the placing of unde-served confidence in the reliability of the technologies that are used.

Chapter 26, in contrast, is for readers who are interested in calibrating Netscape so that they can maximize the use of resources available over the Internet and download and install their own software. There is also a short section on resources useful for keeping up with new additions to Internet resources.

CHAPTER 25

Ancillary computing skills

25.1   Introduction   285
25.2   Using the mouse   287
25.3   Program Manager (Windows 3.X)   288
25.4   File Manager   290
25.5   The clipboard, copying and pasting   294
25.6   A note on saving files   295

25.1   Introduction

This chapter provides a brief overview of how to carry out procedures that you should be familiar with in order to conduct Internet-related work with ease and efficiency. Many readers will already know how to carry these out and can skip this chapter. Familiarity with these procedures is also necessary for the efficient use of all other software applications in a Windows environment.

By working in a Windows environment is meant working on a PC that uses one of the operating systems developed by the American company, Microsoft Corporation, Seattle. An operating system is the software that controls the computer's hardware and software resources. For instance, if you want to load an application, say a word processor, or alter the configuration of a printer, format a disk, or change the screen display options, the operating system acts as the mediator between the issuing and execution of the relevant commands. There are many operating systems available, including DOS, UNIX, LINUX and OS/2. Microsoft has developed a number of operating systems, including MS-DOS (Microsoft Disk Operating System), Windows 3.X (being various versions of Windows 3.0), Windows 95 and Windows NT (New Technology).

In the following discussion, as in the rest of this book, I assume that readers will be working in a Windows environment. For the most part I also assume that they will be working with Windows 3.X. Although this operating system is being phased out, and in three or four years' time, if not earlier, few individuals or organizations will be using it extensively, in most institutions of higher education in the UK it is still the most widely used operating system for IBM-compatible PCs. From the perspective of matters dealt with in this volume, the procedures detailed below are the same for other Windows operating systems, specifically Windows 95 and NT. Functionally, saving files, copying and pasting, the clipboard, drag and drop, and working with windows are identical.

In Windows 3.X files can be moved, deleted or renamed in an application called File Manager. In Windows 95 the functionally equivalent application is called Windows Explorer, whereas in Windows NT it is referred to as Explorer. Also, in Windows 3.X a number of files relating to the same application will be stored in the same directory. In the other two operating systems the functional equivalents are called folders. Although visually the applications may appear slightly different, it will not generally take more than a few minutes for someone familiar with one of them to adjust to using either of the others. In many instances the same features are found on menus with the same name in all three. As far as the discussion below is concerned, even if you are using Windows 95, you should not generally have any difficulty in following its general direction.

The one important difference that does exist concerns the appearance of the desktop and from where you access, or launch, applications. In Windows 3.X, as detailed below, you launch applications (the browser, File Manager, word processors, etc.) from *Program Manager.* In the other two operating systems the equivalent is implemented from either the *Start* menu, the *Desktop*, which is the opening screen once the operating system has loaded, or some other toolbar. As Windows 95 and NT users have considerably more autonomy over desktop appearance and where specific components of it are located on the screen, it is not practical here to use these operating systems as reference points for all potential readers of this volume. In this context, it is easier to move from Windows 3.X to the other two operating systems than vice versa.

Windows operating systems get their name from the fact that applications and subroutines of operations open in their own windows. When you are running a Windows-based software application, say a word processor, you can have open a number of documents simultaneously, alternating your work between them. Each one of these is displayed in a separate file window in the common interface. So, for instance, if you use either of the word-processing packages, Word or WordPerfect for Windows, you can have up to nine documents opened simultaneously. This makes it easy to transfer information between different documents, work on a number of drafts simultaneously, or compile a glossary, bibliography or index while working on the main document, or do all of these things. If you are working on a manuscript that needs a glossary, a bibliography and an index, you can update each of these as you proceed with the main document by transferring between them.

If you are using a Windows environment you can, depending on the specification of your PC, usually have a number of applications open simultaneously. The specifications of nearly all PCs that people are currently using are such that they can have a number of applications running at the same time. The higher the specification in terms of the processing power of the computer and its memory, the more applications that it can run simultaneously. This enables users to move data between them, or work on one while the other is completing an operation.

Thus, to illustrate, someone producing a brochure may want to incorporate text and graphics, some of the latter being clipart and some photographs. The brochure can be produced using special desktop publishing software. The author may want to add special effects to clipart images. This may be executed most satisfactorily by using a dedicated graphics program. Similarly, the retouching of photographs can be carried out particularly effectively with the aid of special photo-editing applications. Instead of working on one set of procedures, closing down the application and then opening another, the work can be carried out more efficiently by having all three open simultaneously. Data can be moved between them by use of the copy and paste facilities that they all incorporate. When you work the Internet you may download files that you want to copy and save portions of, or you may want to save graphics but alter them slightly before you do so. If you have a word processor open at the same time as your Web browser, or a graphics package, you may be able to do so more efficiently than if you first saved and subsequently edited them.

To move between applications that are open simultaneously keep the Alt key depressed and then press successively the Tab key. Each time that you do so an icon representing one of the open applications will appear in a small window in the middle of the screen. When the icon for the application that you want to move to appears release the Tab key. That application will now be active and its interface on the screen.

25.2   Using the mouse

In Windows many tasks relating to features of software applications can be implemented rapidly by using the mouse. Although a significant number may be executed by employing keyboard strokes and others by the selection of menu options, use of the mouse is virtually unavoidable in Windows applications. Most features can be implemented far more rapidly using the mouse than by employing keyboard strokes.

The following discussion applies to a mouse with a left and right button. There are some mice that have only one button, and others that have three. Those with two are the most common. In many applications the majority of features that can be activated by using a mouse are implemented by depressing and releasing the left mouse button. If you have never used a mouse before you will need to practise for a few minutes to become familiar with its operation.

There are three basic operations that you perform with the mouse, invariably with the left mouse button. The simplest is that of selecting some feature to perform, for instance, opening a menu. When you start Windows the mouse cursor arrow will be visible somewhere on the screen. If you move the mouse, the cursor will move. To open a menu, move the cursor over its name (File, Options, Window, or Help in Program Manager, Figure 25.1 below) and gently click the left mouse button. The menu will open. To select a feature on the menu, keep the mouse depressed and move the mouse so that the cursor moves downward. When you get to the feature that you wish to activate, release the left mouse button.

The second operation is called drag and drop. Essentially this involves selecting an item that is located at one position on a screen and moving it to another. The item might be a file, an element of text, an icon or graphic, or other. When you get to the position you want the item moved to, you drop it by releasing your hold on the mouse button. The steps involved are:

1.   Place the mouse cursor over the item to be dragged and depress the left mouse button.

2.   Keep the mouse button depressed and move the mouse so that the item is located at the position where you want it to be.

3.   Release the mouse button.

The third operation is that of launching an application, also referred to as opening or running an application. The procedure involved here is called double clicking. There are also other features associated with particular operations in certain applications that may require double clicking to activate. To launch an application with the mouse you need to double click the left mouse button while the mouse cursor is over the application's icon in Program Manager. This is a feature of using the mouse that many new users find most difficult. Double clicking means clicking on the left button twice in quick succession. The only way to learn how to do this is to practise for a few minutes.

25.3   Program Manager (Windows 3.X)

When you load Windows the interface that appears first on the screen is the Windows Program Manager, illustrated in Figure 25.1.

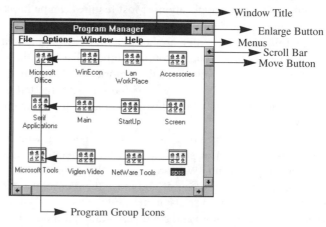

Figure 25.1   *Program Group icon window.*

When opened you will be able to see a number of *Program Group* icons. The number on your system is a function of the number of applications that you have access to, and the way in which these have been configured relative to Program Manager. In Figure 25.1 the Program Group icons featured include *StartUp*, *Main* and *Serif Applications*. When you select one of these icons by placing the mouse cursor over it and clicking with the left mouse button, its name will be highlighted, usually in blue. Double clicking on one of these group icons opens a Program Group. Generally, each Program Group includes a number of icons. In Figure 25.2 there are icons for *Clipboard Viewer* and *Print Manager*, among others. These may all relate to the same software application, or they may be icons linking to different software applications. Not all the icons included may be visible. Use the scroll bars to the right and bottom to reveal any hidden icons. You can either click on the up and down arrows, or place the cursor over the Move button, hold down the left button and move the button up or down. There is no requirement that an icon pointing to a particular application be located in any specific Program Group, or that any Program Group should have a particular name.

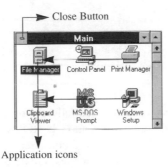

Figure 25.2   *Program Group window.*

Many organizations have a large number of different applications stored on the PCs connected to their network, as do many individual users. If you have exclusive access to the same PC it may be convenient to place icons relating to all those programs that you use frequently in the same Program Group, and arrange for its window to be open when you start Windows. This is quite simple to execute.

● Open the Program Group in which you want to house the frequently used application icons.

● Open the Program Group that includes icons of applications you want to use frequently.

● Place the cursor over an icon you want to move, hold down the left mouse button and drag it into the Program Group window for frequently used applications.

● To ensure that the window in which the icons for frequently used applications are located is open when you launch Windows, select the *Options* menu and check *Automatically Save…. It is essential that you exit Windows normally if you want to save these settings.* By exiting Windows normally is meant that you select *Exit* from the File menu in Program Manager. It is advisable that you always exit normally, rather than simply switching the computer off. If you do the latter while the operating system is performing some function you may affect its proper functioning.

You can open as many Program Group icons as you like. Each one has its own window. If the screen becomes too cluttered, select the *Window* menu and then either *Tile* or *Cascade*. If you select *Cascade* all the windows will be arranged as in a card file index, with just the names of each Program Group icon showing in the title bar, with the exception of the window at the front of the stack. To select any window, just click on it and it comes to the front of the pack. To rearrange neatly, select *Cascade* from the window menu again. If you select *Tile*, the windows will be arranged horizontally and vertically in the Program Manager window. These methods of arranging multiple windows are available in all Windows-based applications.

To close an open window, select the button at the top left of the window (Figure 25.2) and choose *Close*. Although this closes the window, it is much faster to simply double click on that button, rather than open the menu and move down to the bottom of it to select *Close*.

25.4 File Manager

File Manager is an application that is used essentially for ordering files on PC storage devices. These devices are hard and floppy disks, and CD-ROMs. In File Manager you can move files from one directory to another, rename them, alter their properties (read only/archive/hide) and delete them. You can also print files, create directories and delete and rename them. In addition, it is possible to launch applications directly from within File Manager by finding the file relating to a particular application that is its executable file, recognizable by having the extension .exe, as in *something.exe*. When you double click on them they launch the application they are associated with. When you double click on an icon in Program Manager that icon acts as a shortcut to the executable file of the application and launches it. Instead of double clicking on the icon you can launch the application directly from within File Manager.

All software applications involve the use and manipulation of files. Every time you alter a word-processing document and save it you alter the file in which the data is stored. When you download information from the Internet you are downloading a file, a file that you may want to save, rename or eventually delete. All applications save files that are processed by users to a default directory. Although you may have meant to save a file to a floppy disk, or to a particular directory on your hard disk, sooner or later it is likely that you will inadvertently have saved it elsewhere without knowing. Next time that you launch the application and look for the file where you thought it was you will need to locate where it has been stored on your system. The *Search* facility in File Manager can assist you in doing so if you can remember the file name, or part of it.

The File Manager interface is illustrated in Figure 25.3 and is opened by double clicking on its icon in Program Manager.

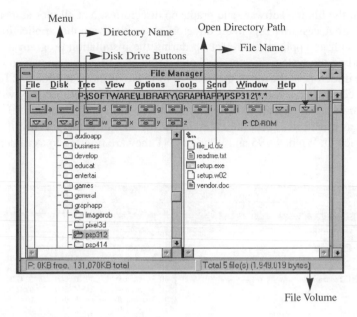

Figure 25.3   *File Manager interface.*

The buttons at the top, a–z, are disk drive buttons. A disk drive is that part of the computer on which data is stored. The disks are referred to as hard or floppy. The hard disk is the main and integral storage component of the computer. A floppy disk is flexible and removable, usually inserted into a drive bay at the front of the PC casing and invariably designated drive A. Most PCs have at least two drives, usually designated C and A, the former being the hard disk drive, the latter the floppy. The CD-ROM bay of a PC is usually designated D or E, depending on whether you have one or two hard disks. The storage capacities of hard disks for the average PC sold today are approximately 4.4 Gb, while that of the traditional floppy disk is 1.44 Mb. If you are connected to a network, you may have access to other drives (file servers) on which data may be stored. The buttons at the top of the File Manager window, a to z, designate the drives potentially available.

If you select one of the disk drive buttons by clicking on it, the directories and files available on that particular drive will be listed in the left and right segments of the window respectively if the *Tree and Directory* option is selected on the View menu. This is the default configuration. A directory is essentially a representational means of grouping files together. (Files in the same directory are not necessarily stored in adjacent sections of storage devices.) An application, say a Web browser, is composed of many separate files. Generally most of the files associated with an application are grouped in the same directory. In Figure 25.3, for example, there is a directory named psp312 in the left-hand window. As this directory has been highlighted, the icon indicates that it is open. The directory path,

P:\SOFTWARE\LIBRARY\GRAPHAPP\PSP312*.*

which appears in the lower title bar in Figure 25.3, indicates the path along the directory tree to the directory that is open. psp312 is on the P drive, and to get to it you go down the hierarchy of the library, software and graphapp directories. Not all files associated with an application are necessarily kept in the directory associated with that application. Some files associated with an application are set up during the installation program in other directories, including the system directory and part of the operating system named the registry.

The directory at the top of the tree is referred to as the root directory. In Figure 25.4 the root directory is c:\. If the drive button A is selected the root directory will be a:\. It is somewhat confusing that all the icons in the left window of Figures 25.3 and 25.4 are referred to as directories, with the exception of the root directory, even if they are in fact subdirectories. In Windows 95 and Windows NT they are referred to as folders rather than directories.

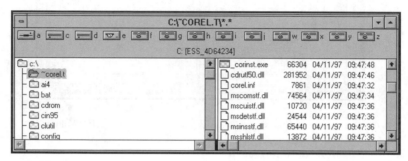

Figure 25.4 *Root directory.*

The operations for copying or moving a file from one drive/directory to another, for renaming a file/directory and creating a directory are all carried out from the File menu by choosing the relevant option. Figures 25.5 and 25.6 display the dialog boxes for copying and moving files.

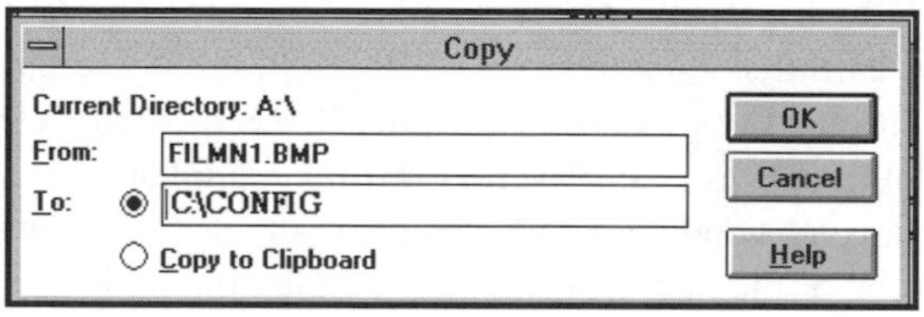

Figure 25.5 *Copy file dialog box.*

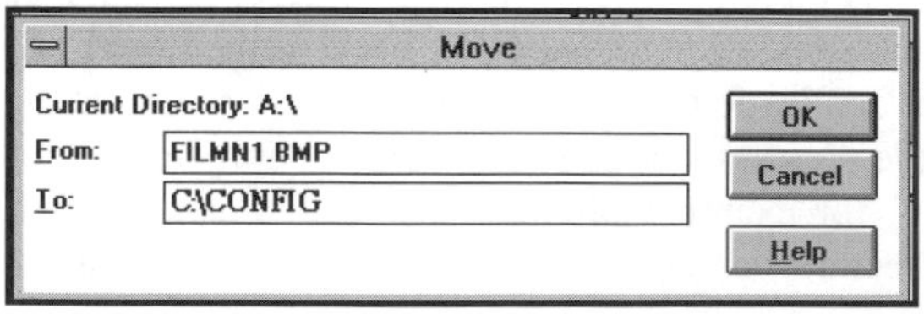

Figure 25.6 *Move file dialog box.*

The file FILMN1.BMP is to be copied (Figure 25.5) or moved (Figure 25.6) to the CONFIG directory on the C drive. A letter followed by a colon and a backward slash indicates the drive. The procedure for renaming a file is virtually identical, involving only the insertion of the new name in the text box. After you copy or move a file from one directory to another you need to select the *Refresh* option from the View menu in order to see the changes reflected in File Manager.

To create a new directory you need first to highlight the directory on whose path you want to create another directory. So, for instance, if there were no cdrom directory in Figure 25.4 but you wanted to create one in the same position, you would highlight c:\ by clicking on it when the cursor was over it, choose *Create Directory* from the File menu, and then enter the name cdrom in the text box, as illustrated in Figure 25.7. If you wanted to create a directory called corel2 under the ~corel.t directory, you would highlight that directory, choose *Create Directory,* and then insert the name in the text box.

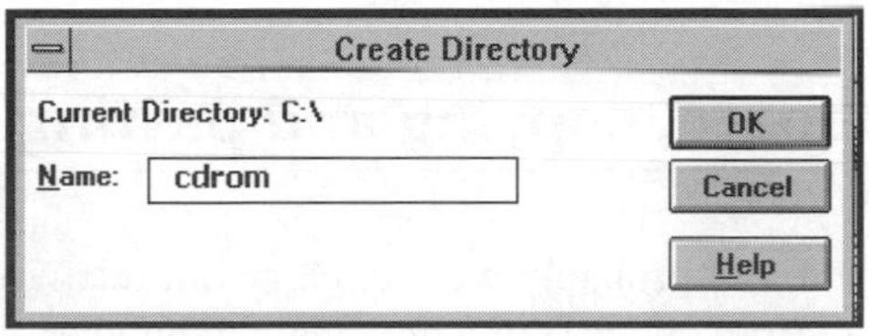

Figure 25.7   *Create directory dialog box.*

The *Search* facility is also accessed from the File menu. Before opening this dialog box (Figure 25.8), open the window of the drive you want the search to be conducted on by selecting the appropriate drive button. Thus if you want to search on the C drive, select the C button so that this becomes the active drive in File Manager. Now highlight the root or other directory on this drive in which you want the search to be carried out. If you want the search to be carried out only in the clutil directory on that drive, select it by clicking on it. Now open the *Search* facility from the File menu. Alternatively, just enter these details in the *Start From:* text box. In the *Search For:* text box enter particulars relating to the file that you are searching for.

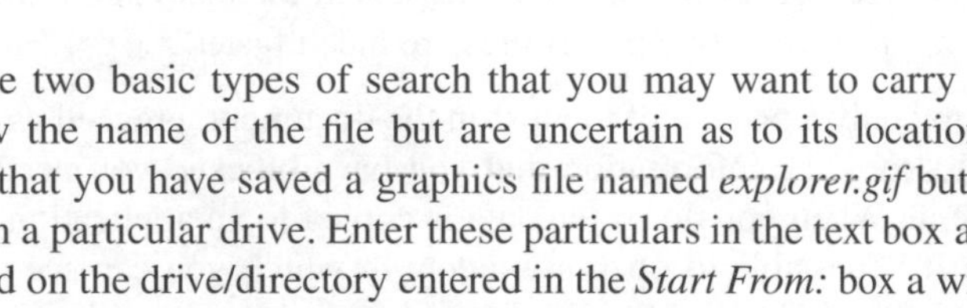

Figure 25.8   *Search dialog box.*

There are two basic types of search that you may want to carry out. The first is when you know the name of the file but are uncertain as to its location. You may, for instance, know that you have saved a graphics file named *explorer.gif* but be uncertain as to its location on a particular drive. Enter these particulars in the text box and select OK. If the file is located on the drive/directory entered in the *Start From:* box a window will open in which the pathway to the file will be indicated. You should note that there may be numerous copies of some files distributed in various directories as many applications use common files.

The second type of search that you may want to conduct is one in which you are certain only about part of the name of the file. Graphics, like other digital files, come in a variety of formats which are indicated by their file extensions. These include .gif, .jpg, .img, etc., for example *something.gif.* If you are certain that you have a file on the C drive called *explorer*, but are uncertain in which format it is, you can conduct a search using what is called a wildcard. The wildcard is signified by an asterisk. This can appear anywhere in the particulars entered in the *Search For:* text box. To locate that file you might insert *explorer.**. In other circumstances you might conduct a search with the query *ex*.** in which the database of files will be searched for files beginning with *ex* with variable extensions.

25.5   The clipboard, copying and pasting

One of the operations you will probably want to carry out relatively frequently is that of copying and moving data from one part of a document to another, or from one application to another. There are three stages involved:

- Selecting the data
- Copying or cutting the data to the clipboard
- Pasting the data in at a chosen position in a document window.

Assuming that you have the document that you want to copy or move data from open and active, you need to select the data that you want to copy or move. The difference between the two operations, of course, is that when copying the original data is not altered; it remains in the same position that it was in prior to copying. If you want to copy the whole document there are three ways of proceeding.

1.   On the Edit menu choose *Select All*. This will block all the text data in the document in the active window. The text blocked will have a black overlay. Note that graphics will not show on an overlay.

2.   Press down the Ctrl key and then the A key. This will block all the text data in most applications in Windows 95/NT but not in Windows 3.X.

3.   You can block the data manually. Place the cursor at the top of the document and then depress the left mouse button. Keeping the button depressed, move the mouse to the end of the document and then release. All the text data in the document will be blocked. The former two procedures are much faster.

If you want to copy only a portion of the text in the document, proceed as in 3 above.

In order to copy the information that you have blocked you need to select *Copy* from the Edit menu. When you do so the data is copied to an application called the *Clipboard*. Although it is possible to open a window in which you can see a document that includes data copied to it, there is usually no need to do so as it works in the background. If you select *Cut* from the Edit menu, the data is also copied to the clipboard but it is also removed from the document from which you have cut it.

Having copied or cut data to the clipboard, to paste it in somewhere else in the same document, in another open document window in the same application or in another application, position the cursor where you want the data to be downloaded to. When you select *Paste* from the Edit menu the data is downloaded. The keyboard shortcut for pasting is Ctrl and V. Hold down the Ctrl key and then depress the V key.

Each time you copy or cut information to the clipboard it overwrites any data that may have been copied or moved there previously.

25.6   A note on saving files

The general procedures for saving files were explained in Chapter 2, pp. 20–1.

In my experience staff and students lose more time through a failure to adopt adequate file saving procedures than they do from many other circumstances associated with the use of IT. Saving files only to a hard disk on a PC, to a file server or to a floppy disk is asking for trouble. You should assume that there is a high probability that the hard disk on your PC or file server will crash and require replacing. Do not expect that it will be possible to retrieve the data, even though there are firms that specialize in doing so, usually at a very high price. Frequently they will not be able to do so. Also, do not rely on network backup systems. Although many servers are backed up, you cannot know whether the procedures have been implemented properly or are checked regularly unless you do this yourself. These systems can and do fail and many IT servicing departments in higher education have a hard time extracting resources to ensure the efficient functioning of such systems until after disaster strikes. Many of the backup systems are frequently housed in the same rooms or sections of buildings as the servers that you are saving your files to. If you have spent a considerable amount of time working on some project stored in digital format you may want to take the trouble of finding out how secure the data actually is.

Floppy disks are not sufficiently reliable as storage devices to trust the security of your work to. The data on them does at times become corrupted and the files unreadable. Here too, restoration procedures rarely work efficiently. Even if you are lucky enough to recover part of the data, the probability that all files will be restored intact is exceedingly small. Accordingly, you should consider saving all your data to at least two floppy disks. These disks should be kept in separate places for most of the time, otherwise they will melt together in the back of the car, be damaged by coffee or other spilt liquids, or disappear along with the car radio.

As far as storage on floppy disks is concerned there is one other problem that crops up regularly. If you are working on a file, save it to your floppy disk and then take out that disk and insert another in its place in an attempt to back up that file you are likely to corrupt the disk. This has something to do with the *File Allocation Table* of the disk, which is like a table of contents. When you saved the file to the first disk the PC recognized that disk's table of contents. When you took that disk out and inserted another and then tried to save it, the PC expected to find the table of contents associated with the first disk, but now finds another. The way that the PC handles this conflict situation can corrupt the data on the disk.

The easiest way to get around this problem is to use File Manager. Having saved the file to one floppy disk, remove it. Open File Manager. Insert the second floppy disk and select *Refresh* from the View menu in File Manager. Now switch to the application that you are working in by holding down the Alt key and pressing successively the Tab key and use the *Save As...* option on the File menu.

You should also back up your work regularly in the process of carrying it out. It is folly to work on a network for hours before saving your work to disk. The network can go down at any moment and unless you or someone else has configured automatic backup procedures the work you have done will be lost. Given that it is so easy to save data to disk, it often perplexes me how many students and staff regularly complain about having lost data when their operating system has frozen, which is not unusual, or the network goes down. There is no reason not to save your work to disk at least once every five minutes.

Whilst I appreciate that much of the above can be taken as symptomatic of advanced IT paranoia, as Laing and Esterson demonstrated some decades ago in their studies of schizophrenia, paranoia is often the flip-side of reality testing. I know of many instances of all the above occurring, both in my own experience, and from regular reports in the professional press.

CHAPTER 26

Additional techniques, applications and resources

26.1	Configuring Netscape	297
26.2	Locating, downloading and installing software	305
26.3	Bookmark applications	309
26.4	Keeping abreast of additions to Web resources	310

In this chapter detailed information is provided on how to configure the more important Netscape settings and how to install software applications. The sections dealing with Netscape settings include details on the use of plug-ins and the configuration of helper applications, both of which are tools that can be employed to read files that browsers cannot handle directly. The sections on software provide information on where to locate programs and how to download, decompress and install them. In addition, there is a brief section on bookmark applications and a section on keeping abreast of new Web resources.

26.1   Configuring Netscape

Introductory comments

When Netscape is installed, either on a PC or on a network, some of the configuration options are already set to their default positions. Others need to be entered so that files can be accessed from Internet servers. If you are working on a network in a university or college, the configuration settings necessary to connect to the Internet will invariably have been inserted by the systems administrator. Those who have PCs at home, or have the browser application loaded on their hard disk rather than picking it up from a network file server, may need to insert the appropriate settings themselves. Many settings can be altered to meet the stylistic and other preferences of users.

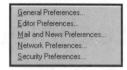

Figure 26.1   *Options menu.*

The configuration settings are accessed from the top section of Netscape's *Options* menu, illustrated in Figure 26.1. The dialog box associated with *General Preferences* is illustrated in Figure 26.2.

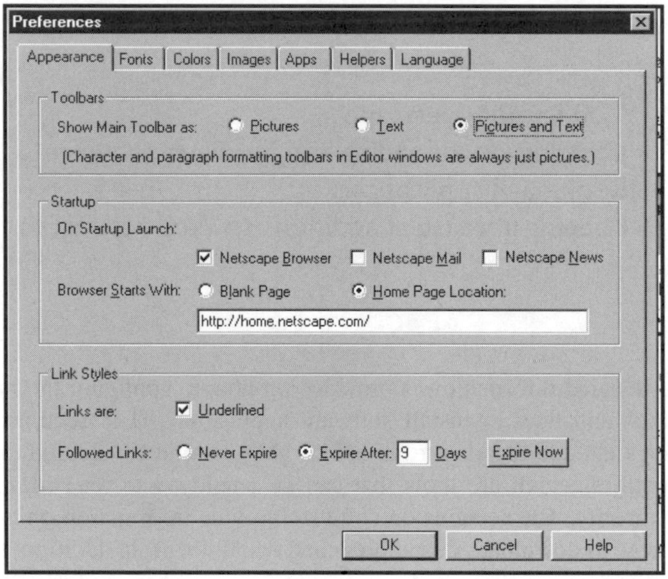

Figure 26.2   *Preferences dialog box: Appearance.*

Appearance

The settings on the *Appearance* tab determine how the toolbar should be displayed (text, image, text and image), the opening file that will be shown in the document window and the appearance of hyperlinks. It is generally not necessary to change the options for *Tool-bars* and *On Startup Launch* from the default configuration shown in Figure 26.2.

The *Browser Starts With* setting determines which document will be displayed in the browser each time you run it, or when you select the *Home* button from the toolbar. Unless your system administrator has already changed this setting, the default will be the Netscape Home Page, which will be downloaded when you run the browser. If you are picking up your browser in a computer lab rather than from your hard disk, there is usually no point in changing the settings for the start page. Every time you launch the browser the default file that has been configured by the system administrator will be downloaded. If you have some control over this feature, you may wish to change the default start page to a file that you have created, or to the bookmark file. If you change it to the bookmark file (see p. 22) then when you load your browser your bookmarks will be listed in the document window as arranged in that file. You can then select the links for the files that you want to access.

Under *Link Styles*, Figure 26.2, the only configuration variable that you may want to change is the *Followed Links: Never Expire/Expire After/Expire Now*. As previously noted, the colour of hyperlinks changes to another colour if you have selected it to enable you to recall which files you have already downloaded. This setting determines the number of days after which the change of colour will no longer hold for the files that you previously downloaded.

Selecting the *Colors* tab from General Preferences provides you with options for customizing the appearance of downloaded files in terms of the colours of the hypertext links and the background colour of the page. My recommendation is not to touch these unless you experience visual difficulties with the default settings. These difficulties some-times arise because of the inadequate html design features of some Web pages where the combination of background and text colours is such that the text is virtually unreadable, or the coding for some features, usually for tables, is incorrect. In such cases you should check *Always use my colors* and select a colour from the palette for *Background*. The best choice is usually white, except, of course, when the text has been set to white. If the text displayed is too small you can adjust its size by selecting the *Fonts* tab.

> If you change any of the Netscape configuration settings, for them to take effect you need to select/click on the OK button to the bottom left of the dialog box. If you have made alterations and then change your mind about having them take effect, select the *Cancel* button. Some changes will only be implemented if you close the browser down and restart it, as with the *Browser Starts With* page, for instance.

Helper applications and plug-ins

Configuration of helper applications and plug-ins, although not particularly complicated, is perhaps best tackled in the first instance by persons with intermediate-level IT skills, or those who do not mind experimenting a bit. It is possible to decrease the functionality of your browser if you inadvertently reconfigure settings inappropriately.

World Wide Web browsers have been developed so that they can display text that has been written in a particular format, *html* (Hypertext Markup Language). This markup language provides the browser with the necessary information so that the text can be displayed in terms of the author's specifications. Documents conforming to this format display directly in the browser window.

Files in html format are only one of the many formats in which files accessible from Internet servers are written. Web pages frequently incorporate graphic, audio and video files. The format of a file can be recognized by its extension (suffix): *html* or *htm* for hypertext markup files, *gif, jpg, bmp* for graphics files, *wav* and *ra* for audio files, and so forth. There are a large number of different file formats in every category.

In addition to files written in html, browsers can display directly ASCII text and the graphics file formats GIF, JPEG and XBM. There are many other file formats that cannot be displayed by Web browsers unless special viewers or applications act as intermediaries, as it were, between them and the browser. Browser and third-party developers have overcome the problems that this causes by allowing for the association of certain file formats with helper applications (see below) and the development of plug-ins (see below). When you select a file format that Netscape cannot display directly, the list of plug-ins that are available is checked to see if there is one corresponding to that format. If there is none, Netscape then checks the list of helper applications to see whether those configured in the Netscape configuration file can handle it. If they cannot, a message appears that asks the user whether they would like to save the file to disk, select an application to associate the file with, or cancel the operation.

Helper applications and *plug-ins* are similar in that both extend the capabilities of the browser by allowing the user to open files in formats that cannot be accommodated directly by the browser. They work differently. When a browser accesses a file format that works via a helper application it will open the relevant application with the file displayed in it. For instance, assume that you have selected a link on a Web page to a WordPerfect document. Netscape cannot read such files directly. It can, however, create its own link to Word-Perfect, if that application is stored on your PC or network. When you select a hyperlink to a WordPerfect file your browser will recognize that it cannot open it directly, will search through the list of configured helper applications, see that WordPerfect is included, and cause WordPerfect to be opened with the file displayed in it. Of course, you need to have an application on your hard disk, or network, that can display the file format that you have selected.

Plug-ins work in a similar way, but with one important difference. If you have a plug-in for the application, once you have selected a file whose format corresponds to that plug-in the file will open in a separate window within the browser. So, for example, you may encounter a file with the extension .pdf, *something.pdf*, this being one of the most popular file formats accessible over the Internet. In order to read a .pdf file you need an Adobe reader, Adobe being the name of the company that developed the PDF file format. If you have this plug-in installed in the correct Netscape directory, when you select a .pdf file on a Web page the browser will open a window within Netscape with that file displayed in it. In other words, with a helper application an additional software package is launched; with a plug-in a window opens within the browser.

Configuring helper applications

If you select the *Options* menu/*General Preferences* and then the *Helpers* tab, the dialog box illustrated in Figure 26.3 will be displayed.

For many of the file types for which users are likely to require helper applications, most of the configuration requirements have already been inserted. You may just have to highlight the relevant one in the list and then fill in the details in the text box to the left of the *Browse…* button, as described at the end of this subsection.

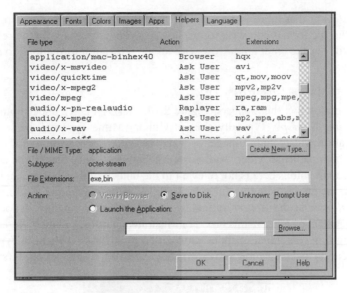

Figure 26.3 *Preferences dialog box. Helpers.*

The data in Figure 26.3 is arranged in rows under three column headings: File type, Action and Extensions. Action refers to the name of the application that will be used to display the file. How this works can be illustrated by reference to the third row from the bottom in Figure 26.3,

audio/x-pn-realaudio Raplayer ra, ram

This row indicates that a file with the extension ra or ram (e.g. *something.ra/ram*) is an audio file, subtype x-pn-realaudio, and that the browser should launch (action) the application Raplayer when a file with such extensions is selected. Most of the entries under the column Action are Ask User. This row, however, has Raplayer inserted, either because the user made the appropriate entries in the dialog box, or because the browser detected the presence of the application on the hard disk during installation and made the necessary entry.

If you encounter a file that needs a helper application, you should first go down the list of helper extensions in the right-hand column to see whether it is included in the list. If it is and you have the relevant application on your hard disk, you can make the necessary entry so that it will launch when a file with that extension is selected. To do so proceed as follows:

1. Highlight the relevant row.
2. Check the entry *Launch the Application*.
3. Select the *Browse...* button.
4. Find the directory folder on your machine where the application is located.
5. Select the appropriate executable file. Executable files end with the extension .exe, like *something.exe*
6. Select OK/Open.

In the event that there is no entry in the table in the Helpers dialog box corresponding to the file format you wish to display, and you have access to the relevant application, you will need to enter a new row with all the relevant information. To do so follow the steps below:

1.   Select the button *Create New Type…*
2.   In the dialog box that appears, Figure 26.4, make an entry under both *Mime Type* and *Mime SubType*. Typically, the entry under Mime Type will be something like application, video, audio image, or text. The entry under Mime SubType will indicate which particular video, audio or image application or file will be actioned. The accuracy of entries here is not relevant to the launch of the appropriate helper application, the entries being useful principally as an *aide-mémoire*. So long as the *File Extensions* and the *Action* variables are entered appropriately it does not really matter what you enter in this box. For illustrative purposes I have entered particulars relating to a conferencing application called FirstClass. The Mime Type entered is Application and the Mime SubType is the name of the application, FirstClass.

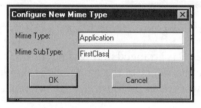

Figure 26.4   *Mime Type dialog box.*

3.   In the *File Extensions* box insert the file extension which will launch the application. (In FirstClass this is fc, files being named *something.fc*).
4.   Check *Launch the Application*.
5.   Select the *Browse…* button. This opens a *Select Appropriate Viewer* dialog box which is similar to a *Save As…* dialog box. Locate the directory in which the application you want launched when files with the appropriate extension are selected is stored. These files will have the extension .exe, indicating that they are executable files, that is, files that launch an application. Highlight the file and select *Open*. The name of the application will be inserted in the Action column. The bottom half of the Helpers dialog box will take the form of Figure 26.5. The icon to the left of the application pathway box is that of the FirstClass client.

File / MIME Type:	Application	Create New Type...
Subtype:	FirstClass	
File Extensions:	fc	
Action:	○ View in Browser ○ Save to Disk ○ Unknown: Prompt User	
	⦿ Launch the Application:	
	D:\fcwin\FCClient.exe	Browse...

Figure 26.5   *Configuring Helpers dialog box.*

Configuring plug-ins

According to the Netscape Handbook:

'Plug-ins are software programs offered by various providers that you can add to the Netscape plug-in folder to supplement Netscape capabilities. Some popular plug-ins are automatically installed with your Netscape software; others are available to users by downloading the plug-in software from the provider's Internet site and following the provider's installation instructions.'

To establish which plug-ins are pre-installed select the *About Plug-ins* option from the *Help* menu. The newer the version of Netscape that you are using, the greater the number of plug-ins that have been pre-installed. There are many other plug-ins available. Plug-ins are ordinarily located in a directory called Plugins in the Netscape/Program path. You can obtain information on plug-ins, their installation, and links to the sites from which you can download them from the following sources:

- Plug-in Plaza at the following site:

  <http://browserwatch.internet.com/plug-in.html>

  This site provides a virtually complete list of plug-ins and hyperlinks to Internet servers from which they can be obtained.

- *WWW Plug-Ins Companion* by Brown *et al.* (1997).
- Netscape's listing and links to plug-ins at

  <http://home.netscape.com/comprod/products/navigator/version_2.0/plugins/index.html>

Internet connectivity

In order to access Internet-linked servers the network options for the browser need to be configured appropriately. These are accessed on the *Options* menu by selecting *Network Preferences*. As noted earlier, if you are on a network these settings will most probably have been set already by the network administrator. If you download a different type of browser to your hard disk, you will need to configure these in the manner indicated below.

Proxies

The dialog box associated with the *Proxies* tab on the *Options/Network Preferences* menu is shown in Figure 26.6.

If you are connecting to the Internet through an Internet Service Provider, you have a direct connection to the Internet and just need to check *No Proxies*. This is the setting that needs to be checked if you are accessing the Internet from home. If you are connecting to the Internet through a Local Area Network, such as that of a company or a university, it is likely that connection to the Internet is proxy controlled. Networks that are proxy controlled have various security devices to prevent outside access to their networks, usually through a software program called a firewall. Firewalls were developed to prevent computers that are linked to the Internet, but are not part of the organization's network, from obtaining access to computers on the network.

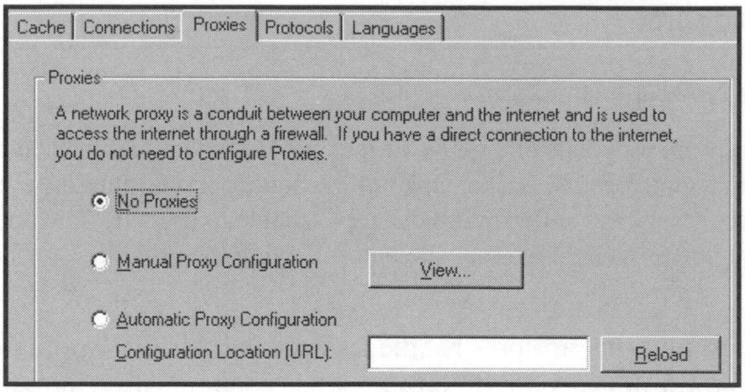

Figure 26.6 *Proxies dialog box.*

If you connect to the Internet through a proxy server, you need to check *Manual Proxy Configuration*, and then select the *View...* button. You then need to fill in the appropriate settings that correspond to each category, as in Figure 26.7.

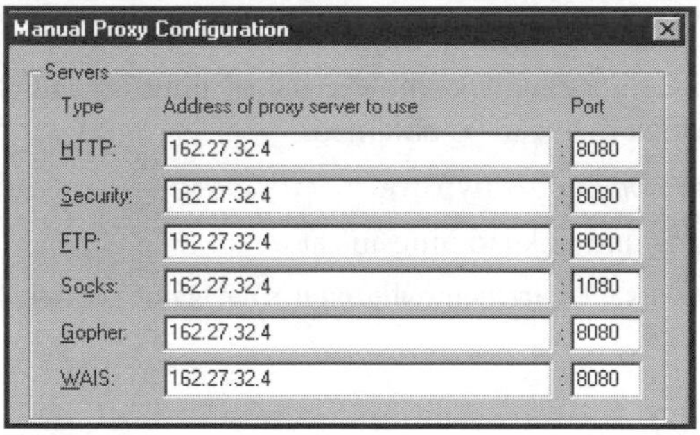

Figure 26.7 *Manual Proxy Configuration dialog box.*

You will need to obtain the correct settings from your system administrator.

Cache

Every time that a file is downloaded through a browser the file is saved, either for the duration of that session (that is, until the browser is closed) or for a more extended period of time, so long as the settings in Figure 26.8 are greater than the size of the page that is downloaded.

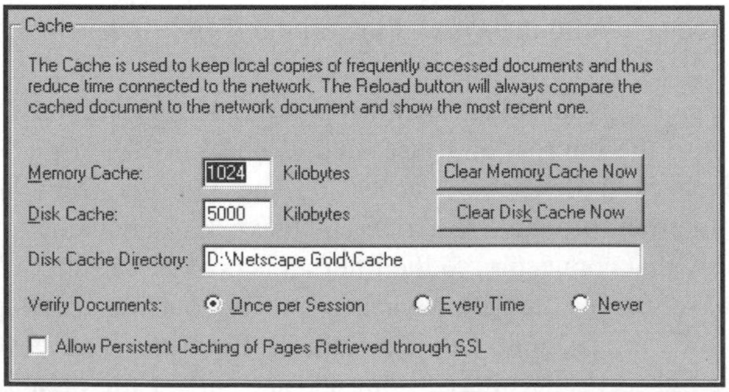

Figure 26.8 *Cache dialog box.*

The caching facility is designed to speed up Internet work. The Memory Cache keeps a copy of the pages that you have downloaded during a session to the volume that you have specified in the text box illustrated in Figure 26.8. If you have downloaded files that are jointly larger in volume than the quantity specified (1024 Kb in Figure 26.8), the files loaded first are cleared to make way for those most recently downloaded.

In addition to the Memory Cache, which stores files during a session, there is provision for a Disk Cache that stores files between sessions. Files will be stored to the volume specified and thereafter files that have been stored longest will be cleared first to make room for those being downloaded.

You can set either cache to any size that is equal to the volume of free disk space that you have available. It is usually not necessary currently to set the volume of Memory Cache above 5–10 Mb (5000–10,000 Kb), or Disk Cache above 15–20 Mb. It is also inadvisable to set the volume to match the amount of free space that you have available, as the PC requires a certain spare volume to carry on working with applications open, or to open them.

When you start a session and request a document with the Verify Documents set to Once per Session (Figure 26.8), the browser will first check to see whether the document is in its disk cache. Next it will check to see whether the source document has been changed. If it has not, it will load the document from the cache. This is quicker than downloading it from the source. If you request a document that you have not downloaded previously, after it has been downloaded it will be stored in the Memory Cache during the session and in the Disk Cache as well. If you request that document again during the session, it will be retrieved from Memory Cache, as this is speedier than retrieving it from Disk Cache.

Further information about Netscape configuration parameters and settings may be obtained from the Netscape Navigator Handbook. You can access this from the Window menu on the interface. At the bottom of the opening page there is an index. You need an open connection to access the help file in all versions prior to Netscape Communicator 4.0 as the file is stored on one of Netscape's servers.

26.2 Locating, downloading and installing software

Introductory comments

There are thousands of software applications that can be downloaded from Internet servers. Many companies and developers allow you to test the software for a certain period of time before you need to make any payments. Some software is made available without the need to pay any fees. As far as fees are concerned there are three categories of software:

1. Proprietary commercial software. Although you may be allowed to test the product for a certain period of time, once this has lapsed you need to pay the licensee in order to continue to use the product. The version that you can test is usually the

full-featured application, but with a built-in time lock so that after the expiry of the trial period it will cease to function. Some applications available for testing may not be full featured.

2.   Shareware. The idea behind shareware is that users download the software, try it out, and if they want to continue to use it they will voluntarily pay the licence fee to the developers.

3.   Freeware. This is software that is made available without charge.

Locating software

There are numerous software archives from which applications can be downloaded. I will mention here three that I have found particularly useful. If you want to track down others, use the Alta Vista search engine with the entry <software +archive*> in the basic search, or <software AND archive*> with advanced search.

1.   Slaughter House at

   <http://www.slaughterhouse.com/>

   This is divided into a number of major categories: Games, Internet, Media, and Utilities, which, in turn, are further subdivided. There is a description of the various applications in each category and a link to the company or a download facility. The system requirements are specified and many are rated out of five, five being the highest rating. There is a search engine facility and a news section that provides information on recent developments under various categories.

2.   TUCOWS, at

   <http://gfn1.genesee.freenet.org/tucows>

   This is very highly rated in terms of the number of site awards conferred. In many respects it is similar to Slaughter House. Information available includes system requirements, revision date, byte size, description, and a rating, the highest being five cows.

3.   Rene Guerrero's Comprehensive List of Freeware, Shareware & Software Sites, arranged by operating system (Windows 3.X, Windows 95, etc.), at

   <http://pilot.msu.edu/user/heinric6/soft.htm>

Downloading software

Having located the appropriate site, find the link named download. When you select it you will ordinarily be asked questions relating to the operating system that you are using, as software applications are generally operating system specific. Having answered these questions the *Save As...* dialog box will appear. Select the directory and file name and then OK/Save. By default the browser will attempt to save the file to a Netscape directory. I suggest that with file manager you create a directory called something like tempsoft to which you can save all applications that you download.

Having downloaded an application you should check it for viruses before installing it. There are various virus protection packages available on the market and many company and university networks provide virus checking facilities. Ask your help desk about virus checking facilities.

Installing software applications

As many software applications are quite large in terms of data, nearly all of them have been compressed in order to reduce the amount of time that it takes to move them over the networks. There are a large number of compression formats. The majority of those that most readers of this volume are likely to be interested in trying out currently come in two formats. They are either self-extracting files or zipped files.

Self-extracting files can usually be recognized by the extension .exe (Note that not every file with the extension .exe is a self-extracting file. Most files with this extension on your PC or network are executable files, that is, files that launch applications. However, applications that you download from software archives, or from software developers that have the extension .exe, are frequently self-extracting files.) Invariably there will be instructions at the site from which you download the file, or there may be a *readme* file if you download the application from an ftp server. To install an application that is in the form of a self-extracting file, proceed as follows:

1. Create a directory in which you want the file to be installed. Although the setup program for the application will by default suggest installing it in a directory that the developers know is available on your operating system, you may find it preferable to install it in a directory that you create. This will allow you easier access to relevant files that you may want to move, delete or alter. It usually also simplifies deleting all files associated with the application if you no longer want it.

2. Double click on the self-extracting file. This can be in either the temporary directory to which the file was downloaded, or the directory which you created and to which you have moved that file.

3. This will have launched the installation shield, which will guide you through the installation procedures. Invariably you will first be asked to agree to licence stipulations. If you want to install the application you will have to agree. Next you will be informed that the application will be installed into the default directory. At this point you should avail yourself of the option of changing this to the directory that you have created for this purpose. You do this by altering the text of the default directory pathway, or using the browse button to locate the directory in which you want the application installed. Many applications have various optional components and the installer is asked whether they want a typical/standard installation, partial installation or custom installation. Unless you are sufficiently experienced it is best to go for the typical installation. You can always reinstall and choose a different option subsequently.

4. At the end of the installation process you will be asked whether you would like a program group to be created. This will be one of the group icons that appear in Program Manager and which contain the icons that launch various parts of the program that you have installed. Respond affirmatively.

The procedures for *zipped* files are slightly more complex. A file that has the .zip extension has been compressed with a software application called PKZIP. To decompress it you can use a software application called PKUNZIP. This application is shareware. Although you can download it without having to pay any fees, after using it for the period specified in its documentation you should register it and pay the licence fee.

Another decompressing utility is a shareware program called WinZip. This application compresses and decompresses a wide range of compression formats, is relatively easy to use, is available as shareware and is inexpensive. It is available for all Windows operating systems. The latest version costs $29, which is not excessive given the range of features that it incorporates. You can download it from one of the sites mentioned above in the section on locating software. Instead of downloading it you may find it worth purchasing a copy of the monthly magazine *Personal Computer World*. WinZip is included regularly on a CD-ROM that comes with the magazine, along with many other useful utilities, including Web browsers.

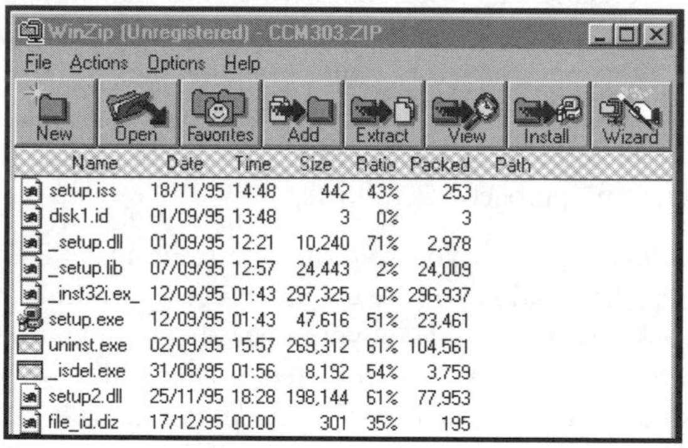

WinZip (Unregistered) - CCM303.ZIP

File   Actions   Options   Help

New   Open   Favorites   Add   Extract   View   Install   Wizard

Name	Date	Time	Size	Ratio	Packed	Path
setup.iss	18/11/95	14:48	442	43%	253	
disk1.id	01/09/95	13:48	3	0%	3	
_setup.dll	01/09/95	12:21	10,240	71%	2,978	
_setup.lib	07/09/95	12:57	24,443	2%	24,009	
inst32i.ex	12/09/95	01:43	297,325	0%	296,937	
setup.exe	12/09/95	01:43	47,616	51%	23,461	
uninst.exe	02/09/95	15:57	269,312	61%	104,561	
_isdel.exe	31/08/95	01:56	8,192	54%	3,759	
setup2.dll	25/11/95	18:28	198,144	61%	77,953	
file_id.diz	17/12/95	00:00	301	35%	195	

Figure 26.9   *WinZip interface.*

The WinZip interface is illustrated in Figure 26.9. (Install it using the procedure for self-extracting files outlined above or from a CD-ROM.) When you double click on a zipped file in the directory to which you have downloaded it, WinZip will automatically be launched and the component files of the compressed application will be shown in its interface, as in Figure 26.9. Alternatively, open WinZip and from the File menu select *Open Archive* and then select the file that you want to be decompressed. Having done either, select the *Extract* button. In the dialog box that appears indicate the directory that you want the files to be extracted to. (If you are using Windows 3.X you will need to have created a directory beforehand; Windows 95/NT will create the directory you name.)

To install the program after the files have been extracted to a directory, open File Manager and double click on the *setup.exe* file (sometimes *install.exe*) in that directory. This will start the installation shield, as described earlier. You can close WinZip down now. Notice that the zipped application will remain in the directory where it was before you decompressed it. You can delete it if you want to save space, or move it elsewhere for future use. You should not delete the application file until you have tested that the application has been installed correctly and is functioning properly. Sometimes errors occur during the installation process that will not recur if you reinstall the application.

An alternative means of installing the program is to use the *Wizard*. You may find that this is easier to implement than the procedure described immediately above.

Figure 26.10   *WinZip Wizard interface.*

Open WinZip. Select the *Wizard* button at the top right, Figure 26.9. From the dialog box that appears select the *Next* button until a dialog box like Figure 26.10 appears. Locate and highlight the file that you want to decompress from the list in the window, or use the *Search...* facility to find it. When you have done this select the *Next* button again. When you do so you will be informed that WinZip will now unzip all the files in the Zip file to a temporary directory and will then run the installation program for the application. When the operation has been completed the temporary files will be removed. In other words, WinZip will launch the installation shield and the program will be installed to the location of your choice, as described earlier.

WinZip is an excellent utility and you can use it also for compressing programs that you do not use frequently as well as for decompressing those that you may download.

26.3   Bookmark applications

In Chapter 2 I described in some detail how to use the Netscape bookmarking facility. In many respects it is similar to the Hot Favorites bookmarking feature of Internet Explorer. Both are relatively easy to use and are free. However, if you are going to be using the Internet extensively for research, teaching or business purposes, you should seriously consider investing in a proprietary bookmark application. The most likely future scenario is one of a considerable expansion in the number of servers linked to the Internet and a concomitant increase in the numbers of publicly accessible files. Even if we allow that only 0.05% of these are likely to be of interest to social scientists, this will still be a very substantial number. Potentially, therefore, many of those using the Internet will want to have relatively easy access to hundreds of Internet URLs that can be catalogued in a variety of ways. As the quantity of information that will need to be digested is extensive, it is also important that detailed descriptions of the resources available at sites can be easily added to and modified.

In my opinion neither the Netscape nor the Internet Explorer bookmarking facilities are sufficiently adequate to meet the likely requirements of intensive Internet users. There are some proprietary bookmarking applications that provide much richer features. You should consult the resources listed in the Locating Software section above to locate and then test run some of these applications. There are two that I will mention here.

- Smart Bookmarks

  <http://www.firstfloor.com/cgi-bin/product_download.cgi>

  The cost of this application is $34.95 and it will work with all Windows operating systems. A detailed description of its features is provided by Bryan Pfaffenberger (1995) – see the Bibliography.

- Internet Bookmarks

  <http://www.eclipse.co.uk/bookmarks/more.htm>

  The cost of this program is £15. It is available only for Windows 95 and NT. You can, however, use it freely for personal non-business use or for 28 days to try it out. If you do not register you are limited to 250 bookmarks. In all other respects it is fully functional.

  This is a richly featured bookmarking program that I cannot recommend too highly. Among the many other things that you can do with it is import bookmarks from Netscape bookmark files, Internet Explorer history files, any html documents, NCSA and CompuServe hotlists, and ASCII text files. This means, for instance, that if you find a page that includes a large number of links that you are interested in you can easily download all these into the Internet Bookmark database. Editing bookmarks in the database is extremely easy and you can output all or a selection of the database in html files without having to know anything about writing html code. The application is regularly upgraded at no cost to those already registered.

26.4　Keeping abreast of additions to Web resources

One of the most difficult aspects of Internet use is that of keeping abreast of new resources and facilities. In practice it is simply not possible to do so in any absolute sense as the rate and volume of change is too great. The sites mentioned below specialize in monitoring new resources that are added. If you check on these regularly you will frequently find pointers to useful materials.

- Internet Resources Newsletter

  <http://www.hw.ac.uk/libWWW/irn/irn.html>

  Heriot-Watt University Internet Resource Centre publishes this newsletter monthly. It provides brief annotations about resources likely to be of interest to members of the higher education community. The links are arranged alphabetically. Back issues from October 1994 are available. This is a very useful and well-produced monitoring resource.

- The Scout Report

  <http://wwwscout.cs.wisc.edu/scout/report/index.html>

  This report on newly available resources is published every Friday and is also available via electronic mail. It now has separate reports on Science & Engineering, Business & Economics, and Social Sciences. It is also available as a bimonthly file and in .pdf format. The Social Science subject file has been available since September 1997 and past issues are available. Back issues of the general Scout Report from April 1994 are available. This also is an excellent monitoring resource.

- Internet Scout Net-Happenings

  <http://wwwscout.cs.wisc.edu/scout/net-hap/index.html>

  This is produced by Gleason Sackman as part of the Scout Project. For the last year it has increasingly focused on providing information on resources likely to be of interest to the K-12 (kindergarten to 12th grade) community. It is still useful for tracking down some other resources, as past postings are archived and the database can be queried with the search engine provided.

Glossary

The terms included below are those that I assume are most likely to be relevant to readers inclined to adopt a utilitarian approach to computer-mediated communications and the Internet. They crop up relatively frequently in the context of Internet and PC-related work. I have included some that have not been mentioned in the text. Also, when appropriate, I have provided the common or colloquial interpretation or use of the term rather than the technical. There is considerable variation in the use of some terms by those professionally involved in IT-related activities.

There are two excellent lexicons that will fill the gaps in this glossary. Both are available as freeware from the same source as self-extracting executable files (see p. 307). Downloading and installing them on your PC will take only a few minutes. I have found that they work on all Windows platforms. The lexicons are called the Internet Lexicon and the PC Lexicon, and are available at

<http://www.firstrain.com/lexicon/>

The commercial version, which includes both and is more extensive, is well worth the investment of $14.95. It is available from the same URL. There are plenty of other dictionaries of computing terms freely accessible, some of which have been mentioned in Chapter 13 on General reference resources.

Items in brackets at the end of an entry signify main or related entries.

APPLET

A program created with the Java programming language that can be embedded in a Web (html) page and downloaded in browsers that are Java enabled, that is, browsers that can read Java. Java programs are cross-platform, which means that if embedded in a Web page they will work on all operating systems (Windows, UNIX, Macintosh, etc.). For security and other reasons some system administrators disable the Java functionality of browsers used on their networks. Although the security risks are real, the probability of being seriously inconvenienced is small. (JAVA)

ASCII (American Standard Code for Information Interchange)

Also known as ISO 646. This is a universally accepted standard for the encoding of character data in binary digits to represent letters of the alphabet, punctuation, digits, a few symbols (e.g. $ and &), and some control characters. The aim was to create a format for information exchange that was stripped down to bare essentials, making it readable on virtually all computing platforms and editors. If you take any file created in a word-processing package, for instance Word or WordPerfect, and save it in ASCII format, all the embedded codes will be stripped out (e.g. columns, bold, italics, tables, etc.).

BANDWIDTH

A term used to refer to the volume of data that can be moved per unit of time over a network. When bandwidth is low the download time is extended relative to that when it is high.

BAUD

A unit that measures the volume of data transmitted per second between a modem and some hardware component, such as a PC or a server. Modems with higher baud rates transmit data faster than those with lower ones. At present the most commonly sold modems have baud ratings of 28,800 or 34,600. The fastest rated modems currently available have a rating of 56,000 and are likely to become the most commonly installed during 1998 as an international operating standard was agreed in February. Many 28,000 baud modems sold since 1996 can be upgraded to 56,000 baud at little or no cost.

BIT

The smallest amount of information that can be stored as a discrete unit on a computer. On computers all data is stored as binary digits and represented by either 0 or 1. The term bit is an abbreviation of binary digit. All letters, digits, and special symbols and characters are represented by these two digits, in much the same way as all letters of the alphabet are represented in Morse code in terms of either a dot, a dash, or some combination of the two. (BYTE)

BITNET

The term stands for Because Its Time Network. It was established in 1981 for the purpose of facilitating exchanges between academics in institutions of higher education in the United States, but has since become a worldwide network. BITNET mailing lists were the progenitors of the thousands of mailing lists currently available. It uses different protocols from those of the Internet although it has long since been gatewayed to it.

BOOLEAN OPERATORS

Named after the nineteenth-century British mathematician George Boole. In computer programming terms these are operators that permit true or false responses. In Internet work they are employed in search engine queries and include the operators AND, OR, NOT. See Chapter 8.

BROWSER

Generally, a term used to designate an application that can be employed to read the content of files. In this sense, word processors or editors, Word or Notepad for instance, constitute browsers. In Internet usage a term synonymous with Web browser, an application used to view content embedded in html (Web-based) files. (HTML)

BYTE

A byte is a group of bits that constitutes a unit of information. Most commonly on PCs a byte consists of eight bits, which together represent a discrete unit of information, such as a letter, a number or a special character or symbol. When you are downloading files from the Internet the number of bytes that have been downloaded relative to the total is indicated in the status bar of the browser if this is visible. The size of an application is represented in terms of bytes. (KILOBYTE, MEGABYTE, GIGABYTE)

CLIENT

A computer program or process that issues commands to another computer or program. A Web browser, for instance, is a client of a Web server. The browser issues commands to the server requiring it to download data. (CLIENT–SERVER COMPUTING)

CLIENT–SERVER COMPUTING

The underlying principle of client–server computing is extremely simple. In distributed computing one part of the framework for distributing data between computers is the client, through which commands are issued to the other component, the server. An FTP (File Transfer Protocol) client, for instance, issues a request to an FTP server to display its directory hierarchy and, subsequently, to download (send) a requested file. The server responds by displaying the directory structure (folders/files) and downloading the file requested.

CLIPBOARD

This is a special area of memory that normally holds data copied to it for as long as the computer is powered up, or until it is overwritten by other data. When you use either the copy or cut command the data concerned is stored in this segment of memory. Data stored in this way may be pasted into other applications. In Windows applications it is not usually possible to append to the clipboard; each copy or cut command executed results in the data previously available in the clipboard being overwritten. There are, however, applications available that permit appending data to the clipboard when using Windows applications. You will usually find such applications in the Utilities sections of software archives.

CMC

Stands for Computer Mediated Communication.

CPU (Central Processing Unit)

'The CPU may be regarded as the unit within a computer that interprets instructions from a program and changes data in conformity with these instructions. In almost all computers the CPU is constructed from a single microprocessor integrated circuit. It coordinates and controls the activities of all other units in the computer system together with the intrpretation and execution of processing instructions, and also performs the logical and arithmetic processes to be applied to data.' (source: Anderson, 1996).

Microprocessor is a generic term used to refer to a piece of hardware that links together various electronic components, all of which are located on a small piece of silicon, hence the term silicon chip.

Pentium and Pentium Pro are names given to microprocessors developed by the firm Intel. Other well-known brands include Cyrix, AMD and Texas Instruments.

DESKTOP

In graphical environments, such as those created by Windows operating systems, and on Macintosh PCs, the term generally refers to the combination and appearance of all elements visible to the user. This includes icons, background graphics and colour schemes, screen savers, document windows, etc. Generally the user can alter the desktop by altering relevant configuration variables in Program Manager/ Control Panel in Windows operating systems. (INTERFACE)

DIGITAL

Any thing or event that is expressible in terms of the integers 0 or 1, or fixed states, on/off (source: PC Lexicon).

DIRECTORY (FOLDER)

Technically, a block of data relating to a particular drive in which links to files are stored. Frequently the files relate to a similar application, topic or procedure. The term is somewhat confusing because, in Windows 3.1, subdivisions of a directory are also referred to as directories. In Figure G.1, for instance, ActiveX, Browser, ... Plug_ins are all subdivisions of the Acrobat3_Reader directory. They are all, however, referred to as directories. Together with those listed further down they constitute the directory tree on drive D. Double clicking on any of these directories will reveal the files or directories, if any, that they contain. In Windows 95 and NT they are referred to as folders rather than directories. Currently the two terms are for all practical purposes interchangeable.

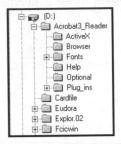

Figure G.1

DOS/MS-DOS

DOS is an acronym for Disk Operating System. Generally presumed to be synonymous with the disk operating system developed for IBM-compatible computers by Microsoft, MS-DOS (Microsoft Disk Operating System). (OPERATING SYSTEM)

FAQ (Frequently Asked Questions)

A term generally associated with newsgroups. A FAQ is a list of questions that are most frequently asked by users concerning a particular subject, along with appropriate replies to them (see pp. 157–8).

FILE PATH

The file path is used to describe the location of a file on a computer storage device. The absolute directory path specifies the location of a file in terms of the drive and folders that need to be opened to get to it on the computer on which it is located. In the Eudora directory/folder included in Figure G.1 (see entry for DIRECTORY) there is a file called eudora.hlp. The absolute file path for it is d:\eudora\eudora.hlp This is also referred to as the absolute directory path of the file.

FILE SERVER

Refers to the computer on a network on which are stored files and programs to be used by workstations connected to it. The handling of files is expedited by this computer being a dedicated file server with a fast, high-capacity hard disk.

FIREWALL

'A damage prevention and security system usually used in WANs (Wide Area Networks) and businesses connecting to the Internet. It consists of code which aliases, hides or blocks the firewalled computer from identification by any other computer on the network. Well-constructed firewalls prevent industrial espionage and sabotage as well as discouraging hackers, and are also used to prevent less knowledgeable users from accessing commands and services which could compromise the integrity of the system.' (source: Internet Lexicon).

FREEWARE

Software for which no charges need be met while the author retains the copyright.

FTP (File Transfer Protocol)

A protocol used to transfer files from one network-connected host to another. There are specialized software applications, FTP clients, which can be used to accomplish such transfers.

FYI

Stands for For Your Information.

GENERAL PROTECTION FAULT

'A peculiar error occurring in Microsoft Windows 3.1/3.11 in which the system detects two programs fighting for the same space in memory and decides that neither of them can have it. Windows closes the program at that point to protect its own integrity, denying the user the ability to save their data before exiting the program. Believed by many to be perhaps the single most arrogant software design decision in the history of personal computing, as it gives the integrity of the operating system priority over the user's own data.' (source: PC Lexicon).

GIF (Graphics Interchange Format)

A file format used for displaying and distributing graphics images over the World Wide Web. It uses compression techniques which have been patented by CompuServe, until recently a major Internet Service Provider. Although one of the most popular graphics file formats, for copyright reasons it is likely to be superseded in popularity by other graphics file formats.

GIGABYTE (Gb)

One thousand million bytes. (BYTE)

GOPHER

A client–server based application that was widely used on the Internet prior to the massive expansion of the World Wide Web. Information stored on gopher servers is arranged in a hierarchical tree structure. Selecting hyperlinks enables the user to move up and down the hierarchy opening directories or files. The gopher protocol, however, does not enable hyperlinking between files or within them. Although there are still a substantial number of documents accessible from gopher servers, this means of storing information on the Internet is falling into disuse.

HITS

Refers to the number of entries included in the database that relate to a query entered by the user searching it.

HOME PAGE

Generally used to refer to the introductory page of a Web presentation, the one to which all other pages are linked, and which, in turn, link back to it.

HOST

A computer on a network that with the assistance of compatible software can communicate with other computers on the network. Other authorities, however, seem to confuse the term host with that of node, interpreting the term as designating any computer linked to the Internet.

HTML (Hypertext Markup Language)

Conceived initially by the inventor of the World Wide Web, Tim Berners-Lee. It is a structural markup language that indicates to specialized software applications that can read it, Web browsers, how the text, graphic images, video and audio files associated with it are to be displayed. HTML is concerned principally with the structure of documents, rather than with their appearance, although the creators of Web pages have been ingenious in using opportunities to maximize their aesthetic appeal with the limited formatting codes provided for. HTML is under constant revision by the Internet Engineering Task Force (IETF), as well as by browser developers who frequently introduce innovations that are subsequently incorporated in the latest HTML standard agreed by the IETF.

HTTP (Hypertext Transport Protocol)

Some experts expand the acronym as Hypertext Transfer Protocol: 'A protocol for tranferring data formats between a server and client. Data formats include plain text, hypertext, images, sound, public or proprietary formats specified as MIME type, and metainformation about the data.' (source: Darnell *et al.*, 1997). Other experts define the HTTP in terms of its mode of connectivity: it 'enables hypertextual browsing through the World Wide Web; the user clicks on links that are established in a Web document and moves to that document.' (source: Gilster, 1995).

HYPERLINK

A method of linking from one file to another by selecting a segment of text in the file (the hyperlink), which, other things being equal, downloads the file pointed to.

In Web pages the segment that constitutes the hyperlink is usually differentiated from the surrounding text by its colour, and by being underlined. Although currently hyperlinks are invariably associated with Web documents, there are many software applications that employ hyperlinks as a means of moving from one section of a document to another (e.g. Word, Adobe Exchange).

HYPERTEXT

Invented in the mid-1960s by Douglas Engelbert. 'The practical and conceptual heart of the Web, hypertext is a system of relating points within and outside a text to each other nonlinearly. Hypertext, as manifested with hyperlinks, moves a user from text to text at will.' (source: Darnell *et al.*, 1997). As it is possible to hyperlink through graphics as well, it is currently becoming common to subsume hypertext under hypermedia.

INTEGRATED SERVICES DIGITAL NETWORK (ISDN)

Refers both to a standard for digital communications directed at carrying data over a standard telephone line at a rate of 128 kilobytes per second, and to the technology and its components that accomplish this.

INTERFACE

The term interface refers to the front-ends of software applications, that is, the combination of windows, toolbars, icons, etc., that appear once the application is launched. Accordingly, a user might refer to the fact that the Netscape interface is more user-friendly (intuitive) than that of Microsoft's Excel.

INTERNET

A term used to refer to the largest and fastest expanding network linking computers in the world. The transmission of digital data in a variety of formats between computers linked to this network is accomplished through the common use of a suite of protocols, the TCP/IP protocols.

INTERNET ACCESS PROVIDER

Refers generally to a private company that provides Internet connectivity to users in return for a subscription fee. Unlike an Internet Service Provider, it does not generally provide other facilities such as discussion groups, financial services, etc.

INTERNET PROTOCOL (IP)

Part of the TCP/IP suite of protocols that govern data exchanges across the Internet.

INTERNET RELAY CHAT (IRC)

A client–server application that enables those who have the client software to exchange messages with other users in real time. The server side of the application receives messages from users who have typed them out and then distributes them to all others logged into the discussion. Any one server can host a large number of discussions, users logging into distinct channels. In many respects the underlying operation is somewhat homologous to that of mailing list management packages.

INTERNET SERVICE PROVIDER

Generic term that covers private companies providing Internet connectivity and additional online services to users in return for a monthly subscription fee. These additional services include various discussion groups and bulletin boards. CompuServe and America Online are two of the more widely known companies that have provided such services. AOL recently purchased CompuServe.

IP ADDRESS

This is the address that uniquely identifies a particular computer (node) on the Internet. Every computer linked to the Internet needs a unique address so that data can be transmitted to and from it. The IP address is expressed in numerical terms, e.g. 158.152.1.122.

JAVA

Java is a programming language developed by Sun Microsystems. The early versions were distributed in the public domain in 1995. The technical definition is somewhat complex and unlikely to be of much interest to most readers of this volume. In practical terms the promise of Java is to deliver executable content over the Internet through Web browsers that are Java enabled; that is, through Web pages that can download Java applets. By executable content is meant software applications. In principle, therefore, instead of a word processor being installed on the hard disk of your PC, it could be downloaded to your PC as a Java program. Once you disconnect from the server that downloaded it, you will not be able to use it further. Consequently, users would not need to have high capacity hard disks as many do at present.

Java, it is assumed, will deliver another dimension to Web content, namely, interactivity. An applet developed by Patrick Worfolk of the University of Minnesota, for instance, simulates graphically and numerically Lorenz equations. The user can manipulate the variables and view on screen the numerical consequences and their graphical representation. As Java is cross-platform, the promise is that software packages can be delivered over the Web for immediate use irrespective of the operating system employed by the user. Whether the promise can be delivered effectively and economically remains a mute question. (APPLET)

JPEG (Joint Photographic Experts Group Format)

One of the most popular graphics file formats used to display images on the Web. 'The palette is large (16 million colors) and the file sizes can be made small with JPEG's variable compression, but the method is lossy, meaning that the original image's detail is not fully restored during decompression. It is used largely for photographs, where the eye makes up for compression loss.' (source: Darnell *et al.*, 1997).

KILOBYTE (Kb)

One thousand bytes. (BYTE)

LAN (Local Area Network)

Generally refers to the network created by linking computers belonging to the same organization together, and the technology and software that accomplishes this. The dividing line between larger Local Area Networks and the smaller end of Wide Area Networks is somewhat fuzzy.

LISTSERV

An abbreviation of LIST SERVer. A software program that stores a list of electronic mail addresses and can execute various commands associated with the management of mailing lists.

MAILING LIST

Subject-based discussion groups implemented through electronic mail, most commonly with the assistance of software programs that automate many of the tasks associated with mailing list management tasks. (LISTSERV)

MEGABYTE (Mb)

One million bytes. (BYTE)

MICROPROCESSOR

See CPU.

MOO

This is a specific implementation of a MUD (see below), and stands for Mud, Object Oriented.

MUD

'Short for Multi-User Dungeon (or Multi-User Dimension), a cyberspace where users can take on an identity in the form of an *avatar* and interact with one another.

Originally, MUDs tended to be adventure games played within enormous old castles with hidden rooms, trap-doors, exotic beasts, and magical items. Nowadays, the term is used more generically to refer to any cyberspace. MUDs are also known as 3-D worlds and chat worlds.' (source: PC WeboPaedia at <http://www.pcwebopedia.com/MUD.htm>)

NEWSGROUP

See USENET.

NNTP (Network News Transfer Protocol)

The protocol used for distribution and retrieval of data relating to newsgroups. (USENET)

NODE

Generally used to refer to any computer reachable over a network, including the Internet. Each computer that satisfies this condition is said to be a node on the network concerned.

OPERATING SYSTEM (OS)

'Operating systems are the programs or collections of programs which act as translators between a computer's processing chips and programs designed to run on them. ... Examples of operating systems are DOS, Windows, OS/2, UNIX, and Macintosh's System/Finder.' (source: PC Lexicon).

PATH

See FILE PATH.

PDF (Portable Document Format)

A document format developed by Adobe, Inc. PDF files are cross-platform, which means that they can be read on any computer, irrespective of the operating system that it is using. In order to read PDF files you need to have the special Adobe Acrobat Reader. This is available as freeware and can be downloaded from the Adobe home page at <http://www.adobe.com>. As many documents accessible over the Internet are in PDF format it is well worth installing this software. The most recent version of Netscape incorporates the Acrobat Reader as a plug-in. To write documents in PDF format you need to purchase the appropriate software from Adobe, particulars of which are available at its site.

PENTIUM

See CPU.

PLATFORM

> See OPERATING SYSTEM.

POP (Post Office Protocol)

> A protocol associated with some forms of electronic mail software that allows users to access and download mail from a server. With this form of electronic mail protocol the mail is downloaded to the computer of the user, rather than remaining on the server. (PROTOCOL, SMTP) POP is also an abbreviation of Points of Presence.

PROTOCOL

> Protocols are established international standards that specify details relating to how computers will interact with each other in relation to the exchange of commands and data governing specific applications and/or procedures.

ROUTER

> A combination of hardware and software used to forward information between computers on or between networks.

SEARCH ENGINE

> Generally, in Internet parlance, the front-end of a large database containing information relating to files (text, graphic, video, audio, software, and combinations thereof) accessible from Internet-connected servers. Search engines vary in their breadth of coverage of Internet resources, their speed of retrieval of information, and the sophistication of the query syntax that can be employed to track down resources.

SERVER

> Used to refer both to a piece of hardware that performs the task of providing specified resources (for instance a file or printer server), and to the server software component in client–server applications, such as Netscape Web Server and Microsoft Peer Web Server. (FILE SERVER, CLIENT–SERVER COMPUTING)

SHAREWARE

> A system of software distribution whereby the user is afforded a trial period to experience the software, usually 30 days, prior to being required to pay for continuing use of it. The author retains copyright throughout. Today there is frequently no difference transparent to the user between proprietary and shareware software, both requiring the payment of a fee and ceasing to function properly, if at all, after the expiry of the trial period.

SMTP (Simple Mail Transfer Protocol)

A protocol that is used for transferring electronic mail between computers.

TCP (Transmission Control Protocol)

One of the suite of protocols that is central to the functioning of the Internet, concerned principally with the accurate transmission of data between Internet-linked computers.

TELNET

A protocol that enables a user to log on to another computer and use it. Access to many academic library catalogues relies on use of this protocol. In effect, the user's own PC is functioning largely as a dumb terminal, issuing commands that are executed by the computer which has been logged on to.

UNIX

A proprietary operating system that was very widely used prior to the development of the Microsoft Windows operating system. It is still very widely used in Local and Wide Area Networks and many professionals consider it to be considerably more reliable and robust than those operating systems most commonly used currently on PCs.

URL (Uniform Resource Locator)

An Internet address. These have standardized formats. The URL specifies the type of Internet service that is being accessed (World Wide Web, gopher, WAIS, etc.), and the file path of the resource being sought. The URL is the entry that is inserted in the location/go to box in a browser.

USENET

Generically used to designate the worldwide network of thousands of newsgroups that are arranged into different subject hierarchies and topics. The software programs that manage newsgroup communications rely on a specific protocol, the NNTP (Network News Transfer Protocol).

WILDCARD

Commonly specified by * or ? in Windows and DOS, this is a character used in searches for information or files, and in copying, moving, filtering and backing up files. Most Internet search engines allow for the use of wildcards in their query syntax.

WORLD WIDE WEB

A hypertext-based distributed information system developed by Tim Berners-Lee at CERN, the European Centre for Particle Physics. CERN was responsible for developing the early agreed standards for the Web and the first command-based Web browser. Originally, the major impetus for the development of the Web was to establish a convenient medium for the circulation of academic documents. It has since become the most important Internet tool.

Bibliography

Anderson, J.A. (1996) *Foundations of Computer Technology*. Chapman & Hall, London.

Brown, M. *et al.* (1997) *WWW Plug-Ins Companion*. Que, Indianpolis, IN.

Comer, D.E. (1997) *The Internet Book*, 2nd edn. Prentice Hall, Upper Saddle River, NJ.

Darnell, R. *et al.* (1997) *HTML4 Unleashed*. Sams.net, Indianapolis, IN.

Gilster, P. (1995) *The New Internet Navigator*. Wiley, New York.

Haskin, D. (1997) *Microsoft Internet Explorer 3*. Ventana, Research Triangle Park, NC.

Keeler, E. and Miller R. (1997) *Netscape Virtuoso,* 3rd edn. Wiley, New York.

Krol, E. (1994) *The Whole Internet,* 2nd edn. O'Reilly, Sebastopol, CA.

Pfaffenberger, B. (1995) *Netscape Navigator*^{TM} *3.0*. AP Professional, Chestnut Hill, MA.

Raggett, D., Lam, J. and Alexander, I. (1996) *HTML 3: Electronic Publishing on the World Wide Web*. Addison Wesley Longman, Harlow.

(See also the Web sites at the end of Chapter 4)

Index

Anderson   5

backbone   8
Berners-Lee, Tim   10
blocking data   294
bookmark/s   22–6
  adding   22–3
  commercial software
    applications   309–10
  downloading file from   17
  folders   23–4
  organizing   23–5
  properties   24–5
  saving bookmark file   25–6
Boolean operators   84–6
browser   10–12
  office   30

client   9
client-server   31
clipboard   294
copying data   294

desktop   286
drag and drop   288

EBONE   8

Favorites   23
  saving   26
File Manager   286, 290–4
  copying files   292

creating a directory   293
disk drive buttons   291
interface   291
folders   292
moving files   292
ordinary search   293
renaming files   293
refreshing   293
search facility   293
wildcard search   294
File Transfer Protocol (*see* FTP)
firewall   303
FTP (File Transfer Protocol)   9

hardware   4
home page   14
hyperlinks   17
hypertext   10
Hypertext Transport Protocol (HTTP) 10

Internet   7
Internet Access Provider   8
Internet addresses (*see* URLs)
Internet Explorer   11
  interface   13
Internet Protocol   7
Internet Protocol address
  (IP address)   9, 34
Internet Service Provider   8
Internet services (*see* Internet tools)
Internet tools   9, 10
IP (*see* Internet Protcol)

LAN (*see* Local Area Network)
Local Area Network   3–6

mailing lists
    archives   113–25
        as resource   113–4
        batch database commands   117–23
        batch database job   117–18
        batch database template   117
        comparison operaters   121
        database lists   122
        date rules   120
        indexes and files   115–17
        keyword rules   120–1
        optional rules   120–3
        output commands   123–4
        search command   119
        summary search query
            procedures   123
    commands   104–9
    contributing to   109–11
    directories of, addresses   100
    directories of, operation   94–100
    non-listserv commands   112
    operation of   93–4
Mosaic   10
mouse, use of   287

Netscapc   11
    abbreviated URLs (addresses)   16
    additional windows   27
    backtracking   17–18
    configuring   297–305
        appearance   298–9
        cache   304–5
        helper applications   299–302
        plug-ins   299, 303
        proxies   303–4
    copying files   19
    Domain Name Server   34
    downloading files   15–16
    enhancing downloading
        efficiency   26–8
    frames   21–2
    Fully Qualified Domain Name   34
    history files   18

    home page   14
    inserting URLs (addresses)   15
    interface   14
    malfunctions   28–30
    page margins of files   19
    page numbers of files   19
    printing dates   19
    printing files   19–20
    printing URLs (addresses)   19
    saving files   20–1
    toolbar   14
Netscape Communications
    Corporation Inc.   10
network
    infrastructure   4
    operating software   4
new Internet resources   310–11
Newsgroups   127–42
    accessing/subscribing   133–4
    archives (*see* also DejaNews)   136
    composing/replying   135–6
    configuring newsreader   130–2
    DejaNews   136–41
    description of   127–30
    flagging messages   134
    graphics   141
    marking as read   135
    newsgroup hierarchy   129–30
    newsreader   128
    newsreader (Netscape) interface   132–3
    newsreaders, commercial   142
    searching for messages   124

operating systems   285

packet switching   5–6
pasting data   294
program groups   289
Program Manager   286, 288–90
protocol   4
push technologies   53

Referencing Internet materials   37–49
    command sequence   41
    electronic mail   43–4
    gopher sites   44

Referencing Internet materials *continued*
    mailing list messages 44–5
    newsgroups 46–7
    synchronous communications 45–6
    telnet 46
    underlying principles 39–42
    viewers 49
    World Wide Web resources 47–9
router 7

saving files 19-20, 295–6
search engines 65–6
    Alta Vista 72
    definition/description 65
    HotBot 74–5
    operation of 67–8
    sites of 70
    types 66
searches
    advanced 83–90
        Alta Vista interface 83–4
        Alta Vista new interface 89
        Boolean operators 84–6
        parantheses 86–7
        ranking queries 87–8
    basic 71–81
        phrases 74
        procedures 74
        query construction 75–7
        refining 77–9
        summary remarks 79–81
    hit ranking 74
    planning 68–70
server 9
software
    downloading 306–7

downloading sites 306
freeware 306
installing 307–9
proprietary 305–6
shareware 306
subject directories 55–64
    Argus Clearinghouse 63
    BUBL 60–1
    definition 55
    Galaxy 60
    InterNIC Directory of Directories 63
    SOSIG 61–2
    WWW Virtual Library 62–3
    Yahoo 57–60

TCP/IP Protocol Suite 4, 7
Transmission Control Protocol 4, 7

URL (Uniform Resource Locator/
    see URLs)
URLs 31–6
    definition 31
    domain categories 35
    Domain Name Server 34
    domain names 34
    Fully Qualified Domain Name 34
    structure of 33–4
    uses of (identification and
        searching) 32–3

WAN (*see* Wide Area Network)
Web page 9
Wide Area Network (WAN) 6 8
Windows Explorer 286
Windows operating systems 285
World Wide Web (WWW) 10